I0214290

CRITICAL PRAISE FOR *WE ARE THE CLASH*

"*We Are The Clash* is an important book in so many ways—and not just because it makes up for a lack of documentation of this period of the band . . . *We Are The Clash* was a book screaming to be written. Andersen and Heibutzki have done a stellar job." —*I-94 Bar* (Australia)

"When you think of The Clash, what comes to mind? Their early days in the London punk scene, perhaps, or the triumphant release of *London Calling*. *We Are The Clash* focuses on a very different moment in the band's history: the point at which the group splintered in the early 1980s, and its members grappled with an onset of reactionary governments around the world." —*Vol. 1 Brooklyn*

"Thanks to what must've been exhaustive research into contemporary bootleg recordings of live shows and articles chronicling the audience response to the performances, Andersen and Heibutzki provide intensely-detailed evidence that this was a band which was firing on all cylinders—especially in a live setting—almost until the very end . . . Seriously: if nothing else, track down *We Are The Clash* and read Chapter Eight, 'Movers and Shakers Come On.' It will reaffirm any fandom you might've once lost for The Clash, and for those who've ever doubted them or considered them 'corporate punk,' it'll give you fresh eyes on the band. It's fucking magical." —*Cinepunx*

"The Clash may have not been the best example of integrity in the music world with their careerist opportunism but their message of hope and possibility, cribbed from reggae and soul music, is all too important." —*Maximum Rocknroll*

"Andersen and Heibutzki have woven a complex, cinematic tale with a lot of heart in *We Are The Clash*, simply by rescuing the unwanted stepchild ending of the story of one of punk's greatest bands from ignominy . . . Maybe Joe Strummer couldn't save The Clash, but this book may save The Clash Mk 2's reputation and legacy." —*Ugly Things*

"When did The Clash quit being 'the only band that matters'? This fascinating book faces a challenge: documenting the final years of the British band that its record label had promoted with that slogan . . . The band may no longer have mattered, but its legacy mattered to the authors, who make it matter to the readers. More than a footnote to the rise and fall of one of the last great rock bands." —*Kirkus Reviews*

"Coverage is specialized, extending considerably beyond mere behind-the-scenes reportage and deeply explores the sociopolitical context in which the band operated; as such, the tone can be intense (read: punk) and professorial. In all, Andersen and Heibutzki's examination of the band's proletarian stance in light of its commercial striving is immensely satisfying." —*Library Journal*

"[O]ne of the most rewarding music books you'll come across this year . . . [B]y focusing as much on the politics that motivated The Clash, *We Are The Clash* becomes a vital political history as much as an account of an underdocumented portion of a band's career. Great music books catalyze critical reconsiderations; *We Are The Clash* does one better, inviting readers to consider what matters to them: the creative commodities that artists produce? Or the ideals, however complexly and clumsily human they may be, that often compel artists to create in the first place."

—*Johns Hopkins Magazine*

"Given the number of books out there about The Clash, this is, as I stated, the only one to take a genuine, unbiased and in-depth appraisal of this era of the band. Given the quality of the writing, this could also be the most essential book about the band."

—*Scanner Zine*

"*We Are The Clash* celebrates the struggle for humanity, both in a band and in the wider world community. Traveling the journey of The Clash's final years is no train in vain. The benefits of understanding history allow readers to see that the future is unwritten, as long as mistakes from the past are not dutifully repeated, but learned from. The Clash, with all of their faults, represented a creative force to be reckoned with. They showed that anger could be power, if one knows how to use it."

—*SLUG Magazine*

"[A] gripping tale of the band's struggle to reinvent itself as George Orwell's 1984 loomed. This bold campaign crashed headlong into a wall of internal contradictions and rising right-wing power."

—*Brooklyn Digest*

"Smash your television and buy this book! *We Are The Clash* proves, once again, the importance of The Clash, even during their rarely discussed and most maligned period. Situated in the Reagan/Thatcher era, *We Are The Clash* illustrates why, when Reagan called women like my mom 'welfare queens,' I bought a ticket to see 'the only band that matters,' and then went on to start one of my own."

—Michelle Cruz Gonzales, author of *The Spitboy Rule*

"The Clash are remembered as much for their blistering music as their gritty yet hopeful message to listeners worldwide. In this first serious look at The Clash's music and meaning, post–commercial success, the authors mix thoughtful reflection with grassroots political analysis in an effort to inspire a new generation of music fans and activists to Cut the Crap." —Craig O'Hara, author of *The Philosophy of Punk*

WE ARE THE CLASH

REAGAN, THATCHER, AND THE LAST STAND OF A BAND THAT MATTERED

MARK ANDERSEN AND RALPH HEIBUTZKI

AKASHIC BOOKS

BROOKLYN, NEW YORK, USA

All rights reserved. No part of this book may be reproduced, stored in a retrieval system, or transmitted in any form, by any means, including mechanical, electronic, photocopying, recording, or otherwise, without the prior written consent of the publisher.

Published by Akashic Books
©2018 Mark Andersen and Ralph Heibutzki

Cover and title page photo: Chris Haskett, The Clash on busking tour, May 1985.

Paperback ISBN: 978-1-61775-293-3
Hardcover ISBN: 978-1-63614-049-0
Library of Congress Control Number: 2017956558
Second paperback printing

Akashic Books
Brooklyn, New York, USA
Instagram: AkashicBooks
Twitter: AkashicBooks
Facebook: AkashicBooks
E-mail: info@akashicbooks.com
Website: www.akashicbooks.com

To my father Merlin and grandfather Otto, who were farmers, ranchers, and coal miners; and to my mother Anna Margaret Vik.

To my son Soren, my daughter Sevgi, and my beloved Tulin.

To Jesús Arias and Martin Jenkinson, both gone too soon.

—M.A.

To "Budgie," my dear wife, Lisa D. Quinlan Heibutzki: your inspiration, love, and support mean everything.

To Anthony Salazar (1965–2005): yeah, you were right, it worked out for the best . . .

To Don Hargraves, Tim Easterday, and John Hilla: the mission continues. Kick down the doors!

—R.H.

So the forces gathered together
against the thorn a-piercing in their side
A brave new world is beckoning
so the olden world must die . . .
—Old English folk ballad, c. 1986

TABLE OF CONTENTS

FOREWORD

JEWELS FROM THE WRECKAGE

BY BARRY "THE BAKER" AUGUSTE, LOYAL CLASH FOOT SOLDIER, 1976–1983

The Baker in action, handing a restrung guitar to Joe Strummer midsong. (Photographer unknown.)

At long last, The Clash's final incarnation has been definitively chronicled. Mark Andersen and Ralph Heibutzki have brilliantly filled in the blanks of the "Clash Mark II" era, including its eventual implosion. And while set three decades ago, the political, social, and economic evils The Clash battled against then are just as relevant today, if not more so. Both Clash fans and general readers alike will be moved by this tale of onstage conquest and offstage turmoil, so deftly woven into the fabric of the charged politics of that time.

Although the seeds of discontent were sown long before, 1983 was The Clash's time of bitter harvest. By one measure, the year held the band's greatest triumph—headlining the first day of the US Festival, before 250,000 people—but also witnessed an astonishing act of self-immolation.

Joe Strummer's DIY film noir *Hell W10*, shot in early 1983 when the band was on break, foreshadowed the tragedy. By the movie's end, the villain, Mr. Socrates—enthusiastically played by Mick Jones—and his empire are wiped out. By September, that would be the case in real life.

The irony is inescapable: Mick freely accepted the villain's role, and would be thus portrayed to the press after his purge. This suggests Mick was a voluntary scapegoat; his expulsion was the purifying remedy for The Clash's maladies, just as that of Nick "Topper" Headon before him.

Mick was axed from the band in a scene plotted long in advance. Few knew it was going to happen. Although valid reasons for the dramatic act were apparent, it hit those close to the band like a death in the family; a killing, even, committed by brothers. There could be no neutral ground. Friends and acquaintances were forced to choose sides, and it would be years before many felt comfortable enough to associate socially or professionally again.

I know, because I lived it. I served alongside Joe, Mick, and Paul starting in the summer of 1976, hauling gear and doing whatever else needed to be done while still a teenager living at home. I signed on shortly after Bernie Rhodes assembled the band, was there when Topper joined in spring 1977, and witnessed Bernie's dismissal in 1978 and his return in 1981, forming a fateful alliance with Kosmo Vinyl, who had become the band's ad hoc mouthpiece in the interim. Aside from the first show at the Black Swan in Sheffield, I was at every show, rehearsal, and recording session.

No one knows what we went through during those years marching up the hill—only us! As Joe once said, "We went to hell and back!" Words are inadequate; it is impossible to convey the anguish of endless months of touring; nonstop revolving hotel rooms; a different town every day; the months of monotony in studios with endless retakes and overdubs; brain-numbing repetition done out of duty and devotion. We had to turn into some kind of machine, or we would have gone mad. Or maybe we did . . . PTSD isn't confined to soldiers. But I'd do it all over again, for such was The Clash's irrepressible sense of mission, a calling I embraced.

That level of dedication always comes at a cost, however. To maintain my own sanity, I ignored the excesses of rock and roll to single-mindedly focus on the equipment and work needed to enable the band to perform, record, and rehearse. I didn't waver from that purpose until September 1983, in a head-on collision of inter-band politics, personal resentments, managerial manipulation, and road-weary exhaustion.

Once reinstated in 1981, Bernie had set about reconstructing the band he had originally created, resurrecting his Stalinist regime from 1976, with Kosmo's assistance. By 1982, the duo was pounding the table about all manner of band diktats, with Bernie barking the orders and Kosmo cracking the whip to keep everyone in line. From Topper's removal; the decision to support The Who and to play the US Festival; to the eventual firing of Mick—the two of them were relentless. Joe found himself caught in an escalating tug-of-war between the band's founding fathers, Bernie and Mick.

Bernie did help the band break through in America, but in the process ripped apart their very DNA. Mick became increasingly isolated, and scarcely helped his cause by acting the prima donna, at odds with the Clash "anti-star" ethos. The contradictions became inescapable: to prove a punk band from the squats of London could conquer the world, The Clash had to become the very thing they set out to destroy. In the end, it just proved too high a price to pay.

This was the "unanswerable dilemma" at the band's heart since its creation: how do you go to the top level of the music business and still stay true—and be seen to be true—to your ideals? As original drummer Terry Chimes had predicted, mass success called everything into question.

The dilemma was unbearable to Joe. In desperation, he adopted Bernie's military platitudes about having to cut off the gangrenous limb in order to save the body, and how we all must be marching in the same direction.

It still confounds people today: how could Bernie even consider that he could fire both Topper and Mick and still have a band? I was one of those skeptics. Yet The Clash, in its purest form, was Bernie, and Bernie was a fundamental extension of them. His relationship with the band was so intimate and personal that, in the end, he would rather demolish it than see it become obsolete. Evolve or die! Tragically, he didn't see that there was more than one way to evolve.

When Mick was dismissed, I instinctively knew I was next for the chop. So I left of my own volition bearing no one any ill will. I had given The Clash more than seven years of my life and had worked as hard and as loyally as anyone could. But I'd done my job and it was time to leave. Regime change required a total purge. I shook hands with Joe and Paul and said goodbye, quietly slipping down the stairs of Rehearsal Rehearsals for the last time.

Like the band, I had given it my all—and then, suddenly, it was over and done. The rupture was painful and complete. After the end of my Clash story, I had no contact with any of my comrades for years, never saw The Clash Mark II perform, and never even heard anything off the album that was created . . . so total was my break with that scene and the people involved.

Eventually, I tried to piece together some of the fragments from my Clash years, but it was a profoundly difficult undertaking. I refused all interviews for over thirty years. Even when I finally decided to speak, I only wanted to contribute to Clash-related projects that would rise above the cheap name-calling and petty finger-pointing that inevitably rise in situations that have run their course. The endeavors needed to have genuine substance, be deeply researched, offer a different perspective, and, above all, exhibit the highest probity, integrity, and honesty.

This book is precisely that for which I searched. Andersen and Heibutzki obviously love The Clash, believe in the band's values, and try to live by them. Their continued passion and idealism is refreshing, a sign that The Clash did not labor in vain, that listeners were touched deeply and indelibly. Both took to heart Joe's plea for his audience to become activists, as is shown by their community work, especially Andersen's involvement with the celebrated punk-activist collective Positive Force DC and inner-city advocate We Are Family. Both take their role as writers and historians equally seriously, as shown in the artistry here and in their other books. They write with care and sensitivity while doggedly pursuing the truth, letting the chips fall where they may.

In reading this book, I found my way back into Clash World, learning for the first time of the trials and tribulations—and grand aspirations—of the last version of The Clash, a Clash I never believed in and of which I was never a part. Astonishingly, I found myself moved, angered, and even inspired all over again. While the world was on the edge of thermonuclear destruction, Central American wars raged, and the coal miners confronted Margaret Thatcher's bully boys, the new Clash struggled to create something real of their own, building upon—but going beyond—past glories.

Now I can see that The Clash Mark II was an attempt to find an answer to the unanswerable dilemma. Even if they didn't locate one, there was drama and value in the effort. I'm tempted to say their flameout was inevitable, but those last two years were an attempt to evolve, to get back to basics, to walk that fine line between commercial success and staying true to your roots.

It is true that an essential chemistry was lost with the firings of Mick and Topper. With all due respect to the skills of Peter Howard, Nick Sheppard, and Vince White, that intangible factor could never be replaced by merely slotting in proficient musicians. Yet, from what I've heard and read, I believe they had a chance to succeed had they just been left alone, to do what musicians do naturally: to gel together, to create an alchemy of their own.

It seems that spark was never allowed a chance to fully flourish, given the managerial dictatorship they had to perform under. Bernie was a visionary, and Kosmo a true believer, but their relentless agitation—in addition to other immense personal and political pressures—ultimately drove the band off the rails, and Joe into psychic meltdown. Yet this book shows that, amid the chaos, something of worth, something recognizably Clash-like was nonetheless forged.

This account of The Clash's final chapter is stark and unsentimental, exhilarating and occasionally brutal, set against the sociopolitical background that impelled the band. Andersen and Heibutzki depict the 1980s world stage with razor-sharp insight, chronicling the gradual surrender to Thatcher and Ronald Reagan's gray, greed-driven vision. It is a cautionary tale, every bit as bleak as Orwell's *1984*, and it is, alas, where we now reside. This is not a story of defeat, however, but a mission to retrieve jewels from the wreckage, so that the future might flourish.

Beautifully constructed and brilliantly written, *We Are The Clash* is a chronicle as complex and powerful as its subject. I was riveted, unable to put it down. No Clash collection will be complete without this epic addition. This book challenges us to recall what was best about "the only band that mattered" and then strive to live up to our own best in this new, frightening, but possibility-filled moment.

Dedicated to Mickey Foote (1951–2018), Clash sound engineer and producer of the first album.

Clash guitar tech Digby, The Baker, and Joe Strummer in the foyer of the Iroquois Hotel, NYC, midtour. (Photographer unknown.)

INTRODUCTION

DROWNED OUT BY THE SOUND

Unused *Cut the Crap* promo poster, late 1985. (Clash photo by Mike Laye; poster designer unknown.)

In 1976, a good many people in the West thought Marxism had a reasonable case to argue. By 1986, many of them no longer considered that it had. What exactly had happened in the meanwhile? Was it simply that these people were now buried under a pile of toddlers?
—Terry Eagleton, *Why Marx Was Right*

Like their counterparts in Hollywood, photographic retouchers in Soviet Russia spent long hours helping the camera to falsify reality . . . The physical eradication of Stalin's political opponents was swiftly followed by their obliteration from all forms of pictorial existence.
—David King, *The Commissar Vanishes*

The air was sweat-soaked and electric. Five musicians could barely be glimpsed amid a mass of humanity. Three men flayed acoustic guitars, while a fourth pounded drumsticks against the metal and plastic of a chair.

The fifth—a flame-haired singer in a green T-shirt with rolled-up sleeves—exhorted the crowd from a slightly elevated perch. Dog tags jangled as he sang without a microphone, his head nearly touching the low ceiling of the cave-like space.

The vocalist provided a visual center to the happening, but his voice was lost in the din. The unamplified guitars were similarly submerged, with only the rhythm cutting through to the back of the small room.

Such technological shortcomings seemed to matter little. Hundreds of voices howled as one: "Breaking rocks in the hot sun / I fought the law / and the law won / I needed money 'cause I had none / I fought the law / and the law won."

The song echoed poverty's desperation, its doomed protagonist reduced to "robbing people with a six-gun." If evoking a mythical American West, its theme also fit with the present locale: Sunderland, a port city in northeastern Britain.

Once Sunderland had been "the largest shipbuilding town in the world," according to the BBC. Now, the ships were gone, factory gates padlocked and rusty, with the area also hemorrhaging mining and other industrial jobs. A battle waged over the past two years to forestall an even bleaker future had not ended in victory.

Yet if the lyrics were grim, the spirit in the Drum Club discotheque on this evening in May 1985 was anything but. Joy met defiance as crowd and band became one giant chorus, spitting in the eye of a cruel fate.

We may have lost, the voices seemed to say, but we are not defeated.

A British rock band called The Clash was the catalyst for that rousing Sunderland night. By the time the group performed this audacious impromptu concert, they had become the single most popular unit to rise out of the UK punk explosion, thanks to their

1982 breakthrough album *Combat Rock*, with its hit singles "Rock the Casbah" and "Should I Stay or Should I Go."

Over the ensuing decades, The Clash's stature has only grown, with commentators regularly placing them in a rock pantheon next to an earlier generation's demigods such as the Beatles and the Rolling Stones. This development—including their induction into the Rock & Roll Hall of Fame—is not without irony, given the band's populist, antistar stance. Nonetheless, as an Arabic version of the antifundamentalist "Casbah" by Algerian rocker Rachid Taha suggests, The Clash's global cultural influence is vast and spreading, as befits a band that consciously strove to think in planetary terms.

In the fall of 2013—nearly thirty years after that Sunderland show—The Clash released *Sound System*, a massive box set. While the long-defunct unit had been the subject of several such compendiums, this one was clearly meant as the final will and definitive testament of one of the twentieth century's most important rock groups.

Described by *Rolling Stone* magazine as collecting "all of its albums," *Sound System* was a vast and weighty document. Designed to resemble that 1980s urban icon—the boom box cassette deck—the set also contained unreleased music and videos, a poster, a book, magazines, badges, stickers, even Clash dog tags. "I'm not even thinking about any more Clash releases. This is it for me, and I say that with an exclamation mark!" band cofounder Mick Jones told *Rolling Stone* at the time.

Yet, for all of *Sound System*'s vaunted completeness, there was a striking omission: the band's sixth studio album, *Cut the Crap*. Although the record cracked the UK Top 20, with a similarly high-ranking single, "This Is England," it was nowhere to be seen. Nor was there any mention that a final version of The Clash, without guitarist Jones and drummer Nicky "Topper" Headon, had played 120-plus shows, nearly 20 percent of the band's total gigs.

Perhaps this shouldn't have been a surprise. The film *Westway to the World* and its companion tome *The Clash*—the other two volumes that, with *Sound System*, effectively comprise the authorized Clash canon—also omitted the same for all intents and purposes. None of the final two years of concerts—such as the Sunderland show—were included in the comprehensive list in the big pink coffee-table book, which credited "Strummer Jones Simonon Headon" as its authors.

It's true that two of those four—Jones and Headon—were absent from *Cut the Crap*. Nonetheless, the record's exclusion was extraordinary, only justifiable from a narrow perspective that has hardened over the years. This view not only dismisses the album but the band's last version itself—popularly known as "The Clash Mark II"—as lead-footed punk pretenders unworthy of serious scrutiny.

According to one Clash biographer, Marcus Gray, The Clash Mark II was drilling out "heavy metal" versions of the unit's classics, "reducing every tune to a primitive staccato stomp . . . with its original melody, subtlety, texture, and meaning hammered into the ground." They are deemed "a Clash cover band" by another, author/filmmaker Danny Garcia. One wag even recorded a reworked version of their latter-day anthem "We Are The Clash" as "We Aren't The Clash."

A few brave souls have dissented from this chorus of dismissal, most notably writer Jon Savage, who described *Cut the Crap* as a "moving state of the nation address." Savage even singles out "This Is England" as "the last great British punk song" in his magnum opus, *England's Dreaming*. Such voices, however, have largely been drowned out by the sound of a naysaying echo chamber.

Over time, the ripple effects of this critical razzing have taken a toll. Ironically, *Cut the Crap*'s roundly panned "electro-punk" production is often held up as proof of the group's lack of talent. Consider this *Saturday Review* summary: "Pathetic stabs at updating the sound with multiple layers of overdubs and synthesized drum machines only point out the limitations of the group's playing abilities." A damning take—yet, as it happens, the record was hardly created by The Clash Mark II as such, and didn't fairly represent their skills or live sound.

Thirty-odd years after the album's release, such attitudes also persist in critics' bibles like the *All Music Guide*, which writes off *Cut the Crap* as "formulaic, tired punk rock that doesn't have the aggression or purpose of early Clash records, let alone the hardcore punk that the new band was now competing with."

Going one step further, *Rolling Stone* entirely dismisses the neo-Clash in a November 2012 "Flashback" column titled "The Clash Say Goodbye at the 1983 US Festival." While admitting that a new lineup continued to play live after Mick Jones's exit, the magazine sneered, "But that's like a Rolling Stones tour without Keith Richards. It doesn't count, and the whole thing has basically been erased from history. The Clash as we know them ended at the 1983 US Festival."

Case closed; roll the credits and be done with it. For many of the band's chroniclers, this post–Jones/Headon version of The Clash is to be classified alongside other egregious artistic faux pas of ego-addled and/or cash-hungry rock pioneers—the Doors going on for two albums without Jim Morrison, the Velvet Underground sans Lou Reed, John Cale, or Nico.

This disdain is heightened by a new reality: in the twenty-first century, zombie versions of once cutting-edge bands stumble on for years after death—Dead Kennedys without Jello Biafra, the Misfits without Glen Danzig, Black Flag without anybody but Greg Ginn . . . the list goes on and on. Except for an occasional compilation appearance of its blazing twilight-era anthem "This Is England," The Clash Mark II has seemed similarly undead, fated to remain one of rock's great untouchables, unfit for public consumption.

Mick Jones famously described his ejection as "the greatest mistake in rock and roll history"—but that might be expected. More curious is the fact it has been hard to find defenders of The Clash Mark II even from those who played in the band.

In his later years, Joe Strummer hardly uttered a kind word about the unit that he more than anyone else created. Clash Mark II axman Vince White wrote *Out of Control*, a blistering exposé of the behind-the-scenes chaos and dysfunctional machinations in the band; in Danny Garcia's book *The Rise and Fall of The Clash*, final drummer Peter Howard bemoans a foregone opportunity to join hard rockers AC/DC in order to stick with the doomed neo-Clash.

While far less vitriolic than White or Howard, guitarist Nick Sheppard has jokingly allowed that this unit might be seen as "the only cover band I've ever played in."

By contrast, Clash cofounder Paul Simonon has reaffirmed the motivation behind the expulsion of Jones, and asserted the worth of the final songs. However, even he doesn't defend *Cut the Crap*, faulting manager/cofounder Bernard Rhodes for undoing the album with his dictatorial ways. Quipping, "If The Clash was the Communist Party, Bernie was our Stalin," bassist Simonon now casts Rhodes as essentially pulling off a musical coup d'état in the studio.

Indeed, in an interview for the *Big Issue* with Jones and Headon after *Sound System*'s release, Simonon claims *Cut the Crap* is "not really a Clash record . . . It hasn't got Mick or Topper on it." Jones then delivers the coup de grâce, joking that "for the benefit of Stalinist revision, [*Cut the Crap*] has been expunged."

Given all of this, it might fairly be asked: should one notice, much less mourn, the exclusion of this one record from this one box set?

The short answer is that the purging of *Cut the Crap*—and a concurrent excision of the neo-Clash era—matters. It not only leaves out a crucial chapter in the story of an entity that has been described as "the only band that matters" but it helps subvert what made the unit much more than simply another pop group.

In fact, the Clash Mark II period is a fascinating window into a band of immense vision and passion—as well as fundamental contradictions—as they wrestle with the meaning of success. In addition, this tale plays out against a backdrop of extraordinary sociopolitical drama, the passing of one era of modern history into another: a vibrant epoch that, nonetheless, is fundamentally more cold and cruel.

The Clash Mark II songs that Simonon defends not only document this moment when the world turned, but can also illuminate a possible better future. Contrary to the many voices that ridicule this Clash era, there is a powerful—if sometimes heartbreaking—story here, together with profound moments, words, and music, including works worthy of standing next to the best that The Clash created.

While we will defend this position with exhaustive, painstaking documentation and tightly constructed arguments, this book began with our own experiences as longtime followers of The Clash. Both of our lives were radically changed for the better by our encounter with the band, its music, look, and ideas, including those on display in its last incarnation.

Of course, personal experience, however profound, can only go so far to provide convincing historical evidence. Another crucial bulwark for this project is more broadly based and impossible to dismiss. As the Internet has enabled sixty-plus bootlegs from the band's final period to be widely circulated, a counterpoint to the "critical consensus"—and The Clash's own rewritten history—has risen. In a striking example of grassroots resistance, a whole segment of Clash fandom now refuses to allow the band's last two years to be "expunged."

These live tapes give the lie to those who dismiss the post-Jones Clash. In short, the passion is palpable, and the performances are compelling, with many of the new songs rivaling the power of the Strummer-Jones classics. These raw documents constitute a lasting rebuke to those who would write The Clash Mark II out of history. They provide not just the foundation of our narrative here; they—as much as live tapes from the earlier Clash years—are also crucial fuel that animate our ongoing personal, creative, and activist endeavors.

Without denying the seamier side of the period, or whitewashing the dysfunction that doomed this last stand, we will strive to take the artistic accomplishments seriously, while also trying to place the failures—or even betrayals—in context, with relentless pursuit of truth and sympathetic assessment of human frailty.

This begins with an honest appraisal of the band's origins. The Clash was mostly assembled from relative strangers by manager/agitator Bernard Rhodes and given a challenging set of orders: in the words of Strummer, "to be bigger than anybody else but still keep our message." That their mission of freedom and anticapitalist revolution was somehow to be brought to fruition via the corporate rock world only serves to highlight what longtime Clash roadie/confidante The Baker has called the band's "unanswerable dilemma."

This profound tension is the taproot of the band's final quest. If The Clash's aims were perhaps doomed from the start, they nonetheless made for an exhilarating ride, one that resonates still, not only for aging fans, but also those discovering the band today. Far from being an embarrassing mistake best forgotten, this neo-Clash era is actually a fascinating and instructive conclusion to their trajectory as a band.

The final phase of this story begins in revolt against basic commercial common sense: the ejection of the authors of two and a half of the band's three hit singles. Even so, it was not insanity. Without a risky course correction, The Clash could easily have become just another gaggle of rock stars lost in an antiseptic bubble, becoming the very thing that they claimed to despise. This final, desperate effort to bottle lightning yet again, in the end, lends an even greater depth to The Clash's saga.

Obviously, "the Clash franchise"—the phrase of Mark II guitarist Sheppard—doesn't believe this. The fervor to scrub away traces of these years is perhaps understandable, given the pain involved. After all, Jones was denounced and summarily purged from a band he helped assemble, Headon's heroin addiction led to his heart-wrenching expulsion, and Strummer then had to live with guilt over what he came to view as his ego-driven betrayal of close friends.

However explicable, the stance is still disappointing. If The Clash exemplified punk's "give us some truth" impulse, then facing reality to find the lesson beyond the pain seems essential. To rewrite history, erasing key players from the scenario in a way not so different than Stalin's falsification of the past—documented in David King's haunting book, *The Commissar Vanishes*—seems unworthy of a band as ambitious, principled, and gifted as The Clash.

Finally, we will place this tale squarely in its sociopolitical context, with the result that figures like Ronald Reagan and Margaret

Thatcher will be nearly as central as The Clash. This approach may not be popular with some more music-centric readers. Indeed, a growing number of people now tend to view The Clash as simply a great rock band: a tendency that, at once, is both obvious and odious.

No less a figure than Topper Headon has suggested that only The Clash's music has stood the test of time, not its politics, which might be acceptably forgotten. With all due respect to Headon's immense contributions, The Clash without its politics is a wretched ghost, for its greatness lay in a willingness to push the envelope on all levels. Its music *and* its message *together* made it a band that truly mattered, significant in a way few other musical outfits could hope to rival.

As such, to ignore the intimate connection of the final version of The Clash to its specific moment would be foolhardy. As forces clashed on battlefields both real and metaphorical, a turning point can be glimpsed. In 1984–85, a conservative counterrevolution that had been slowly building for at least a decade broke through. As esteemed literary theorist Terry Eagleton notes, "In 1976, a good many people in the West thought Marxism had a reasonable case to argue. By 1986, many of them no longer considered that it had. What exactly had happened in the meanwhile?"

While Eagleton jokingly floats parenthood as a possible answer, the matter is at once both more simple and more complex. This query will be as crucial as the question of what happened to The Clash; indeed, the two are quite intertwined.

From this angle, our tale makes much more sense. Jones once summarized his differences with Strummer, Simonon, and Rhodes by noting, "I was going, 'Let's dance'; they were going, 'No, let's riot!'" But while Jones's subsequent success with Big Audio Dynamite is undeniable, so is the fact that others felt the moment cried out for something more pointed than inventive beats and the artful use of samples.

This was a time of frightening military buildup, when tens of thousands were slaughtered with US guns in the name of "democracy," when the Falklands War tipped a nation-altering election.

Markets became God, big business shook off the shackles of regulation, and tax rates of the rich and programs for the poor were both slashed while "homelessness" became a new word in the American lexicon. Meanwhile, US workers joined their British compatriots in feeling the pain, despair, and dislocation behind a single consequential word: "deindustrialization."

If Sex Pistols had warned of "no future" in 1976 with one million unemployed in the UK, how much more grim was 1984 with over three million jobless? With police turned against their own communities, fighting a life-or-death strike with brutality and Orwellian tactics, as the world teetered on the razor's edge of nuclear destruction? Punk back on the barricades made immense sense in this context, and the final version of The Clash gains immeasurably from that reality.

The Clash was ascending the ladder of success as all of this drama unfolded. This breakthrough intensified its inherent tension between message and commerce. Is it victory to be playing huge stadiums but losing any real hope of an intimate or energizing connection to an audience? Is it success to have a hit with a catchy but lyrically vacuous song like "Should I Stay or Should I Go"? To feel the pressures of fame drawing the band further and further into a bubble of unreality that was the antithesis of the Clash punk-populist stance?

Many in the Clash camp felt these growing contradictions, but none more keenly than Joe Strummer. To try to fight back—reinvent and purify—was a chancy but essential course. The singer embraced this path, at least for a time, together with his final bandmates. Whether they succeeded in these aims is, of course, another matter. Yet one lesson might be that failure can be noble, while success can be a threat not only to your soul, but to the world itself.

What then is one punk band, however gifted, successful, or visionary, before the mountain of might, privilege, and raw avarice that Reagan, Thatcher, and the forces arrayed behind them represented? Not much, Strummer admitted in 1984: "The Clash compared to the Pentagon is smaller than the flea on top of a flea!"

Yet Strummer also acknowledged an intangible but still profound power that the group's art and ideas could provide. The Clash represented a passionate rebuke to the conservative advance, while not denying the failures that gave Thatcher and Reagan their initial power and lasting appeal. In certain ways, The Clash was responding to the same challenges, the same gap between rhetoric and reality. For a time, its upward trajectory even mirrored that of its deadly opponents, although The Clash's message would ultimately fail to gain the same social momentum.

If this is in fact so, then the crash of The Clash takes on an even greater resonance. More than any other punk band—or indeed any other rock band—The Clash articulated a vision of a transformed world. If they, like Reagan and Thatcher's shock troops, had measured the status quo and found it lacking, their remedy was quite distinct: the injection of more compassion, more equality, more freedom-in-community, with all this to be understood and applied globally.

The watchword of Reagan and Thatcher, by contrast, was efficiency—read "profits"—at all costs. In a twisted way, the creative destruction that anarchist revolutionary Mikhail Bakunin had called for, that punk had often echoed, was their aim as well. However, the welfare state, government regulation, labor unions, and any impediment to market "freedom" was what they sought to destroy.

Although Reagan and Thatcher evoked a sepia-toned bygone era to win support, their policies bulldozed not only statist bureaucracy but that olden world itself, which had been nourished by shared bonds of responsibility and solidarity. The Sermon on the Mount was outdated; in its place was to be a new gospel of self-interest. *There is no such thing as society*, Thatcher famously declaimed, promoting the idea of individuals acting rationally to advance their interests, guided toward the greater good by their greed, harnessed by the invisible hand of a quasi-divine "free market."

Perhaps some punks and Thatcherites shared more than might at first seem likely, both disavowing the old ways and embracing individualistic rejection of constraints. Yet The Clash instinctively stretched past both navel-gazing negation and the Money God to seek the promise of a "postscarcity" world, where there was enough for all and humans were freed from drudgery to find actualization.

In the hard place where ambitions contended with constraints, utopian visions crashed upon the rocks of harsh reality. "There ain't no need for ya / go straight to hell boys" went one Clash refrain; "Fog drowned towns got to fade / wrong side of a scissor blade" went another, pointing toward the fall of the post–World War II assumption—shared, in some sense, by hippie, punk, and miner alike—of ever-rising living standards for all, with the freedom that could buy.

In the end, we live in a new world where capitalism in its most raw form is ascendant, with diminished material expectations for many. On one hand, there has been untold multiplication of wealth; on the other, inequality has risen to levels not seen since the Gilded Age that dawned after the Industrial Revolution. These disparities are growing globally, crushing the poor and opening a huge divide between the rich and an increasingly precarious middle-slipping-to-lower class.

Even 2008's global economic near-meltdown and the growing specter of climate change may not have shaken the death grip of this iron-fisted version of capitalism. Why not? As Eagleton incisively notes, "It is unlikely that most of the radicals who changed their minds about the system between the seventies and eighties did so simply because there were fewer cotton mills around. It was not this that led them to ditch Marxism . . . but the growing conviction that the system they faced was simply too hard to crack. It was not illusion about the new capitalism, but disillusion about the possibility of changing it, which proved decisive."

In other words—and as Thatcher often argued—*there is no alternative.*

That the period that Eagleton identifies—the decade from 1976 to 1986—is exactly the life span of The Clash suggests a certain synchronicity. And while this is a tale of the last stand of a band with extraordinary ambitions and gifts, it is also the story of their time. This was a moment when The Clash's own struggle to right their internal balance and thus maintain their deeply conflicted upward trajectory paralleled the rise of other actors, whose vision was the dark mirroring of their own, equal in scope and driven by as much passion.

After performing "This Is England" in Düsseldorf, West Germany, in early 1984, Strummer warned his audience, "I'm telling you: pretty soon it is going to be Margaret Thatcher über alles!" If this comparison to the Nazi regime is overstatement common to the performer class, it also carries some truth. It is indeed so that the vision of Thatcher and her political soul mate Reagan triumphed, sometimes for better and often definitely for the worse.

At the same time, the revolutionary traditions The Clash drew upon and extended have not been fully vanquished. Margaret Thatcher to the contrary, an alternative can and must be found, our world still can and must be transformed in a more humane, inclusive, genuinely democratic way. Such belief was always central to The Clash, grounding their artful critiques in authentic, galvanizing hope.

"Find the ace!" Strummer implored, introducing "Three Card Trick" in 1984. This phrase is crucial, for the song portrays capitalism as a grifter's game designed so the dealer will forever win. In such a rigged system, hope becomes a trick that keeps the oppression intact. As each person buys the lie, one by one, they collaborate in their own destruction, down through the generations.

But this was not the whole story. The ace, in Strummer's vision, was the power people can discover by rejecting the lie and banding together: "Who can fight the entire grinding system? Nobody can! *But together everybody could* . . . I am talking pie in the sky here but still that's no excuse to sit back and say nothing."

There is no cheap grace to be peddled here, however. This book is the tale of a punk-cum-pop group, the moment it strained upward and then crashed to earth, the human frailties that led to that, as well as the human costs incurred. As The Clash plummeted, the Reagan/Thatcher vision took flight, soaring to heights that sometimes make it seem inevitable, undefeatable, eternally ascendant.

We Are The Clash, however, is ultimately the tale of how we might yet find that long-hidden ace, the one that enables victory in the game-you-cannot-win, the stacked deck of global capitalism, as well as on other fronts.

As always, it begins simply with the story of a few people, the dreams they had, and what they tried to do to make them real.

CHAPTER ONE
REBELLION INTO MONEY

Top: "Come on, I need some hostility here . . ." Joe Strummer
onstage, US Festival, May 28, 1983. (Photographer unknown.)
Bottom: US Festival, May 28, 1983. (Photographer unknown.)

*Where there is discord, may we bring harmony. Where there is error, may we
bring truth. Where there is doubt, may we bring faith. And where there is despair, may we bring hope.*
—Margaret Thatcher, May 4, 1979

*This here set of music is now dedicated to making sure that those people in the
crowd who have children, there is something left for them later in the century.*
—Joe Strummer, US Festival, May 28, 1983

The scene reeked of glorious rock spectacle.

Once scruffy denizens of British squats, tower blocks, and underground dives, The Clash today occupied the center of the musical universe. Standing on a massive outdoor stage, the band was dwarfed by more than 250,000 people. The roar of the sweating, surging crowd washed over the four slender figures.

From the back of the audience, the musicians seemed tiny ants on a stage, a pinprick of light, sound, and motion. A gigantic video screen provided the only opportunity for most listeners to connect actual human beings to the tsunami of guitar, bass, drums, and voice being flung at them in the darkness of the arena grounds of the US Festival, near San Bernardino, California.

"Unite Us in Song," the festival's advance publicity had said. The crowd, spurred by music, merged into a writhing rhythmic beast. Holy or unholy, some sort of communion was real here at this instant, in this place.

This should have been a moment of triumph for The Clash, a time to savor immense popularity won over seven hard years of touring, recording, and wrangling with an often mystified major record label. But as lead vocalist Joe Strummer strode to the microphone midway through the set, his words and demeanor suggested anything but self-satisfaction.

"I suppose you don't want to hear me go on about this and that and what's up my ass, huh?" the singer sneered. As the crowd cheered incongruously, Strummer continued: "Try this on for size—*Well, hi everybody, ain't it groovy? Ain't you sick of hearing that for the last 150 years?*"

A renewed roar greeted this dismissal, but what did the sound and fury signify? Affirmation? Noncomprehension? Determination to party on no matter what?

Strummer's tone shifted to pained earnestness: "I know you are all standing there looking at the stage but I'm here to tell you that the people that are on this stage, and are gonna come on, and have been on it already, we're nowhere, absolutely *nowhere*. Can you understand that?" The singer nodded to his bandmates, and muttered, "Let's do this number!" The quartet crashed into "Safe

European Home," a sardonic, self-deprecating comment on "third world" violence and "first world" cowardice.

Strummer's words evoked punk's "anti-star" idealism. Yet the members of The Clash stood on that stage as rock stars paid—as the singer boasted later—half a million dollars for barely more than an hour of work.

If the scene evoked untrammeled success, the singer's apparent anguish suggested something darker and more conflicted. Was this evening, ultimately, anything more than a lucrative commercial transaction?

In the eighty minutes The Clash played that night, one could have driven west from the festival grounds on Route I-10 and pulled in front of a handsome mansion in Pacific Palisades, a coastal neighborhood on LA's west side.

This house was where a transplanted Midwesterner had begun a transformation from aging B-list actor to right-wing icon to governor to, finally, the most powerful man in the world: the president of the United States. Now Ronald Reagan was preparing for a final political campaign, one that in eighteen months would determine whether he'd get another four years to consolidate his counterrevolution.

Across the Atlantic in The Clash's homeland, an equally momentous campaign was already well underway. In twelve days, more than thirty million British voters would decide whether to keep Margaret Thatcher as prime minister. Sharing a quasi-religious faith in the "free market" and enmity toward "big government," the two had become partners in what British journalist Nicholas Wapshott described as "a political marriage" that sought to change the world.

Conventional wisdom had dismissed Reagan and Thatcher as fringe figures, unlikely to be elected, much less be successful in implementing their creed. As Wapshott noted in a Reuters op-ed, "When Margaret Thatcher met Ronald Reagan in April 1975, neither was in their first flush of youth. She was fifty and he sixty-five. She was the leader of Britain's opposition; he a former governor of California. It was by no means obvious that either would win power.

They bonded instantly. Although born almost a generation and an ocean and continent apart, they found they were completing each other's sentences."

While both held to a conservative Christian faith that was then beginning to gain political ascendancy in the US via Jerry Falwell's "Moral Majority" movement, they also bonded around another shared inspiration. As Wapshott makes clear, "Both found validation for their convictions in the works of Friedrich Hayek, at that time a long-forgotten theorist even among conservatives."

Hayek was an Austrian economist who had famously contended with Britain's John Maynard Keynes amid the Great Depression over whether government intervention would ease or prolong the economic turmoil. Hayek had extolled allowing the "free market" to correct itself over time. Arguing that "in the long run, we are all dead," Keynes espoused ideas about the crucial role of government action which became the basis for much of Franklin Delano Roosevelt's New Deal.

The vanquished Hayek turned further to the right during World War II. In 1944's *Road to Serfdom*, he argued that not only did government meddling injure the economy but, indeed, was bound to lead to tyranny. Aided by the publication of an abridged *Reader's Digest* edition in 1945, the book found an audience in a slowly building right-wing movement, including with both Reagan and Thatcher.

By 1983 the two were no longer outsiders—they were rulers with immense power on the world stage. They brought this once obscure Austrian economist—and contemporary acolytes like Milton Friedman—into the mainstream. Both now stood at the pinnacle of their respective careers, seeking to dismantle the New Deal and Britain's socialist-leaning "welfare state" postwar consensus.

If punk offered a bleak forecast in 1976, by 1983 that dark possibility was being made real. Virtually all the other early trailblazers had fallen away. Now the successful but conflicted Clash was one of the last gangs in town, standard-bearer for a vision that took the postwar dream for granted, and sought to push beyond.

As such, Strummer might be viewed as the nemesis of Reagan and Thatcher, for the two politicians sought not the fulfillment of that dream, but its death. Yet all three in their distinct ways sought to transcend the post-1945 consensus.

Punk rock had always been about more than simply music. Born largely as a reaction to the self-indulgent excesses and perceived failure of the rock-and-revolution 1960s, it offered a blistering critique of idealism sold out or gone bad.

Punk's "ruthless criticism of everything existing" spared no one, and could slip toward nihilist extremes. That made the idea of harnessing music for radical change a perilous venture. Yet beneath noisy blasts of illusion-shattering negation still lurked an unbending belief in the power of music to transform.

The Clash was defined by this sense of mission. Dubbed "the only band that matters" by record company PR, the band helped crystallize an affirmative, activist vision for punk.

If the early Clash track "Hate & War" encapsulated the band's dismissal of the sixties, the musicians nonetheless borrowed from certain currents of that era. Their jagged, relentless music, close-cropped hair, quasi-military garb, and fierce sense of purpose suggested a marriage of Detroit agit-rock legends MC5 with the Chinese Cultural Revolution.

The Clash was fascinatingly—and sometimes infuriatingly—contradictory. They embodied punk's "year zero" stance, dismissing the Beatles, Rolling Stones, and Elvis Presley in "1977," the B side of their debut single, "White Riot." But if the incendiary songs warned of class war, they were made possible through the largesse of CBS Records, then one of the music industry's behemoths.

"Punk died the day The Clash signed to CBS!" punk scribe Mark Perry famously declared in 1977. Although proved false by what followed, Perry's words nonetheless suggested both The Clash's immense meaning and contradiction: it wanted to be the biggest rock band in the world while somehow remaining "death or glory" heralds of revolution. If this paradox earned The Clash more than its share of criticism, it was also grounded in idealism that was real enough to cause anguish for the man at the center of the maelstrom: Joe Strummer.

Lead singer/lyricist Strummer was not only the elder member

of The Clash, but also its soul. Rising out of the British squat scene, he was fascinated by American folk radical Woody Guthrie as well as the dwindling embers of late-1960s revolt. Active with a rising roots-rock band, the 101ers—named after the band's ramshackle squat—Strummer was wrenched out of his backward-gazing by a blistering Sex Pistols show in April 1976.

Shortly thereafter, he was poached from the 101ers by guitarist Mick Jones and bassist Paul Simonon to front their nascent punk unit. This gifted pair had fallen under the spell of agitator Bernard Rhodes, the catalyst for assembling the band and encouraging them to write about urgent sociopolitical issues.

If Sex Pistols lit the fuse of punk's explosion, The Clash sought to guide the movement's subsequent momentum in a constructive direction, making the implicit affirmation behind "no future" rants more explicit and convincing. "We never came to destroy," Strummer noted to *Melody Maker* in 1978, adding years later in a punk retrospective, "We had hope in a sea of hopelessness."

After the collapse of sixties rock idealism, this was a tricky line to walk. Strummer's ambivalence showed in a March 1977 interview with *Melody Maker*'s Caroline Coon. Asked how potent a band can be in making political change, he responded, "Completely useless! Rock doesn't change anything. But after saying that—and I'm just saying that because I want you to know that I haven't got any illusions about anything, right—having said that, I still want to try to change things."

Although The Clash was careful never to accept a narrow ideological label, it stood on the revolutionary socialist left, as the frontman acknowledged elsewhere. Given this anticapitalist stance, Strummer admitted to Coon—who later would briefly manage the band after the ouster of Rhodes in late 1978—"Signing that contract [with CBS] did bother me a lot."

Despite its underground roots, The Clash was not interested in being captured by a narrow subculture. If the Top 10 beckoned, it was in hopes of bringing a message of radical change to the broadest possible segment of the population.

In retrospect, The Clash's signing to a major label like CBS seems preordained. Capitalism would provide the avenue for reaching the masses that then, in principle, could be mobilized to overturn that same system and build something better. CBS had been home to Bob Dylan, Janis Joplin, and other sixties counterculture icons, and even issued an ad claiming "The Man Can't Bust Our Music" in 1968. Already thinly disguised folderol at the time, by the midseventies, such rhetoric could sound dubious indeed. The Clash pressed on nonetheless.

Punks were not the only rebels who strode onto the world stage in the midseventies, however. At the very moment the Republican Party seemed eviscerated by the Watergate scandal, with the Keynesian postwar order appearing unassailable, grassroots insurgent Ronald Reagan was challenging Republican president Gerald Ford, and "strange rebel" Margaret Thatcher had just captured the leadership of the Conservative Party in the UK.

Reagan came to political prominence with his 1964 "A Time for Choosing" speech on behalf of the presidential candidacy of archconservative Barry Goldwater. While Lyndon Johnson won the contest in a landslide, Reagan used his notoriety as a springboard for a successful race for governor of California.

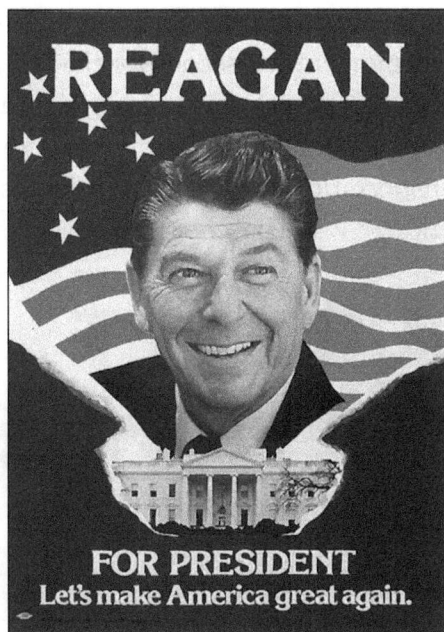

*REAGAN

FOR PRESIDENT
Let's make America great again.

Reagan established himself as the deadly enemy of student radicals protesting the Vietnam War, famously proclaiming, "If there has to be a bloodbath, then let's get it over with." In 1976, Reagan's upstart primary challenge to President Gerald Ford fell just short of victory. Four years later, Reagan defeated Jimmy Carter, who was wounded by inflation and the Iranian hostage crisis. Reagan accomplished what his mentor Goldwater had failed to do nearly two decades earlier: bring a newly radicalized Republican Party into the White House.

Over the same period, Thatcher had gone from Parliament backbencher to minister of education in the middle-of-the-road Tory government of Edward Heath. She slashed milk subsidies to schoolchildren, and showed no remorse when protesters chanted, "Thatcher Thatcher, milk snatcher!"

Thatcher watched not one but two Tory defeats by the militant National Union of Mineworkers (NUM), in 1972 and 1974. Led by rising Marxist firebrand Arthur Scargill, squads of "flying pickets"—unionists dispatched to blockade strategic locations— not only shut down the UK power grid but also brought down the Conservative Party–led government.

While Thatcher absorbed lessons from the lost battles, she was also there to claim the leadership of the party in 1975 in their aftermath. It was a lucky moment to ascend, for the Labour Party would squander its own turn in power amid economic stagnation and social turmoil. Unemployment and inflation rose, mounds of garbage piled up, and transportation was paralyzed by a series of strikes. "Labour Isn't Working" was Thatcher's catchiest campaign slogan.

Left: Thatcher's most resonant 1979 ad, by Saatchi & Saatchi.
Right: A different take on Margaret Thatcher by an anonymous artist.

Capitalizing on the ennui, Thatcher became prime minister on May 4, 1979. She promised healing, quoting the soothing words of St. Francis of Assisi as protesters confronted the police massed outside the compound. Her radical agenda, however, would create divisions not seen in the UK since the 1600s.

Thatcher came to power determined to complete a mission. Sex Pistols manager Malcolm McLaren had approvingly quoted anarchist revolutionary Mikhail Bakunin's dictum, "The destructive urge is also a creative urge," during the heady days of punk's birth. With Thatcher and Reagan's rise, another form of "creative destruction" had now arrived: the "free market."

Ironically, Austrian economist Joseph Schumpeter had derived the term from the work of Karl Marx. For Marx, "creative destruction" meant that capitalism sowed the seeds of its own downfall. But the phrase became used within "neoliberal" (a.k.a. "free market") circles to describe actions like slashing jobs at a company in order to increase its efficiency and, in principle, also that of the larger economy.

This process had been at the heart of the wrenching transformation generated by the Industrial Revolution, and was central to capitalism. If essential for economic growth and progress, the cost in human terms could be immense.

This conservative surge provided the backdrop for The Clash's rise. The tension between the band's aims and its means led to new groups such as anarchist trailblazer Crass. While inspired by The Clash, these bands were hostile to their compromises, with Crass cofounder Penny Rimbaud noting that "CBS promotes The Clash—but it ain't for revolution, it's just for cash." Strummer countered by calling Crass "a storm in a teacup," deeming their do-it-yourself stance as "self-defeating, 'cos you've got to be heard."

The Clash's third album, *London Calling*, challenged a version of punk that could seem ever more narrow. As Strummer groused, "I don't want to see punk as preplanned and pre-thought-out for you to slip into comfortably like mod or hippie music or Teddy Boy rock and roll. In '76 it was all individual. There was a common ground, it was punk, but everything was okay. Punk's now become 'he's shouting in Cockney making no attempt to sing from the heart and the guitarist is deliberately playing monotonously and they're all playing as fast as possible so this is punk' . . . God help us, have we done all that to get here?"

To Strummer, punk was a spirit, an approach to life, not a set of clothes, a haircut, or even a style of music. This was possibly convenient for the band's commercial aims, but his critique rang true. Soon many of The Clash's hard-core underground punk critics would find themselves striving to transcend self-made straitjackets.

With *London Calling*—released only six months after Thatcher's election—The Clash began to stake its claim on the broader arena of mainstream rock and roll. The musicians abandoned their early disavowal of prepunk sounds for a fervent embrace of the many forms and faces of rebel music. Spurred on by a catchy but lyrically lightweight hit single, "Train in Vain," the album rose almost into the American Top 20, an unprecedented level of success for a left-wing punk band.

The band's ambitious vision was made even clearer by the following triple-album set, *Sandinista!* It sought to articulate—with wildly varying degrees of success—a world music that spanned jazz, salsa, reggae, funk, rap, folk, steel drum, disco, and rock, united only by a common grassroots focus and radical politics.

The latter was announced by the album's title, an approving nod to Nicaragua's Sandinista Front for National Liberation (FSLN). Popularly known as the Sandinistas, they were Marxist revolutionaries who had overthrown a US-backed military dictatorship in a popular insurrection in 1979.

Strummer first learned about the Sandinistas from an old friend, Vietnam veteran/activist Moe Armstrong. Later he recalled, "Moe [gave us] info that was quite hard to find out. A bunch of teenage Marxists oust your favorite dictator? The establishment don't want to know!" Impressed by the quasi-punk spirit of the youthful revolutionaries, as well as initiatives like a mass literacy campaign and health care advances, Strummer and the band took up their cause.

The song "Washington Bullets" provided the album's title, rebuking the US—as well as the UK—for supporting dictatorships. It was no simple anti-American screed, for it also celebrated Jimmy Carter's commitment to human rights that had led the US not to intervene to stop the Sandinistas' victory. Articulating a consistent anti-imperialist stance, Strummer also skewered the Soviet invasion of Afghanistan and the Chinese occupation of Tibet over a bubbling salsa beat.

Left: Augusto César Sandino, who fought against the US occupation of Nicaragua, 1927–33.
Right: Massive crowd in the main square of Managua, Nicaragua, after the Sandinista victory, July 20, 1979.

By the time *Sandinista!* was released in the US in January 1981, however, the Carter administration and its human rights policy were on its way out. In its place was the newly elected Reagan administration, whose more muscular approach was driven by a rabid anticommunism that viewed conflicts around the world through the prism of superpower competition with the Soviet Union.

"Dictatorships and Double Standards," an essay by Jeanne Kirkpatrick, a former Democrat turned neoconservative hawk, informed Reagan's Central American policy. Kirkpatrick argued that Carter's human rights emphasis was fatally misguided. By abandoning authoritarian allies like Anastasio Somoza in Nicaragua or the shah of Iran, the US was naively opening the way for the expansion of Soviet-backed totalitarianism, and thus not only injuring our strategic interests but also, ultimately, the cause of human rights and democracy.

Reagan's decision to make Kirkpatrick his ambassador to the United Nations—an institution that she largely held in contempt—

sent a clear message that human rights was no longer a priority for US foreign policy.

While the Sandinistas had ample reason to worry about this shift, an ugly preview of bloodbaths to come first materialized in neighboring El Salvador. Kirkpatrick had already identified that country—which bordered Nicaragua, and was in the throes of its own nascent civil war, with Marxist-led guerrilla groups fighting a military-backed regime—as the next battlefront in a global war against Soviet communism. With Reagan's 1980 victory, his spokespeople made it clear that there would be no hands-off approach in El Salvador as with Carter in Nicaragua.

According to Robert White, Carter's ambassador in El Salvador, Salvadoran elites took Reagan's victory as a green light for a murder spree shocking even for a country where Archbishop Oscar Romero had been assassinated only eight months before. In swift succession, the leadership of the peaceful opposition was abducted, tortured, and killed, followed by rape and murder of four North American churchwomen, and, finally, the execution of the head of the Salvadoran land reform agency and two US advisers in the lobby of the Sheraton hotel.

When White spoke out against these horrors and subsequent efforts to cover up the role of the Salvadoran military, he was summarily dismissed. Reagan swiftly put forward a request for millions of dollars of military aid for the government. The conflict intensified and the body count mounted, rising quickly into the thousands.

The Reagan administration's savage debut could hardly be expected to pass unnoticed in the Clash camp. A response would be forthcoming, but the band was then preoccupied with other matters.

The Clash had created headaches for its corporate sponsors as early as 1977 with "Complete Control," which lambasted company machinations in brutally direct terms. Likewise, the band won few friends at CBS with its insistence on first putting out the double-LP *London Calling* for the price of a single album, then upping the wager with the three-for-the-price-of-one *Sandinista!*

CBS had grudgingly agreed. But *Sandinista!* held no breakthrough singles on any of its six sides, had received mixed reviews, and sold no better than *London Calling*. The band had foregone royalties in order to get its bargain price. Now debts to the record company were mounting.

As pressure built, a management shake-up pushed by Strummer and Simonon brought Bernard Rhodes back in early 1981. It would prove to be a fateful shift.

Rhodes was hardly a typical rock impresario, and his approach was anything but diplomatic. According to Clash insider The Baker, "The fundamental mistake everyone makes is in viewing Bernie as just the manager. But it was Bernie's vision that inspired the entire concept of The Clash. He crafted them, fathered them, pulling them one by one from their respective situations and putting them together like ingredients in a grand recipe. Their early political ideologies, fashion concepts, and total image were a statement of Bernie's thought processes."

If Rhodes was central to The Clash, his roughshod manner had alienated most of the band—especially Jones—and led to his firing. The Clash flourished artistically and commercially during his exile, with first Coon and then sixties holdover Blackhill Enterprises in the managerial role. Yet the growing tension between radical intent and commercial ambition left Strummer in particular feeling uneasy.

In Rhodes's absence, Jones had assumed control in the band. Strummer felt sidelined and—after the critical savaging of *Sandinista!*—concerned for the band's direction. As The Baker recalls, "The excesses of Mick's musical domination resulted in angst-ridden turmoil within Joe. Certain that The Clash had deviated badly from their intended goals, he turned to the only person that he felt was still championing those original political and cultural ideologies: Bernie Rhodes!"

At the same time, band mouthpiece Kosmo Vinyl argues simply, "Bernie was brought back to break The Clash in America, and I worked with him to make that happen." However counterintuitive this may seem, The Baker agrees: "Bernie was given a mandate: make the band huge, sell as many records as possible, get the message out to as many people around the world as possible—but do that without having the band's message watered down to puerile pop nonsense."

This seems an unlikely role for the abrasive radical. But Strummer believed Rhodes could accomplish this breakthrough while somehow keeping the band true in a revolutionary sense more than could the "professionals" at Blackhill.

In 1982, Strummer would explain to journalist Lisa Robinson, "It's like having a split personality. I want The Clash to get bigger because you want people to hear your songs, you want to be successful . . . But on the other hand, I'm pretty wary of that, of having it get too big to handle. You always think you can handle it, but you never know."

The Baker elaborates: "Joe wanted The Clash to reach the top, and yet not become part of the industry that they so despised. It was a tall order, and a very noble cause. Elvis, Beatles, and the Rolling Stones—they all became product, packaged and sold. Could it be avoided? Joe wanted to try."

In The Clash's 1978 anthem "White Man in Hammersmith Palais," Strummer had written about other punk bands "turning rebellion into money." If The Clash did break through, how could it evade that trap? Strummer wasn't sure—but regarding Rhodes not only as a political catalyst but as a surrogate father, he trusted him to navigate the treacherous straits.

Jones was not as hopeful that Rhodes would bring commercial success, but he also was not as nervous about the idea of rock stardom. Indeed, he had groomed himself for just such a role, as a kid from a broken home, living with his grandmother in a tower block. Vinyl—who had been with Blackhill, but who continued on with The Clash after the return of Rhodes—explains, "Mick was one of those kids who locked himself in a room, listening to the Stones, Mott the Hoople, whomever, practicing his guitar, dreaming of living that rock star life."

The Baker agrees: "Joe was from the squat scene, Woody Guthrie and all that, but Mick came from an old-school rock background, openly idolized bands like Mott the Hoople and the Stones." When asked why "1977" declared, "No Elvis, Beatles, or Rolling Stones," by a fanzine writer in October of that year, Jones grinned and replied, "Well, you gotta say all that stuff, ain't ya?"

Both Vinyl and The Baker hasten to add that this did not mean Jones was not committed to the Clash political vision, only that his attitude toward the fruits of success was much less fraught than that of Strummer or Simonon. Such differences meant little when the band was an underground punk phenomenon, but would become a flash point as its popularity grew.

As The Clash considered its next steps, Thatcher was recovering from a bruising year where her popularity had dropped to historic lows amid a deep recession. The contraction had been caused largely by her monetarist economic policies, bitter medicine intended to cure a rising cost of living.

Beyond inflation, Thatcher had ripped Labour for the high rate of unemployment. Yet joblessness had been rising ever since her election. It neared three million by 1981's end. Her critics were hardly surprised when urban riots broke out in Brixton and other low-income areas. Yet Thatcher was undeterred, asserting, "The lady's not for turning," despite pressure from within her own Tory ranks.

The pain was immense and undeniable: over two million jobs were lost in 1979–81. Particularly hard-hit was British Steel, the government-owned enterprise headed by Thatcher-appointee Ian MacGregor. He had returned after decades of living in the US to serve in this moment of "creative destruction" with downsizing, privatization, and closures high on his agenda.

MacGregor had presided over similar wrenching cutbacks in places like Youngstown, Ohio. As factories were shuttered, only to reopen with cheaper labor overseas, this US region gained a new nickname: the Rust Belt.

Thatcher was determined to "privatize" industries such as steel that had been nationalized after World War II as part of building a socialist state that sought to protect citizens from the cradle to the grave. Seeing only inefficiency and waste in this method, Thatcher valued MacGregor's hard-nosed approach to labor relations and improving profitability, and brought him on the team to do this specific job. But dismal poll numbers suggested that she risked being not only the least popular prime minister in UK history, but also a short-lived one.

Thatcher promised "a short, sharp shock" as her policies went into effect, with renewed growth and vitality to come. Many were not convinced.

As disaffection and upheaval in Great Britain were building, the Rhodes-led Clash had become the toast of New York City and Paris, turning residencies at the Bonds nightclub and Theatre Mogador into artistic and publicity triumphs. The Clash was especially captivated by New York, and had begun work on a new album.

Vinyl recalls the recording sessions themselves going smoothly—but not so the efforts at mixing or finalizing the record. Jones was even more dominant in the sessions than usual. He presented a finished double album tentatively called *Rat Patrol from Fort Bragg* that Strummer, Simonon, and Rhodes considered lightweight and too long. So producer Glyn Johns, renowned for work with the Who, the Stones, and other big names, was brought in on a rescue mission.

An impressed Johns later recalled to *Tape Op* magazine, "Joe let me rip it to pieces!" The result was a stripped-back single album that left Jones angry and aghast. Strummer was unapologetic: "I brought in Glyn Johns and I think . . . well, it isn't all good but he shook some real rock and roll out of that record."

If the musical disagreements were ominous, a more urgent crisis was the growing drug dependency of drummer Topper Headon. Drug addiction was a rock and roll cliché by now, and one The Clash had blasted with some regularity, despite the band's obvious affection not only for alcohol but also marijuana—a predilection made public in a 1979 feature in pot bible *High Times*.

In that article, Strummer identified heroin as a bane to the counterculture, echoing the longstanding Yippie distinction between "life" drugs like pot and psychedelics and "death" drugs like speed, cocaine, and, above all, heroin. Clash antiheroin commentary dated back to "Deny" on the first album through "Hateful" on *London Calling* and "Junkie Slip" on *Sandinista!* as well as a new track,

"Ghetto Defendant." Yet Headon fell prey precisely to this drug.

On an early 1982 tour of the Far East, Strummer confronted Headon: "How can I be singing all these antidrug songs with you stoned out of your head behind me?" Headon was unmoved, and the issue remained unresolved after the band's return, through the drama over the new album's length and production.

Then on April 21, 1982—three weeks before the new record was to be released and only days before a UK tour was to commence—Strummer disappeared.

Much has been written about the time the singer was missing in action. The disappearance had its genesis in a stunt suggested by Rhodes, apparently worried about weak advance ticket sales on the UK tour. But it turned into a genuine reflection of Strummer's desperation over pressures from the band's growing popularity, the deepening tension with Jones, and Headon's addiction.

Although Vinyl was able to locate Strummer in Paris after three weeks and convince him to return to do a lengthy US tour, the price was Headon's ejection. Original Clash drummer Terry Chimes stepped in with five days' notice before the two-month tour began on May 29, 1982, in New Jersey.

It was a challenging development, most of all for Headon, who felt betrayed and abandoned. Vinyl recalls, "Topper was the best drummer of his generation, but he had no interest in giving up drugs. We had no choice." The Baker disputes this, but admits, "The band couldn't just wait for Topper . . . things were moving so fast."

Strummer would later bitterly regret his decision, and date the demise of The Clash to this moment. Yet it's hard to see what else could have been done—not if the band intended to preserve its credibility.

By the time this drama had played out within The Clash, the political ground had shifted—starting when Argentine military forces invaded and occupied the Falklands Islands on April 2, 1982. The Falklands were a somewhat embarrassing vestige of the faded British Empire. They were situated just off the coast of Argentina, which claimed them as "Las Malvinas." While this Argentine assertion had history and geography on its side, the Falklands had been a British colony since 1841, and were largely populated by descendants of British settlers.

A series of errors had sparked the war. Budget cuts pushed by Thatcher led to British ships being removed from the South Atlantic, sending a signal that the Falklands were no longer a priority. Reagan emissary Vernon Walters subsequently assured the leadership of the Argentinian military dictatorship that in case of an invasion, "The British will huff, puff, protest, and do nothing." And the Argentinian dictatorship apparently felt that reclaiming the Falklands/Malvinas would distract attention from economic troubles and political repression at home.

In the last instance, the junta was proved correct, at least at first. Argentinian nationalism was sparked by the bold act, and approval of the government soared. But the first two assumptions would prove less sound.

Given that Thatcher's decisions had helped precipitate the Falklands conflict, the war could have dealt a deathblow to her unpopular regime. Thatcher's risky decision to dispatch a naval task force on April 5 to retake the islands raised the stakes even further. But this gamble would be her political salvation.

As British troops went into combat, nationalist fervor built in the UK, especially as the war went well for the home team. A popular tabloid newspaper, the Sun—mouthpiece for right-wing media mogul Rupert Murdoch—offered a simple huge "GOTCHA" as a headline in response to the sinking of the Argentinian ship General Belgrano, at the cost of 368 lives. The Sun adjusted the headline after the immensity of the death count became known, but the paper—like most of the British press—continued its gung ho war coverage.

Vinyl saw this war fever engulf a pub that the band had long frequented: "It was really ugly. We had been drinking beside these guys for months, and felt they were alright geezers. All of a sudden they were cheering Thatcher, cheering for the deaths of hundreds of human beings, all because they were 'the enemy.' It was a bit sick, really, and we decided to take our business elsewhere."

Thatcher adamantly opposed any resolution short of outright Argentinian surrender. This tested her relationship with Reagan, who was torn between their alliance and his support for the anti-communist Argentinian military dictators.

When Reagan sided with Thatcher, the outcome was certain. After ten weeks, and with nearly one thousand dead, the Union Jack once again flew over the Falklands. Thatcher emerged victorious, with dramatically increased popularity not only at home but abroad as well. The Argentinian dictatorship was soon deposed in a return to democracy, but for Thatcher the message was chilling: War works.

Among the many repercussions from this episode was a small one involving The Clash. At the last possible moment, Strummer decided to call the new album Combat Rock, intended as an oblique comment against the war then raging. It was a sign that Strummer's artistic gaze—largely diverted to Central America, Vietnam, and New York City—might soon come to rest back home.

For now, there was little time for reflection. Combat Rock was released on May 14, 1982, and the reunited original version of The Clash hit the road two weeks later. The shows tended to downplay Sandinista! in favor of the new record, the London Calling LP, and early nuggets like "Career Opportunities" now containing a revised line: "I don't want to go fighting in a Falklands street." "Charlie Don't Surf" was a key Sandinista! track aired from time to time, with Strummer explaining, "We thought this song was about Vietnam, until we discovered it was about the Falklands."

The band played virtually every night for two months. Although Chimes was not Headon's equal as a drummer, he was skilled and tireless, providing a hard-hitting foundation for the songs. One seasoned observer, Rolling Stone critic Mikal Gilmore, complimented the band on "some of the best shows in years."

Any doubts about the Clash trajectory were quickly overwhelmed by the imperatives of touring. After the US tour, The Clash had only two weeks off before making up the UK dates dropped when Strummer went AWOL. After three weeks and eighteen gigs, The Clash went back to America for another three months.

Combat Rock itself could be seen as a more concentrated version of the musical formula debuted on *Sandinista!*, largely eschewing straight-ahead rock numbers for more angular and open compositions. When Rhodes critiqued the new material he heard in rehearsal as long meandering "ragas," Strummer slyly incorporated the remark in the opening line of a new song, "Rock the Casbah."

The album also echoed *Sandinista!*'s themes. That record had been given the catalog number "FSLN 1," another nod to the Nicaraguan revolutionaries; *Combat Rock* now took "FMLN 2" as its number, a reference to the Salvadoran guerrilla coalition, the Farabundo Martí Front for National Liberation (FMLN).

The group was named after Salvadoran Communist leader Farabundo Martí, an ally of Nicaraguan revolutionary Augusto César Sandino, for whom the Sandinistas were named. Martí had led a peasant uprising against the military and oligarchy in 1932. It ended in *"La Matanza"* (The Massacre), with perhaps thirty thousand killed—including Martí—in less than a month in retaliation for the rebellion.

This slaughter found an echo in the mounting atrocities committed by the Salvadoran military, armed by the Reagan administration. In just one example, the Atlacatl Battalion—trained and advised by the US military—killed as many as one thousand men, women, and children suspected of supporting the guerrillas in the northern village of El Mozote on December 11, 1981. This single massacre equaled the entire death toll of the Falklands War.

When *New York Times* reporter Raymond Bonner helped expose these killings in January 1982, Reagan officials viciously attacked his objectivity, denying the atrocity had taken place. Amid intense pressure from the administration, Bonner was transferred to another post, and the slaughter went on.

If most of the US populace looked away, The Clash was paying attention, with sixties icon Allen Ginsberg adding references to Salvadoran death squads to *Combat Rock*'s "Ghetto Defendant." As with *Sandinista!*, the ghost of the Vietnam War hovered over the record, even as El Salvador was in danger of becoming another such

WE ARE THE CLASH » 51

quagmire, with the US drawn again into defending a corrupt and brutal ally in the name of "fighting communism."

Behind the scenes, the CIA was working to unify fractious anti-Sandinista counterrevolutionaries—known as "contras"—into a fighting force to harry and ultimately overthrow that regime. Using clandestine allies like Israel and Argentina, Reagan extended his backyard offensive throughout the Central American and Caribbean region.

As The Clash pressed its own campaign on the concert trail, a seismic shift was occurring. *Combat Rock* was garnering strong reviews, but even greater sales. First, "Should I Stay or Should I Go" ascended the charts, replicating the success of "Train in Vain" three years earlier. Then a new video music channel, MTV, sent a second single, "Rock the Casbah," into the Top 10. The endless gigging was exhausting, but The Clash was breaking big in the largest market in the world, headlining larger and larger venues.

Then The Clash got an unusual offer: the Who wanted the upstart unit to join a "farewell" American tour. Commercially, this was a no-brainer, exposing The Clash to an audience far beyond their existing one. Artistically, the appeal was less certain. The Who represented the "dinosaur rock" The Clash had set out to displace, and the band would be on enemy turf, playing huge stadiums.

The Baker knew where he stood: "We were packing up the gear after a show and [Clash guitar tech] Digby said to me, 'What's going on in the dressing room? The door is locked and there's no fans in there.' I ran back to the dressing room and found the band in heated discussion with Bernie and Kosmo about the prospect of supporting the Who. At the time it seemed to me that Mick was for it, Paul was on the fence, and Joe seemed to be just listening, undecided. I couldn't believe what I was hearing and resolved—against my better judgment—to offer my own protest even though I knew I was in danger of being told it was band business."

The Baker cited all the obvious drawbacks, but to no avail: "The Bernie/Kosmo force majeure was pounding the table about 'taking it to the next level' and 'competing with the music business on its own playing field.' Tempers flared—I couldn't believe we had come this far holding onto some of the most precious tenets of the early days, only to give in to big business. I was accused of being 'unrealistic' and trying to live in the past."

When Rhodes shouted, "This ain't fucking 1976!" The Baker gave up and stormed out of the dressing room. If beaten in the argument, he remained skeptical: "I felt Joe knew they were making a mistake but that there was nothing else to do. His unshakable trust in Bernie's instincts once again won the day."

In the end, the band decided it couldn't turn down the money or the challenge. But it was one thing to decide to do it, and another to actually play on gigantic stages to a distant audience, many of whom had not come to see The Clash, and who were impatient to see the headliners.

The Clash had played to big crowds before, including some 80,000-plus in London's Victoria Park for Rock Against Racism on April 30, 1978. That gig, however, had a political urgency and purpose, helping to defeat a rising neo-Nazi threat in the form of the National Front, amid acts of racist violence.

One of those in attendance was a teenage Clash fan named Billy Bragg. Years later, Bragg would recall, "That was the first political activism I ever took part in, and I went because The Clash were playing. It totally changed my perspective. There were 100,000 kids just like me. And I realized that I wasn't the only person who felt this way. It was that gig—and that audience, really—that gave me the courage of my convictions, to start speaking out."

Bragg was not alone in feeling the day was a transformative experience. In 2008, leading UK newspaper the *Guardian* wrote, "For those who attended the concert in 1978 it was a show that changed their lives and helped change Britain. Rock Against Racism radicalized a generation, it showed that music could do more than just entertain: it could make a difference."

Victoria Park carried an extraordinary resonance—but Strummer found that stadium shows rarely had such a vibe. They were engineered to include as many fans, and make as much money, as possible, with little thought to the quality of the experience. Bands would generally be visible only on gigantic video screens, blurring the line between experiencing live music and watching TV.

This meant hard work for any group serious about connecting with its audience, often resulting in an exhaustion that was more psychic than physical. The Clash was a band that fed off its fans, enjoying the chaos and spontaneity. The businesslike tick-tock of these huge shows was alien to them, and the immense distance from the audience took its toll.

At New York's Shea Stadium, Strummer chided the crowd for chatting during the songs. After another gig, a visibly exhausted Strummer—sitting slouched over and hiding behind sunglasses—was asked about the band's responsibility to the fans. He responded curtly, "I'm not strong enough to carry anything like that right now." When the interviewer followed up with Jones, asking how he felt about the music industry, he replied, "It's not any worse than any other prostitution business."

That Jones would say this is striking because, of the band's original cohort, he was perhaps the one most open to this level of success. It did not mean, however, that he handled the breakthrough well.

Jones had never been known for punctuality—in the movie *Rude Boy* he is scolded on camera by road manager Johnny Green—but after *Combat Rock* broke big, it got worse. Whether this was due to his late-night lifestyle or a power play is not clear. Whatever the cause, Jones regularly left the band waiting. Added to existing musical and ideological differences, a chasm was growing.

When the seemingly endless tour finally concluded just before Halloween 1982, The Clash was on top commercially, but battered spiritually. Moreover, Chimes did not wish to continue as drummer—nor did the band want to record new material with him, according to Vinyl.

After one last show in Jamaica on November 27, 1982, the band settled in for a lengthy break. Before recording *Sandinista!* the band had come off the road energized, eager to go to work writing new material, and even *Combat Rock* songs had come swiftly. Now everything felt different. There was no move to replace Chimes, and no plans were made even for rehearsals.

Ever eager for the stage, Strummer played a series of gigs with old friends—including Mole and Richard Dudanski from the 101ers—in an impromptu combo called the Soul Vendors. Both the band's name and the raw roots-rock it played suggested the deep ambivalence Strummer felt about the commercial status and musical direction of The Clash, increasingly driven by Jones, whose interest in hip-hop and electronic music was growing.

Jones had begun using a guitar-synthesizer hybrid that Vinyl derisively dubbed "the dalek's handbag," referencing evil extraterrestrials in the *Doctor Who* TV series. Jones's adventurous spirit had catapulted The Clash past most of its peers, asserting punk as far more than a static set of chords, hairstyles, and clothes. Now, it was not clear whether Strummer or Simonon wished to continue on that journey, at least in the direction Jones proposed.

When Strummer suddenly decided to make a ragged but engaging film noir, *Hell W10*, in early 1983, he enlisted friends and bandmates for the DIY endeavor. Strikingly, Jones was cast as the villain. For some participants like The Baker, the clues were too obvious to miss: "It was as if Joe knew that the only way they could keep working together was by not playing music."

In the midst of editing the film, a call came with an astonishing offer: The Clash had been offered $500,000 to headline the first night of something called the US Festival, to be held near San Bernardino in Southern California.

The US Festival, which aspired to be "the Woodstock of the 1980s," was the brainchild of American entrepreneur Steve Wozniak, cofounder of Apple Computers. The mountains of money being made in this emerging sector was contributing to fundamental shifts in the US and global economies—and allowed Wozniak to bankroll a huge festival costing untold millions of dollars.

Could that cash buy The Clash? The band had made a reputation by not being overly impressed by money and its temptations, even rebuffing the UK hit maker *Top of the Pops* because it required lip-synching. But if stadium shows were difficult, playing such a festival was a whole other animal.

In the sixties, the rock festival represented a "gathering of the tribes," a communal celebration of the counterculture transcending a simple commercial transaction. Many were free, exemplifying a belief that music is for the people more than profit, for communion more than commerce.

But the intimate context that fed punk—with audience and band on essentially the same level—was worlds apart from the mass scale of rock festivals. Vinyl later noted, "Festivals are a hippie's dream, but a punk's nightmare."

In 1989, Strummer articulated the punk ethic in praising the original 9:30 Club in Washington, DC, which had a legal capacity of 199: "I like tight spaces like this one where the crowd can feel the sweat splashing off the stage and you can look one another dead in the eye, take each other's measure. It makes it all real, you know? Whatever it is, we're doing something together, right in this spot, right now. It ain't luxury, but it has some soul, like it was made for people, not cattle."

The US Festival was going to be the sort of massive rock spectacle that made powerful communion difficult at best. But perhaps this was the moment for The Clash to take on the music biz on its own turf, a chance to stand up for "revolution rock." Or maybe the money and momentum propelling them into the mass arena was too great to resist. Whatever the mix of motives, The Clash signed on.

Immediately the band faced a problem: there was no band. Seeing "the row brewing between Mick and the other two," Chimes had definitively stepped back. Headon was still lost in his addiction. As a result, The Baker—none too excited about the show in the first place—was tasked with finding a skilled, relatively unknown replacement that could fit The Clash's music, look, and mission.

The Baker knew there was no time for lengthy auditions. (The Clash had tried out perhaps one hundred drummers after Chimes left the first time, before settling on Headon in April 1977). He placed an ad in the April 23 issue of *Melody Maker*, and Peter Howard was one of those who answered the call. As The Baker remembers,

"From the moment Pete walked into rehearsal he was so right for the Clash that it was an open-and-shut case . . . Musically, stylistically, and culturally, he was perfect for them."

Howard was young, just twenty-three, but skilled. Although a casual fan of The Clash, he was not a devoted follower. "I'd seen The Clash, and I liked them, but I was not overawed. Headon was great, but my drum heroes were mostly prog-rock guys like Bill Bruford or Alan White, so I wasn't intimidated."

It was a high-pressure moment to be joining The Clash, and the managerial team of Rhodes and Vinyl were scarcely warm and fuzzy. Yet Howard seemed to hit it off with his rhythm-section mate Simonon, as well as The Baker who recalls, "With Pete's arrival, it appeared possible that the dynamism, energy, and creativity could once again be ignited with the introduction of another element into the mix."

As the Clash machinery revved up again, Strummer got some life-changing news: his partner Gaby Salter was pregnant. As Strummer's relationship with his own parents was strained—having been consigned to boarding school, and losing his older brother to suicide—the immensity of becoming a father hit home.

Other members of The Clash were also experiencing massive changes in their personal lives. According to The Baker, "Paul had flown out to the US after we'd got Pete Howard and married his girlfriend, Pearl Harbour. Joe was now a father-to-be and was obviously feeling all the tensions that go along with that. Mick was fully ensconced at home with [his girlfriend] Daisy exploring new ground with his own alternative set of friends and their 'creatures of the night' scene which obviously flew in the face of the Bernie/Kosmo/Joe/Paul axis."

As Strummer absorbed the big news, and The Clash hurried to break in the new drummer, another momentous change had taken place. On March 28, Thatcher's new National Coal Board director was announced: Ian MacGregor.

MacGregor had headed British Steel since 1980, presiding over a radical restructuring: 166,000 people had jobs when MacGregor arrived; by the time he left for the Coal Board, only 71,000 were still there. More than 60 percent of the jobs in this British industry had just . . . disappeared.

Enterprises sheltered by government subsidy could run deficits eternally, bleeding the coffers dry. But not everything worth having showed up in the bottom line, of course, and there was serious social value to the jobs created.

For Thatcher, it was not worth the trade-off. In the long run, all would be best for the most, as the market made its magic happen—or so went the creed of the neoliberal faith. The choice of MacGregor to head the Coal Board meant the same medicine that had been given to steel was now to be administered to another pillar of the British economy. Arthur Scargill—now union president, having won election in 1981 with over 70 percent of the votes—declared, "The policies of this government are clear: to destroy the coal industry and the NUM."

Meanwhile, Reagan had taken his rhetorical confrontation with the Soviet Union to an ominous new level. Speaking on March 8 to the National Association of Evangelicals in Orlando, Florida, Reagan extolled the power of prayer, and religion's role in the founding of America. These paeans to the faith-based "greatness and the genius of America" were delivered while the administration was underwriting savage repression in El Salvador and beyond.

After denouncing abortion and supposed infringements on religious freedom by government bureaucrats, Reagan shifted to a new topic: the nuclear freeze movement trying to arrest the escalating arms race between the US and USSR.

Reagan claimed, "As good Marxist-Leninists, the Soviet leaders have openly declared that the only morality they recognize is that which will further their cause, which is world revolution." He then asked the crowd to oppose a nuclear freeze that would only serve "the aggressive impulses of an evil empire . . . and remove yourself from the struggle between right and wrong and good and evil."

Such terms made war seem inevitable. While nuclear conflict might appear unthinkable, Reagan had argued in 1981 that such a war might be contained to Europe—a grim prospect for those who recalled World War II's devastation.

As the stakes were rising on both sides of the Atlantic, The Clash hit the road, doing a series of smaller-scale shows in Texas and Arizona, warming up for the US Festival. The band was rusty, but Howard was proving himself as the new engine of the machine, with the power of Chimes and the finesse of Headon. The Baker: "In a way, Peter was a mix of the two . . . he fit like a glove." Vinyl: "There were issues, there always are, but it was clear he could do the job."

Yet tensions in the band were simmering. As Howard recalls, "I was the new guy, so I wasn't privy to everything, but I could tell that Mick and Joe seemed hardly on speaking terms." The choice of "Garageland"—a "we won't forget where we came from" anthem written in response to signing with CBS—to open the first shows seemed to acknowledge a growing disconnect. Strummer was keen to demonstrate that The Clash remained true to its original mission.

Playing shows seemed to help ease the strain. The Clash was starting to hit its stride by the final warm-up in Tucson, Arizona. Strummer confronted overly aggressive security from the stage and joked about "the MTV curiosity seekers" in the packed house, but the band was hot and the crowd rapturous.

With the warm-up shows successfully completed, The Clash was on its way to the festival with spirits high, when reality hit them in the form of a huge Budweiser billboard in the desert promoting the US Festival. Such sponsorship was hardly unknown in rock and was rapidly becoming much more pervasive. Having signed to CBS years before, The Clash was by no means innocent of corporate marketing. Yet the band sought a certain distance to avoid compromising their politics and art.

The ad showed exactly what the band had signed up for, and The Baker remembers the mood on the bus darkening palpably. Strummer had already been joking about the juxtaposition, taking jabs at the other headliner, heavy metal party band Van Halen—which was getting $1 million to play, twice The Clash's payment—from the stage at the show in Wichita Falls, Texas.

Today · Tomorrow · Together

'83

GLEN HELEN PARK
SAN BERNADINO, CA

The   Festival

May 28, 29 & 30

Saturday
THE CLASH
MEN AT WORK
STRAY CATS
THE ENGLISH BEAT
FLOCK OF SEAGULLS
OINGO BOINGO
WALL OF VOODOO
INXS
DIVINYLS

Sunday
VAN HALEN
SCORPIONS
TRIUMPH
JUDAS PRIEST
OZZY OSBOURNE
JOE WALSH
MOTLEY CRUE

Monday
DAVID BOWIE
STEVIE NICKS
JOHN COUGAR
PRETENDERS
MISSING PERSONS
U2
QUARTERFLASH
BERLIN
LITTLE STEVEN & THE DISCIPLES OF SOUL

TICKETMASTER
213-480-3232
$20.00 per day

Gates Open at
8:00 a.m.

Buy in Person at Music + Plus · Federated · Sportsmart   Buy Early, Tickets Higher at the Gate

Now Rhodes tried to help by going on the attack. The festival's techno-hippie vibe made it an easy target, and the decision was made to test the organizers' utopianism. Although Wozniak would end up losing a huge amount of money on the festival, at the time that wasn't anticipated. Rhodes challenged him to pony up $100,000 for a camp for at-risk youth or The Clash wouldn't play.

Wozniak resisted what he saw as blackmail, given that The Clash had already signed a contract to play. At a last-minute press conference, the band pressed its threat not to play unless Wozniak came through with the donation. The audience was left waiting for nearly two hours until a compromise was found: the festival would give a token $10,000 contribution, and the band agreed to go on.

The band members were scarcely relaxed as they ran onstage, taking places in front of a gigantic banner proclaiming, *THE CLASH NOT FOR SALE!* If this seemed to protest too much, Strummer nonetheless greeted the massive crowd with a sardonic, "So here we are in the capital of the decadent US of A!" as the band plugged in.

In an earlier press conference with numerous other performers—where Van Halen lead singer David Lee Roth ribbed The Clash for being "too goddamn serious"—Vinyl had declined to comment on the festival itself, while making it clear "from the moment we hit the stage till the moment we leave, we will have something to say." The band was no more than thirty seconds into the show, but the truth of Vinyl's statement was apparent.

Perhaps thinking of his impending fatherhood, Strummer dedicated the Clash set "to making sure that those people in the crowd who have children, there is something left for them later in the century." Then the band was off, igniting "London Calling," followed swiftly by a fiery "Radio Clash" and a haunting "Somebody Got Murdered" with Jones on lead vocals. Strummer's guitar was mixed higher than usual, providing an appealingly abrasive sound, with his ragged chording adding a raw edge to Jones's more pristine tones.

Strummer had clearly come onstage intending to challenge the huge crowd as much as the event organizers. As soon as the third song died away, Strummer was back on the offensive: "Well, I know the human race is supposed to get down on its knees in front of all this new technology and kiss the microchip circuits, but it don't impress me over much . . ." The singer hesitated, then launched another salvo: "There ain't nothing but 'you make, you buy, you die'—that's the motto of America. You get born to buy it . . ." Leaping from critiquing consumerism to racial and economic inequality, Strummer continued: "And I tell you, those people out in East LA ain't going to stay there forever. And if there is going to be anything in the future, it's got to be from all parts of everything, not just one white way down the middle of the road!"

If the words were perhaps a bit incoherent, Strummer's passion was plain. As the crowd tried to absorb the message, the singer tossed off one last exhortation—"So if anybody out there ever grows up, for fuck sake!"—and the band was off into their hit single "Rock the Casbah," followed by the hard-hitting numbers "Guns of Brixton," "Know Your Rights," "Koka Kola," and "Hate & War."

Slowing the pace, Strummer introduced "Armagideon Time" as "the F-Plan Beverly Hills reggae song," referring to a fad diet popular at the time. This quip turned serious as Strummer evoked the famine building in the Horn of Africa by extemporizing about "the Ethiopian Diet, lose five hundred pounds, success guaranteed, or your money back—yes, your money back" over a spooky dub groove. As he returned to the "a lot of people won't get no supper tonight / a lot of people won't get no justice tonight" refrain, the band—led by Jones—brought the song to an ominous close with splashes of dissonant guitars and drums.

If the music was strong, the singer found the audience response wanting. As applause washed over the stage, Strummer retorted, "Bollocks, bollocks! Come on, you don't have to fake. You spent twenty-five dollars to go out there, so do what you like . . ."

The puzzled crowd responded uncertainly. Strummer upped the ante: "A lot of you seem to have speech operations, can't talk or shout back or anything." Balling up his fists, seeming desperate to somehow touch the distant mass, the snarling frontman baited the audience: "Come on, I need some hostility here . . . RRRRAAAWRRR! I need some feeling of some sort!" Then his tone lightened: "As it's Sunday tomorrow, I hope you will join me . . ." The zinger led into a rollicking version of *Sandinista!*'s "The Sound of Sinners," an amiable—but eminently forgettable—bit of gospel rock and roll. Self-deprecation, spoof, and sincerity mixed freely in lines like, "After all this time to believe in Jesus / after all those drugs / I thought I was Him," before concluding, "I ain't good enough / I ain't clean enough / to be Him."

It seemed something of an odd choice. Strummer, however, had a spiritual side, with radical bits of Christianity coming in largely through the Rastafari faith that imbued the band's reggae covers. His past inspiration, Woody Guthrie, sang of Jesus as a revolutionary standing against the powers-that-be: "Jesus said to the rich / give your goods to the poor / so they put Jesus Christ in his grave."

This view was backed up by history, and was shared by many believers. Priests and nuns served in the Sandinista government, for example, and had sacrificed their lives in El Salvador, part of a "liberation theology" that reclaimed this radical Jesus. While Thatcher and Reagan wore Christianity on their sleeves, The Clash's stand with the dispossessed was more consistent with Christ's life and teachings.

Unlike "Armagideon Time" or "Police and Thieves," however, "The Sound of Sinners" did not seem like heavy message music. Yet clearly the song meant much to Strummer, and its comedic disavowal of messianic pretension sparked his most vulnerable appeal of the evening. The singer dismissed rock stars and their glamour, pointedly including himself in that "nowhere" crowd. His anguished outcry aimed to bridge the chasm between The Clash and its audience and, in so doing, perhaps to mend the similar gap widening within the band's heart.

Schizophrenia nonetheless remained apparent. After a frantic stretch of blazing rockers—"Police on My Back" (with Jones again on lead vocals), "Brand New Cadillac," "I Fought the Law," and "I'm So Bored with the USA," with Strummer pausing only to spit "Oh so you're still there?" at the audience—the band segued into the pop love song "Train in Vain," their first US hit.

Next the band brought the funk of "Magnificent Seven," spinning its tale of workaday desperation before downshifting into the brilliantly bleak seven-minute epic "Straight to Hell." The song gained further poignancy from Strummer's extended rant against drug-addled rock stars. Such, the singer noted, made enough money to get their blood changed when their lifestyle grew too toxic, caring not a whit that they were leading others down a dead-end path—a clear reference to an apocryphal story then circulating about Keith Richards.

Strummer brought his improvising to a close with bitter lines like "Hey, man, let's just party / while our friends are dying / let's just party / hey, where's the party at?" before spitting out the song's aching final verse. Yet, after this sobering, artful challenge, it was back to the lightweight hit "Should I Stay or Should I Go."

The shifts were jarring—but then it was over. The band went off the stage, returning for a short encore of "Clampdown." Strummer once again launched into a tirade, blasting complacency about atomic weapons and nuclear power. The song drifted out across the multitude, moving some, no doubt mystifying others.

The band stepped back, intending to return for a final encore. When organizers moved to preclude that by dismissing the crowd, Vinyl tried to grab the mic. A fracas erupted, with the band in fisticuffs with the festival staff. As this unfolded, an emcee took the microphone and called out derisively, "The Clash has left the building," echoing the fabled Elvis exit announcement. The show was over.

Likely the festival's most dynamic set, it was surely the most unsettling. The Clash had flung itself against the wall of rock-biz hypocrisy and audience expectation, while being sure to showcase all its hit singles. In its inimitable fashion, the band simultaneously played the game and sought to burn it down.

It was one of their greatest performances. But if The Clash intended a righteous challenge to "business as usual," it didn't necessarily come off this way. To many, their behavior was simple rock star ego, self-servingly couched in revolutionary rhetoric. The Clash's half-million-dollar fee seemed at odds with its concern for the poor. Why didn't they donate some of their take? And if they didn't like the festival, why play in the first place? While the band made noises about returning to California to play a free show, this didn't stem the criticism.

As The Clash returned home with contradictions worsened and internal divisions unhealed, the crucial UK general election loomed. Thatcher's popularity had dipped from its post-Falklands high but remained well above where it had been a year earlier. In part, this was due to an economy that was bouncing back in some areas—though not in Britain's hard-hit north, reeling from industrial closures.

Meanwhile, the Labour Party had splintered. Dissident elements had formed the Social Democratic Party that allied itself with the middle-of-the-road Liberal Party. Thatcher's opponents could not have done her a bigger favor.

Thatcher got a smaller percentage of the vote than in 1979—dropping from 43.9 percent to 42.4 percent—but thanks to the fractures on the left, the Conservatives swept Parliament. This meant Thatcher now had a vast, veto-proof majority—and a free hand to pass right-wing legislation—even though she had won considerably less than half the overall vote. It was an ominous portent, made worse by the news of rebounding popularity for Reagan, readying his own run for reelection.

Meanwhile, the members of The Clash had gone their separate ways after returning from the US Festival. No one seemed to know what the next step was.

June and then July passed with no movement. As The Baker remembers, "I started calling everyone in an attempt to find out what the next move was, but it seemed like no one knew or no one was talking. No matter who I called—Kosmo, Bernie, Joe, Paul, or Mick—I was met with a resolute, 'I don't know,' or, 'I haven't heard from anyone.' It seemed insane." A conspiracy of silence had descended over the band, with clandestine meetings being conducted behind closed doors.

The Baker finally got a grudging agreement to restart rehearsals— the essential first step toward writing new songs—but with only limited results: "We set up the backline at Rehearsal Rehearsals and put the kettle on just as we did for previous occasions, but it was like flogging a dead horse. One day Paul would turn up, hang around for a while, and go home. The next day Mick would arrive late, miss Joe, and leave again, and so on. Poor Pete Howard was going out of his mind, having succeeded in getting the chance of a lifetime, only to have it turn out like this. I can't actually remember a complete rehearsal that August."

Unbeknown to The Baker, pent-up frustration, stoked by the pressure of mass success, was about to splinter The Clash. Jones was soon to be purged from the band that he, more than anyone save perhaps Rhodes, had built.

"The day Mick was fired, the air was thick with tension," The Baker recalls. "Bernie came into the studio early, then left. Then he would call: 'Anyone there yet?' 'No.' Click." When Strummer and Simonon turned up, nothing was revealed to them, and they went across the road to the pub with Rhodes.

The Baker was told to have Jones come straight over on arrival: "Mick arrived suitably late and I told him they were waiting in the pub. He ruffled his feathers and asked me, 'What are they all doing in the pub?' I told him I didn't know."

After only about fifteen minutes, Jones came back from the pub and without a word proceeded to put one of his guitars into its case. The Baker: "I was busy doing something on the other side of the room and heard Digby say, 'Do you want me to take the guitar for you, Mick?' Then Mick said, 'They've asked me to leave the group!' Digby interjected, 'They can't do that, it's your group, isn't it?' Mick said, 'They don't want me in the fucking band anymore!'" Jones then picked up his guitar and left Rehearsal Rehearsals for the last time.

It had been an excruciating choice, and perhaps it was the right one. But The Baker articulates the first reaction of many observers: "What did I think when Mick was kicked out of the band? I thought The Clash was over and done."

Yet how could The Clash end at the height of its popularity, with a battle of historic proportions looming? Was there a way to rebuild, to reinvent, to right the course and get on with its mission? Strummer, Simonon, Rhodes, and Vinyl were determined to find out.

CHAPTER TWO
WHAT IS CLASH?

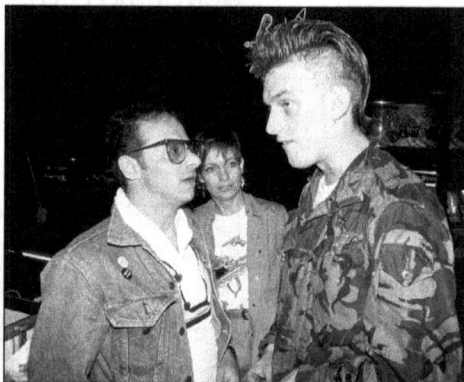

Left: Strummer and Simonon return to their punk roots, late 1983. (Photo by Mike Laye.) Right: Bernard Rhodes and Kosmo Vinyl, with Peta Buswell, head of the NYC Clash office at center. (Photo by Bob Gruen.)

We have two choices. We can give in and watch social destruction and repression on a truly horrific scale, or we can fight back . . . Faced with possible parliamentary destruction of all that is good and compassionate in our society, extra-parliamentary action will be the only recourse left for the working class.
—Arthur Scargill, NUM conference, July 4, 1983

We've been away for two years—and I've been trying to come to a decision. I've been thinking, What the fuck am I doing living? What am I supposed to do with it? How come you all come see it? Where is it going, what was it going, what is Clash, where is Clash, who is Clash?
—Joe Strummer, Barrowlands Ballroom, February 10, 1984

On Saturday, September 10, 1983, readers of *New Musical Express* (NME) were startled to learn that The Clash—as they had known it—had ceased to exist.

A band statement read simply, "Joe Strummer and Paul Simonon have decided that Mick Jones should leave the group. It is felt that Jones had drifted away from the original idea of The Clash. In future it will allow Joe and Paul to get on with the job The Clash set out to do in the beginning."

Clash biographer Marcus Gray later wrote that the news "hardly came as a surprise," but it was to at least one person: the author of the NME press release, Kosmo Vinyl. "I was shocked by this," the Clash spokesperson insisted years later. "I was not part of the process that decided whether or not this was going to happen—or maybe I was, but I wasn't aware of it."

Vinyl was well acquainted with the tensions, but never believed it would come to this. Yet it now fell to him to somehow help reassemble that most alchemical of creations: an ambitious and successful rock band that had ejected the authors of two and a half of its three hit singles in slightly more than a year.

Vinyl: "In the end, the situation was presented in a certain way: 'Are you on board with this, or not?' And I decided to go with that. The band, what it represented—it all was too important for me to stand aside."

This was no small decision—and other members of the Clash camp made different ones in the "him or us" atmosphere that developed after the purge of Jones. The Baker recounts, "I decided to wash my hands of the whole situation. I never told Joe or Paul that I quit, but I said goodbye and left. They never called me, and I never called them."

Equally committed partisans came to different conclusions. Like Johnny Green, The Baker had been suspicious of the upstart. Vinyl, however, had earned their grudging respect. Now, as Rhodes's consigliere and a band mouthpiece second only to Strummer, Vinyl was key to meeting the challenges ahead.

"Now Mick's gone, and we're thinking, 'We have Joe and Paul and a drummer,' you know?" Vinyl recalls. "So we're not starting from scratch here. How are we gonna go forward now?" If the exact path wasn't immediately apparent, one agenda item was: a new guitar-slinger, with both the needed skills and of sufficiently stalwart ideological stock.

Five days after the news of Jones's expulsion, seven people gathered for a meeting at 10 Downing Street. If far less publicized than the internecine strife in The Clash, the meeting would prove considerably more consequential.

The public would only learn about this secret conclave more than thirty years later via a newly released document, marked, "Not to be photocopied or circulated outside the private office." Attended by Margaret Thatcher and her closest aides, the meeting concerned Ian MacGregor's plans for the British coal industry.

British Steel had already undergone drastic layoffs. Now coal mines—known in the UK as "pits"—were on the bull's eye. According to the meeting notes, MacGregor's closure program had "gone better this year than planned: there had been one pit closed every three weeks," with the workforce shrinking by 10 percent.

This was wrenching amid the worst downturn since the Great Depression, but the Coal Board now meant to go much further: "Mr. MacGregor had in mind that over the years 1983–85 a further seventy-five pits would be closed . . . The manpower in the industry would be down to 138,000 from its current level of 202,000." *Almost one-third of all coal miners stood to lose their jobs in the next two years.*

This was political dynamite, as was made clear by the precautions taken to avoid disclosure of the plan: "There should be no closure list, but a pit-by-pit procedure," the notes record before coming to the final paragraph: "It was agreed that no record of this meeting should be circulated." Another memo written a week later stated that the group would continue to meet regularly, but that there should be "nothing in writing which clarifies the understandings about strategy which exist between Mr. MacGregor and the secretary of state for energy."

The secrecy was essential, for the plan was ruthless. As the BBC reported in 2014, "Two-thirds of Welsh miners would become redundant, a third of those in Scotland, almost half of those in northeast England, half in South Yorkshire and almost half in the South Midlands. The entire Kent coalfield would close."

It was precisely this sort of wholesale assault that Arthur Scargill feared. While some disliked him as a Marxist firebrand, Scargill's landslide victory for the union presidency in 1981 reflected both his popularity and the rank-and-file sense that a decisive showdown with the government was coming.

The sweeping Tory election victory raised the stakes. In 1981 Thatcher had backed down before a NUM challenge; now her position was strengthened considerably.

At the NUM national conference held shortly after the Tory landslide, Scargill issued a call to action. Warning that Thatcher sought to destroy the industry not only due to lack of profits, but for revenge, he evoked the specter of fascism in 1930s Germany: "We have two choices. We can give in and watch social destruction and repression on a truly horrific scale, or we can fight back."

NUM president Arthur Scargill, with United Mineworkers of America hat. (Photographer unknown.)

Scargill made his position clear: "I am not prepared to quietly accept the destruction of the coal-mining industry, [or] to see our social services utterly decimated. Faced with possible parliamentary destruction of all that is good and compassionate in our society, extra-parliamentary action will be the only recourse left for the working class and the Labour movement."

These were powerful words—and they would be used against him. Scargill matched Thatcher as a polarizing figure, with the same air of righteousness. Like the Tory leader, he inspired fanatical followers, but also bred determined enemies and could alienate less-convinced sectors.

Scargill's call for "extra-parliamentary action" was simple reality: Thatcher controlled Parliament, so the only way to resist now lay outside that institution. Still, darker notions of a Communist coup d'état would be spun out of the same thread, as the Tories portrayed the matter as a struggle for democracy, not jobs.

Thatcher was not above fearmongering, sketching Scargill as a dangerous radical out of step not just with Britain but with his own rank and file. MacGregor echoed this, describing Scargill's speech as "a declaration of war" from an antidemocratic bully seeking to overturn the duly expressed will of the country.

This conveniently overlooked the fact that a majority of British voters had never pulled the lever for Thatcher. Even though the vagaries of the UK system had awarded the Tories a veto-proof majority in Parliament, their support in 1983 had actually dipped to 42.4 percent, some 700,000 less votes than in 1979.

Moreover, if Thatcher was so assured of the legitimacy of this path, why not share the plans with the public? Clearly she feared the consequences—so she and her minions would subvert the open discussion essential for democracy by never admitting to the true scope of the sweeping mine-closure program.

While there were reasonable arguments to be made over the economic health and future of coal as an industry, the central thrust of the Tory scheme was political, as was made clear by the existence of something titled, "The Final Report of the Nationalised Industries Policy Group."

Nicknamed "The Ridley Report" for its author, Nicholas Ridley—Tory free-market evangelist and close Thatcher ally—this plan was drawn up in June 1977, just as punk was exploding across Jubilee-era Britain. The report contained many contentious suggestions, but most explosive was a two-and-a-half-page "Confidential Annex" entitled, "Countering the Political Threat."

This addendum identified the nature of the "threat" and suggested a solution. Like Thatcher, Ridley took for granted that the NUM—by virtue of its organized militant strength and unique importance as the provider of electricity that ran the entire British economy—had become even more dangerous than the Labour Party itself. Any successful Conservative government in the future would need to tread carefully, aware that confrontation was more than likely.

Ridley did not fear this struggle. But he did seek to ensure that the battle would come on terms favorable to—or even chosen by—the Tories.

Ridley urged that coal stocks be increased to prevent power cuts in the event of a prolonged strike. Plans should be made to import coal from nonunion foreign ports, with nonunion drivers recruited by trucking companies, and with dual coal-oil generators installed. While these measures would increase costs, they would significantly reduce the miners' leverage.

Police would also need to be equipped with riot gear and trained in mobile tactics to counter "violent picketing," i.e., the flying pickets. Legislation should be passed to make such picketing illegal to whatever extent possible. The police force was to be readied to use as a blunt instrument in what was ultimately a political battle.

The Ridley Report was a map for winning a war with the unions, especially the NUM. Such inflammable material is hard to keep secret, and the plan was soon leaked, appearing in the UK press in early 1978.

That error had become a learning experience. Now that the game was afoot, a much tighter lid was clamped on preparations for the coming war. The election had given the leverage needed to put the Tory plans into action—all that stood in the way of the free-market renaissance they craved was the NUM.

While Thatcher was drawing up battle plans, so was Joe Strummer—and his weapon was The Clash. But for many people, that entity no longer existed: The Clash was Strummer-Jones-Simonon-Headon. Vinyl called this the "John-Paul-George-Ringo Syndrome"—a band was certain people; no less, no more.

This purist idea was widely flouted in an industry ever more fixated on money. Still, it spoke both to an artistic reality—the mix of certain people could have a unique magic—as well as a compellingly romantic notion of rock bands made of friends who rise from the garage to the world stage together.

Jones himself had raised this question with rock journalist Mikal Gilmore in June 1982 by noting that the post-Headon Clash "feels like a new band now," even wondering aloud if they should be called "Clash Now" or "Clash Two." Such musing seemed odd given that The Clash had started out with their then-current drummer Terry Chimes, recording their first record with him. Moreover, The Clash had played the landmark "Anarchy" tour with Sex Pistols, Heartbreakers, and the Damned—as well as other key shows—with drummer Rob Harper.

Jones's idealism shines here, as such attachment to specific members had become unusual. By the 1980s, most bands freely shed members, even losing central catalysts like Syd Barrett (Pink Floyd) and Brian Jones (Rolling Stones), but still rolling forward on artistic and, of course, commercial terms.

But what if "The Clash" was more than a band—if it was an idea? Was it the specific people or the mission that mattered? Jones's rival Clash cofounder Rhodes believed in the latter notion, which was, in its way, just as idealistic as its opposite.

Rhodes was taken by the idea that The Clash could be like an army platoon, with no soldier irreplaceable and the shared objective paramount—a metaphor that Strummer and Simonon also embraced at the time. Indeed, Strummer would soon go so far as to argue, "I hope that if I start acting funny, I'd be fired, and The Clash would roll on without me."

This could be taken to an extreme. The Baker skeptically re-called Rhodes's admiration of the Puerto Rican bubblegum pop band Menudo whose members shifted at the whim of their pro-ducer/creator Edgardo Diaz. He later laughed: "Of course, Bernie would like that—it gave him all the control!"

This comparison might seem ridiculous. Yet the original Clash had hardly come together as teenage friends in some mythical ga-rage. It was manufactured out of Jones's striking musical vision, but equally assembled by Rhodes's instincts and ideology. Miracu-lously, this fairly mechanistic mating had actually worked.

The Clash coalesced more deeply than Malcolm McLaren's Sex Pistols, whose self-destruction was more or less assured. Strummer and Jones had chemistry as a writing team and—with Simonon added to the onstage mix—as an arresting live juggernaut. Headon soon added to this, helping to propel their ascent.

Could lightning strike again? For Strummer this was no aca-demic matter. While marching in step with Rhodes, he also knew there was something more mysterious and organic required; more than anyone else, it would be up to him to make the new "platoon" cohere as an artistic and spiritual entity.

The pressure was immense. Strummer admitted he "was think-ing all the time . . . maybe too much." He had a depressive nature and in 1982 had spoken of "some bad times, dark moments when I came close to putting a pistol to my head and blowing my brains out"—an ominous admission given his brother's suicide.

Although Strummer hastened to add, "If you ain't got anything optimistic to say, then you should shut up," his bouts with dark-ness might have been the natural result of a brain that refused to shut off. He now had more than usual to contemplate, as doubts about his decision to eject Headon and Jones nagged him.

The burden had a practical aspect. After his exit, Jones would pointedly question how The Clash might forge ahead without him, saying, "I hope that their new guys help them write the material." Strummer hardly needed to be reminded of the hole in the band's creative core, acknowledging, "If your song ain't good, you ain't gonna triumph." He was already hard at work to meet this challenge.

Michael Fayne, the young recording engineer brought in by Rhodes in 1981 to work at Lucky Eight, the studio at their Camden haunt, Rehearsal Rehearsals, saw the pressure on Strummer up close. "Joe would come in to demo a song, you could tell he was nervous. He would run through the song, just him and guitar. As he did, he'd kind of sneak a peek at me, see how I was reacting."

Fayne didn't remember being that impressed by the new songs, but did recall that one tune with the words "This Is England" caught his ear. If Strummer picked up on the lukewarm reaction, he was not deterred. The singer continued to knock out new tunes, to be fleshed out once the band was whole again.

Strummer's plans were helped when a new guitar player was found via auditions hastily arranged by Vinyl: Nick Sheppard, former lead guitarist of the Cortinas, a defunct first-wave punk band from Bristol in southwest England.

Though the auditions were for an unnamed band, Sheppard had a pretty good idea who it was. As the guitarist recalls, "I was out at a pub not long before the audition came up and ran into Joe, Paul, and Kosmo. I happened to overhear them talking a bit, going on about 'he's got to go.' Had no clue at the time, but in retrospect, it was pretty clear who the talk was about."

Hundreds came to the auditions, but Sheppard stood out. He was from the same original punk generation as Strummer, Simonon, and the rest. The Cortinas had been popular enough to earn their own brief liaison with CBS in the late seventies, but not so high profile as to be a distraction. Sheppard: "We had the same influences, came up in the same school, if you will . . . We understood each other."

While the Cortinas scarcely shared The Clash's politics, Sheppard had solid left-wing credentials: "I grew up in a family of trade unionists and Labour supporters, and I was, in that respect, politically aware—I knew what side I was on." Finally, Sheppard was a big Clash fan, having seen the band live many times.

Once Sheppard was in the fold, the band went into intense rehearsals. Strummer unveiled more than a dozen new songs, which the new lineup began to hammer into shape. Their work, however, was shadowed by rumors that Jones and Headon were readying their own version of The Clash.

While this prospect gnawed at Strummer's self-doubt, a less sentimental Rhodes saw it as a direct threat. Jones had been critiqued for working through lawyers while in the band; how much more likely was legal action now?

In strictly commercial terms, "The Clash" had become a lucrative brand, and Rhodes wanted to preempt counterclaims. He urged Strummer to make it clear in song that nothing from Jones and Headon could be the real item.

Sheppard witnessed the dynamic: "You got the sense then that some new songs were 'made to order' in a way, that Bernie had said to Joe, 'We need a song called this or about that.' Joe would listen, but he is a serious writer, right? So what he would come up with would be his own vision in the end." The process produced a song that would define the new band to fan and foe alike: "We Are The Clash."

The title was a bit obvious. Even for a band renowned for self-referential anthems like "Clash City Rockers," "Radio Clash," "Last Gang in Town," and "Four Horsemen," it seemed a step too far. Predictably, it would be swiftly lampooned as a laughable echo of "We Are The Monkees," the theme song of another manufactured band favored by Rhodes.

While the song may have started out in that territory, Strummer took it to a deeper and more resonant place. He understood Rhodes's desire to protect the Clash "brand," but such an angle struck him as altogether too businesslike. For Strummer—as with Rhodes, ultimately—The Clash was something far more profound than a commercial venture, more than even a band . . . but exactly what?

The surge of right-wing power added urgency. "The world is marching backward fast all the time!" Strummer declared at the time. "Everything I read is bad news, apart from the Sandinista thing in Nicaragua." A tantalizing idea began to percolate out of his soul-searching. Strummer's thoughts intersected with Rhodes's directive, but went beyond.

Strummer's inspiration began with the Clash audience. Ever eager to engage with fans, Strummer had been touched by encounters on the 1982 tour of the Far East. In Japan, for example, one conversation had turned to family members killed in the US atomic attacks on Nagasaki and Hiroshima. Strummer was already riveted by the nuclear danger; this made it even more real.

Strummer shared another anecdote from the tour with Sheppard, who recalls: "These aboriginal guys came to talk to him after the [Queensland, Australia] show about their situation. And then he got a phone call saying that the police had gone and busted up their house, because they'd dared to go backstage and talk to these white guys." The ugliness of the incident, the deep racism it represented, and the courage of the fans "really left an impression on him," according to Sheppard.

The Clash had once articulated voices from Brixton, Camden Town, Notting Hill, the West Way. Now they had come to embody something broader, rising up from the global grassroots: a rainbow of peoples, united by a shared spirit. The fans' enthusiasm and ability to relate their struggles to themes in Clash songs affected Strummer, fueling the band's own ambitious musical and topical trajectory.

This growing fusion also reflected the fact that The Clash came alive in concert—in Strummer's words, "working together with the audience." Keeping all of this in mind, the singer wrote a couplet that became the central metaphor of the new song: "We can strike the match / if you spill the gasoline."

First heard as a demo recorded at Lucky Eight in November 1983, "We Are The Clash" utilized blunt yet cannily arranged butcher-block chords to stake its claim. Propelled by Howard's powerful drumming, its chorus asserted, "We are The Clash / we can strike the match" with the follow-up line "if you can spill the gas" repeated twice and drawn out, the focus shifting from artist to audience, to what could be created together. Fittingly, it seemed designed for a gigantic sing-along.

The song was now less about "protecting the brand" than making it clear that—as Strummer would later insist—"when I say that 'we are The Clash,' I'm talking about considerably more than five people." The song was an example of how a nudge from Rhodes could result in something profound in Strummer's hands.

This exploded the concept of The Clash, launching it past the realm of "rock band." If the song embodied Strummer's punk populism, other lyrics tied the fate of this fusion to larger global struggles. "We don't want to be treated like trash," the song insisted—yet across the world so many were, in so many ways.

The end of 1983 was a particularly powerful moment in this regard, for reasons both practical and symbolic. Strummer had long been a fan of writer George Orwell. This independently minded British socialist had authored the dystopian classic *1984*, which portrayed a suffocatingly oppressive world where language itself had been corrupted to serve as a tool of social control.

Orwell's blistering critique—aimed equally at fascism and Stalinism—reflected his belief that relentlessly seeking and speaking truth was central to human liberation. The idea resonated with Strummer, as did Orwell's critiques of British imperialism and the violence of poverty, and his desire to abandon his privileged background to be in solidarity with the poor and working classes. The singer's emphasis on truth telling as the core of The Clash's revolutionary mission echoed Orwell's own imperatives.

The references were everywhere: the band's debut single "1977" ends with a spooky echoed "1984!" On the embattled "Anarchy" tour, Strummer had refitted "Protex Blue" with lyrics that warned, "Big Brother is watching you." Graphics from the film versions of *1984* and another Orwell masterpiece, *Animal Farm*, appeared in The Clash songbook and on the cover of 1978's "English Civil War" 45, respectively. Strummer had even revised history once, suggesting that the 101ers' name was a reference to Room 101, *1984*'s torture chamber.

Orwell had intended *1984* less as prophecy than as a warning of what was already unfolding in the late 1940s when the book was written. Still, its impact imbued the year 1984 with a sense of destiny. Much like 1977—the year when "two sevens clash," according to some Rastas—the fast-approaching new year had an ominous sense of converging, perhaps even world-rupturing forces.

"The Clash," then, might not simply be a band and its audience, but also this charged moment, carrying the sense of an era's turning, for good or for ill.

This conception of The Clash could seem pretentious, yet was of a piece with the band's immense ambition. It suggested why, in Strummer's mind, The Clash was urgently needed right now, not simply as a politicized pop group, but as a cocreated project of artist and audience, as a spirit of struggle.

The high stakes and global sweep involved were evoked by the existing words of "We Are The Clash." The song opened with a list of peoples—"Russians, Europeans, Yankees, Japanese, Africans"— invited to a "human barbecue," where "twenty billion voices / make one silent scream." This Edvard Munch-like image suggested worldwide nuclear war, a final showdown that no one could truly win.

To Strummer, Reagan appeared to be preparing for just such a conflagration, embarking on the largest military buildup in post-WWII history, while cutting taxes for the rich and slashing programs for the poor. Furthermore, never-ending war against a shadowy enemy provided the justification for 1984's totalitarian control. This, in part, already existed. Both US and Soviet military planners justified their massive budgets by pointing to the danger posed by the other, a circular logic that drove ever greater expenditures and made war all the more likely.

On September 1, 1983, tensions between the US and the USSR hit a scary crescendo with the downing of Korean Airlines flight 007 (KAL 007). A commercial flight from Alaska to South Korea, KAL 007 strayed into Soviet airspace for unknown reasons and was shot down, with a loss of 269 lives.

The Soviets had made a terrible error—one repeated when the US shot down Iran Air flight 655 in July 1988, killing 290—out of paranoia fanned by US bellicosity. This meant no less in terms of human suffering, but it mitigated the supposed barbaric intent, and highlighted the perils created by superpower tensions.

Amid all of this, the US invaded the Caribbean island of Grenada in October 1983. Touting a supposed Communist threat to the region, Reagan used the chaos following a bloody coup against Grenadian leader Maurice Bishop—a Cuban ally—to intervene. The supposed aim was protecting American students on the island; the result was the installation of a new US-friendly regime.

For the first time since the Vietnam War, the US was asserting its imperial prerogatives over its "backyard." The message to the Sandinistas and their Cuban and Soviet supporters was clear.

George Orwell's *1984* hung heavy over Clash-land. (Artwork by Eddie King.)

As 1984 approached, catastrophic confrontation seemed increasingly inevitable. Strummer expressed this fear in another new song, "Are You Ready for War?" Musically, this was one of the strongest of the new batch, and analogous to the bracing punk-reggae of "Police and Thieves." The song rose off a funky groove but also brought the punk hammer down, creating something new and exciting. Sheppard contributed cutting-edge "DJ scratch" hip-hop guitar noise.

The demo's other dozen songs cataloged additional concerns. Some were new takes on old topics: the personal and political dangers of drugs ("Glue Zombie" and "National Powder") and US foreign policy ("The Dictator"). Others like "Sex Mad War"—an attack on rape and pornography from a feminist perspective, riding on a hopped-up rockabilly chassis—explored newer lyrical territory.

A notable focus on the trials of the British working class came through in a trio of hard-hitting songs. "This Is England"—the song that had caused Fayne's ears to prick up—began as a folky dirge spinning out dark images of "a gang fight on a human factory farm," only to rev up by song's end, with galloping guitars, bass, and drums driving home a bleak commentary on Thatcher's Britain.

The use of the term "factory farm" was striking. These words had been popularized by UK animal rights activist Ruth Harrison: "Factory farms are often owned or highly influenced by corporations and the guiding principle of these businesses is efficiency, producing the most produce and hence profit for the least expense," with little regard for the consequent suffering—a trenchant critique of Thatcher's aims.

A second song, "In the Pouring Rain," opened with clarion chords, followed by words that portrayed a gray vista, drenched in a downpour that evoked the hopelessness settling over the depressed north of England: "I could see as I rode in / the ships were gone and the pit fell in / a funeral bell tolled the hour in / a lonely drunkard slumbering . . ." While the music started off a bit stiff, not quite bringing the aching words to life, dynamic guitar interplay after the chorus lifted the song.

Best of all—musically and lyrically—was the blistering "Three Card Trick," which likened the capitalist system to a famously fixed card game, three-card monte. The song opened with crushing power chords propelling a stark indictment: "Patriots of the wasteland / torching two hundred years." Strummer struck directly at the claims of Thatcher and Reagan to be making their countries "great" again, while creating a desert of deindustrialization and unemployment.

This was not overstated. Journalist William Kleinknecht would later describe Reagan as "the man who sold the world," a critique that could just as easily apply to Thatcher. The duo preached the gospel of "creative destruction": clearing away the old and exhausted to make way for that which was new and improved.

Such claims were not far from punk's "Year Zero" rhetoric, but Strummer was having none of it. His focus was on people, on their pain, as "Trick's" follow-up lines show: "Bring back crucifixion / cry the moral death's head legion / use the steel nails / manufactured by the slaves in Asia."

As with the best of Strummer's lyrics, these lines pack a book's worth of critique into nineteen words. Subtly equating the Nazis and the Moral Majority, the Clash frontman undercuts the right-wing Christian "law and order" agenda by evoking their crucified founder, while tearing the veil off the interconnected realities of first-world deindustrialization and third-world exploitation.

A more succinct indictment of the Thatcher-Reagan project was hard to imagine. More concretely, the steel references in both "Three Card Trick" and "This Is England"—as well as earlier in "Straight to Hell"—show how Strummer was aware of the devastation of British industry, and what it represented: the unraveling of a social compact forged in the fires of the Industrial Revolution.

Strummer was ambivalent about the cost of that bargain, as his lyrics elsewhere comparing factory work to slavery suggest. The singer argued, "For the past two hundred years we've all been had by an industrial society . . . that only needs workers to fuel its factories and furnaces and whatever. I feel [humanity] has a better destiny . . . There's a better life to be lived for everybody and by everybody."

Yet Strummer saw the immense suffering created when factories, mills, and other enterprises closed, taking jobs with them: "Supposedly technology and science was going to save the world, and we should be going forward into a bright future, but [instead] it's recession, close a factory down, put people out of work."

To be fair, these trends had predated Thatcher and Reagan, and resulted from globalizing forces that were extremely difficult to resist. But Thatcher in particular was an unapologetic defender of cutting the lifelines for many struggling industries—and those who worked there—in the name of efficiency.

In "This Is England," Strummer encounters a female mugger holding a blade made of "Sheffield steel," referring to the most renowned UK steel town, now devastated by cuts. The reference was clear: most of those workers left jobless saw Thatcher as the one who had slashed their industry's throat.

Steel had been one of the pillars of the British economy since the Industrial Revolution, and its decline could rightly be viewed as a national tragedy. Still, there was one commodity that was even more fundamental: coal.

Orwell noted this in *Road to Wigan Pier*: "Our civilization is founded on coal. The machines that keep us alive, and the machines that make machines, are all directly or indirectly dependent upon coal. In the metabolism of the Western world the coal miner is a sort of caryatid upon whose shoulders nearly everything is supported." Even steel depended on coke—a coal derivative—for its manufacture. Without coal, the lights went out, metaphorically and literally.

The work could be horrific. Untold thousands had been lost in mining disasters and from diseases like black lung. This underlined the cost at which our world had been built, and who paid the price. As such, coal miners' rights to better conditions and pay resonated across history—especially in British society.

Once British miners had built a strong union, their unique combination of moral claim and practical power gave them a status unmatched in the country's workers' movement. Given their historic role, the miners would tend to have public opinion on their side, and a direct way to inflict pain on the government by causing power cuts—unless proper preparations were made in advance.

By late 1983, Thatcher was keen to complete just this. According to Charles Moore's authorized Thatcher biography, "Preparations for the inevitable confrontation continued. 'The first priority,' Mrs. Thatcher told the meeting, 'should be to concentrate on measures which would bring benefit over the next year or so.'"

Aware of the growing tension, the miners took action. As Moore notes, "The first rumbles of confrontation were felt on 31 October 1983, when the NUM began an overtime ban in protest at the current pay offer and rumors of pit-closure plans. In a meeting of ministers two days later, which Mrs. Thatcher chaired, it was agreed that the danger of a strike was 'likely to increase in the second half of 1984.'"

If anything, the NUM's prohibition of overtime—which would effectively cut miners' pay, but also slow government efforts to build up surplus coal stocks to guard against a strike—was late in coming. Although Moore reports, "Ministers assumed that the NUM would not be so foolish as to begin a strike in the spring just when demand for coal would fall," this seems disingenuous, for the Tories would surely seek to provoke a strike at the most advantageous moment.

As Thatcher baited her traps, The Clash seemed to have bounced back in record time. While a couple of cuts on the demo seemed hardly advanced from the rattletrap grit of the 1976 Clash—or even the 101ers—the tape as a whole suggested a promising new unit. Far from a narrow punk fundamentalism, the songs conveyed a stronger rock foundation while still leaving room for other flavors.

Strummer knew that, despite any loftier intent, The Clash would rise or fall on its power as a band. Interviewed at Lucky Eight after the demo's completion, he seemed resurgent, offering paeans to rock's power: "The real things came off the street, invented by lunatics, madmen, and individuals, they're the ones that last. I'm talking about your actual rock and roll, rockabilly, even psychedelic insanity rock and punk rock—these things weren't created by the industry. The industry was running after these things, going, 'What is it? Where can I get some?'"

The singer sounded ebullient about the new lineup: "In this place, seven years ago, we decided we were going to be bigger than anybody else—but still keep our message. And, in a way, there was no way of avoiding those things that we fell into. So, it's been good rebuilding The Clash here because we've really come full circle, starting out here and coming back here now."

Strummer then turned philosophical: "You mentioned that it was 'unfortunate' that we had to go through these things but I think that is the wrong word. I think it was *inevitable*. You don't get issued with a map about how to avoid these things. I think it's a question of learning, of being burned by life and learning from it."

Asked finally to share his greatest thrill about The Clash, the singer said: "I get a kick out of it when someone comes up to me and says, 'Because of your group I went and retook those exams that I failed and passed them all!' I get a kick of hearing how we influenced people's lives. 'Because of your group I am majoring in political science.' I get a lot of stuff like that."

This power was real, but the responsibility it entailed was immense. For now, Strummer laughed at the thought that this role might bring him unbearable pressure.

Pieces seemed to be falling into place. Not long after the demo's completion, however, a wild card was introduced: Greg White, who was living in Finsbury Park, was suddenly drafted as the second guitarist in the new Clash.

This most likely began as an effort by Rhodes to reduce Strummer's burden. Vinyl was startled but supportive: "I don't remember exactly where it came from, but I'm thinking it came from Bernard. Joe would not play guitar as much onstage and we would get two guitar players." And, Vinyl noted, "there were five in the original Clash lineup," recalling the early guitarist Keith Levene.

Vinyl was surprised by this sudden turn, but it hit Sheppard much harder: "Was I happy? Of course not. One day it was just announced that another guitarist would be joining us. I had no say, and it was hard not to take it personally, even if it made some sense musically, and there had been five in the beginning."

The move acknowledged another reality: Strummer was a spirited but rudimentary guitar player who, by his own admission, was able to "jam out a few chords but couldn't do any fiddly bits." In the heat of a performance, his playing could become even more hit-and-miss, as he lost himself in the moment, "looking for the ultimate wipe-out," as he once described his attitude toward performing.

In 1982, Jones noted this challenge: "Joe stops playing the guitar a lot, and those are moments where the instrumentation could use a bit of embellishment, so me hands are going all the time." Though Jones tried "to hold it all together," he did so with only mixed success, as live tapes from that era sometimes showed.

Live performance is not entirely about hitting all the right notes. Nonetheless, there was wisdom in the idea that songs written for two guitars should be played by such. This interplay was part of the power generated "when two guitars clash" as Belfast's Stiff Little Fingers put it in a tribute to the band.

This promised to be a boon to Strummer, who was now freed "to go loopy," as he laughed later. The rub came in finding the right person for this job.

If Sheppard had been a somewhat known commodity, White was anything but. Later Sheppard would admit to uncertainty about whether White had ever played publicly before his gigs with The Clash. White actually had, but he acknowledged the largest pre-Clash crowd he had faced was perhaps less than two dozen. Even so, he had the skills and the looks—and a serious attitude. That's likely what won him the job.

Feeling lost in a dead-end life, working at a warehouse, White was intrigued and annoyed in equal measure by a NME ad in that read, "Wild Guitarist Wanted." He passed an initial telephone interview, and joined dozens of guitarists summoned to audition for an anonymous band.

Unlike Sheppard, White only had a vague notion of what band he might be joining. "They kept it very hidden," he recalls. "I wasn't totally sure, but there was a rumor that it was [The Clash]. Some people were saying it was Tenpole Tudor, and a few people were saying it was somebody else."

Auditions took place on The Clash's Camden Town stomping grounds, at the Electric Ballroom. There, White and the others cooled their heels until it was time to play with a prerecorded backing track. Strummer and Simonon were nowhere to be seen, leaving Rhodes and Vinyl to run the proceedings.

Bored by the process, White entertained himself with a few beers he had smuggled in. He took the stage angry and a bit drunk, swiftly breaking a string, but playing straight through what White later described as "a load-of-crap electronic rhythm-and-blues track," then stalking off in a huff.

By musical standards, it was hardly a successful audition. But while White's skills couldn't match those of some of the other players, his aggro caught the attention of Rhodes and Vinyl, who tailed him outside to get contact information. Later Rhodes triumphantly told Strummer and Simonon, "We found a real street punk!"

The move was not entirely ludicrous, as White had been a fervent fan of the band and often in its audience. He no longer dressed "punk," but that was easy to address. As White later laughed, "When I joined The Clash, I basically reverted to how I had looked a few years before, as a teenage punk!"

This daring choice showed how unbusinesslike The Clash remained in key regards, operating by punk instinct rather than commercial calculation. Yet it was not without danger. Sheppard noted a bit ruefully later, "The problem is, when you choose someone for their attitude, that's what you get: *their* attitude."

There was little time for reflection, for Rhodes was not allowing much time for the new platoon to solidify. His aim was to get back on the road quickly, returning to the vicinity of their embattled last show with a tour of California in late January.

The original idea had been to play a free gig to erase the lingering bad taste of the US Festival. That was now deemed impractical, given legal worries and the need to make money to fuel the retooled Clash machine, so a seven-date tour was planned instead. As White officially joined the band just days before Christmas, this gave them less than a month to get ready.

One further adjustment was needed. "Greg" was deemed an insufficiently punk name, so White was redubbed "Vince" in honor of early rock heroes Gene Vincent and Vince Taylor. White went along with the change grudgingly, seeing it as evidence of a controlling—and superficial—image consciousness. It was not the last time that he would be dissatisfied with life in The Clash.

The new Clash amid the worst joblessness since the Great Depression, early 1984. (Photo by Mike Laye.)

Less irksome to White was a rigid antidrug line, newly instituted within the band. The edict did have some omissions. "Since alcohol was not on the list of banned substances, it was no skin off my nose, really," White later recalled with a chuckle. Sheppard: "We were set down early on as a group and Joe and Paul made it clear that we weren't to be doing these things." Dropping drugs beyond alcohol was also not a big issue for Sheppard: "I had been considering giving [pot] up anyway, for what it does to your short-term memory."

This stand made sense, given the desire for a new start for the band. Yet the ban was striking because it included marijuana, a longtime Clash staple.

Some were skeptical, suspecting a Rhodes edict or yet another dig at Jones, whose fondness for pot and cocaine was well known. Perhaps these dynamics played a role, but more likely this was a natural evolution out of long-standing concerns.

Early punk had denounced drug-addled hippies and similarly impaired rock stars. Some in the movement like Rhodes and Vinyl saw such stances as serious and self-evident, but many punks simply seemed to disdain "other people's drugs" while indulging in their own faves.

The Clash had long inhabited this ambivalent space. Strummer critiqued heroin in 1976's "Deny," and "Complete Control" took a swipe at "punk rockers controlled by the price / of the first drugs we must find." Yet the singer referred to himself as a "drug-prowling wolf" in "White Man in Hammersmith Palais." Speed came up matter-of-factly in "London's Burning" and "Cheat" had similarly offhand chemical references. Strummer's relationship with drugs was clearly complicated.

During a spring 1977 interview with NME journalist Tony Parsons, Strummer even defended drug use, claiming he "can't live without it," yet admitting, "If I had kept doing what I was, I'd be dead." This could have been just a bluff; Strummer is noticeably aloof during the interview, and letting down his guard with the media would have been off the Clash party line at the time. Still, there may have been more truth than sullen bravado in Strummer's admission.

One of the few substances Strummer roused himself to critique to Parsons—who would later slam all drugs save speed in *The Boy Looked at Johnny*, the 1978 punk broadside cowritten with fellow NME writer Julie Burchill—was glue sniffing, then widespread in Scotland and various lower-income environs.

The new song "Glue Zombie" picked up that thread, reading almost as a belated rejoinder to the Ramones' "Now I Wanna Sniff Some Glue" and "Carbona Not Glue." Its riff mimics the unsteady lurch of a member of the living dead, with words sketching an unsparing portrait of addiction's deadly grip: "I am the rebel with the stare of the glue bag / I lost my friend to the smell of gasoline . . ."

Headon's crisis had pushed Strummer along the antidrug path, as had his own addictive tendencies. According to Chris Salewicz, on the same 1982 tour where Strummer confronted Headon over heroin, the singer—and Jones—had burst into tears upon arriving in Japan to discover pot would be nearly impossible to get.

This new Clash antidrug line joined with a "Sex Mad War" critique of the sexual revolution to bluntly challenge the common "sex, drugs, and rock and roll" mantra. This stance came from a deep if unexpected source.

In Strummer's revealing chat with Mikal Gilmore in June 1982, he grounded his growing opposition to drugs in rock idealism: "Music's supposed to be the life force of the new consciousness, talking from 1954 to present, right? A lot of rock stars have been responsible for taking that life force and turning it into a death force. What I hate about so much of that sixties and seventies stuff is that it dealt death as style . . . To be cool, you had to be on the point of killing yourself.

"What I'm really talking about," Strummer continued, "is drugs. If the music's going to move you, you don't need drugs. If I see a sharp-looking guy on a street corner, he's alive and he's making me feel more alive—he ain't dying—and that's the image I've decided The Clash has to stand for these days. I think we've blown it on the drug scene. It ain't happening, and I want to make it quite clear that nobody in The Clash thinks heroin or cocaine or any of that crap is cool."

"I just want to see things change. I don't want it to be like the sixties or seventies, where we saw our rock stars shambling about out of their minds, and we thought it was cool, even instructive. That was death-style, not lifestyle. Those guys made enough money to go into expensive clinics, get their blood changed—but what about the poor junkie on the street? He's been led into it by a bunch of rock stylists, and left to die with their style."

In the end, Strummer sounded humble yet committed: "I guess we each have to work it out in our own way—I had to work it out for myself—but The Clash have to take the responsibility to stand for something better than that."

Simonon echoed this when Gilmore asked why The Clash had been able to persist: "You're talking about things like corruption, disintegration, right? I tell you what I've seen do it to other groups: drugs. I've been through all sorts of drugs. At one time I took them just for curiosity, and I learned—it's not worth it. It's like a carrot held in front of you, and it's the downfall of a lot of bands we've known."

The bassist bluntly stated a new Clash directive: "We just cut it out—we don't deal with that stuff anymore. I'd much rather use the money to buy a record, or a present for me girlfriend, or phone me mum up from Australia." Asked if the band would share that position with Clash fans, Simonon was again direct: "Sure. I don't see why not. I think that's part of what we're about, is testing our audience."

Neither Simonon nor Strummer was addressing drugs here in a facile, practiced way, as if under orders. These parallel insights, shared separately in mid-1982, when Jones was still in the band, suggested why the duo continued on together.

This orientation could help to purify a Clash sullied by drugs and rock-star behavior, and provide solid footing amid the moment's immense challenges. It suggested deep soul-searching about what The Clash was meant to be, for what it should stand. Of course, the spirit could be willing, but the flesh might yet prove weak.

The test was to begin when the new Clash met its old audience, beginning at the 2,000-seat Arlington Theatre in Santa Barbara on January 19, 1984. To some, this California tour made little sense. Sheppard: "I thought it was ridiculous that we went straight onto big stages. I said, 'Why don't we do some small club gigs, unannounced, just to find our feet?'" Rebuffed, Sheppard was nonetheless excited to play live, which tended to wash away his doubts.

His equanimity was not universal. While the band had begun to click in practice, White was nervous about playing out. Sensing this, Strummer took the young guitarist aside. As White wrote later, "Joe began talking about a return to basics . . . a new blistering Clash burning with the fire they'd had at the beginning. A new Clash rising up from the ashes with a bunch of short, sharp songs that would redefine what the band was about and reestablish its credibility."

This was Strummer's new gospel, soon to be shared wherever

he went, and it was galvanizing. That the singer segued quickly from inspiration to asking the guitarist to get a haircut didn't matter. "I was convinced," White later wrote.

Having conviction helped, but playing with The Clash—even in a relatively cozy venue like the Arlington Theatre—was an enormous jump for the twenty-three-year-old guitarist. White winces at the memory, recalling missed chords and blown cues, overwhelmed by the hurricane of sound and humanity, not able to move and jump as he wanted while trying to play the songs.

Sheppard recognized the challenge: "Vince was completely out of his depth . . . I had played in big spaces as a support act in the Cortinas, but those stages are huge. You can just get lost." White nonetheless found the show amazing, partly for the same reason—everything was so hectic and very nearly out of control. As it happened, "Out of Control" was the name of one of the band's most rocking new numbers, one that White favored.

While the song had not made the cut for the live set, "Out of Control" became the motto of this tour and the new Clash in general. Its energy appealed to White, and reflected the lack of commercial calculation involved with the ejection of Jones and Headon and the return to raw, unfashionable punk rock.

As Simonon would later explain, "We feed off the reaction we get from the audience, then we send it right back out, and the whole thing just spirals out of control in a good way. The tour is called *Out of Control* and that's kind of why. It's really a bit of a wind-up of the press."

There was another meaning as well, reflecting the band's unsettled legal situation. According to Clash graphic artist Eddie King, "The *Out of Control* logo was simply photocopied from a *Commando* comic book and was placed next to *The Clash* in all flyers and posters in case of possible lawsuits over the use of the band name. Bernard wanted the possibility to either have the word *are* flyposted between *The Clash* and *Out of Control* so that they could tour as *Out of Control*, or simply have *The Clash* cut from the top of posters rather than have to set up a whole new print run."

Taking aim at those who saw the new Clash as wrecking its

commercial future, Simonon continued: "We're portrayed as this band that goes about smashing shit up, and for us . . . the music is the only thing that's out of control. We like it to be. What good would it be if we just stood there like dead men onstage?"

Backstage after the show, Strummer perched uneasily next to Simonon for a TV interview, smoking a cigarette and wearing a military hat with *Out of Control* emblazoned on it. Despite postgig exhaustion, the singer was bursting with a barely contained energy, seemingly ready to leap out at the interviewers.

Asked how the show went, Strummer took a drag, made a fist, and launched: "This is the first of many, now we begin. We wanted to strip it down to punk-rock roots and see what's left, see how it progressed from there." Slicing the air with his hands, Strummer went on: "I looked around over the past year at all the folks doing shows and making records and I realized that they'd all gone over-produced . . . I realized there wasn't any piece of vinyl I could hold on to and leap out of a space shuttle with yelling, feel satisfied with like some real piece of rhythm and blues, a Bo Diddley record." The singer grimaced and balled his fists intently. "You could just hold it in your hands forever!"

Asked how fans responded to this new, raw Clash, Strummer responded, "I think they were took aback a bit maybe because they see us rushing, rushing with the nerves showing in our faces. But we want to take that nervous energy and turn it into power . . . We want our music to deal with reality, and not skip around it."

As the interview progressed, Strummer's targets were varied—corporations, drugs, Reagan, Thatcher, current pop music, heavy metal, musical imperialism—and the verbal blows didn't always connect. Still, the passion was palpable, and the central message clear: "People want something real . . . everything is blando, blando, blando—let's have a revolt from the bottom up!"

After Strummer rattled off a long list of upcoming tour dates, the interviewer innocently asked about vacation plans. Strummer reared back in disgust, while Simonon retorted, "We haven't got time for vacation, we're there for working!"

Strummer jumped in: "There is no time for vacation! Ronald

Reagan and Margaret Thatcher, their fingers are like that over the button"—hands shaking, mocking an orgasmic eagerness to set off nuclear hell—"there is no time for vacation. It's time to get down to it, to have responsibility, to use your vote!"

When the interviewer commented that both musicians seemed happy with the new Clash, Strummer agreed: "We are excited, because at last we don't have to waste our energy on internal arguments. We don't have to waste our time begging someone to play the damn guitar!"

After more whipping of Jones's ghost by both musicians, Strummer unleashed a storm of words: "Now is the time to cut out everything that has been wasting your time, time to get serious. You should have high standards . . . I wish everyone would run into street and smash all their records and burn every record store down . . . tell the business we don't want something they invented . . . Our flesh is about to be flayed off our faces by a firestorm, we haven't got time to listen to white people play fake black music . . . Don't support stadium dog rock!"

The fervent, jumbled rant leaped from Strummer's mouth as if a dam were bursting. The singer was desperate to communicate—to justify the new Clash? To address this scary moment? To rally the troops to action? It's hard to tell.

Yet both Strummer and Simonon—in his gentler way—communicated an urgency that was far too often missing from the popular music of 1984. Indeed, more passion was on display in this interview than many of their contemporaries evidenced onstage. As Simonon curtly noted, "So much music these days is so tame, you might as well just go back to bed!"

If Strummer and Simonon sensed an impending "Armagideon time," others acted as if 1984 was nonstop party time. Culture Club's Boy George and bands like Duran Duran, Spandau Ballet, and Wham! celebrated jet-set lifestyles and club-land glamour, spinning out lightweight synth-pop dance tunes that were highly profitable but eminently dispensable.

Sheppard later dismissed such music: "It's like people watching the big musicals in the thirties—it's escapism, isn't it? People trying to avoid thinking about the hard times." Mick Jones had aligned himself on the "dance" side of the "dance vs. riot" polarity, illuminating what helped lead to the break as 1984 approached.

While The Clash disdained the club crowd, the band also had to account for its own misadventures—beginning with a confrontational appearance on America's pop showcase, *Entertainment Tonight* (*ET*), filmed during the California tour.

ET cohost Dixie Whatley laid it out: "The Clash have returned to the concert trail for the first time in two years. In that time the politically outspoken group has lived up to their name both inside and outside the band. Two members left, with one of them embroiling the group in a bitter lawsuit. The Clash has also had to endure severe criticism stemming from . . . last year's US Festival where they accepted a payment of $500,000 in the face of their stance as revolutionaries."

A defensive Strummer first responded with a shot at Boy George and the new pop scene, then unleashed a passionate sermonette: "There are people out there [who] are sick to their souls. They have been at a party too long, they have been taking drugs too long . . . Drugs are over from this minute now!"

A skeptical Whatley shot back: "You don't take any drugs at all?"

Strummer raised his hands as if to wave the thought away: "I stopped . . . Six months ago I wouldn't have any more damn pot!"

Whatley: "Is that true for your whole band?"

Strummer: "They're not into it either. And we've come over here and we are telling people if they want to listen."

Simonon leapt in: "To get sharp, there is no use in taking a spliff or anything like pot, because it just clouds your mind up."

Whatley shifted gears, but stayed on the attack: "You've been a very outspoken group, but some people say it's a gimmick."

Strummer: "Look, there is no time for gimmicks . . . There is only one thing that young people are listening to. They aren't reading Sartre, poetry is a bore, in school they don't listen . . . They are only listening to one medium, and that is rock and roll."

The frontman's vehemence, paired with live footage of the new band doing "Clampdown" and "I Fought the Law," made a powerful statement, despite the interviewer's skepticism. As a snarling Strummer said at the outset of the segment, with the rest of the band flanking him: "Something should be started. We are here to bring up reality and push you in the face with it!"

The Clash brought that confrontational attitude to seven thousand people at San Francisco's Civic Auditorium. The set was not lacking for rough spots—"Safe European Home" opened as a discordant mess, grating feedback marred "Dictator," guitars repeatedly went out of tune, and a Simonon-led "Police on My Back" came off flat. While Sheppard did a fine job taking lead on "Should I Stay or Should I Go," the song's inclusion struck a false note, even to its singer: "To be honest, I didn't feel comfortable singing it . . . [I felt] a bit stupid, really." The Jones-linked song would soon largely disappear from the set list.

Strummer was in fine form, bantering with the crowd. Not all was lighthearted; he introduced "Sex Mad War" by shushing the crowd and urging them "to focus all your minds on sex!" Perhaps anticipating racy rock talk, the crowd cheered.

Strummer cut savagely through the revelry: "Every boy in this world has gone sex mad, there ain't no satisfaction. This is dedicated to all the victims of the sex-mad war—the women, the women, the women . . ." On cue, the song exploded to life, earning its place on a set list heavy with the band's early anthems.

Likewise, Strummer segued from joking about the uncontrollable feedback—"We have no intention of playing avant-garde music that sounds like this . . . so we'll just have to drown it out by some old-fashioned human and wood stuff"—to railing against "Ronald Reagan's favorite hobby: *smashing Central America to fuck!*"

Having blitzed through the first show on "pure adrenaline, pure nerve," Sheppard felt better about the outcome in San Francisco. So did White, whose opening-night jitters—"I didn't know what I was doing onstage"—gave way to utter abandon: "I just threw caution to the wind. I remember cutting my hand to pieces . . . doing these Pete Townshend windmill things, just fuckin' going mad."

The intent was to present a rougher version of The Clash, with

Strummer's passion cranked up to cover the band's raggedness. The patchy parts were to be expected, given that the five had been playing together for a month.

Some observers were unconvinced. In the *San Francisco Examiner*, Phillip Elwood argued that the "new Clash lacks some of the old fire," faulting the new lineup for lack of identity overall, and Strummer for erratic onstage delivery. The *San Francisco Chronicle*'s Joel Selvin hammered Sheppard and White: "Neither proved exceptional . . . Even keeping their guitars in tune proved a problem for these two green additions to the world's most famous punk band."

The quintet continued on the road, playing spaces as out of the way as the Spanos Center in Stockton, California, and as massive as the Long Beach Arena—capacity 13,500—followed by Santa Monica's Civic Auditorium. Mixed reviews continued, with Ethlie Ann Vare complaining that the new lineup "shows more energy than finesse." Her verdict was stark: "Yes, the new Clash are taking off in a direction. Trouble is . . . that direction seems to be backward."

Such slams didn't discourage the new recruits, who hadn't been tasked with replacing Jones as much as staking a new claim with punk bravado. Sheppard: "With hindsight, we went out very much challenging what The Clash had done before. [At this point] we weren't being as musical. We were very in-your-face."

Some critics reveled in the defiant energy. After seeing the San Francisco and Santa Cruz shows, Johnny Whiteside of *Beano* fanzine declared, "This is The Clash, with their beauty and firepower intact, albeit bruised and scabby . . . The [absence] of Jones makes barely a shred of difference." The *Los Angeles Times*' Richard Cromelin agreed, saying Jones's loss "hardly seems as crucial as the departure of Keith Richards would be from the Rolling Stones."

In Santa Monica, Strummer paused to scorch the skeptical critics, exhorting the crowd: "We're standing here, you're standing here, so let's get on with it!" New songs now made up about one-third of each set, sprinkled through the evening, with the shows improving day by day. In a sign of growing confidence, the band unveiled an embellished "Guns of Brixton," with a haunting har-monica intro from Simonon and jagged lead guitar line courtesy of White. All the venues save the massive Long Beach Arena were sold out, and the crowd reaction was strong.

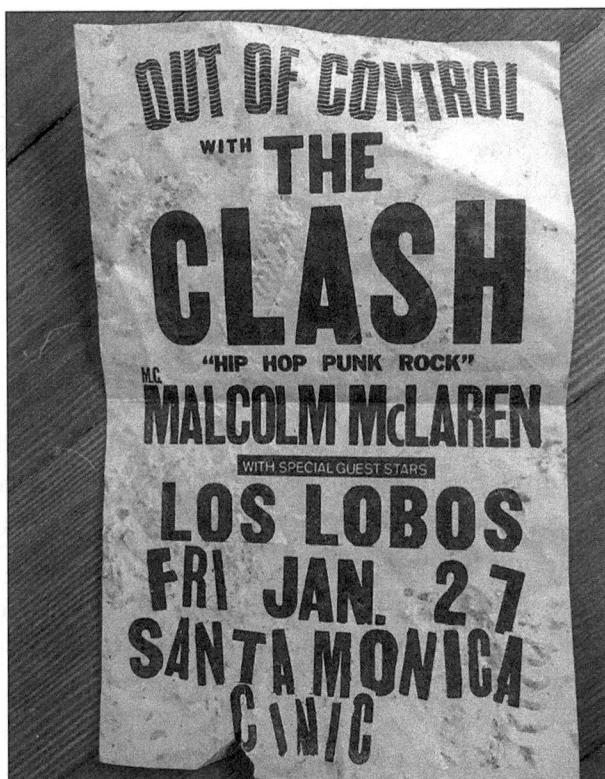

Kosmo Vinyl would later print DIY Clash shirts with the words *Hip Hop Punk Rock* on them, foreshadowing a musical shift. (Flyer courtesy Kosmo Vinyl.)

Yet Strummer was eager for more direct feedback, even stopping the Santa Monica show to ask the audience to rate the band: "Okay, now we need your vote here . . . Come to the voting section where you shout 'rubbish,' or you shout 'not bad,' or you shout 'good,' or you shout '*excellente*'!" If Strummer's ritual was done with a wink and a grin, it also suggested residual doubt.

This was not his only cause for concern. As usual, The Clash had carefully chosen opening acts, showcasing Malcolm McLaren's hip-hop/world music and a then-largely-unknown Latino band, Los Lobos. Despite the return to "punk roots," Strummer fiercely opposed cultural segregation, seeing such divides as part of an exploitive global system that kept apart people who needed to be together.

Strummer was eager to expose his largely white US audience to a broader world. He took aim at Top 40 radio and MTV for racism, calling the crowd to protest: "Until they hear your voice, they will keep giving you what they've been giving you!" At another show, Strummer noted "Police and Thieves" was not "white reggae," scorching Police singer Sting for ripping off Jamaican music.

This echoed his critique of Jones for becoming a musical "imperialist." Yet even the new Clash was walking a tricky line. Their version of "Armagideon Time," for example, had little musically to distinguish it from the original Willie Williams reggae version. Such tunes were not unlike what the Police were doing.

Yet the presence of these songs was critical. The racial divides in music had become massive, especially in the US. Rock was increasingly a white phenomenon, with disco and rap reviled by some rockists as "nigger music." This ugly mentality was evident at the Clash's Long Beach show, at which McLaren was harassed by the audience's less-enlightened denizens. For Strummer, the incident was a flashback to the brutal roasting of hip-hop pioneer Grandmaster Flash when he opened for The Clash at New York's Bonds Casino.

Strummer would recall the Long Beach incident as a snapshot of the intolerance behind the Reaganite facade of a cheerfully colorblind, classless society—and a suggestion of how much work remained in getting his message across. After seeing Clash fans shout "You nigger-music lover!" at McLaren, he snapped to one reporter, "That goes straight to Joe Strummer's head."

The band wouldn't brook such racism. As one Stockton audience member recalled, Los Lobos "was getting booed and the audience was throwing things at them. Two songs into their set, Joe Strummer barges out from backstage, the band stops playing. Strummer yells at the crowd, 'Shut the fuck up! These guys are going to be great someday and you are going to regret it.' He marched back behind the curtains, the band fired up again, and everyone got into the music."

The Clash wound through California, finally arriving at the Fox Theatre in San Diego on February 1. The show started late due to a standoff with authorities who insisted on a barrier in front of the stage in the 2,800-capacity venue. The band balked, despising such divisions between it and the audience.

Unable to get the powers-that-be to remove the barrier, Strummer channeled his anger, leading the band through a rousing show. While the newer songs came across well, many of the set's high points were Clash songs from 1977–78, songs that Jones had disdained playing, calling them "like the nagging old wife." Strummer, however, had never given up on the tunes, knowing they were important not only for the fans, but for reminding the band of its initial mission.

Toward the end of a blistering version of "White Riot"—a song that had once brought Strummer and Jones to blows when the latter refused to play it as an encore—were the lines "Are we going backward / or are we going forward?" This echoed the challenge Jones likely would have put to the band. But to Strummer, sometimes you had to go backward to get back on the right path to move forward.

The crowd's fervor had grown so intense by the encore that Strummer stopped the show to plead with people to back up so as to prevent anyone from getting crushed on the unwanted security fence. Despite the chaos, the show was a hopeful tour finale. Save for a ragged "Rock the Casbah"—Strummer stopped the song, had the band start it over, only to muff it himself after the last chorus—the group kept up with their singer, and the trek ended on a high note.

The real test was about to come: a return to their fervent—and demanding—British audience. Such fans could be jealous of the band's success abroad, and had noticed its lack of focus on home-front battles on recent records.

London was British pop's beating heart. Going north to the Barrowlands Ballroom in Glasgow made sense as The Clash sought to defy commerce and reconnect to its base. Few places throbbed with as much raw anti-Tory sentiment as this rough-and-tumble city, nestled in a hard-hit industrial region. Yet Scottish crowds could be uncompromising, more than willing to confront unsatisfying performers.

Strummer was ready to present his own challenge. After a spirited introduction by Vinyl, The Clash hit the stage with "London Calling's" stirring chords, only to be met with a thin, persistent rain of saliva.

Gobbing—as this ritual of spitting on bands was known—was one of the less pleasant UK punk habits, and the singer loathed the practice. Even as most of the crowd began singing along, Strummer suddenly halted the song, and bluntly urged other fans to "find the saliva and punch it in the face."

Hygienic boundaries reasserted, the band was back into "London Calling," followed swiftly by "Safe European Home." As the song ended, Strummer leaped forward, yelling, "House lights, house lights!" When the lights rose on the audience, and the guitarists tuned up behind him, Strummer greeted the crowd with a jaunty, "Good evening to you all! Welcome to the first of this mob in the UK . . ."

The crowd cheered, and Strummer launched into one of the most emotionally naked raps of his long career: "Yeah, we've been away for two years—and I've been trying to come to a decision. I've been thinking, what the fuck am I doing living? What am I supposed to do with it? How come you all come see it?"

As the sweat-drenched singer grasped the mic, the last six months of soul-searching poured out of him: "Where is it going, what was it going, what is Clash, where is Clash, who is Clash? These are decisions, you know, I'm thinking . . ."

If Strummer had sometimes strained for coherence in California interviews, now he cut to the bone: "Become activists! Yeah, any damn thing is better than nothing. Read Che Guevara, paint furniture pink and superglue it onto the sides of city buses. Anything! Become an activist! Turn off the bloody whatever it is . . . Turn off the *Jewel in the Crown* or *Brideshead Revisited*. Fuck that! Get off the drugs and all—a waste of time. *Get rid of Thatcher before she gets rid of us!*"

As the crowd roared its approval, Strummer insisted, "I'm serious!" After a quick band introduction, he leaned over to challenge the crowd: "And down here? Yeah, down here we got the future . . . If anyone has got any guts, let's take it!"

Immediately, gentle chords announced "Jericho," one of the strongest of the new songs, drawn from the biblical tale of city walls brought down by a trumpet blast. After a couple quiet measures, the band paused for a second only to erupt into full force, the twin guitars lashing out like barbed-wire whips.

In "The Sound of Sinners," Strummer had mused about "looking for that great jazz note / that destroyed the walls of Jericho." Tonight he seemed intent on enacting just that. With references to seemingly imminent nuclear war—portraying Thatcher hiding in a bunker as bombs fell—the song measured up to the Clash classics that preceded it, putting sinew behind the charged words.

With barely a pause, the band went into two other new songs, "We Are The Clash" and "Sex Mad War," followed by "Clampdown" and "Guns of Brixton," both benefiting from the additional muscle of two guitars. Then it was back to two more new songs, "Three Card Trick" and "Glue Zombie."

After "Zombie's" last chords faded, a knot of fans started a Mick Jones chant, causing a wrangle in the crowd. Strummer paused, peering into the darkness, trying to sort out the scene. After listening for a while, the singer wryly remarked, "Perhaps we can have a battle after . . . Perhaps we can have a pro- and anti–Mick Jones fight. Yeah, you might think about that . . ."

Strummer then led the band into a defiant "English Civil War." A huge chorus rose from the audience as the song took flight. Then, as if to silence any doubters, The Clash ignited a mix of new and old songs like a string of firecrackers. The response was intense, generating a massive sing-along. Bum notes popped up and the twin guitars occasionally slipped out of sync—but the spirit was powerful. The band ended with a blazing-fast "White Riot" played almost as a vow: Mick Jones might be gone, but The Clash is here.

As White later wrote, "It was one of the most exhilarating shows I played with The Clash. And it was all down to the audience, their energy. Just bordering on complete destruction. But there was a good thing in there too . . . a spirit there that seemed authentic and true and unlike so many other places we played. They really laid it on the line. And it inspired you—you stepped over the line with them."

White's words paid tribute to the "We Are The Clash" idea, how performer and audience together could create something nearly miraculous: "I wasn't from a socially deprived background, but I understood desperation. Desperation is a state of mind. Where nothing makes sense and there's pointlessness in being alive. But in that moment you were released from something. You touched a source of some kind where . . . life made total sense for a couple hours."

Yet if such liberation lasted only briefly, it was limited, even illusory. Could it persist, to change lives, even help change the world? In the face of the looming life-or-death confrontations between Thatcher and the miners, the US and USSR, in Central America and beyond, such power would be sorely needed.

The search for identity, for renewed meaning, had brought a reinvented Clash back home to begin making its stand. Strummer meant the new songs and the new band to be a match for the moment—and the real battle was just about to begin.

CHAPTER THREE

READY FOR WAR

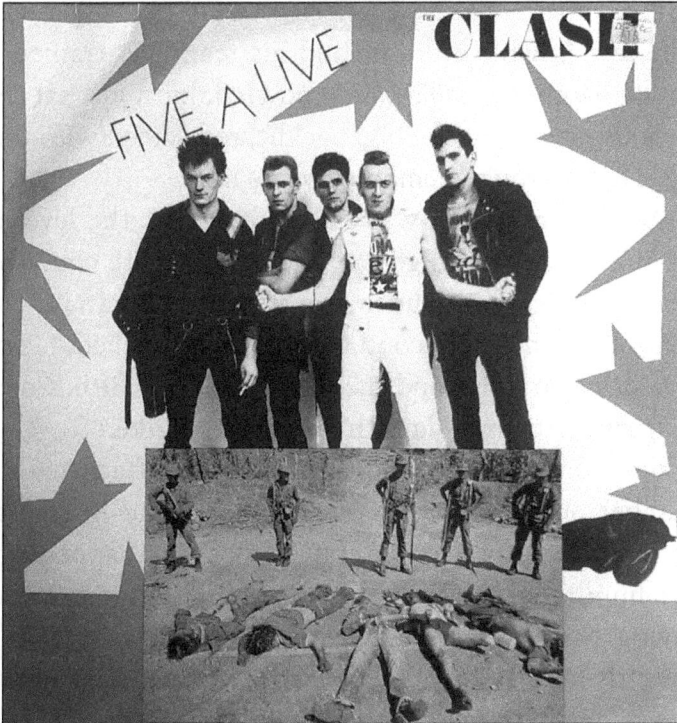

Bootleg of the Stockholm show on February 17, 1984, with a photo of The Clash by Jan Bengtsson/*Schlager* magazine, and a photo of the Salvadoran military with victims.

The logical consequence of the preparation for nuclear war is nuclear war . . . If the world were to fall prey to such a disaster, we will take with us not only all present life, but the magnificent heritage [past generations] bequeathed . . . We hold in our hands the ability to destroy creation. It could happen any day.
—Helen Caldicott, Missile Envy, 1984

Every war, before it comes, is represented not as a war but as an act of self-defense against a homicidal maniac. The essential job is to get people to recognize war propaganda when they see it, especially when it is disguised as peace propaganda.
—George Orwell, 1937

A siren was screaming. Red lights were blinking on and off. It was just past midnight, September 26, 1983, deep in Serpukhov-15, a secret bunker outside Moscow. The message from the Soviet early warning system was clear: a nuclear missile attack from the United States was underway.

Stansilav Petrov—the lead officer on duty that night—froze in place. The unthinkable event he and his team had trained for appeared to be happening. "The siren howled, but I just sat there for a few seconds, staring at the big, backlit, red screen with the word 'launch' on it," Petrov remembered years later.

The Oko alarm system was telling him that the level of reliability of that alert was "highest," indicating there could be little doubt that America had launched a missile. "A minute later the siren went off again. The second missile was launched," Petrov explained. "Then the third, and the fourth, and the fifth. Computers changed their alerts from 'launch' to 'missile strike.'"

But something didn't seem right. Why an attack with such a small number of missiles? The Soviets feared the Reagan administration intended a first strike, but if that was happening, there should be hundreds, maybe thousands of missiles in the air.

Knowing that his system was new and relatively untested, Petrov swiftly checked with colleagues staffing the radar early warning systems. No missiles had been sighted on their screens. Which assessment was right?

Petrov's duty was to report this alert. Every second counted, given that US missiles, once launched, could reach Russia in minutes. He was, however, well aware that Soviet forces were on high alert, and that a false alarm might set off a cascade of nuclear dominoes that could end human life on earth as he knew it.

His career—and millions of lives—was on the line. Petrov made his decision, choosing not to report the alert up the chain of command. The next twenty minutes were agony, but when no missiles landed, Petrov knew he had been right.

It was later discovered that the "missile launch" had been simply sunlight reflected off the clouds, shockingly misinterpreted by the Oko system. In the twenty-first century, Petrov would be feted as "the man who saved the world" and September 26, 1983, would be "the day the world almost died."

At the time, however, Petrov's gutsy call resulted in a reprimand for disregarding protocol and subsequent early retirement. Nothing would be said publicly about the incident, which deeply embarrassed the Soviet military machine. Many years passed before anyone outside of the USSR's nuclear program knew just how close the earth had come to annihilation due to mechanical error.

Petrov took it philosophically, loyal to his country but secure in the righteousness of his action. Meanwhile, the world continued to teeter on the abyss of nuclear holocaust, with most people blissfully, willfully unaware of the danger. Not everyone, however, was willing to accept this quietly, without words of protest.

Flash forward five months to Colston Hall in Bristol, England, 1,900 miles east of Moscow: named for Edward Colston, a well-known philanthropist who had made his money in the slave trade, this concert venue was packed with two thousand paying customers on the night of February 13, 1984.

The crowd was restless. The lead singer pacing back and forth in the spotlight—resplendent in a bright-red Mohawk—knew it. After sparring with some outspoken show-goers, the slender figure stepped to the front of the stage, defiant, eager to confront: "What you see here is one rat shouting . . ."

Few might guess that this man was identifying himself with one of the victims of the rat-catcher of Hamelin, the Pied Piper, who—legend has it—ended that town's infestation by leading countless rodents to their deaths with his hypnotic music.

The hubbub continued unabated. The singer ignored the catcalls and continued on: "What you see here is one rat making his piteous moan!" As the crowd struggled to make sense of this, he unleashed a jarring denouement: "Okey-dokey, the Pied Piper of Hamelin can be found . . . I'll be ready for war!"

With that, the four figures shrouded in shadow behind him sprang into action, hurtling into the light with sound and motion. The funky drums and clipped chords of "Are You Ready for War?" cut through the sweat- and cigarette-soaked air, and the "rat"—Joe

Strummer—flung himself into the swirl of word and beat.

For reasons both topical and musical, "War" had come to sit early in the nouveau Clash set, usually in the third slot after "London Calling" and "Safe European Home." The tune operated on multiple levels. Listeners might find their feet moving to the rhythm, and their minds opening to a frightening reality. This could be a song for those who wanted to both dance *and* riot.

"War" was made for this scary moment, speaking powerfully to the danger that faced the world in the early days of 1984. "Free your mind and your ass will follow" funk pioneer George Clinton had proclaimed more than a decade earlier. While this song sought the same kinetic connection with its audience, it offered not trippy idealism but urgent reality, targeting the Pied Pipers of world war.

The words were nursery-rhyme simple, but made their point: the nuclear competition between the US and USSR endangered the entire world. "No use running in a mobile home / everywhere is a target zone / hell is ringing / on a red, red phone." There was no escape, only urgent confrontation. As Strummer said elsewhere at the time, "The atomic age is upon us already, it's time to wake up!"

This "sea shanty," as Nick Sheppard described it, sported an infectious beat with two guitars crunching and slicing in quick succession—a spoonful of sugar to make the bitter medicine go down. When the song asked, "Are you ready for war?" it was a cautionary tale about possible destruction and a call to arms.

Onstage, Strummer wore a T-shirt designed by longtime Clash ally Eddie King that went well with his new hairdo. *Mohawk Revenge*, the shirt proclaimed, with an anonymous Mohawked punk and ghostly *1984* hovering in the background. The actual front of the shirt—Strummer wore it back to front—was equally striking. Two American paratroopers with hair trimmed into austere Mohawks stood face to face, evoking the infamous Sex Pistols "gay cowboys" shirt.

Instead of shocking with sexually graphic juxtaposition, however, this shirt suggested deadly serious resolve, for these men were preparing for the D-Day invasion of Nazi-occupied Europe. The scene captured them grimly applying war paint to each other, with a giant boom box added by King as a backdrop.

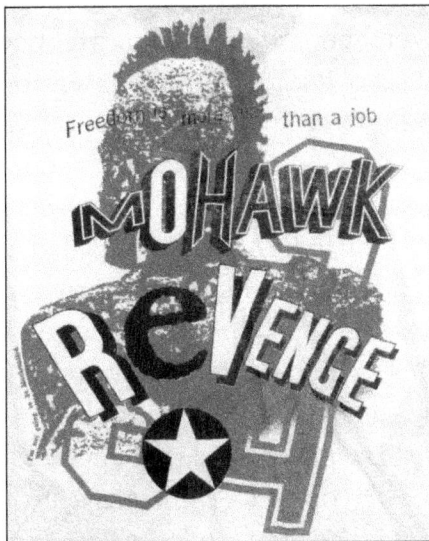

Left: Repurposing the *Stars and Stripes* photo as The Clash prepare for D-Day.
Right: *Freedom is more vital than a job, Mohawk Revenge,* 1984. (Both T-shirts by Eddie King.)

First published in the US military journal *Stars and Stripes* in 1945, the photo had been brought to King's attention by Paul Simonon some years earlier. "Kosmo knew me from when I worked next door to him at Stiff Records," King recalls. "We became friends, and through him I met the rest of the band."

King assisted Julian Balme with *Combat Rock*–era Clash graphics, designing T-shirts and record sleeves. King helped Balme turn one of Vinyl's drawings into perhaps the most gripping and resonant of all Clash images: the words KNOW YOUR RIGHTS nestled beneath an open book with THE FUTURE IS UNWRITTEN written in bloody letters on one page, juxtaposed with a pistol-shaped hole on the other. The stark tableau was itself flanked by a large red star that evoked the band's socialist orientation.

The new shirt had been a collaborative effort with roots stretching back to 1982. As King says, "Paul gave me a copy of the 'Mohawked' D-Day paratroopers and said, 'Put this on a shirt!'" This motif had struck a chord within the Clash camp. Impressed by the vehemence of the Mohican-wearing Travis Bickle character in the film *Taxi Driver*, and unsettled by their pop breakthrough, first Vinyl and then Strummer adopted this militant look early in the *Combat Rock* era.

However, the shirt did not materialize immediately. "I did a sketchbook design using the photo and came up with the slogan *Mohawk Revenge* with the intention of producing a T-shirt," King recalls, "but I never got around to it." As the band drifted, paralyzed by internal divisions and the ambivalent impact of their Top 10 success, King moved on to other endeavors.

In late 1983, King was called up for a new tour of duty: "Bernard conducted an informal interview up in Camden. Flipping through my sketchbook, Kosmo spotted the design and said, 'Can I show this to Joe?' who was rehearsing across the road. Ten minutes later he came back: 'Joe wants this on a T-shirt!'"

The motif gained yet another facet when the band read about Peter Mortiboy, an eighteen-year-old punk who was fired in late 1983 from his job at Rolls Royce. The cause of Mortiboy's termination? His spiky Mohawk that—according to a Rolls Royce spokesperson—represented a "safety hazard." Angered by this injustice, Vinyl and others in the Clash camp got involved helping Mortiboy.

Fired For Dangerous Hair

Punk rocker Peter Mortiboy, 18, was fired by Britain's Rolls Royce because the company believed the four-inch spikes of his hairdo endangered the eyes of his co-workers. His attire usually includes 18 earrings, a studded dog collar, steel armlets and a stud through his nose.

Left: Eddie King (in a photo by Nick Sheppard) created edgy, provocative graphics that complemented the neo-Clash's raw style. His T-shirt for *Mohawk Revenge* (see page 105) used a photograph of the back of Peter Mortiboy's head. Right: A newspaper clipping of Mortiboy. (Photographer unknown.)

While nothing ever came of plans mooted for a band or a record with Mortiboy, King designed a T-shirt as a tribute. It used an image of the back of Mortiboy's head, with *Mohawk Revenge* as well as *Freedom is more vital than a job* juxtaposed with the photo. *I'm not going to be blackmailed* could also be glimpsed in small type on the edge of the image.

According to King, "Mohawk Revenge then became the theme as opposed to just a reference to the D-Day photo." The slogan was multifaceted, he explains, drawing together "this Native American element, hardcore punk, and the military aspect, as well as this sense that an uprising is being attempted, a fight back."

A deeply politicized artist, King was energized by his conversation with Rhodes and Vinyl, and eager to sign on to the new campaign: "Bernard really doesn't like the way things are, he really, really does want a revolution! That inspired me, and I was excited to work on the shirt and anything else the band wanted."

Clearly Strummer agreed, as the *Mohawk Revenge* shirt would almost always be on his chest for Clash shows over the next few months. With the front photo of the paratroopers now emblazoned with *The Clash* and *Out of Control*, the shirt suggested that the band found itself in its own D-Day moment.

While Europe, appropriately enough, was soon to come on the itinerary, The Clash followed its Barrowlands concert with dates in Manchester, Leicester, and Bristol. The shows quickly sold out, and audience reaction was strong, if not universally positive. While devotees of Mick Jones or British pop were likely unsatisfied, this rough-and-ready Clash was proving to be blisteringly good.

Given that it had less than two months under its belt, the band was on top of its game, and Strummer was in good spirits. The vocalist's freshly cut Mohawk signaled confrontation, beginning with his own audience. In Leicester, he wrangled good-naturedly with some fans—including die-hard gobbers—and introduced himself as "Mick Jones" before "Are You Ready for War?"

Near the end of the set, shouting erupted in the crowd as Strummer announced "Tommy Gun." The singer waved off the band and stopped to listen. Hearing a litany of Jones-related complaints, Strummer spoke gently: "Can I ask you one question? Who understands why we had to change?" When only a few people raised hands, he responded, "Well, that means I have to tell the rest of you . . ."

With that, Strummer's voice shifted, rising from a conversational tone to a near scream: "The Clash was going nowhere—it was going to DIE! *GOODBYE!*" When this explanation failed to settle the matter, the singer challenged with biting humor: "What's *your* contribution to the scheme of things? What color are your underpants? This is the question that must be answered! I'll have the [tabloid scandal rag] *News of the World* on you . . .."

Satisfied with his repartee, Strummer then let the music talk. A twin-guitar crescendo ensued, heralding the long-delayed song, followed quickly by an equally fiery "I Fought the Law." This one-two punch was intended to leave anyone hard-pressed to deny that a genuine Clash was in the house.

Skepticism nonetheless was easy to find—and not simply due to the absence of Jones. In truth, the four big UK music weeklies—*NME*, *Sounds*, *Melody Maker*, followed by *Record Mirror*—had for years tended to savage anything The Clash did. Sheppard laughs: "Somebody asked me once, 'Were you hurt by the bad reviews that The Clash got in England?' And I said, 'Well, they haven't had a good review since the first album—and that got panned by some people!'"

It was not surprising when the first review—by Jim Reid of *Record Mirror*—found lots to criticize about the Leicester show. Decrying a "stultifying lack of imagination," Reid wrote, "The reconstituted Clash—three young blades, a Marlon Strummer, and a Mean Boy Paul—are five punky curators with a traveling 'Museum of '77.' Muscular, energetic, and ultimately pointless."

Reid wrote that the powerful show put Leicester "under punk rule" for two hours, and allowed, "The issues The Clash deal with are important," before delivering the coup de grâce: "It's just that the form they express them in has become meaningless . . . When Strummer screams 'White Riot' it doesn't mean anything."

Despite this, one gets the sense that—under his cynical pose—Reid liked the show, ranking new songs like "This Is England" and "Three Card Trick" alongside "the early—and best—Clash." Conceding that "a Clash show is nothing if not spirited," Reid concluded with a backhanded compliment: "As an exercise in nostalgia it sure dumps on the Alarm," a punk-inspired band then making waves alongside the likes of Big Country and U2, who were also summarily dismissed.

Hardened by past criticism in the weeklies, the band shrugged it off. Vinyl later made it clear the new Clash was "wasn't meant for them," as the unit was not interested in the pop-novelty merry-go-round ridden by these publications. "The Kleenex scene," scoffed Strummer. "Blow your nose on it and throw it away."

Another skeptic was harder to dismiss. Since the Victoria Park "Rock Against Racism" show, teenage Clash fan Billy Bragg had begun to make some riots of his own. Bragg: "There was a time in 1977–1978, everyone seemed to be in a band, and every door seemed to be open to young nineteen-year-olds with attitude and short haircuts. It was like a cultural revolution. It was going to change the world—particularly, The Clash were going to change the world. I fervently believed that."

Taking the folk troubadour stance and marrying it to an acerbic punk aesthetic, Bragg had won a growing, passionate following as a solo artist. Wielding an electric guitar, a romantic's heart, an irreverent sense of humor, and a big mouth, Bragg laughed, "When I started out, I wanted to be a one-man Clash!"

Perhaps because of the band's role in inspiring him as an artist and budding activist, Bragg had been bitterly disappointed with their trajectory: "It seemed that The Clash had completely lost the fucking plot with *Sandinista!* I didn't really even listen to *Combat Rock*." He sees this as part and parcel of a broader ennui: "By the mideighties, I'm becoming very disillusioned with all my hopes for punk in general. What's happening is that the focus is moving toward the New Romantics. Style is starting to reassert its dead hand over content."

Wincing at the thought, Bragg continues: "All of the things that I dressed like an idiot for seemed to be coming to nothing—we just seemed to have cleared the way for Spandau Ballet! Everything else was going more and more stylish, more and more huge productions—the idea of going the opposite direction, just one guy with turned-up jeans and white T-shirt and a beaten-up electric guitar was a classic 'zag' when everyone else was 'zigging,' you know?"

This was largely the critique that had led to the new Clash's birth. Nonetheless, Bragg began to roast The Clash in his live performances. Bragg: "I'd been saying onstage that the new band that are out on the road—it would be simpler if they just drop the 'L' from the name and just called themselves 'The Cash.'"

He later admitted—with a sad laugh—"That was a really nasty thing to say, wasn't it?"

The irrepressible Vinyl makes short work of the slam: "Say what you will about the last version of The Clash, but it wasn't designed in any way as a money-making maneuver. The record company would have been a lot happier with Mick still there . . . What a daft thing for Bragg to say!"

Billy Bragg and Joe Strummer, Colston Hall, Bristol, UK, February 13, 1984. (Photographer unknown.)

Daft or not, Bragg then found himself being asked to open for the same band he was publicly criticizing at Colston Hall in Bristol, the day after the Leicester show. On one hand, this made sense. Strummer had said, "I wouldn't cross the road to buy a record," except "maybe Billy Bragg's one."

The band had another agenda as well, however. Bragg—who had never met Strummer or Simonon before the show—found himself on the hot seat that night after sound check. "Joe and Paul buttonholed me about what I had been saying when we met, and I had to kind of sheepishly admit my wrongdoing."

Yet Bragg was not really that chastened by the sit-down: "I was already a heretic, so it didn't really matter." But when he saw the band live that night, Bragg was transported: "I was dancing in the aisles . . . The spirit was still there, Joe still had the passion, and I thought they were great, actually. They were more musical than the old Clash, I felt—maybe the additional guitar helped."

This was no small concession, for as Bragg freely admits, "I was such a Stalinist about The Clash. If they were shit, I would have been, you know, mortified, and sulked off somewhere. The fact that I was bopping in the aisles . . . Clearly, they were still The Clash, whatever else was going on."

After seeing the band in action, Bragg also understood their tête-à-tête more deeply: "It seemed to be clear that Joe and Paul really wanted to make a point of proving that they still had it, which is why they were buttonholing me."

The new Clash was ready to push the envelope. Pressed to explain what the band gained under its new two-guitar regime, Sheppard—interviewed for Radio West before his hometown debut in Bristol—didn't hesitate: "A bit of desperation, a bit of energy—a *lot* of energy—and a bit of new blood. What they need."

That no-nonsense ethic held true for other aspects of Clash affairs too. Asked if joining such a successful band meant not having to carry his own gear anymore, Sheppard responded, "I don't like poncing around while somebody does stuff that you could quite easily do . . . What you [can] do, you do."

But many skeptics remained as their campaign prepared for continental Europe. In the face of this, Strummer tried to encourage Sheppard and White. As road manager Ray Jordan recalls "Joe [told] them, 'If the audiences give you any shit, just give it to them right back . . .'" While Jordan was skeptical himself of the new band, he admitted, "[Nick and Vince] put themselves on the line."

It was not simply the guitarists. All the members of the new Clash were fighting for their lives on artistic terms—even as they were doing the same, in some sense, for *everyone's* lives, endangered by the threat of imminent nuclear war.

Strummer had told Mikal Gilmore in 1982, "We ain't dead yet, for Christ's sake! I know nuclear doom is prophesied for the world, but I don't think you should give up fighting until the flesh burns off your face." By singing "Are You Ready for War?" night after night—with lines like "I ain't gonna lay down and die / playing the global suicide"—Strummer was pressing the issue the best way he knew how.

In California, Strummer had argued rock music was the only way to reach young people. Few issues could be more critical than the nuclear arms race. As Vinyl noted later, "We supported groups like CND"—Campaign for Nuclear Disarmament, touted on their 1980 "The Call Up"/"Stop the World" 45—"but at same time, they seemed very middle-class, university-intellectual types. We wanted to reach the kids they weren't reaching."

The single had risen to #40 in the UK, so was only marginally successful in this aim. The songs were gripping nonetheless. "Stop the World" was a raw stream-of-consciousness screed warning of atomic devastation. While "The Call Up" mostly spoke against the draft, it also evoked the Doomsday Clock created by *The Bulletin of Atomic Scientists* to dramatize the danger of nuclear holocaust.

When the Clash single came out just after Reagan's election, the Clock stood at seven minutes to midnight. In January 1984, however, the hands were moved to only three minutes to midnight, the closest they had been since 1953. While the *Bulletin* criticized Soviet actions that increased the danger—such as the 1979 invasion of Afghanistan and deployment of SS-20 intermediate-range nuclear missiles in Eastern Europe—by 1984, it was especially alarmed by US policies.

Ronald Reagan was the Pied Piper that Strummer had warned of in Leicester. The singer was connecting the same dots as influential antinuclear activist Dr. Helen Caldicott, who called Reagan the "Pied Piper of Armageddon" for his disarming style, which made his warmongering seem friendly, even parental.

Caldicott later elaborated: "At a fundamental level people enjoy being cared for by supposedly strong leaders. This gives them the freedom to avoid the true responsibilities and autonomy of adulthood, with all its attendant details. They can then behave as adolescents needing a father or a mother figure. And Reagan fit this pattern. It was a pity that the father the American people had chosen was not a creative, vital figure, but such a destructive one."

Caldicott spoke from direct experience, for she had met with Reagan in December 1982, thanks to the intervention of his daughter, Patti Davis. Reagan found Caldicott to be a "nice caring person . . . but she is all steamed up and knows an awful lot of things that aren't true." The doctor was horrified to discover the president was apparently unable to distinguish between *Reader's Digest* allegations and top-secret intelligence data. Reagan's emphasis on building more bombs as to prevent nuclear war seemed delusional to her.

"Peace through strength" was Reagan's key talking point. He was a member of the Committee on the Present Danger (CPD), an advocacy group of powerful right-wing hawks who believed that the US had slipped dangerously behind the USSR in military power. This was not true—but once in office, Reagan acted on this belief by vastly ramping up arms spending, alarming the Soviets.

The danger was heightened by Reagan's skepticism about arms control talks. For him, as for the CPD, such agreements were essentially meaningless. The Soviets couldn't be trusted—the US had to be stronger than the Soviets, so its rival would not risk an attack. Ergo, Reagan and his ilk were the real peace activists, their preparations for war the most effective way to prevent it.

A novel interpretation, and perhaps it was true. Still, Reagan's words recalled the prescient warning issued by George Orwell about "war propaganda . . . disguised as peace propaganda."

After speaking with Reagan, Caldicott agreed. She saw the flaw in his argument: military buildup would make the Soviets fear attack from a stronger America, so they, in turn, would build more weapons. The US would do the same—and on and on, with tensions building toward a breaking point.

This unending arms spiral was insanely expensive, foreclosing more socially beneficial uses for the money. It also held other dangers, for its momentum would almost inevitably lead to war. In Caldicott's 1984 book *Missile Envy*, she argued, "The logical consequence of the preparation for nuclear war is nuclear war"—a direct rebuttal to Reagan's assertions in their meeting.

Reagan claimed to be misunderstood. Yet it is more likely that he believed—at least at the outset—that it was in America's best interest to scare the Soviets with tough talk and military buildup.

In Reagan's home state of California the previous month, Strummer had lambasted the leader: "His job is trying to press that button. And when he presses it, he wants 900 million missiles, not nine thousand. He wants the Fourth of July from here to Timbuktu! And he's going to get it unless people snap out of it."

This might seem wild overstatement—but the administration's lavish wish list of superweapons gave ballast to Strummer's claims. Reagan, as one wag put it, "had never met a weapons system he didn't like."

Perhaps the most destabilizing weapon of all would be the one Reagan touted as a bid to end the arms race: the Strategic Defense Initiative (SDI), announced in late March 1983, two weeks after his "evil empire" speech. Intended to intercept incoming Soviet missiles, SDI was derisively dubbed "Star Wars," and dismissed by many experts as an insanely expensive boondoggle that could never work.

Reagan portrayed SDI as a defensive shield that could prevent a Russian first strike. To the Soviets, however, it appeared to facilitate a first strike, allowing the US to attack without fearing retaliation, thus fatally undermining the Mutually Assured Destruction (MAD) doctrine at the heart of deterrence.

This was dangerously destabilizing, given that MAD had arguably prevented nuclear war for more than three decades by making it unthinkable, since both sides would be destroyed, no matter which struck first. According to analyst Marc Ambinder, "By November of 1983, Russia was convinced that US nuclear doctrine had been changed to include a tilt toward launch-on-warning or first strike posture." This meant the margin for error was frighteningly slim.

The *Washington Post* later described 1983 as "the most dangerous year" of the US-Soviet face-off. Despite growing support for a nuclear freeze, the shooting down of KAL 007 on September 1 kicked off ten weeks of unprecedented peril. The overkill possessed by both sides, the fever pitch of anger and fear in the absence of ongoing dialogue, all made for an extraordinarily volatile cocktail.

Left: Reagan and Thatcher star in a 1984 satirical movie poster. (Designer unknown.)
Top right: *Civil Disobedience Is Civil Defense* button, 1984. (Courtesy of Greg Carr.)
Bottom right: *The Future in Our Hands* button. (Courtesy of Mark Andersen.)

This is the context in which Stansilav Petrov made his fateful decision. Arms expert Bruce Blair asserts the US-Soviet relationship "had deteriorated to the point where the Soviet Union as a system—not just the Kremlin, not just [then–Soviet leader Yuri] Andropov, not just the KGB—but as a system, was geared to expect an attack and to retaliate very quickly. It was on hair-trigger alert. It was very nervous and prone to mistakes . . . The false alarm that

happened on Petrov's watch could not have come at a more dangerous phase in US-Soviet relations."

The same was true of Able Archer 83, a massive NATO military
exercise held near the Soviet border shortly thereafter. Thanks to
a long-classified document finally released in 2015, it has come out
that the president's Foreign Intelligence Advisory Board had reported, "In [November] 1983 we may have inadvertently placed our
relations with the Soviet Union on a hair trigger."

While this near miss was long suspected, the document erased
all doubt. According to the *New York Times*, "The fact that the War-
saw Pact's military response to Able Archer was 'unparalleled in
scale,' the board concluded, 'strongly suggests that Soviet leaders
may have been seriously concerned that the US would use the exercises as a cover for launching a real attack . . . Soviet forces were
preparing to preempt or counterattack a NATO strike.'"

As the report concludes, "This situation could have been extremely dangerous if during the exercise—perhaps through a series
of ill-timed coincidences or because of faulty intelligence—the Soviets had misperceived US actions as preparations for a real attack."
Such misperception was glimpsed, but then sidestepped, thanks to
the cool head of Lt. General Leonard Perroots at Ramstein Air Base
in West Germany, who, according to the report, made a "fortu-
itous, if ill-informed" call to not escalate in response to the Soviet
moves.

The board's report quotes Reagan describing the situation as
"really scary" in June 1984 after he read "a rather stunning array of
indicators" of Soviet war preparations compiled by the CIA in the
wake of Able Archer. While Reagan felt America's good intentions
should be self-evident, the world was not so trusting.

Only one nation had ever used nuclear weapons: the United
States. The Soviets knew this and, given Reagan's words and actions, assumed the worst. The Foreign Intelligence Advisory Board
warned, "It is an especially grave error to assume that since we
know the US is not going to start World War III, the next leaders
of the Kremlin will also believe that—and act on that belief."

The fear was hard to avoid; even network TV paid heed. *The*

Day After—an ABC dramatization of the aftermath of nuclear war—debuted on November 20, 1983, mere days after Able Archer had brought the world to the brink for the second time in three months. More than 100 million people watched the program during its initial broadcast, making it the highest-rated television film in history.

Rarely did a film seem so in tune with a specific moment, coming at the end of what were perhaps the most dangerous months of the Cold War. One of the film's viewers was Ronald Reagan. Genuinely moved, he wrote in his diary that the film was "very effective and left me greatly depressed."

Few had the chance to know as many of the specifics at the time as Reagan, but many made reasonable guesses about the gravity of the situation. Joe Strummer was a serious student of the nuclear threat and was thus reasonably terrified.

After the January 19 show in Santa Barbara, he gruffly challenged a skeptical interviewer—*Record*'s John Mendelsohn, a self-described "long-ago college radical"—about American complacency in the face of US-backed savagery in Central America and the nuclear arms buildup. Strummer: "Every American is responsible for what their government does—if it ain't being done in your name, whose name is it being done in? I read all about the Committee on the Present Danger, and I know they are the ones calling the shots. Why doesn't every American know this? Why are they all on drugs and goofing off?"

Unimpressed, Mendelsohn dubbed Strummer "the mouth that roared," comparing him with a rabid dog running at "full froth," and calling The Clash "the most shrilly self-righteous boors in pop history." In retrospect, Strummer appears to have been largely correct. Reagan's pursuit of policies promoted by the Committee on the Present Danger had brought the world into the gravest danger imaginable.

Words carried a deadly logic. If the USSR was simply an "evil empire" as Reagan said, acting outside the bounds of human decency, what option did the West have but military confrontation? Such language fed the feedback loop now spiraling the world toward nuclear holocaust.

Saner voices challenged both superpowers to stand down.

In October 1983, in what UK activist E.P. Thompson called "the greatest mass movement in modern history," nearly three million people across Western Europe protested nuclear missile deployments and demanded an end to the arms race. The largest crowd of almost one million people assembled outside the Hague in the Netherlands.

In London's Hyde Park, 400,000 people participated in what was probably the largest demonstration in British history, opposing the arrival of US nuclear-armed cruise missiles. While Thatcher had asked Reagan to delay the deployment until after the 1983 election, they were due to arrive at the Greenham Airbase in early November, just before the Able Archer exercises began.

Despite knowing that British public opinion opposed the cruise missiles, Thatcher refused to bend. Thatcher biographer Charles Moore reports, however, that even she was worried by the escalation in rhetoric and the danger of war. This concern didn't stop Thatcher from authorizing spying and harassment against the peace movement or suggesting that it served Soviet interests.

The new Clash ventured into this maelstrom of fear and mobilization with an eight-date tour of Europe. Vowing to "outwork those heavy metal bands" with relentless gigging, Strummer and the others wound their way through Norway, Sweden, West Germany, Belgium, Switzerland, Italy, and France.

Before the tour's second show—at Johanneshov Isstadium in Stockholm, Sweden—the unit posed backstage for a photo that captured the confrontational spirit of the moment. The Clash stood starkly outlined against a white backdrop in dark-colored quasi-commando gear. Strummer is in white, flanked by the others. With a newly trimmed Mohawk and brandishing his *Mohawk Revenge* shirt, the singer has a snarl on his lips and his fists balled up, as if ready for a rumble.

A casual observer could have been forgiven for wondering if the band was on a mission of mayhem rather than peacemaking. In fact, The Clash had long been ambiguous on the question of war and peace; the same Strummer who composed lines like "when violence is singing / silence the sound" and "I don't want to kill" also wrote "I want a riot of my own" and "I don't mind throwing a brick" and wore a Red Brigade/Red Army Faction T-shirt at the biggest UK show they ever played, the Rock Against Racism rally in Victoria Park.

Moreover, The Clash's support for armed guerrilla movements such as the Sandinistas and El Salvador's FMLN was well documented. As already noted, the martial-sounding "Are You Ready for War?" hardly came across as a pacifist ballad. One observer approvingly noted, "They looked and moved like a guerrilla unit onstage." A more skeptical one groused, "For a group so against the machinations of violence they still get an awful lot of mileage from its imagery."

The ambivalence was real. Strummer would argue, "Real revolutions are in the mind," while in the next breath asserting, "Mind you, I think there's really going to be an armed struggle between the have-nots and the haves of the world."

Asked by one interviewer about the band's "army surplus terrorist chic" clothing, Strummer responded, "It's just self-defense." With his questioner at a loss, he elaborated: "You take a Green Beret, who's this well-trained killing machine, which is what we're against. So how do we express what we're opposite to—by dressing like some shambling hippie stoned on acid? The point is, if you're going to defend yourself, you've got to be as fit and tough as the opposition."

Before a sold-out crowd of eight thousand in Stockholm, The Clash seemed ready for the fight. After Vinyl's rousing intro, the band kicked off with "London Calling," "Safe European Home," and "Are You Ready for War?" with "Know Your Rights" thrown in. The intense reaction led Strummer to briefly stop the show to urge the audience to step back, lest folks in front be crushed.

The show had some rough patches—a muffed, out-of-tune opening to "Complete Control," a sluggish "Dictator"—but overall the band was hitting its marks. The tension of playing amid the expectations of the UK home crowd was absent, and no Jones advocates made themselves known. Strummer remained spirited, speaking with brevity and passion on topics like Central America, police brutality, and race relations. He also interjected shouts of "1984!" into "I Fought the Law" and "White Riot," and called out Reagan by name in "Are You Ready for War?"

When the band returned for its first encore, "Glue Zombie," Strummer provided fly for the ointment, shouting, "I'd like to say something to stop you all cheering at once—I say, from now on, drugs are crap!" If the rhythm was a bit static, the singer's throat-shredding invested the tale with pathos, suggesting sympathy for—even identification with—the addict's plight.

Meanwhile, Mick Jones was making himself present via the legal injunctions that—according to Clash scholar Marcus Gray—were greeting the band at every stop. The notices were ignored, and the shows went on, but it was getting harder to brush off rumors of a rival Clash, especially once concert impresario Bill Graham reported getting a call from Jones promising to bring "the real Clash" to tour Stateside.

So when The Clash returned for a second encore that night amid a sea of flickering cigarette lighters—a concert ritual Strummer found tiresome—this was on his mind: "We are about to play a song entitled 'We Are The Clash.' You way well have heard there might be two or three or four Clashes. I DON'T CARE. Let there be five hundred! As long as there is one real one . . . We need to hear TRUTH!"

The band then crashed into the song, which now featured a new opening verse evoking the 1982 conversations with fans in Australia and Japan. While a kinetic call-and-response revamp of the chorus tried on recent dates had been dropped, the song was a bit less stiff than the studio demo, with stirring guitar lines.

There were also less-fortunate adjustments, especially to the chorus. Before, the "We are The Clash" line had been used once, the focus being on "We can strike the match / if you spill the gasoline." Now, "We are The Clash" was repeated three times, with the "strike/spill" couplet split apart and de-emphasized. The song's title had been its weakest link; now it was front and center.

The song now seemed less about cocreation with the audience, and more about staking a simple claim to the name. If a brutal power still shone through, this lyrical shift confused the tune's intent and undermined its resonance.

On this night, however, any doubts were dispelled by the set's momentum, with blazing renditions of "Brand New Cadillac," "Armagideon Time," and "Janie Jones" following "We Are The Clash." When the third and final encore of "English Civil War" and "White Riot"—introduced as an "old English folk song"—was over, there was a sense of well-earned triumph in the air.

As the crowd called out for more, an ebullient Strummer shouted a goodbye and strode off the stage. Gray panned the performance, but a Swedish newspaper's verdict seemed closer to the mark: "Everything works for the 'new' Clash."

Nya Clash
— utmärkt

CLASH
Drammen,
OSLO
MUSIK

Nya CLASH låter utmärkt.
JOE STRUMMER gjorde rätt
när han sparkade MICK JONES.
Nya Clash har mer av allt —
tyngd, tempo och passion.

Bandet når Stockholm och Isstadion i kväll. De inledde Europaturnén i går kväll inför 5 000 stol- och rökbombskastande norrmän. Men vildast av alla är Joe Strummer.

I sista numret kastar han sig huvudstupa från en förstärkare. Det slutar i blod och en mycket stor bula.

— Nu kan väl ingen tvivla på vår inlevelse, var hans kommentar till Expressen i natt.

Han är stolt över Drammenkonserten. Med all rätt.

Det är den nya sättningens trettonde konsert, ändå låter Clash säkrare än någonsin. Mick Jones är ersatt av två gitarrister, Nick Sheppard och Vince White. Den utmärkte trummisen Pete Howard är också ny.

Några soulouppvisningar är det aldrig tal om, och tack och lov inte heller mycket av de gamla reggaeimprovisationerna.

Nya Clash är kort sagt skärpta.

Strummer har antytt att bandet skulle vända tillbaka till den aggressiva punkten från första LP-n. Men så är det inte. Under en och en halv timme gör de 24 låtar. Fem är nya, bland resten finns bandets alla fem tidigare plattor representerade.

Mick Jones hade en stor utstrålning. Men Clash kan även utan honom se bra och farliga ut. De har ju alltid sett ut och rört sig som ett första klassens rockband.

Grått och svart

Scenen går i grått och svart. Nio TV-apparater sänder ut suddiga och förvirrande bildsekvenser ovanför bandets huvuden. De fem är klädda i svart och vitt, är punkigt kortklippta och dansar runt varandra på ett sätt som bara kan betyda en sak: nya Clash är kul.

De inleder med "London calling" och slutar med "White riot". De slarvar bitvis

och **Paul Simonon** gör en hemsk munspelsversion av sin "Guns of Brixton". De fem nya låtarna är svåra att bedöma efter bara en lyssning, men inriktningen är gammal rock'n'roll.

Även om det sviktar stundtals slår det klart att nya Clash är en seger för Joe Strummer och hans idéer.

Och numera är till och med ljudanläggningen korrekt inställd.

— Vi blir bättre för varje spelning, sa Joe i natt. Tricket är att kunna släppa loss på scenen utan att musiken blir lidande. Joe kliar nackbulan och ler.

Nya Clash kan.
— MÅNS IVARSSON

Foto: VERDENS GANG

EN SEGER FÖR STRUMMER. Joe Strummer (bilden) bevisar att han gjorde rätt när han sparkade gitarristen Mick Jones. Nya sättningen av Clash låter utmärkt.

Big crowds and rave reviews in Europe—"New Clash Is Excellent," from a newspaper in Oslo, Norway.

Offstage matters were considerably less copacetic. "You can forget Joe, you can forget Paul, you can forget everybody," White snapped later. "Bernie was the man with the controls. He was the one dictating. I was in a situation where I had to listen to him." This was hardly encouraging, as Rhodes tended to be a drill sergeant at the best of times, albeit one of the Marxist variety, with perhaps hints of Asperger's syndrome. Sheppard: "You'd come off-stage feeling good, but there would be Bernie to bring you down . . . Nothing was ever good enough."

Rhodes's approach was intended to foster "self-criticism." Knowing that rock nourished hedonism and ego-tripping far more readily than revolution, Strummer defended the value of the practice: "Every star surrounds himself with yes-men—we'd rather have a team with internal self-criticism."

This reflected the influence of Chinese Communist leader Mao Tse-tung. In the 1940s, Mao had written, "Conscientious practice of self-criticism is still another hallmark distinguishing our Party . . . To check up regularly on our work and in the process develop a democratic style of work, to fear neither criticism nor self-criticism—this is the only effective way to prevent all kinds of political dust and germs from contaminating the minds of our comrades and the body of our Party."

In principle, the practice was both common sense and revolutionary. Self-criticism was adopted by elements of the New Left in the late sixties and early seventies. Perhaps the best-known exponent was the Weather Underground, a splinter faction of Students for a Democratic Society, the most important US student organization of the 1960s. In 1969, the group—who soon made its name with a series of bombings, including of the Pentagon and US Capitol—put striking new lyrics to the holiday standard "White Christmas": "I'm dreaming of a white riot."

Whether Strummer or Rhodes knew of this turn of phrase is unclear, but they were aware of the group. While the courage of the Weather Underground was undeniable, its effectiveness was less certain. Self-criticism in their hands soon appeared to be less a tool of democracy than a means of control. This was not so different than in Mao's China—or, some felt, within The Clash itself.

As Strummer touted self-criticism, he denounced groups who operated like businesses. He noted, "We did eight gigs with the Who and looked at them and thought, 'Is that the end of the road? Four complete strangers, going on for an hour and then off?'" Strummer's stand was clear: "I want to be friends with the members of my band . . . I want [us] to be a real team, not a stage-light team."

Like self-criticism, this made sense in principle. However, the regular hectoring by Rhodes—in practice the main critic, and rarely of himself—undermined morale.

So did the gap between Strummer's pronouncements and the fact that the three newer members were paid minimally—£150 a week, about $225—and often felt treated like hired help; janitors wielding a "guitar broom," as White put it. The trio swiftly grew to dislike the band meetings in which Rhodes held forth on all manner of perceived failures and sometimes goaded others to do the same.

It was not an easy situation. The Clash was an unlikely combination of Top 10 pop stars and would-be revolutionaries. Howard, White, and Sheppard knew they could not expect to play a fully equal role in the band immediately. To suggest by word and deed that such full membership depended on working hard to earn the necessary trust hardly seemed out of bounds, and they granted as much.

Nonetheless, a practical reality was that The Clash, legally, was now a limited liability company whose members were Strummer, Simonon, and Rhodes. This reinforced a second-class status for the others that chafed against the oft-stated desires to have a fully bonded platoon and contribute to genuine equality in the world.

Nor did it make much sense to treat members of the team so harshly that at least one—Peter Howard—began to call band meetings "Bernie's dehumanization sessions." If onstage The Clash set such contention aside in order to try to give it all to the moment, such unnecessary abuse didn't make matters any easier.

Given punk's antiauthoritarian inclinations, this was also incentive for acting out, such as White's impromptu bathroom liaison in Stockholm with Rhodes's girlfriend. At best, this was White's effort to strike back at Rhodes—who he had quickly grown to loathe—in the most painful way possible. At worst, it suggested that White had the impulse control of a three-year-old. Neither option was glad tidings for a band with such an ambitious agenda, in such a challenging moment.

This discord in the ranks wasn't visible onstage. With the band playing night after night, the five began to truly gel musically. As the tour crossed Europe, The Clash continued to draw large crowds and enjoy ecstatic fan reactions.

The home front was never far from Strummer's mind. Before a crowd of seven thousand in Düsseldorf, West Germany, he paused after "This Is England" to note acidly, "I'm warning you, very soon it's going to be Margaret Thatcher über alles," referring to the German national anthem that was associated with the Nazis.

Once again Strummer could be accused of hyperbole, yet some truth lurked. While all may have seemed quiet back home, it felt to some like the calm before the storm. Ever since the NUM had banned overtime, close observers were waiting for the other shoe to drop. That shoe fall would not be long in coming.

Yet while the war dance between Thatcher and the miners was worrisome, other developments were even more alarming. In Milan, Italy, Strummer dedicated the song "Jericho" to "all of you who went to Comiso and stood there in the pouring rain, to tell them we don't play a Yankee game . . ." The Comiso military air base was the Italian equivalent of the UK's Greenham, receiving US cruise missiles and thus becoming the venue for mass protests.

By the time Strummer spoke, the missiles had already arrived at Comiso despite the outcry, as they had at Greenham and Molesworth in the UK. Their mid-November arrival caused uproar in the British Parliament. Labour leader Neil Kinnock called it an act of "reckless cynicism . . . that makes Britain a more dangerous place today than it was yesterday." Thatcher responded that it was "not true" that deploying cruise missiles meant escalating the nuclear arms race.

Referring in part to a recent decision by NATO ministers to rid the alliance's stockpiles of outdated nuclear weapons, Thatcher claimed that there now were 2,400 fewer US nuclear warheads in Europe, even with the new arrivals. While technically true, this conveniently overlooked the fact that cruise missiles—small, easily movable, difficult for radar to detect as they could hug the ground, yet far more powerful than the bombs that destroyed Hiroshima and Nagasaki—were qualitatively quite different than the decommissioned weapons.

The Soviets recognized this and, as a result, threatened to walk out of long-delayed Geneva arms control negotiations if the cruise missiles were deployed. Thatcher was losing the argument with the public, as polls showed that 59 percent of the British opposed taking cruise missiles. Nonetheless, she pushed back against the Greenham Women's Peace Camp's round-the-clock protest outside the base, with police regularly making arrests and evicting protesters.

As all of this was unfolding, Joe Strummer's personal life was about to change fundamentally. Two days after the Milan show, on February 29, his father Ronald Mellor died suddenly of a heart attack during a gall bladder operation. While Mellor had dealt with heart difficulties for some time, the death was nonetheless shocking.

The news reached Strummer at the band's final European date, a Paris show that had been rescheduled to March 1 when an earlier gig was scrubbed by a transportation strike. It would take some time for his band to find out, however, as Strummer played the show without telling the other musicians what had happened.

His father's wake and funeral happened two days later on March 3, when The Clash was booked to play a gig at the Edinburgh Playhouse in Scotland. Strummer went to remember his dad, then got in a car and rode to the show. Most of his bandmates still didn't know what had happened.

Strummer had become a father and lost his father in a matter of months. Sheppard: "Becoming a parent and losing a parent—these are two of the biggest life changes imaginable. Joe was dealing with them in the midst of trying to resurrect The Clash. The pressure— and grief—must have been immense."

Vinyl agreed: "Looking back at it now—and not from my point of view at the time—[the rebuilding of The Clash] is really not happening at the right time for Joe in his personal life, he and Gaby are starting a family, his parents are not well. It happens all the time in a band, a gang, whatever . . . At some point, the other side of people's lives is going to take over, it's going to develop. And gang life becomes secondary, in certain aspects. Then you're trying to juggle, you know?"

Vinyl also knew Strummer carried deep pain from his childhood and his relationship with his parents—often absent due to his father's work overseas in the British foreign service—but not much beyond that. Vinyl: "Joe's childhood was a real off-limits subject. Even to somebody like myself, who was fairly close to him."

In a late-1976 interview with Caroline Coon, Strummer let down the wall a bit: "The only place I considered home was the boarding school my parents sent me to. It's easier, isn't it? I mean it gets kids out the way, doesn't it?"

The bitter words masked a more complex reality. Strummer's father lost his own parents in a car crash at an early age and grew up in an orphanage with his brother. One can only speculate how this trauma factored into the decision to place Strummer and his brother in boarding school at the ages of eight and ten. In any case, the pain appears to have been handed down to the next generation.

Strummer spat out adolescent venom to Coon: "[Boarding school] was great! You have to stand up for yourself. You get beaten up the first day you get there. I'm really glad I went because I shudder to think what would have happened if I hadn't gone . . . I only saw my father twice a year. If I'd seen him all the time I'd probably have murdered him by now. He was very strict."

The harsh remarks hinted at Strummer's fraught relationship with his father and, by extension, his mother, Anna MacKenzie. While Vinyl senses that much had been left unsaid between the two Mellor men, he declines to speculate further.

Nonetheless, a man whose childhood was marked by long separations from his parents while at a stern boarding school, who lost his only brother to suicide during that time, would likely carry lasting wounds. Such a person might feel special guilt leaving his own newborn for long stretches as well—but this is exactly what would happen if The Clash were to be tireless road warriors as promised.

In a sign of how dysfunctional intraband communication could be, Sheppard, White, and Howard only learned about Strummer's loss a week later. Sheppard: "There was a big to-do about something or other, and all of a sudden Bernie is laying into us, screaming about how we always complain. 'Look at Joe, he's just lost his father and you don't see him moaning about it.' I was just floored."

Strummer didn't ask for any support with what he was going through, and would have been unlikely to get it anyway. The pace of Clash life was fast, and—as in war—there was little time for comfort or condolence. Even Vinyl himself now bitterly regrets his lack of attention to his friend on this level: "There was just so much to do. We were on a mission. Much like somebody working on a sports team is not that interested in whether one of the star players is having a second child or whatever, do you know what I mean? The guy is thinking about winning the trophy, getting the form back, or whatever it might be. He's not thinking about their private lives and their fulfillment on that level, you know?" While Vinyl hastens to add, "I've changed a lot since then," at the time, Strummer carried the burden largely alone.

This meant charging into heavy fire on his own Normandy beach: London, where the band had started, and could expect to face the most skepticism. Shows in Edinburgh, Blackburn, Liverpool, and Portsmouth had gone well. Anticipation was high, and so were ticket sales: two shows at the Brixton Academy—capacity five thousand—on March 8 and 9 sold out so quickly that three additional shows were added, with postponed Irish dates in Belfast and Dublin sandwiched in between.

Yet another front was about to be opened. On March 1, as Strummer was absorbing the news about his father, the director of the South Yorkshire Coal Board announced that the Cortonwood coal mine would close in six weeks. This sudden pronouncement angered miners employed there, as the coal vein in their pit was not exhausted, and the enterprise remained profitable.

Immediately, agitation for a strike there began, and on March 5 a vote was taken to authorize work stoppage. As the Cortonwood miners went on strike, Ian MacGregor announced that more than a dozen other pits would close in 1984, for a net loss of over twenty thousand jobs. Furious, Arthur Scargill warned that this was just the beginning of a full-on assault that would close more than seventy pits, decimating the industry.

While this indeed was the plan, Thatcher's government denied it loudly and consistently, painting Scargill as a hysteric. Nonetheless, the Cortonwood strike spread to other pits. More and more miners came out, determined to make their stand. By March 12, so many were out that Scargill declared it a national strike.

This decision was swiftly attacked as illegitimate by the Thatcher government, which pointed out that a national vote of the entire NUM membership to approve such strike action was required. In this, Thatcher hoped to split the miners and short-circuit the strike. It is possible the NUM would not have gotten the required majority in a vote, given that a significant portion of Nottinghamshire miners—whose pits were thought to be safe from closure—opposed this action.

However, other miners whose jobs were on the line resented the possibility that those whose jobs were safe might stand aside and watch their brothers go on the dole. As a Cortonwood miner said, "We won't give them a vote on whether or not we lose our jobs." If this was understandable, some worried it was a strategic error by the NUM. Thatcher would batter them for waging an illegitimate strike, thus justifying what would be ruthless tactics to undermine and destroy the NUM.

Far less convincing was the argument that the NUM was foolhardy to begin a strike as spring approached. MacGregor—and behind him, Thatcher—had struck the first blow. Whether shared with the public or not, there was now a death list. Once these mines were closed, they would almost certainly never reopen—so it was now or never if thousands of jobs were to be saved.

Thatcher had shrewdly chosen the optimal time for the confrontation. Given what was at stake, however, the miners could not afford to wait for a better moment, which would likely never come. The miners knew it was do-or-die. They took to the picket lines determined to save their communities and defeat Thatcher.

Top: The Clash take a five-night stand at Brixton Academy. (Poster by Eddie King.) Bottom: "Resistance"—the band's live fury at Brixton Academy as the miners strike begins. (Photographer unknown.)

* * *

As pickets went up in mining communities across Britain, The Clash brought their heavy artillery to the Brixton Academy. This was home, and the band was prepared to fight to retake this ground.

The NME had put the group on the cover of its February 25 issue in preparation for the homecoming. The resulting article by Richard Cook did not neglect the hard questions, but mixed witty jabs with a sense of taking the band seriously. Cook posed his essential query early in the article: "In nin'een-ady-FORE The Clash are back again. Do we want them back? Do we need them?"

This seemed the perfect setup for yet another takedown. Astonishingly enough, what emerged instead was a genuine give-and-take, where Cook allowed himself to be touched by Strummer and Simonon's persistent passion.

Cook challenged Strummer's bashing of Boy George and similarly androgynous UK popster Marilyn, saying, "They are doing what you say you want to do, changing people's attitudes," albeit in a different way. At the same time, Cook was clearly taken with Strummer's call for punk to once again be like a blowtorch incinerating the dismal pop landscape.

Strummer was in fine fettle, ripping drugs, apathy, and right-wing politicians: "It's all rubbish! With Reagan and Thatcher strolling away to victory . . . That's why we are back. We're needed!"

Simonon: "Basically [we're] getting on with the job . . . it's risky. But we are a band that takes risks."

Strummer jumped back in: "I aim to outwork all those people and get rid of them. We'll smash down the number-one groups . . . Pop will die and rebel rock will rule."

Strummer paused, then unleashed a final salvo: "I'm saying stop the drugs. Vote. Take responsibility for being alive. I'm prepared to dive back down the pavement again—give me an old guitar and some shoes and I'll fuck off . . . [but] The Clash has been elected to do a job and it has been neglected. I'd rather have a stab at it with a fresh team. That's the path of honor for me."

Cook found himself grudgingly convinced: "It's a heroic manifesto, a tidal wave of convictions—and maybe we need a loud-mouth bastard like Strummer just as much as we need a boy in braids who says be yourself . . . Their opportunity, at a time when pop is in its most lachrymose and indulgent doldrums, is to recreate their epiphany." Although Cook felt "this is their last chance," he also somewhat incredulously concluded: "Is 1984 the year of The Clash?"

The band was hoping to make this so. The five Brixton shows proved to be fairly epic, with packed houses every night and over-the-top response. Its weapons sharpened by six weeks of steady gigging, the new Clash knew it had to deliver, and it did. The Irish shows were similarly spirited, with massive, joyous crowds.

Nonetheless, reviews in the UK music weeklies were anything

but raves. Lynden Barber of *Melody Maker* picked up where *Record Mirror*'s Reid left off, spewing negativity. Allowing that Strummer's "heart was (and is?) in the right place," Barber lacerated with descriptors like "pathetic" and "farce," terming the whole affair "nothing more than a reactionary surrender to the forces of nostalgia."

Some slams were strikingly personal: "Poor old Joe Strummer. It's 1977 all over again up there onstage and he desperately wants us to believe in it. Moreover, he desperately wants us to believe in him because it ain't too nice when people get cynical and think you don't mean anything anymore, especially when you privately realize that they've probably got good reason."

Not to be outdone for anti-Clash cred, NME published not one but two slams. A review of the opening-night show—Gavin Martin's "Jail Guitar Bores"—tipped its hat ever so slightly to Richard Cook's relatively upbeat take, then burned it all down: "This new Clash are no big departure, they are still entangled with all the old faults . . . The calisthenics, the heroic posturing, the riot scenes and war footage are all still there . . . [They are] still hung up on self-aggrandizement."

On one hand, The Clash was "posed perfect rebels" engaged in "hollow myth-making." On the other hand, substance was no-go as well. Strummer's "disparate declarations on everything from the White House, to welfare, to women's sorry lot," only led Martin to complain that the singer "labors his points unnecessarily—a Clash audience (even though mostly white males) knows well the level of political import and intent without having it rammed down their throats." Describing the night as "the heaviest and most orthodox rock show I've ever seen the Clash play," Martin concluded: "Mostly they were terrible."

Lola Borg's short, savage review of the fourth Brixton show dismissed The Clash as "mucho butcho as ever" and denigrated the audience for its "total hero worship." Spending as much time discussing the "classical Greek" interior of the Academy and Strummer's "hideous demi-mohican" as the music, Borg found little of value. While she professed to be turned off by the band allegedly ignoring brutal bouncers, there is little indication Borg took the night seriously in any way.

While The Clash had little reason to expect kind—or even fair—treatment by these trend-obsessed rags, this gusher of venom was still a bit shocking. Such critics would hardly have convinced Strummer to rethink his agenda, however, let alone retreat. "The thing that Joe got from seeing the [Sex] Pistols was that you don't have to go out there and say, 'Please like us,'" Sheppard says. "You go out and say, 'This is what we do. If you don't like it, the door's at the back.'"

Likely far more significant to Strummer was the review delivered in person by Johnny Green, his longtime Clash brother. Crucial to the Clash road machine for years, Green had parted ways with the band in 1979, feeling matters were becoming too businesslike. Green didn't dismiss the possibility that The Clash could continue on in a valid way without Headon or even Jones; however, he simply wasn't impressed with what he saw onstage in Brixton.

Green: "I thought it was very sterile, and kind of like a cardboard cutout, really—two guitarists trying to pick up Mick's pieces. Joe seemed to be diminished. I mean, Joe put his heart and soul into it, of course, but he wasn't bouncing off the other members of the band. They weren't playing as a team, you know? It was Joe and—to a lesser extent—Paul, playing with three guys who looked real good, *too* good, you know? Almost like someone had made 'em up to be in The Clash."

Here, Green seems to echo one insight from Borg's slam: "Joe Strummer is clearly in charge and the band follow his orders." This was quite a contrast to when Strummer, Jones, and Simonon had dodged and dived with one another out front, presenting a sense of equality and teamwork. Yet to say that something is different is not the same as demonstrating that it is worse. Indeed, the new Clash was slowly finding its own onstage interplay that could prove equally dynamic.

Another Green critique seems less solid. Green claims that the new Clash "had these wooden springboards that enhance the lift of the athletes put by the side of the drum riser, so the guitarists could jump in the air, like Mick used to do, you know? And I thought, 'Bloody hell—the lengths that people go to, to reenact something that was entirely natural and spontaneous, once upon a time!'"

Asked about this, Sheppard bristles: "I respect Johnny Green enough to be surprised that he'd believe a story like that." It does seem hard to believe, as both Sheppard and White—now that he had found his stage legs—exhibited unaided athleticism night after night while playing the songs.

Green also seemed to share a Jones complaint: "How can [the new guitarists] play those songs with conviction? They haven't lived them." Sheppard's terse response: "I played those songs with the conviction that I had for them. And I did love those songs. I made no bones about it, I was a big fan of The Clash. There wasn't a song that I didn't want to play, you know?" Left unsaid was that, by the end of his tenure, Jones didn't wish to play quite a number of Clash songs.

In any case, Green found his way backstage, dodging a disapproving Rhodes and running into Strummer in a hallway. As recounted by Chris Salewicz in his epic Strummer bio, *Redemption Song*, "Having rid himself of his heroin demons, Johnny had put on a large amount of weight; he hardly fit into the only suit he had to wear. 'That's a terrible suit,' Joe told him. 'It's not as bad as your group,' replied the Clash's plainspoken former road manager."

Salewicz explains, "In the forthrightness of the Clash posse, an extension of punk's professed honesty, there was sometimes an element of 'dare,' incorporating a subtle mind game. But Johnny's remark cut Joe to the quick. In front of him, in the backstage corridor, Joe burst into tears."

Green recalled, "I said to Joe, 'What are you doing this for, for fuck's sake?' He burst into tears, and he said, 'I don't know what else to do.' Bernard came by, and said, 'Don't talk to him, Joe, he's yesterday.' [Joe] said, 'Fuck off, Bernard, or I'll smack you. You don't understand friendship, you don't understand loyalty.'" Green soon hustled off, leaving Rhodes in command, but his words still resonated.

Strummer's tears were no doubt real—but what did they mean? It could have just been the sign of a man under immense pressure, bone tired. Maybe he was grieving in ways too deep to express, at least for a man raised in stiff-upper-lip England, internalizing the destructive demands of masculinity. Perhaps it meant Strummer feared that what Green said was true, that the new band was not up for the mission, and that he had betrayed a friend to pursue a fool's errand. Maybe it just meant that Strummer was insecure, even becoming unmoored amid irreconcilable demands . . . or some combination of all of these.

Despite the apparent wrestling with profound self-doubt, it is hard to find fault with Strummer's performances at Brixton Academy, or of the band as a whole. If the heavier sound was not for everyone, it was nonetheless powerfully realized. As another longtime ally Julian Balme recalls, "They were fantastic, really, really good . . . All the new songs live sounded brilliant. With two guitarists *and* Joe, it was like, *WOAH!* They weren't pussyfooting around. It wasn't apologetic; it was turn it up to eleven and right in your face! There was nothing lacking in the live performances at all."

Nor should there have been any doubt about the band's continued relevance, the sniping notwithstanding. Beyond the trenchant outcry of numerous new tunes, several of the older songs seemed so on target they might well have been composed for precisely this moment. Arguably the most powerful was "English Civil War." While written amid the neo-Nazi scare that Rock Against Racism helped turn back, it also fit the drama unfolding in 1984 like a glove.

Strummer knew this. In the final encore of the last Brixton show, he chose to dedicate the song to "the cold coal miner out on the picket lines, freezing his bollocks off." The statement suggested he saw the strike not simply as a fight between the Tories and the miners, but a struggle for the soul of the country. If Thatcher was to be stopped, it had to happen now; it had to happen here.

At Colston Hall, Strummer had paused to query the crowd before igniting a crushing version of "Clampdown," another song seemingly tailor-made for this urgent moment: "Does Britain exist? Is Britain a dream or a nightmare?"

As Thatcher's clampdown began to descend on William Blake's "green and pleasant land," this was an unavoidable question.

The fight would require much, and victory was not guaranteed.

It was unclear how great of an impact a band could possibly have. As the miners stood on picket lines, The Clash was about to take its own war across the ocean for an extended US tour. They would do so carrying news from the UK, while wrestling with peculiarly American challenges as Reagan revved up his 1984 reelection campaign.

So much was now at stake: for the band certainly, but much more for millions of human beings. The battle was on, and the world seemed about to turn—but in what direction? It was time to find out.

CHAPTER FOUR
TURNING THE WORLD

Strummer perched on TV monitors during US tour. (Photo by Bob Gruen.)

Ever since the Founding Fathers of our nation dreamed this dream, America has been something of a schizophrenic personality, tragically divided against herself. On one hand we have professed the great principles of democracy. On the other we have practiced the very antithesis of those principles.
—Martin Luther King Jr., 1964

Live your beliefs and you can turn the world around.
—Henry David Thoreau

The crowd's applause was deafening, exhilarating. Already drenched in sweat only two songs into the night, Joe Strummer stepped to the microphone. Smiling, clearly lifted by the power of the people in the room, he shouted one word: "Lights!"

Instantly, the glow radiating from the stage was swallowed up as powerful house lights revealed a packed audience of nearly four thousand at the Sunrise Musical Theater near Fort Lauderdale, Florida. The division between performer and audience dissolved and all stood joined together by the wash of incandescent lighting.

As the other members of The Clash prepared their next salvo, Strummer spoke: "I'd like to welcome you here tonight. I'd personally like to thank each and every one of you for showing up, proving that maybe the world can be turned!"

The crowd roared again. After introducing the rest of the band, the ebullient singer quipped: "And, last but not least, my name is Ratso Rizzo!" As this reference to *Midnight Cowboy*'s doomed antihero seemed to fly over the heads of most of the audience, Strummer gathered himself and chanted a simple mantra: *"Take drugs—don't vote—get ready—for war!"*

Knowing this as the count-off to the next song, the band returned to the fray.

This was only the third date on a two-month tour, but the new Clash was already hitting its stride. The opening "London Calling" and "Safe European Home" had always been performed fervently, but now they came across with a sort of swing, the clear sign of a band coming into its own.

Strummer's curt intro to an equally kinetic "Are You Ready for War?" had outlined the tour's message—and it was hardly a happy vision. Yet his hopeful energy also resonated, suggesting a rallying cry behind the critique.

The Clash had left behind a homeland just entering into what would prove to be its biggest conflict since World War II. The huge country they were about to traverse over the next months was itself at a crucial crossroads.

Reagan had defeated incumbent Jimmy Carter four years before. Now, as the world teetered on the edge of a catastrophic war, poverty in the US was on the rise, racial tension simmered, and desperation festered where once a mighty industrial economy had thrived. As a result, millions loathed Reagan.

Yet many—even some of those displaced by the economic tides—found pride, even hope, in the unapologetic vision of national renewal put forward by this conservative revolutionary. The question once asked by Reagan hung in the air: *Are you better off than you were four years ago?* A bitterly divided American public would render its verdict in a little over seven months.

Beyond the politics, America held a special fascination for Strummer and the rest of The Clash culturally. "I'm So Bored with the USA" notwithstanding, it was—as Vince White noted—"the home of country music and rock and roll!" So much of Strummer's own inspiration came from there, from Woody Guthrie, the blues, the MC5, even political figures such as Martin Luther King Jr., whose speeches the singer would sometimes listen to in order to get psyched up to perform.

As such, Strummer brought a conflicted passion to the band's US tours. "We appreciate lunatics and individuals and madmen," he told an interviewer after the new Clash's first show in California. "America had millions of them. All the lunatics and madmen in the entire world came to America at one time!"

But if this once-upon-a-time USA had been an inspiration, the present was less uplifting. Strummer: "So why have these corporations got in their little boardrooms, and made all these rules and anybody who breaks these rules gets fired? And nobody wants to get fired . . . Where has the pioneering spirit gone?"

America remained more than cookie-cutter corporate consumerism to Strummer. Onstage at the historic Township Auditorium in Columbia, South Carolina, five days after their blistering Fort Lauderdale show, he paused to pay tribute to "James Brown, Otis Redding, and all the greats" who had performed there.

While some called the band hypocritical for dismissing the US while so obviously besotted with it, this was not entirely fair. As Strummer would note later, there were at least two Americas: King and Reagan, the dream and the nightmare, freedom and control, pioneering innovators and corporate conformists.

Ironically, in a way, the musicians were themselves employees of a huge American corporation. Part of their spark came from that dynamic tension, a rub of ideal vs. real, as they walked the fine line separating them from their own critique of corporate power. The Clash waged war from that ambiguous space.

There was also a commercial angle. The band was venturing back into the vast American market—the biggest in the world, one that made and broke bands.

Two short years ago The Clash had gone from successful cult band to one of the biggest draws in the world on the *Combat Rock* tour—a jaunt that almost didn't happen due to the internal crisis with Headon. Success had nearly swallowed the group; it had also provided muscle to push back against their overlords.

This tour itself might be seen as an example. The Clash had returned, trawling across this vast country—but in blatant violation of basic rock business mores, and much to the dismay of their label, they had no new record to flog. Asked about this, Strummer responded, "We're just going out and playing for the hell of it. We all have a common goal now: we want to become a *real* band."

Strummer also felt the moment required The Clash, not as some abstract idea, but as a signal to rally the troops before it was too late. It was no accident that the frontman introduced himself as "Paul Revere" at one of the US dates. "We've been elected to do a job here," Strummer insisted. "It takes commitment."

Yet the band was not surrendering its pop ambitions. As Strummer had told Richard Cook, "We want to take rebel rock to Number One!" This was less for the money than for the impact. Calling US underground punk heroes Bad Brains and Black Flag "closet cases" because they were on independent labels and thus might not get heard by most, Strummer wanted to get his message out to all.

Likewise, Vinyl saw no point in aiming too low. *Combat Rock* "was just a foot in the door," the rooster-haired rabble-rouser declared to one interviewer. "What's the point of getting enthusiastic about selling a million when Michael Jackson's sold thirty million, and is probably selling another million while we talk?"

How this was going to work was unclear, and Cook had understandably been left a bit stumped. America had never embraced punk as the UK had done—and even in Britain, it was now often seen as yesterday's news. The only punk-related acts that had made it big in the US—Blondie, the Police, even The Clash—had done so with songs that were hardly incendiary "rebel rock."

While "Rock the Casbah" was far more substantive than any of these, its serious message was masked by its novelty appeal. This was intentional, for Strummer had often decried "preachy" performers, even noting, "I put some jokes in ["Are You Ready for War?"] so it wouldn't be too depressing!" Flashes of humor added balance and accessibility to hyperserious themes.

However, none of the band's relentless new material fit the "Casbah" mold, much less that of the poppy love songs "Train in Vain" or "Should I Stay or Should I Go." This tour was a leap of faith, continuing the job that The Clash had set out to do. With forty-plus dates packed between March and May, it was also hard work.

In part, the aim was to build solidarity within the new lineup. The Clash had begun its tour in the South, slowly working down and up the Atlantic seaboard in a no-frills bus. As White recalls, "The whole tour was by Greyhound bus. No flying was allowed. It was structured this way so that we had a down-to-earth real traveling experience. We weren't allowed to be pampered rock stars."

Strummer celebrated the road warrior vibe: "We got a Greyhound bus, without a bunk, without a TV, without a bar . . . We just sit on the bus, we drive fourteen hours straight. We fucking road hog it!" Not everyone was so enthused. "I hated being on that hellish tin can," Howard says.

For most, however, there was a "we're all in it together" spirit as the tour set off. Eddie King—who was doing video for the band—recalled a determined vibe on the bus: "We were listening to a lot of Bo Diddley, the first Run-DMC album, and a song that used the Malcolm X 'No Sell Out' speech in a loop. That was on the tape deck all the time, it became a kind of theme: *No Sell Out*."

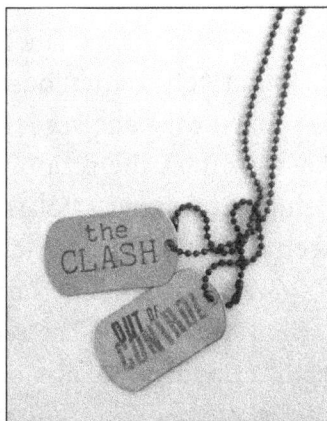

Left: "Rebel punk" Paul Simonon on US tour bus. (Photographer unknown.)
Right: Prototype for Clash dog tags, never produced. (Designed by Eddie King.)

The spartan approach had an aim—to share hardship and build cohesion, as in an actual military unit. The entire band now wore dog tags, items originally used to identify dead or wounded soldiers. As Sheppard explains, "The dog tags were given to us by some fans that had painted them up before [the three new members] joined . . . beautifully done, with enamel paint. It was all part of the whole *Combat Rock* image, and the gear that we were wearing."

Strummer told one journalist: "In my mind, I liken us to a new platoon and we're going to go out and crawl right in front of enemy lines, get fired upon, and then look at each other to see how we're bearing up. Can I rely on this guy when my gun jams? We're under fire and we're sharing that experience."

If the metaphor was presumptuous, it signaled the band's serious intent and special challenges. This Clash was a new entity, thrust almost immediately into an extremely demanding position by the band's popularity. To succeed required intangible but very real glue, what analyst Jennifer Senior has called the "psychologically invaluable sense of community and interdependence" that comes "only during moments of great adversity [where] we come together."

For Senior, the experience of combat illustrated this: "War, for all of its brutality and ugliness, satisfies some of our deepest evolutionary yearnings for connectedness. Platoons are like tribes, [giving] soldiers a chance to show their valor and loyalty, to work cooperatively, to demonstrate utter selflessness."

Given this, she argues, "Is it any wonder that so many soldiers say they miss the action when they come home?" But if the theory behind Strummer's "platoon" analogy was sound, it remained to be seen how it would work.

Given the fan base built over the long *Combat Rock* tours, expectations were high. The reengineered Clash aimed to exceed them. While Gavin Martin had scorched the band for its "massed light banks, three-prong guitar chunder and video screen backdrop," *Washington Post* rock critic Mark Jenkins had a different take after seeing them in front of a sold-out crowd of five thousand at George Washington University's Smith Center on April 8.

Jenkins was often hard to please, and had been left dissatisfied by the band's two previous DC shows: "When I first saw The Clash, they were trying that amazing everything-coming-together-on-the-edge-of-falling-apart sound they had pulled off on their first album—but it didn't work very well live. They'd be racing around onstage and you'd suddenly think, 'Where'd the song go?' It was very entertaining to watch but the music didn't really come across."

Jenkins was impressed by the new lineup's energy and its music: "It was 'the Joe Strummer show' for sure, but with two guitar players, he didn't have to worry about doing anything but calling everyone to war or whatever. The band had their commando 'state of attack' theatrics but the musical presentation was far better than the Jones-era Clash, and the new songs fit nicely with the older ones."

Jenkins sensed an outfit with a future: "The Clash had been a bit like a club band that hadn't figured out how to play to arena crowds. This was the first time they seemed able to project in the necessary way to be convincing at this level."

Although two guitars seemed like overkill to some, they did bolster the Clash attack, making the sound savage and direct. Sheppard: "We were playing two Les Pauls, very loud, very punk, you know, very rock and roll—a bit too rock and roll for some people." The twin guitars not only generated extraordinary sound and fury, but also—as Jenkins witnessed—reproduced the full power of the songs' original arrangements which had sometimes suffered amid Strummer's stop-and-start playing and Jones's overly busy, effects-laden approach.

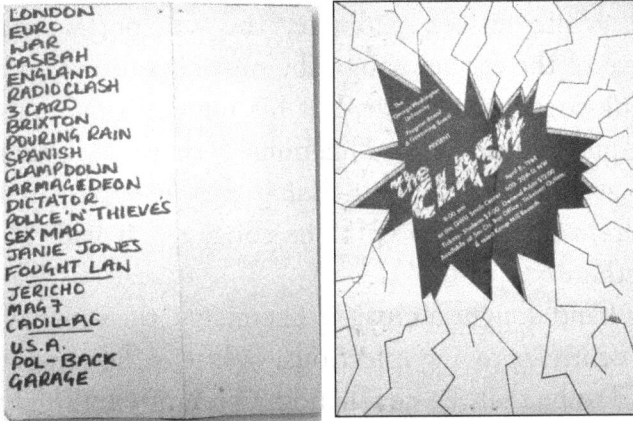

Left: Strummer's set list from Smith Center show, Washington, DC, April 8, 1984.
Right: Flyer for the show.

Not all observers were as taken with the new Clash—understandably enough, given how central Jones had been. White had his own criticism of Strummer and a white suit that he sometimes wore onstage. While the *Mohark Revenge* T-shirt remained, the bulky suit coat suggested a Mohawked lounge singer. The guitarist derided Strummer's "deep-orange hair and white suit under the spotlight, cabaret entertaining in an *Out of Control* shirt . . . the solo star. He'd become a bit of a caricature of something."

To Howard, the singer's sartorial displays suggested "a banana republic dictator" or "Captain Scarlet meets something out of [the Woody Allen film] *Bananas*." The drummer laughs: "Sometimes, honestly, he would walk in the room and me, Nick, and Vince would look at each other: *What the hell is he wearing today?*"

Strummer offered few apologies. "We need an image," he insisted. "I'm out there fighting like tigers against all these slinky, funky, junkie mothers. I'm out there in a three-ring circus, I need an image to grab some attention." He had a point, and White—in the band, but often its biggest critic—allowed, "Despite everything, the shows continued to be good. There was something there. I felt it."

The band also exercised artistic self-criticism, adjusting both the set lists and the song arrangements. There still was no sign of "Should I Stay or Should I Go," and "We Are The Clash" and "Glue Zombie" had also disappeared.

While White missed "Zombie," he was not worried about the absence of the former song. The musician didn't embrace the song's punk-socialist message, but his main critique was artistic: "The song just felt lumpen, with a nursery rhyme sing-along chorus . . . I felt stupid singing it." Echoing this, Sheppard notes, "We tried different approaches with the song, but it had never really come together."

As the band sought a creative chemistry, the sense of mission remained central, proving infectious. White: "The general consensus seemed to be that the new band had reignited. [This] return to the basic primal sound of The Clash [had] energy and conviction where two years ago there had been boredom."

Skepticism still remained, especially among more mainstream outlets, which seemed less willing to let the departed Jones go easily. For Boston After Dark's Doug Simmons, songs like "Sex Mad War"—one of three new ones aired at the Worcester Centrum—struck him as a paler echo of The Clash's original intensity. He questioned how this revamped band could breach the pop mainstream without sound musical reinforcement: "Without fresh tunes, and for that matter, fresh lyrics, Strummer's radical message is not going to sink in."

The negative write-ups often struck Sheppard as reflecting an old-fashioned generation gap: "The decision had been made to go out and be a punk rock band. It doesn't surprise me that [mainstream] reviewers would find [the new approach] a bit much. Presumably, they'd be older, not able to keep up with it."

There may have been some truth here, for college papers tended to be more sympathetic to the ferocious new Clash. "Clash Is a Smash," the Hofstra University Chronicle proclaimed. The reviewer wrote: "Guitarists Nick Sheppard and Vince White and drummer Pete Howard proved the band's regrouping successful. They performed the . . . songs with excellent showmanship and musicianship."

Chronicle Arts

Hofstra Concerts

Clash Is A Smash

By Carol Brooks

Eardrums were on the verge of popping on Saturday, April 14th, with the Clash in concert at the Physical Fitness Center. The band, featuring original Clash-ers Joe Strummer and Paul Simonon and three new members, rocked the rafters of the PFC with their boisterous brand of music.

It was loud, but great! Of course, there were those who couldn't appreciate the rowdy sound, but Clash fans abounded—standing on chairs (if they had a seat) and bopping to the beat, or they crowded towards the stage, swaying with the tide of bodies.

Oddly enough, though one might expect anything from a band like the Clash, the group did not sign their contract until the night of the show. Since they had done the same thing at the US Festival, one may come to expect this "last minute detail" to become a common practice for them.

Prior to the band's entrance, Kosmo Vinyl, personal manager for the Clash, got on stage and asked those with general admission tickets standing in the aisles to move back one step, explaining that the barriers in the back of the PFC would then be removed. After asking for the crowd's cooperation two or three times, there was a slightly noticeable motion backwards from the mass and the barriers were taken down—only to cause more confusion and shoving to get closer to the stage once again.

Finally taking the stage at 10:45 p.m., the Clash appeased their anxious audience with "London Calling" and "rocked" them dead throughout the entire show with the Clash classics like "Rock The Casbah," "Spanish Bombs," "Police On My back," "Brand New Cadillac," and their infamous remake of "I Fought The Law."

Guitarists Nick Sheppard and Vince White and drummer Pete Howard proved the band's re-grouping successful. They performed the old Clash tunes with excellent showmanship and musicianship. Joe Strummer, sporting a divine blond mohawk, belted out the hits with phenomenal stage presence while Paul Simonon

played his bass guitar with equal energy.

The band played very few new songs and the ones they did include in the show didn't go over as well as the older material. Most of the audience knew the lyrics of the old tunes and sang along with Strummer, which is probably why the new songs were not wholly accepted. Nevertheless, "In The Pouring Pouring Rain" and "Sex Mad

War," two songs featured on the forthcoming Clash LP, *Out Of Control*, were decent and showed a great deal of effort from the revamped band.

Some amount of musical change must be expected from the Clash since the "departure" of guitarist Mick Jones from the band. Jones, who has filed suit against

(continued on page XX)

Clash members (left to right) Paul Simonon, Pete Howard, Vince White, Nick Sheppard and Joe Strummer.

Concert review in Hofstra University's *Chronicle*, April 1984.

Reviewing the Colgate University gig, Robert Capiello agreed: "Any pretensions of funk, reggae, or pop [are gone, replaced by] power strumming." Though he wondered how The Clash might convert listeners chiefly concerned with "obtaining a comfortable corporate position and a large record collection," to him, the band seemed up for the task: "If their new music, particularly a song called 'This Is England,' is any indication, a new album will be worth hearing."

Other observers—especially European ones—criticized The Clash for a US-centric approach, assuming a monetary motivation. This was not entirely wrong. The band had to pay its bills, and the income from tickets and merchandise sales was considerable. While the absence of a new record was felt, the shows generally sold out, mostly in college venues ranging from three thousand to ten thousand in capacity.

Strummer often exhibited a disarming self-deprecation, telling a North Carolina audience, for example, "You've probably come to realize you're not watching a slick operation, selling hot dogs and T-shirts as they go, spreading boredom in their wake! No, indeed, it is real human beings fucking up before your very eyes!"

The singer also offered more lofty aims, however. Challenged by one skeptical interviewer, Strummer sounded a messianic note, evoking Christ's journeys amid prostitutes and other "disreputables." Such urgency might seem pretentious; it was also real. The US was not only the world's biggest music market—it also held the earth's fate in its hands. What happened here inevitably affected the entire world—and here The Clash must thus take its campaign.

This seemed especially true as the US election drew nearer. Having rebounded from their 1982 doldrums, Reagan and his campaign coterie were sharpening their rhetorical knives for the race. At the same time, the Democrats were in the midst of the contentious process of picking their standard bearer.

Edward Kennedy, the great liberal hope, had declined to run. In his absence, the front-runner was Walter Mondale, a Minnesota Democrat who had been Carter's vice president. If hardly charismatic, Mondale was a centrist Democrat with a reputation for integrity. A large pack of other candidates had been winnowed down on March 13—dubbed "Super Tuesday" for its concentration of primary contests—leaving Mondale neck-and-neck with a new contender, Gary Hart of Colorado.

Youthful and relatively unknown, Hart styled himself a "New Ideas" candidate, railing against Mondale as a continuation of "failed policies" that had brought Reagan to power. This tact foreshadowed the "Third Way" movement that would bear mostly sour fruit in both the UK and US in the 1990s.

On March 17, however, a "dark horse" scored an upset victory in the South Carolina primary. African American minister Jesse Jackson electrified audiences with powerful oratory, resurrecting the hopeful energy of the civil rights and antiwar movements. A former lieutenant to Martin Luther King Jr., Jackson saw himself as the candidate of a "Rainbow Coalition," a grassroots movement aiming to mobilize an increasingly diverse America to defeat Reagan, remake the Democratic Party, and realize an unfinished American revolution.

Jesse Jackson 1984 campaign button.

Not surprisingly, Jackson found favor with Strummer, and the Clash singer endorsed him in interviews as the "only real opposite to Reagan." Yet Jackson was a long shot at best, and hurt his cause with anti-Semitic remarks to a *Washington Post* reporter. Nonetheless, Jackson's presence helped push an inclusive and progressive agenda, suggesting the kind of vision that might be needed to challenge the Republican president's crowd-pleasing narrative.

Strummer saw Reagan as less a rousing leader than an undeserving recipient of an accidental gift, tracing his 1980 victory to a sad legacy of the 1960s: "Ronald Reagan is the product of the drug culture. The two are synonymous in my mind. Reagan is there because we didn't care. We kept goofing up, we copped out, and we let Reagan in. Same with Thatcher in England."

This argument illuminated Strummer's words onstage in Florida, making explicit his connection between drug taking and a warmonger in charge of the world's deadliest arsenal. While this remained arguable, it is true that the sixties countercultural politics—which included a celebration of drugs as liberation—fed a backlash that helped bring elements of the working class to support Reagan.

These so-called Reagan Democrats had voted against their party—and their own economic self-interest—amid post-Vietnam/Watergate ennui, the humiliation of the Iranian hostage crisis, and the sting of "stagflation," a deadly combo of increasing prices and lagging growth. Reagan's promise to "make America great again" had convinced enough such voters to send him to the White House.

Would they do so again? Did 1980 herald a historic realignment of the US electorate like FDR's 1932 election, or was it an aberration? No one yet knew.

Strummer was aware of how Thatcher's breakthrough victory in 1983 presaged the life-or-death miners' strike now nearing its third hard-fought week back home. However, under the cloud of possible nuclear war, he saw the stakes as even higher in the US election: "Maybe we have to be burned to learn. Hopefully people will be less apathetic about it now, or nothing will be left."

While Strummer had no vote in this coming election, he was determined to put his thumb on the scale as much as possible. Over the past months, the singer had often urged his listeners to engage in the electoral process. He had told an Italian crowd, "Please, I ask you to use your vote—use your vote before we die!" Similar statements peppered surprised crowds on this trek across America.

Such public service announcements might seem odd coming from a band that celebrated a "White Riot" and the "Guns of Brixton." For many on the revolutionary left, voting was often seen as a feeble, even counterproductive endeavor. It also could seem uncool for a radical rock band: "If voting could change things / they'd make it illegal," sang the Lords of the New Church. "Whoever you vote for, government wins," warned Crass.

Strummer was aware of the limitations of the ballot box. His new song "The Dictator" lampooned what historian Peter Kuznick termed "death squad democracy" underwritten by the US: "Yes I am the dictator / my name is on your ballot sheet / But until my box has your cross / you know this form is incomplete."

Strummer was referring in particular to El Salvador. To justify the military aid being sent to turn back a growing guerrilla movement, Reagan had called for elections to shore up his allies. Human rights groups like Americas Watch questioned the validity of voting amid the horrific ongoing violence, the vast majority of it committed by the US-backed government forces.

Reagan nonetheless pushed forward, and the vote duly endorsed the preferred party, enabling military aid to continue.

The election, however, was widely criticized. On March 7, 1984, the *Christian Science Monitor* reported, "Two days before balloting, the [Salvadoran] Electoral Commission estimated 720,000 people would vote. But the official count was 1,551,680—out of a voting population estimated by the US State Department at 1.5 million."

Reagan shrugged off such inconvenient reports. The pretense of democracy had been preserved, even as death squads roamed freely. This was not surprising, as the US had a long and sordid history in the region. As Martin Luther King Jr. had warned, America had something of a schizophrenic personality: "On one hand we have professed the great principles of democracy. On the other we have practiced the very antithesis of those principles."

Like King, Strummer was outraged by the hypocrisy, saying, "The Clash believe in freedom—even in Central America," and noting, "American taxes are supporting quite a few [dictators] right around the world at the moment."

The singer was scarcely less acidic about his own country's foreign policy. Describing the UK as "the little island that once crushed the world in its fascist grip," Strummer explained his anti-imperialist stance: "How do you think I come to write these songs? We [British] are the fucking experts."

The US and the UK were hardly alone in organizing sham elections or supporting oppressive regimes. Such "realpolitik" was distressingly common, and the Soviet Bloc had regularly rigged polls as a way to justify faux "people's" governments.

Why then would an aspiring revolutionary like Strummer suggest voting as a way to dislodge Reagan or any other malefactor? Simple political realism, grounded in a sense of the utter urgency of the moment.

The calculation was simple, but compelling. Absent a mass movement like that of the 1960s, the only way to stop Reagan was at the polls. Just as the miners' victory was essential, so was denying Reagan more time in office to complete his conservative counterrevolution.

Screaming "Revolution now!" was a self-indulgence that the world could not afford, not in this moment of nuclear danger. So, night after night, Strummer would temper his rabble-rousing to advocate the mundane act of voting as an essential way to prevent war and turn the conservative tide.

In this, the band was also acknowledging a hopeful development. Even as the band had been preparing for the US tour, Reagan's Undersecretary of State Lawrence Eagleburger wrote an internal memo about "an important problem we face with our European allies," warning, "The steady decline of public confidence in US policies is a real concern and one we must all work to correct."

Nor was it just a European "problem." Arms Control and Disarmament Agency director Eugene Rostow—a hawk, notwithstanding his title—worried that "there is participation [in the freeze movement] on an increasing scale of three groups whose potential impact should be cause for concern. They are the churches, the 'loyal opposition,' and, perhaps most important, the unpoliticized public."

Nuclear Weapons Freeze buttons. (Courtesy of Mark Andersen.)

The power of the grassroots peace movement was becoming worrisome to Reagan as it spread from the fringes into mainstream America. White House communications director David Gergen later noted, "There was a widespread view in the administration that the nuclear freeze was a dagger pointed at the heart of the administration's defense program."

But if the band could sense this shift in popular opinion, and sought to boost it rhetorically, it did not take the next step: inviting voter registration tables to their shows. Only moral support was being given, divorced from practical politics, despite the stakes of the presidential campaign.

The impending election and possible nuclear cataclysm were not the only issues on Strummer's mind. In Fort Lauderdale, the singer had introduced "This Is England" by saying, "We like to provide you with some information, we like to bring you the news straight from England . . . Here it is, England 1984, underneath the worst government we've had in living memory!"

While Strummer had a broad range of complaints about Thatcher, the strike now stood at the forefront. Simon Parkes, owner of the Brixton Academy, recalls, "At first things went well for the miners. Much of the country rallied behind them, responding to the message of livelihoods lost and communities destroyed." But, he continued, "Thatcher's Conservatives had prepared for this battle. They were not going to fold in the face of industrial action as previous governments had."

Sheffield and Cortonwood delegations at "Support the Miners" march, 1984. (Photographer unknown.)

A divide in the NUM helped them. While the vast majority of miners were on strike—160,000 strong—most in Nottinghamshire refused to join. The constant official drumbeat against "mob rule" and "violent" picketing encouraged this. Local courts, in turn, limited free speech, even banning picketers from decrying their errant workmates as "scabs," leading to numerous arrests on dubious grounds.

The mines in the Nottingham region were relatively new and profitable, thus safe from closure. Why then, some asked, should we risk our jobs for the others? In addition, a national strike vote still had not been called. This crack in the miners' solidarity was a godsend to Thatcher, one upon which she would capitalize.

This was not the main topic of conversation on the Clash tour bus, however. "Being on tour," Sheppard says, "is like being in your own little world . . . It's hard to pay attention to anything else." King agrees: "England was not on my mind much, I remember feeling really cut off. Once you hit the road and start moving, you just get swallowed up, consumed by it all."

Nonetheless, events in the UK weighed heavily on Strummer. Almost every night, he would preface "This Is England," "Three Card Trick," or "In the Pouring Rain" with an explicit nod to the drama. In Atlanta, Strummer took it further, coupling "Rain" with "an old English folk song"—1977's "Career Opportunities." This description not only underlined the continued relevance of the Clash catalog, but suggested how it connected to a centuries-long struggle for economic justice.

Although Strummer was generally skilled at balancing the "edutainment" equation, not everyone in The Clash was happy. White recalls, "Joe was pushing the political thing really hard," adding, "I didn't give a shit, I just wanted to play music." If this suggested growing alienation from the band's agenda, it also carried truth. Like any band, the new unit would rise or fall on its musical power.

For Strummer, it was a delicate balance: "We're not being really preachy. First I want to rock and roll, to hell with the lyrics! But if the words come in handy, if they are topical, if they mean something to real life, that's extra." At a Worcester show, Strummer lambasted the likes of Culture Club and Wham!, shouting, "Music can do something more than put a poster on a thirteen-year-old girl's bedroom wall!"

But what was that "something"? As The Clash took on a journey that sought—in Strummer's mind—to help "turn the world," it seemed likely that music's power would prove insufficient to the task.

Such ambition was not new, however. It had helped win The Clash its famously fervent following. A Clash not straining toward "death or glory" wouldn't be the genuine article. But a stretch of such magnitude was likely to fall short. It also might come at some real human cost.

For now, there were more mundane challenges—getting to the next show on time or keeping bandmates on good terms. Shadowing them all was a simple fact: The Clash soon needed to make a new record—a great one. As Cook had pointed out in NME, only this could solidify, define, and justify the new Clash: "They have to wipe the slate of years of their own torpor. They have to make astounding rock and roll records, iron-hard music."

This was exactly what Strummer had in mind. Taking his moody guitarist aside, Strummer told White the US tour's deeper purpose: to help finance the recording of a new album, while building the unit's cohesion and shaping the songs. "We've gotta get into the studio as soon as possible and bang it out raw," Strummer explained. "I don't want to make the same mistakes we made in the past."

Once again, the skeptical White was swept up in the force field of Strummer's passion, envisioning a "brilliant, raw, exciting album like the first." Despite legal challenges presented by Jones's blizzard of injunctions, this was the goal toward which all the exertion was aimed. "We're gonna get this album out by the end of the year," Strummer told White. "We've got to."

Strummer would relate the same ambition to whoever would listen. All the struggle and stress of the road, the building of this new platoon under fire was "what is going to make our [new] record great!" Strummer told *Creem*'s Bill Holdship after the Detroit show.

Holdship was a hard sell, as was his publication. For those in the know, *Creem* was "America's only rock roll magazine." It had been home to trailblazing critics like Lester Bangs and Dave Marsh. In a 1971 issue, Marsh coined a new phrase to describe a raw garage-band sound: punk rock.

As rock aficionados, The Clash loved *Creem*, but they had a stormy relationship with it. Holdship was also skeptical of them. Once "an idealistic college kid who believed rock and roll could 'save' the world," now he had adopted the "meet the new boss / same as the old boss" credo of the Who's "Won't be Fooled Again."

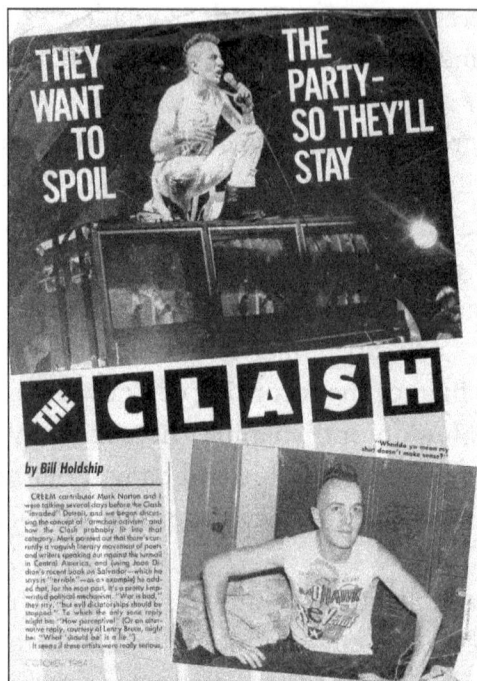

Bill Holdship article from *Creem* magazine, October 1984. (Photos by Bob Gruen.)

Holdship spoke for a lot of older rockers who now questioned activism's value, especially related to music. First critiquing The Clash as "armchair activists" who should emulate Ernest Hemingway—or George Orwell—in the Spanish Civil War by donning actual military uniforms to fight for their Central American causes, Holdship then flipped to embrace resignation: "As I grow older, I'm beginning to believe that there simply are no political solutions . . . Things rarely change."

Holdship's fatalism echoed UK writers like Martin and Barber whose "I'm older and wiser now" stance came off more as self-serving cynicism rather than insight. One can almost hear them straining to vanquish their younger, more idealistic selves.

Martin mourned the "seven long years since I first ripped that T-shirt, scowled that scowl, and danced that dance." Barber evoked "the good old days" when "we could actually believe that The Clash were some sort of radical force," claiming Strummer "still seems to think he can shoot Margaret Thatcher dead by commanding one of his guitarists to thrum an E chord like a machine gun in the direction of the House of Parliament."

Their dismissals seemed aimed as much at reassuring themselves over convenient choices made and dreams abandoned as assessing the band's performance. Nonetheless, Holdship's "million-dollar question" for Strummer hit home: "What does an orange Mohawk have to do with changing the political structure in the 1980s?" Holdship suggested that symbolic actions were not enough. In this, he—as well as Martin and Baker—surely had a point.

"Music isn't a threat, but the action that music inspires can be," argued Chumbawamba, a group of Crass devotees then building its own underground following.

As any self-aware punk might agree, 1984 was no time for anyone to expect a band to fight your battles for you. Strummer told Holdship he wanted fans to "get out from under our shadow, be your own person. I'm proud to inspire people, and from then on, they should take it from there." This, of course, could be a cop-out. What exactly was The Clash doing to aid its fans in making this crucial next step?

Yet Strummer's patience with tough questions won Holdship over, as did the passion of the band's performance. While the writer wasn't impressed by many of the new songs, he allowed "the new band sounds tighter and better than the old lineup." Holdship grudgingly granted, "Maybe Joe Strummer was right. Maybe we do need The Clash . . . A little optimism ain't a bad thing."

One of the themes Strummer hammered with Holdship was the band's antidrug stance, as he did consistently on the rest of the tour: "We're not born again or anything like that. All we want to do is think clearly, and you can't think clearly on any drug. And I've found that my life is much better."

There were broad implications here. After the rousing DC show, Strummer had once again linked drugs to Reagan's ascent, while paying tribute to a punk antidrug movement inspired by the DC hardcore band Minor Threat: "I'm pleased to see there is a straight edge scene . . . It is something separate from us, yet we happen to be traveling on parallel paths. It reinforces my belief that it is right."

Ironically, at that moment, another antidrug movement—one far less grassroots in conception—was taking shape within a building less than a mile away at 1600 Pennsylvania Avenue NW. After a visit to a Brooklyn drug rehabilitation facility during the 1980 campaign, Nancy Reagan had made fighting drug abuse her central cause as America's first lady.

"Just Say No" was about to become her mantra. Legend suggested Reagan came up with it spontaneously in response to a child's question. According to *The Yale Book of Quotations*, however, the slogan "closely identified with Nancy Reagan" was "originated by the advertising agency Needham, Harper & Steers."

Agency representative Carolyn Roughsedge told the *New York Times* in 2016: "Bob Cox and David Cantor came up with 'just say no' because that's what a little kid would say." When Mrs. Reagan visited the agency in October 1983, "they presented it . . . and she absolutely loved it," Roughsedge said.

The Just Say No campaign would be announced later in 1984, and clubs touting the slogan would soon sprout at hundreds of schools around the country. Nancy Reagan's initiative was surely well intended and driven by genuine concern about a very real problem. Meanwhile, however, her husband moved forward on a more ominous tack.

In October 1982 Ronald Reagan had revived the "War on Drugs," an initiative first launched by the Nixon administration for reasons that went far beyond concern for public health. "The Nixon campaign in 1968, and the Nixon White House after that, had two enemies: the antiwar left and black people," former Nixon domestic policy chief John Ehrlichman told *Harper's* writer Dan Baum in 1994. "We knew we couldn't make it illegal to be either against the war or black, but by getting the public to associate the hippies with marijuana and blacks with heroin, and by criminalizing both heavily, we could disrupt those communities."

This initiative had more than symbolic consequences, Ehrlichman made clear: "We could arrest their leaders, raid their homes, break up their meetings, and vilify them night after night on the evening news."

By the time these quotes surfaced in 2016, Ehrlichman was dead, and his family disavowed his words. In any case, the "War on Drugs" revived by Reagan would have a far more dramatic effect than "Just Say No"—one not so far from what Ehrlichman suggested.

This was not the only disturbing twist in this particular tale. As Reagan denounced drugs, some of his contra allies—with US support cut off by a disapproving Congress—were using cocaine sales to help finance their attacks on the Sandinistas.

Some of these drugs made their way to American streets as something new called "crack": cocaine cooked solid then chipped into rocks meant to be smoked, not sniffed. Crack would soon generate panicked headlines as a cheap, highly addictive drug spreading violence and community disintegration.

While crack's carnage was very real, the most destructive drugs in American society remained far more mundane: alcohol and tobacco. The Reagans were painted as hypocrites by some observers for opposing drugs, yet indulging in martinis and the like. The Clash shared this contradiction. Strummer's love for alcohol and tobacco was well known. He saw nicotine as a spark for creativity and alcohol as a "revolutionary drug" because it got people talking.

Clash biographer Salewicz even suggests that as Strummer's pot use dropped in 1984, his alcohol consumption went up—and he was not alone in this excess. While the band limited alcohol before a show, afterward copious amounts of it helped them wind down, often in bars where they encountered their fans.

For Strummer, this was part of his punk ethic. He liked being accessible to his audience, often listening more than talking. Yet the toll of such heavy drinking was significant. White's girlfriend would josh him at the end of the US tour about the belly he had developed despite the almost daily shows. The abuse of bodies with alcohol, lack of sleep, bad food, the grind of constant traveling . . . it was bound to take its toll. This was especially so for Strummer, still harboring the grief over his father's death as well as aching over the distance from his wife and child.

Perhaps having a young daughter was making Strummer more sensitive to other issues, as suggested by "Sex Mad War." Like many of the best Clash songs, the tune was a bit of glorious jumble: whip-sharp punkabilly with a blistering feminist message that Strummer underlined nightly with stinging onstage commentary.

Aware that The Clash was seen as a "lad's band" with a mostly male following, the Clash frontman began to talk about a "new man"—or "a new human being"—who was "antiracist and antisexist." Strummer encouraged female involvement, pausing to honor "some brave girls down here" in front of the stage in Eugene, Oregon.

That night Strummer also expressed his hope "that some men here will realize that pornography is rape, which the women already realize . . . and they can't walk [safely] in the dark!" He was echoing feminist activists such as Robin Morgan who asserted, "Pornography is the theory and rape is the practice," and Andrea Dworkin who saw it as part of what she would later describe as a "war on women." This line of argument could be disputed—and was, even by other feminists—but regardless, "Sex Mad War" was not your average rocker.

The song also resonated in a moment where concerns about sexual violence were rising on college campuses, the main venues for the Clash tour. Strummer had even rewritten the opening lines—"Going to the party / never made it to the party / she's gone"—making the song even more relevant to college communities where "Take Back the Night" marches were becoming more widespread. If the musical vehicle was hardly groundbreaking, the message was—at least for a popular all-male rock group—and the song evoked an eerie atmosphere of violent foreboding with jagged stop-and-start guitar, bass, and drums.

At least some Clash members, however, felt a twinge of conscience about the tune. Sheppard: "We didn't treat women that well, did we?"—a sentiment sadly seconded by White. If The Clash rhetorically was miles away from rockers such as Mötley Crüe—who *Creem*'s Holdship scorched as "morons" yelling out witticisms like "We love fucking the girls in Detroit because their pussies taste so good!" from stage—it was not entirely divorced from the groupie scene.

White had started out keeping to himself, excited by touring. He soon grew wary: "The great United States of America—miles and miles of synchronized bland nothingness. For me, it got essentially boring pretty quick." White also bristled at controlling behavior like the enforced regimen of certain music and artists on the tour bus.

Playful high jinks could help ease the tension. For example, the Mohawk imagery that dominated on the tour's T-shirts, posters, and handbills took on a life of its own. In Hartford, the band started up a good-natured debate with its Texan road crew. "One of the guys had really long, luxurious black hair," Sheppard recalls. "We started kidding him in the bar: 'You should have a Mohawk.' So he said, 'Well, hell, if you give me a thousand dollars, I will.' In five minutes, there was a thousand dollars on the bar—and he crapped out. He wouldn't do it."

Just then, however, one of the truck drivers agreed—if the money could go to his favorite charity, "which was homeless [children], or something like that," Sheppard continues. "So we all trooped off to this local bar that had a stage, set up a chair, and starting giving Mohawks to all and sundry."

The same had happened a couple nights earlier, before the band's April 22 show at the Philadelphia Spectrum. The band found themselves sharing the same hotel as the Grateful Dead, whose own hair could stand a bit of shearing—or so ran the thinking in the Clash camp. Sheppard laughs: "Kosmo went on a Mohawk spree that night. By the next day, he had a bagful of hippie hair that he'd cut." But the Dead's locks were not among the trophies.

Not all diversions were as benign, however. As tedium set in, and alienation from the rest of the band grew, White began embracing casual sex with the band's followers. Egged on by twin groupies, White even indulged in that most clichéd of rock star antics, trashing his hotel room and hurling a TV out the window. He had to pay for the damage, getting a Vinyl tongue-lashing to boot.

White had taken matters to an extreme, but he was hardly alone in acting out. Given that hedonism had long been one of rock's core pursuits, this was hardly headline news. Still, a banner of "If it feels good, do it" hung uneasily on a band touting "a new antisexist man"—and Sheppard and White knew it.

One man stood at the center of the operation, carrying immense weight. How was Joe Strummer doing? It was hard to tell, as he tended to keep his deepest thoughts and feelings to himself. The singer may have been taking his own measure as much as the band's in telling one reporter, "Yeah, let's go for the top, let's take it all on at once—that's always been our speciality!"

Occasionally, telling bits would slip out. Coming offstage after a frenetic, soul-drenched New Jersey show in late April, a momentarily unguarded Strummer told someone close to the band, "You know, sometimes I almost believe in this!" The self-doubt exposed by Johnny Green had clearly not disappeared.

Salewicz reports that after the Long Island show Strummer shared his darker side with longtime friend Jo-Anne Henry: "The death of his father was still in his thoughts, and now Joe was beating himself up for being away while Jazz was a baby. 'I could be any bloke going off and leaving her,' he said," Henry recalled. "Jazz being born brought up tons of stuff about his childhood . . . Deep down he seemed to be in a really awful state. There was this anger that he was not able to let come out, the swirling emotions inside him that he couldn't admit to."

As with the others, touring wearied Strummer. He had to summon enormous amounts of energy and passion every night. In one TV interview in late April, Strummer was asked how he felt about the new band. Flanked by the other members, Strummer responded: "Great!" Then, as if to underline his point, he leaned forward and repeated even more loudly: "*GREAT!*" His defiant response seemed intended to convince himself more than anyone else.

Behind this shout, Howard suspected, was a person struggling to deal with a growing array of demons—personal, social, and professional—that the relentless tour schedule wouldn't allow a chance to address. "He was getting quite mental, quite desperate, and he was drinking an awful lot," Howard says.

Yet the near-nightly shows seemed to help Strummer focus. Whatever his private qualms, the singer didn't let them show on-stage. Even critics rarely found Strummer's performances anything but convincing.

Changing things up helped with this. Three weeks into the tour, another song disappeared from the set: "In the Pouring Rain." A live version from the April 14 show at New York's Hofstra University suggests why. While featuring powerful lyrics and music that blasted off after the chorus, the song was hamstrung by a clunky beginning. Other bands, notably Gang of Four, had overlaid dark social observations atop dance beats—a sound that some writers took to calling "plague disco." But the chunky, repetitive funk riff chosen to drive home "Rain's" message actually served to undercut its intense lyrical bent. The result seemed a bit herky-jerky and off balance, having never fully blossomed from its original demo.

Shaking up the set a bit, Strummer got the band to work up "Broadway" in its place. Since the new band had never played the song, "We had to go out and get a record to figure it out!" Sheppard laughs. At the same time, "Junco Partner," "Jimmy Jazz," and "Koka Kola" were also brought up from the basement. None were among the stronger of the band's catalog—not really a match for the newly dropped "In the Pouring Rain," or maybe even "We Are The Clash" and "Glue Zombie"—but they added variety, helping Strummer keep his performing fresh.

Unlike with "We Are The Clash," Sheppard wasn't satisfied to see "Rain" disappear: "Some songs have space, you can find your way into them, do you know what I mean? I found the way in on 'Pouring Rain.'" Stripping out Strummer's rhythm guitar, Sheppard had experimented with a different arrangement that opened with graceful, descending chords. Slowly shaping it up, he'd shared his ideas with White and the others during free time at sound checks.

As the tour wore on, Strummer leaned on his absurdist humor. At one show, he dedicated "Armagideon Time" to "anyone who has turned down a Hostess Twinkie and felt the better for it." In a stiflingly hot Chicago club, he kicked off "White Riot" with a wry query: "What I'd like to know, judging by the temperature in this room—if this is the Windy City, where's the fucking wind?"

Above all, Strummer sought solace in his Clash platoon—or at least his romantic conception of it. In New York, he motioned to the rest of the band, telling the crowd, "We ain't pretending to be friendly with each other when we are standing in front of you. When we go into the back room, we actually are friends. I tell you a lot of famous groups hate each other's guts, they won't even get in to the same car with each other . . . I don't want to go forward into that situation."

When the entire band was interviewed by a cable TV show in Toronto, Strummer took this one step further. Asked about his personal life, the singer blurted out, "If you are really serious, you haven't even got time for a personal life!" Later in the interview, he added, "I have no friends."

The interviewer asked the obvious follow-up: *Why not?* "Because when we started this group we realized we had to dump everything that we'd had previous, and that included everybody we've known, everybody we'd lived with." As Simonon seconded that, Howard jumped in: "Yeah, that's why we don't need a personal life outside this group, because this is it. *This is it.*"

The reporter probed: "Why don't you have any friends, is it because your views are so pure that you can't let in any outsiders?" Strummer nodded: "You can, but it is weakening in some way. You're getting at it with what you said about 'pure'—when we put the group together, we tried to reinvent the world from scratch."

The journalist persisted: "But when you reinvent the world, you have to invite some other people to come with you . . . ?" Strummer clenched a fist and launched an empathic rejoinder: "Yeah, but I mean 'reinvent the world' because we are looking for an idea, not because we are throwing a party!"

The vision Strummer and the band put forward was a demanding one—the platoon, whole unto itself, tight-knit, self-sustaining, unstoppable. The image presented in the interview was not exactly untrue. The band had surely come together musically, as well as somewhat on a personal level. For example, Simonon and Sheppard had bonded enough for a jealous White to notice.

However, there were worrisome elements. Strummer seemed to share his inner life with no one in his band. By pushing down the feelings, channeling it into his performances, he might be a riveting frontman—but was he happy, healthy, centered? If not, his creative momentum was not likely to be sustainable.

Another unresolved tension remained. After soldiers endured punishing boot camps, real effort was made to build group solidarity. This was not so in The Clash, where boot camp never ended. As King ruefully admitted, "Bernard wanted it uncomfortable, he wanted it vital and raw, at each others' throats. He kept you edgy, on your toes—he would antagonize just to make something happen." If this approach could accomplish some things, it hardly fostered unity.

Other factors also tended to divide, including money—specifically, why there wasn't more of it, especially for the newer members. White tried to get Sheppard and Howard to join him to press Rhodes for more pay midtour. "Fucking socialism in action, I thought," chortled an unrepentant White later. Finding no takers, the guitarist went to Rhodes anyway, only to be flatly refused and left feeling like a "greedy capitalist."

At the band meeting later that day, White expected to get roasted by the irascible manager. To his surprise, Howard instead became the focus of fire from both Rhodes and Strummer for supposed lack of commitment, in what White later described as a "mafia meeting." Invited by Rhodes to either shape up or find new employment, Howard walked out.

While Howard was brought back in time for the evening show, the incident suggested the internal band situation was more complicated than Strummer let on. That was underscored when White and Howard came to blows onstage at the May 25 show in Denver. Henry David Thoreau—one of those uniquely American "lunatics, individuals, and madmen"—had argued, "Live your beliefs and you can turn the world around." If so, how well was The Clash doing this?

If aspects of the new Clash appeared dodgy, the music was not. The strongest proof was a refurbished "In the Pouring Rain" which returned to the set in Dayton on May 8. There could hardly have been a more appropriate moment for its reappearance, as the show began a swing through America's Rust Belt.

The song had been inspired by what Strummer called the "ghost towns" of the northern UK, devastated by an increasingly globalized economy, accelerated by Thatcher's polices. It fit the similar doldrums of this once-vibrant heartland. This descent into rust had been worsened by Reagan's policies. A global "race to the bottom" was underway, one that slashed American jobs in favor of foreign workers who received slave wages while corporate profits boomed. Though cheaper consumer goods also resulted, this was little comfort for previously comfortably middle-class workers who now couldn't afford even inexpensive products.

"Rain" was immensely strengthened by the revamp. The verses breathed and built momentum throughout the song. Even if the postchorus blastoff was missed, something extraordinary was coming together, a song worthy of its weighty subject matter: the wrenching pain and dislocation felt in such hard-hit communities.

Strummer carefully linked Rust Belt tragedy to the ongoing struggles at home, telling one audience that the "situation is bad in the UK, just like this country." Back on the British picket lines, neither side had been able to strike a knockout blow. A grim war of attrition was developing, a situation that might not favor the miners.

Realizing this, Scargill decided to target the Orgreave coking plant with mass pickets. Thatcher feared this would become a reprise of "The Battle of Saltly Gate" where striking miners joined with other workers to close the Saltly coke works in Birmingham and effectively win the strike in 1972. Determined to prevent this, the Tory leader put pressure on the police to increase roadblocks to stop flying picketers, and embrace mass arrests and other rougher tactics—effectively outlawing dissent and easing the way for brutality.

Locked in their alternate reality, The Clash was unaware of much of this. The musicians were now racing toward the end of their sojourn in the US—a tour that, despite the obstacles, had been a significant success.

Strummer's exhaustion was starting to show. Introducing "In the Pouring Rain" in St. Louis on May 21, he was boozy and bereft: "All the towns are dead! I mean it! I've been in more towns the past eight weeks that I can even think of and they are all dead! They are all dead in Europe, they are all dead everywhere! This is 'In the Pouring Pouring Motherfucking Pouring Rain,' jacko!" His outburst muddled the song—not all towns were dead, only those whose hearts had been ripped out by free-market policies—and suggested the singer's ragged spiritual state.

The performance was nonetheless potent, and Strummer showed no further signs of strain that night. He was back on message over the week, announcing "Rain" as "news straight from England!" Audience tapes capture the fan reaction: in St. Louis, one deems the song "fucking great"; in Eugene a few days later, a woman can be heard gasping, "That was beautiful!" at the song's end.

So it was. With three weeks of continued growth and polish, "In the Pouring Rain" had become a stunning achievement, on the level of truly great Clash songs like "Straight to Hell," "Complete Control," and "White Man in Hammersmith Palais." Sheppard's descending chords drew listeners into the tale, and White's leads added to its pathos. The guitars played off one another, conjuring a sense of utter desolation, as if lost in a driving storm, drenched to the very soul.

Could there be a way to turn this tide, a current that seemed as relentless and unforgiving as the English weather? Perhaps. In the US, it was becoming clear that Mondale—a longtime union supporter who spoke passionately against Reagan's economic policies—was to be the nominee of the Democratic Party. In May 1984, he also pledged his commitment to ending the nuclear arms race, reaching out to activists like Helen Caldicott to press the issue on the campaign trail.

Reagan's team was watching closely. National Security Adviser Robert McFarlane later admitted, "We took [the nuclear freeze] as a serious movement that could undermine congressional support for the nuclear modernization program and potentially a serious partisan political threat that could affect the election." It would not be easy, but most observers thought Mondale had a fighting chance to defeat Reagan, denying him a legacy-sealing victory.

Meanwhile on the UK picket lines, pressure was growing day by day, as a decisive confrontation loomed. As in America, a bitter contest for the country's future was underway. Who would emerge victorious remained to be seen.

The Clash was winding up its US campaign, bone-tired and homesick, but justifiably proud. In Seattle, Strummer sparred with overzealous security while shepherding a fervent crowd so no one got hurt. Communing with three thousand souls packed into the Paramount Theatre, the singer led his bandmates through a blistering set.

After four months of intense touring, the group was a rock dynamo, with new songs played with a ferocity and skill that made the promise of an amazing new record seem real. The band's eighty-minute set was clockwork paced, with the final half hour a breathless sprint through highlights of the band's catalog.

Just before the show—the second to last on the tour—Simonon mailed a postcard to old friend Moe Armstrong in California: "Howdy! Well, after two months and 20,000 miles of American roads, we are now ready for home!"

Were they really ready? Outwardly, the collective mood remained as bullish as ever. "We certainly don't fall into the category of people that are willing to shut up," Vinyl offered backstage at the University of Oregon. "We like to get in an argument, right? Once you get a big argument going, you get all kinds of people involved, and then you get—maybe you get a few answers."

But had the band found its own answers? The unit was not truly unified, and a costly bill for unresolved issues would soon come due. Meanwhile, the band was headed back to a country on the brink of something close to civil war.

CHAPTER FIVE

OUT OF CONTROL

Police charge miners at Orgreave, June 18, 1984. (Photo © John Sturrock/reportdigital.co.uk.)

We had to fight the enemy without in the Falklands. We always have to be aware of the enemy within, which is much more difficult to fight and more dangerous to liberty.
—Margaret Thatcher, July 19, 1984

Either the human being must suffer and struggle as the price of a more searching vision, or his gaze must be shallow and without intellectual revelation.
—Thomas de Quincey, 1845

The riot shield came down hard, with a sickening crunch. Hit from behind, Arthur Scargill pitched face-first to the ground, knocked senseless.

It was barely past eleven a.m. on Monday, June 18, 1984. Chaos swirled around the unconscious union leader as riot police and mounted officers assaulted miners picketing the Orgreave coking plant near Sheffield.

The attacks had been coming in waves for two hours. Many miners had taken off their shirts in the morning heat, shedding their only protection against the savagery. Amid what was effectively a police riot, an impartial observer might have been forgiven for thinking that George Orwell's *1984* was coming to pass.

NUM member Arthur Wakefield witnessed the unprovoked assault on Scargill. Ironically, it came mere moments after the union president had rebuked some miners who—angered by the earlier attacks—were throwing stones at police lines.

The repeated brutal charges sowed panic in the mostly peaceful ranks of picketers. Wakefield recalled, "The lads were climbing the fence on the opposite banking, some of them falling down, being chased by the police on horses and with dogs . . . The 'cavalry' are first as usual, then the riot squad."

Lesley Boulton, a strike supporter armed only with a camera, was helping a bloodied miner only to be targeted herself by a mounted policeman. John Harris's camera captured the moment the baton came down. Clash biographer Marcus Gray spoke for many in calling this photo of the officer leaning out to take a full swing at the unarmed female spectator "the most memorable image of the miners' strike."

"I felt the truncheon go past me—just missed by the skin of my teeth," Boulton explained. "The police were actually having a very good time, they were laughing and joking, enjoying this huge exercise of brutal authority . . . You got the sense that they were just out of control, completely carried away."

Such bare-knuckled displays contrasted with the bland assertions of government white papers: "The traditional approach is to deploy large numbers of officers in ordinary uniforms in the passive containment of a crowd." The real aim, however, was shared in police tactical manuals: to "incapacitate" the miners.

The Labour Party paper, June 22, 1984—one of the few media outlets to publish this photo. (Photo © John Harris/reportdigital.co.uk.)

The day had dawned with electricity in the air, but little sense of the carnage to come. In the biggest face-off in the now fourteen-week-old strike, perhaps ten thousand miners and supporters stood across from more than five thousand police, including riot squads and mounted officers.

The union had been targeting Orgreave for three weeks, seeking to turn the tide in what was not only the biggest industrial dispute in recent British history, but a true struggle for the country's future. Previous days had been confrontational, with injuries and arrests, especially on May 29, when the riot squads had made their first appearance. At the time, Scargill argued, "The intimidation and the brutality that has been displayed are something reminiscent of a Latin American state."

Now the NUM intended to make its stand, shutting down the

plant, blocking trucks, and cutting off the supply of coke to the nearby Scunthorpe steelworks. To do this, the union needed massive numbers of picketers to overwhelm police lines. Their call had been answered. As Wakefield recalled, "I'd never seen so many of our lads all together, it brought tears to my eyes." The police had similarly bolstered their ranks.

This meant a struggle for control at the gates of the plant, one that would begin once trucks were sighted. The strikers didn't have long to wait. Wakefield: "There was a lot of shouting going on as the lorries went in. It's eight forty-five a.m., the lads started the chant of 'Here We Go' and there was one big push against the police lines"—a literal push by massed miners against a similar clump of government forces. It was turned back, and the first wave of trucks swiftly rolled through.

This contest was commonplace by now, repeated daily over the past three months. Although very physical, it generally followed certain unspoken rules that limited injuries on either side. Today would be different.

While some stones had been thrown from deep in the miners' ranks earlier, there was little happening when suddenly the lines opened and a phalanx of mounted police emerged with blood in their eyes. Wakefield: "This time the police went berserk and the riot squad charged up the field with the 'cavalry' [and] they did something that I had not seen them do before, they turned to where we were standing peacefully picketing and started hitting whoever they came across. I'm thinking, 'This is it' . . . I'd never seen anything like it."

The police even pursued picketers into the nearby village, brutalizing at will. Broken and bloodied, the miners scattered. "The battle kept going on and off until one p.m.," Wakefield remembered. "It was like 'Monday, Bloody Monday.'" There were seventy-nine people hurt and ninety-three arrests, including a shaken but unbowed Arthur Scargill, wearing a United Mineworkers of America baseball hat sent as a sign of solidarity from across the ocean.

Seventy-one miners would soon be charged with "riot," an offense carrying a possible life sentence. If this penalty seemed extreme, given that most had done nothing except be on the receiving end of a truncheon, "The Battle of Orgreave" showed how just far Thatcher was willing to go to defeat the miners.

Meanwhile, the band whose first single was entitled "White Riot," whose new songs "This Is England" and "Three Card Trick" warned of batons dishing out bloody "law and order," and whose singer had just crossed America evoking the unfolding British drama night after night, was doing . . . what exactly?

The Clash had been home for two weeks from its triumphant US tour, the journey intended to solidify the band and shape up the new songs in preparation for a triumphant "return to form" record.

The group was now razor-sharp musically, with nine new songs battle tested and well honed. Some unaired demos like "Galleani" and "Out of Control" also had strong potential. If this was not quite enough ammunition for a new album, the reimagined "In the Pouring Rain" suggested that the unit—or at least Strummer and Sheppard—might be able to create other potent new songs in short order.

Indeed, Vinyl had tried to kickstart the collaboration by bringing the two together in a hotel room on the US sojourn. A tour can prove a difficult venue in which to midwife new material, however, and there were no results from the meeting. "I took it as a compliment," recalls Sheppard, "but it seemed a bit forced really."

Given that finding a new songwriting partner could relieve some of the weight on Strummer, it seemed worth a second try. Yet no such opportunity for swift entry into either a studio or creative collaboration appeared to be in the offing. As White bitterly recounts, after the band's return "it was just pointless rehearsals for me, Nick, and Pete. Joe was nowhere to be seen. Nor Paul."

White allowed that, initially, Strummer's absence did not seem worrisome. Even before America, the singer "was turning up less and less to rehearsals. I don't think it was because he couldn't be bothered, but more that he was extremely self-conscious about his voice . . . He seemed more comfortable singing in front of forty thousand people than four." But as days stretched into weeks, concerns mounted.

Sheppard remembers how an uncertain stasis became the new reality: "As soon as we got back from America, it started to get very weird, dysfunctional, straightaway. Joe disappeared from rehearsals . . . We didn't really see him. Paul was around sometimes, and not around other times."

This was a jolting turnabout from the constant motion to which the new members had become accustomed. More to the point, it seemed at odds with the talk of a platoon bonding under fire, the urgency of The Clash's unfinished job, the promises of a new record knocked out swiftly, with fire and finesse.

One key player was not making himself scarce, much to the chagrin of White: "Bernie began turning up more and more at rehearsals . . . delivering spiteful verbal tirades at the three of us, making sure we knew how inadequate we were, how tenuous our situation was, how we had to be more 'happening.'"

While Sheppard and Howard were perhaps more immune to Rhodes's harangues than White—"I tried to build a thick wall in my brain against [the attacks] but it kept falling down"—it left all of them even more confused and demoralized.

Rhodes was privy to a bigger picture and perhaps feared Strummer was slipping out of his control. In part, this was because family life had reclaimed its priority upon the singer's return. Strummer surely needed time to regenerate and reconnect with his wife and daughter, but such concerns had little place in Rhodes's vision for The Clash—hence his squeeze on those still in his grip.

According to Chris Salewicz, "Bernie didn't believe that the group was yet ready to record." Rhodes: "The live thing was working, but Joe wanted to rush into the studio. He was worried when he heard Mick was getting [a new band] together."

Both Rhodes and Vinyl also believed the band simply didn't yet have enough top-notch tunes. As the latter explains, "After the US tour, Joe was trying to come up with material and do lyrics. Meanwhile, the other guys were in rehearsal with on-site recording facilities—and what did that produce?"

Sheppard, White, and Howard unanimously agree that they were never encouraged to write new songs, but instead were asked to rearrange existing Clash songs or record covers. Vinyl remembers it differently: "All of them were asked to record something they wanted to record. It turned out to be covers because there wasn't anything else to record . . . It became apparent that they were not songwriters," at least not of the caliber that The Clash required.

The situation bred contrarian responses. Sheppard: "I recorded The Temptations' 'Just My Imagination' because it was the least punk thing I could think of." Vinyl admits that the trio "weren't taken on board as songwriters," but still insists, "The opportunity was there." Sheppard's response: "I worked on a funk riff at nearly every sound check on the US tour hoping that Joe would pick up on it, but he never even noticed, to my frustration."

Sheppard understood a deeper challenge, the result of being a latecomer to the band: "If you're going to write songs with someone, you need to be their equal. Your voice needs to be heard and appreciated. There is also the question of the magic that needs to happen, and that needs to be allowed to happen." The perpetual boot camp created by Rhodes hardly nurtured creative expression.

The main exception had been "In the Pouring Rain." Vinyl granted, "Something good had become even more impressive" thanks to Sheppard and the others. Even so, "The time it took to happen was too long . . . We just didn't have the time."

Sheppard had his own analysis: "I need to be able to hear something in a song that inspires me to take it somewhere. With some of Joe's songs, I didn't—and when I did, the ideas were apparently not good enough," at least for Rhodes.

This remains—in Sheppard's words—"a bone of contention" within the neo-Clash camp. It is true that, despite later missteps, Jones had helped set a very high artistic standard. Vinyl: "It *was* intimidating. Look at what you are competing against—that immense Clash catalog! No one thought it would be easy."

This was a key crossroads for the platoon. That this collaboration really wasn't even tried suggests either cynicism underneath the idealistic rhetoric or—more likely—exhaustion.

Whether by design, miscommunication, or necessity, Strummer now felt the creative weight resting on his shoulders alone. Vinyl: "I don't think Joe thought it was going to be as hard to come up with material as it turned out to be. As Joe came to see more was on his plate than he realized, the pressure compounded."

Sheppard: "With the benefit of hindsight, I've no doubt that huge amounts of thought were being given to how the record would be made. Of course, no one communicated this to us; it would have been too direct and sensible." As it happened, he was correct—but in ways no one could have guessed.

The germ of a shocking twist was growing in Rhodes's mind. Unbeknown to all save perhaps Vinyl, the manager had begun to doubt the wisdom of a return to the sound of the first record. Rather—in an ironic echo of his nemesis Jones—Rhodes now wanted a great musical leap forward.

This ambition fell within the best Clash tradition, and Vinyl would later claim that "a return to the first record was never our intent." This contradicts Strummer's own words, but also begs a fundamental question: how could this be done? Given Strummer's own raw rock proclivities, and the reality of personnel chosen to undergird the "back to basics" drive, it was hard to see how a vaguely imagined reinvention of The Clash could be realized.

Rhodes did not yet have answers for this conundrum. It may have served his purposes for the momentum of the US tour to ebb, and for Strummer and the band to remain—for now—in creative and personal stasis.

Meanwhile, the miners remained stalwart, but the defeat at Orgreave convinced their leadership that the present course was untenable. While left-wing critics like Alex Callincos and Mike Simons of the Socialist Workers' Party (SWP) argued, "The Battle of Orgreave could have been the beginning of a real attempt to win the strike by mass picketing," soon the pickets were sent elsewhere.

The coking plant would never again see mass picketing. As the SWP duo lamented, "In the wake of the police riot at Orgreave, many people were sympathetic to the argument that the police were now unbeatable. The miners had tried to use the methods of 1972, and had failed."

Although Callincos and Simons disagreed with the idea that the miners should concentrate on "winning wide sympathy . . . building a broad alliance around their objectives," it was hard to deny that Thatcher had learned the lesson of Saltley Gate. Her newly militarized police force had proven its worth in turning back the miners—and now Thatcher sought to win the public relations battle as well.

She got unexpected aid in this mission when the BBC implicated the miners in sparking the Orgreave violence by inaccurate editing on its evening broadcast. By placing images of miners fighting back before images of the state-sponsored brutality, the program suggested the police were simply acting in self-defense. While a later edition corrected the order of events, the damage was done.

A mock-up of the blocked *Sun* cover. (Artist unknown.)

This error was mild compared to the daily deceit dished out by British tabloids, chief among them the *Sun*, owned by right-wing media mogul Rupert Murdoch. Sensationalist in their coverage and hewing only loosely to journalistic ethical conventions, these newspapers were also entertaining and popular.

Following Murdoch's lead, other tabloids excoriated alleged union corruption and violence. One planned *Sun* cover portrayed Scargill as Adolf Hitler, raising his arm in a Nazi salute next to the headline "Mine Fuhrer." While this cover was ultimately scrapped thanks to the refusal of the unionized *Sun* workers to print the paper, others nearly as provocative appeared regularly at newsstands.

This relentless assault by right-wing scandal sheets was effective in swaying public opinion. They were aided by the timidity of the more mainstream press, whose "objectivity" often appeased the government. The clearest evidence of this came when only one of the seventeen major UK papers published the iconic John Harris photo of the unprovoked police assault on Lesley Boulton at Orgreave.

The result was predictable. On June 30, the *Economist* reported that only 35 percent of the British public supported the miners. A Gallup poll in July showed that 79 percent disapproved of the methods used by the NUM. Both confirmed—in the words of Thatcher biographer Moore—"a growing view that the NUM, and Scargill in particular, were committed to unjustified violence."

This was precisely the narrative that Thatcher sought to foster. On May 23—before the confrontations at Orgreave—she spoke of "an ugly streak of violence" that "has disfigured our television screens night after night. Reports appear of those who have been intimidated because they seek to go to their place of work, to pursue their occupation, and to support their families . . . Trade unions were founded to protect their members from threats and bullying. And yet there are leaders who could say the word to stop violence, but who fail even to condemn it."

This spin was inspired, reframing flying pickets as "violent" and the maintaining of union discipline as "intimidation." Even as police roadblocks made a mockery of freedom of movement and speech, and Thatcher unleashed the power of the state to tap phones and sow chaos inside the NUM, the true threats to freedom and democracy were . . . miners struggling to save their livelihoods.

The police even claimed that Scargill was not attacked, but had simply fallen down and hit his head. In the highly charged atmosphere, it was hard to know what to believe, unless one witnessed events directly. With the combined might of the state, the police, and the corporate media, Thatcher and Murdoch were able to largely control public perceptions in ways that Orwell had warned about.

Yet as Callincos and Simons note, "The defeat suffered by the miners at Orgreave had a contradictory effect." Even as the skewed coverage led much of the public to question the strike, the brutality led a smaller but still significant group "inside and outside the mining communities to think about [the strike] in much more general political terms, as a broad class issue."

The miners, then, had potential new allies. While most were from the larger labor movement, others came from more unlikely sectors. This solidarity from a committed minority of the broader public gave hope to the striking miners.

"The battle is getting hotter," Strummer sang in "Armagideon Time," and there could be no truer summation of Great Britain in the summer of 1984. Yet as the moment cried out for action, the singer was paralyzed. After eight months of nonstop motion, he was exhausted, hurting, brooding about choices made.

Gaby Salter was overjoyed to have her husband back, even if he seemed dogged by shadows she didn't quite understand. "Initially I thought perhaps he was out of touch through living in the bubble of the world of The Clash for so long," Salter recalls. "I never doubted Joe's integrity at the time but I do think that he was pretty naive and allowed himself to be hoodwinked, especially by Bernie . . . I sat back silently waiting for [the new Clash] to implode."

This could surely happen—but Strummer might come apart first. Salewicz: "Joe [was] coming out with all that stuff about going back to basics, but if you look at him, the state of his soul [was] fairly evident. You're not convinced that he's convinced. He also seems extremely angry . . . actually imploding with anger."

In "Clampdown," Strummer argued that "anger can be power." Clearly that emotion had driven many of his greatest achievements.

But anger directed within can turn poisonous. Salter: "It wasn't till later that I recognized what was happening: Joe was depressed."

This was not a new issue. In 1982, Strummer had spoken about his ongoing struggles with Mikal Gilmore: "Suicide is something I know about. It's funny how when you feel really depressed, all your thoughts run in bad circles and you can't break them circles. They just keep running around themselves, and you can't think of one good thing, even though you try your hardest." While Strummer added, "But the next day it can all be different," his road had remained rocky. Salter also knew what few others did: Strummer had returned home to find his mother was likely terminally ill, facing a struggle with cancer.

Vinyl also knew about this latest heartbreaking development, but wasn't in a supportive mind-set. Similarly exhausted by the uphill grind, and burned out on the music business rat race, Vinyl had put Rhodes on notice of his desire to leave. He had not yet told Strummer or Simonon, fearing that they would feel betrayed and even more burdened—especially the struggling singer.

As Vinyl remembers, "The situation in the band at the time didn't take into account any domestic or personal issues . . . Joe was not in a sympathetic environment at all. We were pushing toward something crucial and everything else was secondary." The consigliere later admitted, "That lack of support is very hard and ultimately not sustainable. But that wasn't my perspective at the time, I wasn't thinking of sustainability at the time—none of us were."

Strummer was stretched to the limit. Salewicz: "Now his mother has got cancer, Joe's going to visit her regularly. He's been in a crisis really ever since Mick's kicked out of the group, but it's like . . . there's a succession of kind of plunging ravines that he's crashing down."

Strummer might not have acknowledged this, for as Salewicz sadly suggests, "He'd run a mile to get away from his emotions." This was the unreconstructed masculinity shared by most in Strummer's peer group, heightened by his fraught history with his parents and his harsh experiences of English boarding school.

"Joe went to public school—not what they are in the US, but these elite boarding schools—and the British public school boy of that time had the bit of your brain that connects to your emotions severed on your first day," Howard says. "Anybody who feels any emotion is bullied mercilessly . . . it's not seen as the proper thing to do. I know quite a few public school kids of Joe's generation, and they haven't got a fucking clue what's going on in their own heads and bodies. They're not allowed to be in touch with it."

Howard continues, "Such kids are usually wealthy enough, or arrogant enough, or educated enough, or connected enough, that feeling or expressing their emotions isn't essential—they're protected from on high. It becomes a habit, hard-wired into you, that you can push all of that down . . . because there are other things that'll help you through, like money and property."

Strummer was never in this crowd's top echelon, and had stripped away as much of his privilege as possible. But some bits went too deep for easy extraction. Feeling desolation, yet wishing to project positivity, Strummer rarely admitted to his darker emotions. When he did, it was sometimes expressed in artistic terms.

As ex-Clash comrade The Baker explained, "The concept of 'not minding that it hurts' [was] something Joe was very conscious of." Evoking the example of Lawrence of Arabia "and the abuse he allowed and willingly encouraged at the hands of the RAF-enlisted men after the war," The Baker went on to recall how "Joe went through his own short phase of masochistic indulgence when in 1977 he would slick back his hair, dress like a Teddy Boy, and go off to rockabilly shows and pubs that were famous for being in Teddy Boy territory."

As the "Teds" were the deadly enemies of punks, this risked violent attack. Indeed, The Baker recounts, "This tempting of fate, of pushing the envelope further and further, resulted in Joe being badly beaten one night by a Ted in the toilets at the Speakeasy." When visiting at London's Western Hospital, The Baker asked the battered singer about deliberately courting assault: "I remember vividly Joe's response: 'If you want to create, you need to suffer.'"

Nineteenth-century British essayist Thomas de Quincey put the notion in more lofty terms: "Either the human being must suffer and struggle as the price of a more searching vision, or his gaze must be shallow and without intellectual revelation." This idea was central to Strummer's creative impulse, and part of why he remained deathly afraid of the isolating, cocoon-like life of rock stardom.

The "redemptive suffering" motif wound through many of the singer's inspirations. Jesus proclaimed, "Blessed are the poor in spirit," and his path was known as the "Via Dolorosa," the way of suffering. Rastafarian reggae pioneers like Bob Marley celebrated the "sufferers," the poor in the shantytowns like Jamaica's Trench Town.

Strummer found great power in music created out of such oppression. In one interview on the 1984 US tour, he linked reggae and the blues in this regard: "When I heard those blues singers I knew it was for real. 'Cause what did we [British] have? Cliff Richard, Lonnie Donegan, Straightsville. But Howlin' Wolf, he shouts to the top degree; everything comes out. It's not feeble, it's *gnnrr-raaahh, gnnnrrraaah*, and you know it is born out of sufferation."

"Sufferation" is a Rasta term meaning suffering, especially due to poverty or repression. Strummer explained, "Down in Jamaica, sufferation is like something that's in the air." When he tried to outline to the interviewer why The Clash had lost its way, he reached for similar metaphors: "We lost that ghetto direction, the direction of the sidewalk, of concrete, and of hunger."

The intertwined roles of pain and anger became obvious when Strummer explained his approach to writing: "I tell you what I do—I plug into the world. When I hear about the terrible things that are going down, it throws me into a rage and so it prompts me to write and sing songs about it."

This explanation made sense. Yet Strummer's life was on a trajectory away from the street, ghetto hunger, and sufferation. Even if he did not act or look a stereotypical millionaire property-owning father with a wife and a young child, this was his life now. This longtime squatter who had emulated Woody Guthrie's hobo life was drifting back toward the privilege he had scrubbed away.

184 « MARK ANDERSEN AND RALPH HEIBUTZKI

There surely was pain in that realization. But what if this agony—fearing that one had become a hypocrite, a failure, a sellout—paralyzed instead of catalyzed? Can this burning-fear-verging-on-self-loathing be turned into art that matters, that can change lives, maybe even change the world?

Strummer struggled to find that revelation as anger and pain threatened to boil over in his homeland. Thatcher was pressing her offensive against the miners on several fronts at once. In principle, the strike was a simple dispute between workers—the NUM—and their employer—the National Coal Board—with an impartial police and judiciary merely refereeing. Yet few doubted that Thatcher was truly the general commanding the entire campaign, bending public institutions to serve her wishes.

Seeking to encourage a trickle of striking miners returning to work as their hardships grew, Thatcher pushed the police out of relatively friendly environs like Nottinghamshire into areas solidly behind the strike. The resulting hostile occupations bred backlash. Callincos and Simons: "Whole mining communities rose up in revolt with women often playing a leading role . . . On July 9 the first pitched battles between police and Yorkshire mining communities occurred."

Thatcher encouraged two Nottinghamshire miners who were bringing a legal case claiming that the NUM had attempted to embroil them in an unlawful strike. If favored by the court, this would allow the Tory government to "sequester" the union's funds, crippling its ability to meet the needs of its striking miners.

Strikers don't get their wages, only a meager union stipend, so many families were already eating at community soup kitchens. Their prospects became even bleaker on July 26 when Parliament enacted the Trade Union Act. As a result, neither striking miners nor their families were entitled to state benefits. The children of strikers could not receive free school meals or social security help with school uniforms.

The growing suffering fed fury at those who crossed picket lines. In August, the Rhymney Valley Miners Support Group issued a front-page editorial, "What Is A Scab?" in the *Rhymney Valley News*.

To the authors, the dictionary definition—"an unpleasant crust of dead tissue"—seemed apt to describe those returning to work: "Such a person is a scab on the face of the community. As far as the miners of [South] Wales are concerned, there is nothing so low as a man who will stab his fellow workers in the back by strike-breaking."

The barely contained fury of those words foreshadowed agonizing fractures to come. As hunger became rife, miners faced a dilemma: return to work and be viewed as a "scab," ostracized in your own community; or stay out and live primarily on the most meager of handouts. The vast majority chose the latter.

When a dock strike in mid-July opened a second front, the miners' hopes rose. The Tory government was in danger of defeat—and was preparing extreme measures to prevent that eventuality. As the *Guardian* reported years later, "Margaret Thatcher was secretly preparing to use troops and declare a state of emergency . . . out of fear Britain was going to run out of food and grind to a halt."

The Clash on the docks, mid-1984, before Strummer's disappearance. (Photo by Mike Laye.)

The prospect that a broader Britain would face the deprivation that miners and their families endured daily no doubt cheered some—but it was not to be. Under immense pressure from the To-ries, the dock strike collapsed within two weeks.

Nonetheless, the threat of union solidarity remained. As Moore recounts, "Scargill at Orgreave exorcised for Mrs. Thatcher the de-mon of Scargill at Saltley twelve years earlier. It did not automat-ically follow, however, that the government would win. It remained possible that key trade unions would combine successfully against it."

Britain's north was now in turmoil, with the strike impacting the daily lives of millions. Although the south was less contested, the chaos was spreading. Thatcher aide Andrew Turnbull allowed, "'The Battle of Orgreave' recalled 'the Wars of the Roses'"—an ad-mission that something akin to civil war had broken out.

He was not the only one to come to this conclusion. As Moore writes, Thatcher aide David Willetts "recalled that when working for Mrs. Thatcher during the miners' strike the comparison with a civil war was apt. 'You would be in a meeting with Mrs. T on some other subject and messengers would come in with reports like "Kent is solid . . . Nottingham is with us . . . Yorkshire is in rebellion." It did feel like a scene from one of Shakespeare's history plays.'"

Thatcher again sought the rhetorical high ground, painting the miners not simply as her political opponents but enemies of the country. According to the *Times of London*, "Speaking at a private meeting of the 1922 Committee of Conservative backbench MPs at Westminster [on July 19], Mrs. Thatcher said that at the time of the Falklands conflict they had had to fight the enemy without; but the enemy within, much more difficult to fight, was just as dangerous to liberty."

Such rhetoric had consequences. As Moore admits, it "gave Mrs. Thatcher the permission . . . to have some of the strikers' ac-tivities monitored by the Security Service . . . Stella Rimington, who later became the head of MI5, classified Scargill—whose phone had been tapped for years because of his links with the Soviet-backed Communist Party of Great Britain—as 'an unaffiliated subversive.'"

While Moore agrees with Thatcher's use of the phrase "the en-emy within," he distances himself from its impact by noting the obvious: "Being a declared enemy of the government led by Margaret Thatcher did not of itself make anyone a subversive," i.e., an enemy of democracy.

Even though the details of the "dirty tricks" campaign would not be exposed for years, any careful observer saw the scale of the Tory offensive. It might have been expected to break the will to resist—but the miners persevered. They inspired allies from around the country to organize support groups that channeled food, clothing, and money into the hard-hit mining communities.

Nick Sheppard's parents joined one such group, which provided a much-needed outlet for the frustrated guitarist. Sheppard: "Vince, Pete, and I worked pretty much a five-day, ten/eleven a.m.-to-six/seven p.m. week rehearsing and doing whatever busy work Bernie devised. We were set various tasks: record a new Clash song—I did 'Pouring Rain,' and was told there would be no 'disco' on the new record—record a cover, fix guitars, dig a hole, fill it in . . . Mind-numbing repetition, really."

This would have been trying at any time. But with Britain on fire, this disconnect was incomprehensible and infuriating. Sheppard: "I had gone on marches for the miners . . . and I do remember asking Bernie if we were gonna do any benefits for the miners, because I really couldn't believe that we wouldn't. And I wasn't given an answer then . . . That was difficult."

Instead, the guitarist for the most popular revolutionary rock band in the world did a benefit for the miners' strike—arranged by his parents. Sheppard: "My mum and dad live in Bristol, which was close to Wales, one of the centers of the strike. And I did a benefit they helped organize with some other bands and friends of mine. Not as anything to do with The Clash—I just went down to Bristol to play at a benefit to specifically help this one particular town in Wales." If the show scarcely had the impact of a Clash gig, it at least eased Sheppard's conscience.

Sheppard was not the only musician whose personal support for the miners' cause had begun to turn toward acts of concrete solidarity. The Clash's anarchist nemesis Crass played a miners benefit in July in what turned out to be its final show. Other artists like

Chumbawamba, Redskins, Paul Weller, New Model Army, Bronski Beat, and Billy Bragg were preparing to do the same. Even relatively apolitical bands such as New Order joined the cause, as did Music for Miners, a group of writers, artists, and filmmakers aiming to activate the youth.

This fit well with a new strategy of the miners' movement. With the loss of Nottinghamshire, the defeat of mass picketing at Orgreave, and setbacks in the public relations war, it was becoming clear that the NUM needed broader support to outlast Thatcher. This meant aid from other unions, but also went far beyond.

Peter Carter, the British Communist Party's industrial organizer, argued, "Trade-union solidarity alone is not enough. A wider public support has to be won for the miners . . . A major industrial dispute of this character cannot be won by industrial muscle alone in the face of hostile public opinion. The miners should concentrate on winning wide sympathy, building a broad alliance around their objectives."

While reiterating his support for mass picketing, Scottish NUM vice president George Bolton similarly argued, "The government and the [National Coal Board] have consistently tried to contain the argument to the question of mass pickets, violence, and law and order; and they have avoided like the plague any discussion of what the dispute is all about. That tells you that they have a real fear of a mass understanding by the British people of what the dispute is all about . . . The question of the arts is very important. We need to get the world of entertainment identified with us, not least because they get mass audiences."

Bolton's words suggested precisely the sort of alternative news network that Strummer and Rhodes had envisioned with the "Radio Clash" concept, and that the band had endeavored to fulfill in its own way. At this perfect moment to push the idea, however, Strummer remained MIA, with The Clash consequently dormant. As Sheppard ruefully recalls, "In terms of discussing the miners' strike with Joe, on any level, it just didn't happen . . . because I didn't see him."

If Thatcher and Reagan were the "enemy without" for Strummer, he was now contending with his own "enemy within." Depression was made worse by his addictive tendencies, not only with alcohol, but his old frenemy marijuana.

Strummer had foresworn pot loudly, publicly, and repeatedly. Those closest to him knew it wasn't that simple. Years later, Salewicz claimed, "Bernie may have said there was a 'no drug policy' but Joe was smoking spliffs all the time!" Interviewed in 1999, Strummer agreed: "[The anti-pot line] was Bernie's new regime. It didn't last long. After two weeks, we were gagging for it."

Strummer's self-deprecating sense of humor may be at play here. None of The Clash's newer members witnessed such drug use, so Strummer was clearly keeping it close to his chest. Such corrosive secrecy could breed self-loathing as one did in private what one denounced in public. In the same 1999 interview, Strummer copped to "feeling like a no-good talentless fuck" during this period.

The vehemence of his antidrug stand in 1982–84, and the depth with which it was articulated, suggest that Strummer actually believed it—but couldn't live it. Far from being something forced upon him by Rhodes, Strummer's stance came from self-knowledge. On the US tour, the singer had spoken of "little gems of wisdom" learned from harsh experience: "I know how to take care of myself a bit more—like I have two beers instead of eight, stuff like that."

But for an addict such lessons are often beside the point. Bill Wilson, cofounder of Alcoholics Anonymous, argued, "The actual or potential alcoholic, with hardly an exception, will be absolutely unable to stop drinking on the basis of self-knowledge." Strummer's ability to translate insights into changed behavior was limited. His most revealing, articulate, and convincing discussion of his antidrug stance—his June 1982 conversation with Mikal Gilmore—was itself lubricated by copious amounts of alcohol, as the writer's blow-by-blow makes clear.

Strummer was more cognizant than most that human beings can be intellectually aware of some truth without that knowledge producing a change in behavior. The mere fact that Strummer found it so hard to stop using—even for a short time, even when he was publicly committing himself to his audience as well as privately to his band—suggests addiction.

Asked directly about this, Strummer's friend Salewicz gently notes, "Pot can help you get through a lot." Strummer was sliding back into self-medicating to ease his pain. While better than his brother's way, Strummer knew drugs could be "slow suicide." "I kill my soul / each and every day" ran a line from an early version of "Glue Zombie," and Strummer now found himself slipping into this limbo.

Salewicz: "The pressure must have felt enormous. The very last thing you would have thought [Strummer] wanted to do was go on the road, breaking in a new group, though . . . this might have been exactly what he did want to do." Now, Salewicz argues, Strummer was back home and could hide no more from his feelings. "Over the ensuing months he would come close to cracking under their pressure, unable to avoid the messages they were sending him."

Drugs, like pain, could be a catalyst for creativity—but they could also crush the spark. Strummer found himself in a hurting place, and not an easy spot from which to live out his lofty vision. So he didn't. He hid away, hoping the pain would somehow translate to inspiration. But months passed, and Strummer remained stuck, isolated from his band and desperately in search of his muse.

In late August, something finally shook loose. Vinyl recalls, "London was feeling oppressive for Joe and I, so we decided to just take off, no agenda except getting out of Dodge for a few days!" Once the penny-pinching Rhodes was convinced to fork over some money, the duo went to the airport and flew to New York City.

Vinyl: "That night in New York we hatched a plan—nothing preconceived—that we would go to Los Angeles and make a record, totally on the fly." The next day they were off. "I got somewhere cheap to stay and looked for a cheap demo studio out of the back of the LA Weekly while Joe worked on some material—I'm not sure if it was something he had or just made up on the spot."

The next day, they recruited a mariachi trumpet player and percussionist found at a Sunday brunch. Vinyl: "When I was on the phone with the percussionist, Joe shouted, 'Tell him to bring all the gear that he usually isn't allowed to play!'" With musicians in hand, the pair took off to a tiny demo studio for a swift session.

As Strummer hadn't even brought a guitar, the studio provided one. Much to the dismay of Strummer, it was a jazz-rock guitar with a built-in keyboard, similar to an instrument that Jones sometimes used. "The studio guy was showing us all the sounds it could make," Vinyl says, laughing. "And finally Joe just said, 'We ain't in search of fucking Spock, mate . . . Just make it sound like a guitar!'"

None of the studio folks or musicians connected these scruffy Brits to a Top 10 rock band. Vinyl: "We said we were hustlers just trying to make a quick buck." Of the three or four songs that the makeshift group knocked out in a few hours, "Three Card Trick" was the only song Vinyl recognized—though this incarnation was adorned heavily with Latin trumpet and percussion.

The impromptu session completed, the duo flew back to New York to remix the demo at another fly-by-night joint—"some place out of the *Village Voice* classifieds," says Vinyl—and were off to London the next morning, the entire adventure completed within a long weekend.

It was a startling burst of creative energy, especially given the stalemate Strummer had found himself in for the past three months—but it would go nowhere. Vinyl: "We played the tape for Bernard and he was very taken aback because he thought we were just out getting drunk."

This "go in and bash it out" session echoed what Strummer had touted as his plan for the new Clash record—only the larger platoon was not involved in any way. In any case, Rhodes was not impressed. Vinyl: "We gave him the tape and it was never talked about again, other than when I once mentioned an arrangement from the session. Bernard was not happy that I brought it up."

While Vinyl describes the adventure as "great fun," he is also clearly pained that the tracks simply got filed away. Given Rhodes's desire for control of all things Clash-related, the outcome is not surprising. Still, it came as yet another blow to Strummer's shaky creative confidence.

This stasis was costly for The Clash, as well as Strummer personally. As the brutal Thatcherite response to the miners' strike cast a shadow over the entire UK, the moment seemed ripe for the band to shine. Other performers like Billy Bragg were knee deep in strike support. But as Bragg asked later, "Where was The Clash? They were AWOL, missing in action, nowhere to be seen."

Bragg was not the only Clash fan who felt let down. Recalling the savage assault by mounted riot police at Orgreave, Clash biographer Marcus Gray noted, "'Three Card Trick' and 'This Is England' reflect the brutal face of contemporary policing, batons are wielded willy-nilly in both," only to mourn that "The Clash missed a real opportunity to attach themselves to the miners' cause at this crucial time."

It was a massive burden for any person to carry, but Strummer could not escape it. "I really enjoyed being a bum again. I wish I could do it every day, really," Strummer had told Gilmore in 1982, referring to his disappearance to Paris. "But I can't disappear anymore. Time to face up to what we're on about."

That time was coming around again, for Strummer returned to London to learn that The Clash had been booked to play five shows in Italy as part of the "Festival of Unity." This was an annual cultural extravaganza sponsored by the Italian Communist Party, an exponent of "Eurocommunism," which sought to recapture the movement's original aims, challenging both the US and USSR.

White, Howard, and Sheppard were overjoyed. White: "We were just [feeling], 'Thank God, we're going away and doing something, instead of fucking around in a studio every day.'" Sheppard was ideologically pleased as well: "The Communist Party held these huge festivals every year, featuring all different kinds of music, partly to generate funds for the party on the local level—they operate politically at a town council/county council level, with a network throughout Italy—but also to enhance the cultural life of the country."

The venue, however, posed more questions about the band. As Gray wrote, "The Clash of '76 had managed to generate a righteous anger and capture the imagination of the country's youth on far less fuel than [the miners' strike]. The Clash of '84 remained on holiday until September of 1984. When they did reconvene it was to play a series of gigs for the Communist Party. In Italy."

Gray would claim, "The motive was chiefly financial," but this seems unfair. Three months had passed since The Clash last graced a stage. The battle had grown hotter, but no new songs had appeared, no recording had commenced. Like Strummer, The Clash was nearing a point where stasis becomes disintegration.

The decision to return to the band's fountain of energy and inspiration—the Clash audience—seemed essential. While it might have been better to be focused on the home front, these shows would help determine if, indeed, a band still existed.

The summer of 1984 had held high drama for Thatcher, with the chances of victory or defeat shifting like the weather. The Coal Board and the NUM were now in talks. One of Thatcher's biggest worries was that MacGregor would fold under the miners' pressure and agree to what she saw as an unsatisfactory settlement.

When talks broke down just short of agreement, Thatcher recalled later, "I was enormously relieved." The government assault was intense and multipronged, and Thatcher's sense of righteousness remained undiminished, but the miners were proving to be a far more tenacious foe than the Argentinians.

As her authorized biographer Charles Moore recounts, "So uncomfortable did the situation seem that President Reagan took the step, highly unusual in an ally's purely domestic political difficulty, of writing to Mrs. Thatcher." Reagan purred encouragingly: "I have thought often of you with considerable empathy as I follow the activities of the miners' and dockworkers' unions. I know they present a difficult set of issues for your Government . . . [but] I'm confident as ever that you and your Government will come out of this well."

Reagan—a leader of the actors' union in his more liberal days—had faced down many unions himself. Indeed, his destruction of the air traffic controllers' union in 1981 had been an inspiration for Thatcher, as had his ability to co-opt other unions such as the Teamsters to support his agenda.

He had his own challenges, however. The day after Reagan

wrote his soothing words to Thatcher, Walter Mondale mounted the stage at the Democratic National Convention in San Francisco to accept the nomination for president.

Evoking the diversity in the room—"black and white, Asian and Hispanic, Native and immigrant, young and old, urban and rural, male and female, from yuppie to lunchpail"—Mondale dismissed Reagan and his party as "a portrait of privilege" while describing the Democrats as "a mirror of America." To underline this point, Mondale chose Geraldine Ferraro as his running mate, the first time a woman had gained the vice presidential slot for one of the two big parties in the US.

"Over the next one hundred days, in every word we say, every life we touch, we will be fighting for the future of America," Mondale proclaimed. "Four years ago, many of you voted for Mr. Reagan because he promised you'd be better off. Today, the rich are better off. But working Americans are worse off."

Describing the Reagan regime as "a government of the rich, by the rich, and for the rich," Mondale reached out to communities hit hard by deindustrialization: "Three million of our best jobs have gone overseas. To big companies that send our jobs overseas, my message is: We need those jobs here at home. And our country won't help your business—unless your business helps our country."

On foreign policy, Mondale promised to "reassert American values," pressing for human rights in Central America, the removal of US military advisers, and an end to "the illegal war in Nicaragua"—a direct attack on the current policy in the region. He also blistered Reagan over the nuclear arms race: "Every president since the Bomb went off understood that we have the capacity to destroy the planet and talked with the Soviets and negotiated arms control. Why has this administration failed? Why haven't they tried? Why can't we reach agreements to save this earth? The truth is, we can . . . [and] we must negotiate a mutual, verifiable nuclear freeze before those weapons destroy us all."

Mondale then evoked one of Joe Strummer's favorite themes: truth. "Americans want the truth about the future . . . Whoever is inaugurated in January, the American people will have to pay Mr.

Reagan's bills. The budget will be squeezed. Taxes will go up. Anyone who says they won't is not telling the truth.

"Let's tell the truth," Mondale called out, building to a crescendo. "It must be done, it must be done. Mr. Reagan will raise taxes, and so will I. He won't tell you. I just did." As the crowd roared its approval, Mondale returned to the attack: "There's another difference. When he raises taxes, it won't be done fairly. He will sock it to average-income families again, and leave his rich friends alone. And I won't stand for it. And neither will you and neither will the American people."

It was a rousing speech, a powerful vision for America. Clearly relishing his newfound role as truth-teller, Mondale—long criticized from the left as a timid and centrist "old news" Democrat—seemed ready to take the fight to Reagan.

Across the ocean, another vision had risen. SEX STYLE SUBVERSION read the banner across the back of the stage at Stadio Simonetta Lamberti, a soccer stadium in Cava de' Tirreni, a small city adjacent to Naples in southern Italy. The provocative yet vague banner—not glimpsed since its debut at the US Festival—seemed an odd match for a socialist band playing a Communist festival.

As a crowd of 15,000-plus roared approval, a slender man with spiky hair strode to the microphone and let loose: "*Hip-hoppers! Punk rockers! Young ladies! Show stoppers! The . . . Clash . . . are . . . out . . . of . . . conttrrroooollllllll . . .*"

As the words reverberated through the stadium, Kosmo Vinyl walked away, his words followed by the spaghetti western tune "Sixty Seconds to What?" While the music swelled, the staccato chords of "London Calling" split the night air. The crowd erupted in waves of pogoing as The Clash burst into the light.

The sound was tight, seemingly unstoppable. Few outside the band's inner circle could have guessed that the very first time that the entire five-man unit had been together in over three months was several hours earlier for sound check.

Sheppard recalls, "We didn't rehearse once for the shows in Italy. We just went and did 'em. We didn't see Joe until he was sound-checking in Naples."

As it happened, Strummer had arrived in Naples days earlier, but passed up connecting with the band to go out with some locals. Italian fan Luca Lanini remembered, "Joe was in Naples a couple of days before the gig and became friends with some juvenile delinquents of a notorious central slum named Quartieri Spagnoli. He roamed around town with them on the back of their scooters."

The company Strummer was keeping and his somewhat rumpled appearance led to trouble when he tried to visit the National Archaeological Museum. Lanini: "Joe wasn't allowed to enter because of his Mohican haircut and his lion-tamer jacket." After a frantic series of calls, journalist Federico Vacalebre—who had written the first Italian book about The Clash—was summoned and succeeded in getting Strummer into this hall of hallowed antiquities.

The band knew none of this. Asked if Strummer offered any explanation or apology for his extended absence, Sheppard responded simply, "No, he didn't." The sound check itself consisted of Strummer barking out "'Be-Bop-a-Lula' in F sharp!" and the band doing a swift run-through of the Gene Vincent classic.

Given all of this, the show went off astonishingly well—a tribute, surely, to the work Howard, White, and Sheppard had put in on their own, with an occasional assist from Simonon. The set didn't stray far from that established on the US tour, although several key new songs like "Pouring Rain," "Jericho," and "The Dictator" were missing. The night also saw the return of the much-maligned "Should I Stay or Should I Go" in the second encore.

The most intriguing moment came six songs into the set when Strummer stopped to query the crowd: "You must know that we are English, right? *Inglese* . . . This is what it is like in England tonight!" On that cue, Sheppard hit chunky guitar chords reminiscent of the Modern Lovers' protopunk classic "Roadrunner" and the band launched into a revamped "This Is England." If not nearly so fully renovated as "Pouring Rain" had been, the song—which could sometimes seem a bit stiff—benefited from the more even tempo and improved dynamics.

Beyond showing that the newer members had continued to stretch and shape the songs, this suggested that—all appearances to the contrary—Strummer was following events on the home front closely. He was nonetheless barely more engaged with the band on this tour than he had been since June, traveling on his own, regularly drinking to excess, seeming detached and aloof.

To White, Strummer was "out in the stratosphere . . . not exactly a space cadet, more like the galactic general." Sheppard was a bit kinder if no less concerned: "Joe was drunk pretty much all the time. Sometimes it was good value, other times he was best to avoid. I think he was really upset, hurting."

An interview with Vacalebre after the Naples show provided a glimpse of Strummer's bleak frame of mind. Asked about the *Sex Style Subversion* backdrop, the singer offered a laconic response: "These three words represent us, we can't do without it."

When Vacalebre brought up the Campaign for Nuclear Disarmament and the Greenham Common Peace Camp, Strummer dismissed the groups, saying, "We are not interested in them," explaining darkly, "War is everywhere, inside us, there is no other peace than what we have now, which is armed, nuclear. Our life is at the maximum peace we could possibly have, unfortunately."

Strummer then expressed similar disdain for the massive marches a few months before, saying simply, "Bob Dylan sang about it in 1963." This seems a reference to "Blowin' in the Wind," a protest song steeped in despair; in the words of rock critic Mick Gold, it was "impenetrably ambiguous: either the answer is so obvious it is right in your face, or the answer is as intangible as the wind."

Strummer—allegedly hard at work on new songs for months—also had some startling words to share on that front: "After the tour we'll concentrate on writing new material. You'll be surprised when you listen, you'll snap your fingers, you'll howl with wonder, it will be different from what you've heard to date. Maybe it will be pop, at least in part, and will appeal to women too. You have my word."

Strummer only became genuinely effusive when speaking about his recently made comrades, mixing praise for them with a swipe at his home city: "Those street kids have become my friends, introduced me to Naples, such an old, charming city . . . I saw where they live, where they have fun, what problems they have finding work, or having sex with their girlfriends. I liked Naples, it's alive, sunny, carnal, sensual, not depressing and boring like London."

Strummer sounded fatalistic and unmoored, but there was one upbeat development when the band finally came back together. Much to Sheppard's pleasure, "Joe wanted us to stretch out musically . . . He was really pushing us to jam at the gigs, maybe to test our suitability for the planned new Clash record."

This began to show on the second night, September 7 at the Palasport Arena in Rome, another spacious stadium filled with fervent fans. "London Calling" once again opened, this time featuring an extended guitar intro with first drums and then bass phased in bit by bit. The music built gradually and then pulled back to welcome Strummer—fully two and a half minutes into the song—before blasting off.

An extended quiet section also appeared late in "White Man in Hammersmith Palais." As with the opener, this was a powerful addition, making space for a graceful crowd sing-along and some melodic guitar passages.

Strummer was very animated onstage, trying out more of what White called his "pidgin Italian" to engage the crowd. He gave an apparently spontaneous—and somewhat off-color—introduction to "Rock the Casbah," asking the crowd if they know what a "casbah" was. With no answer forthcoming, Strummer held forth: "The casbah in the Middle East is where you go to get down with something, maybe hear some dirty rhythm or something funny with a snake or if you want to do something with a donkey!" Regardless, this proved to be another powerful show, maybe even better than the night before.

While the band grew more musically assured with each day, Strummer was in a downward spiral. Salewicz writes, "Joe went on a three-day bender, guzzling bottle after bottle of brandy. Raymond Jordan was appointed to babysit Joe through this crisis." Howard remembers Strummer "screaming in the hotel bar," and both he and White recollect band meetings where Strummer outdid Rhodes in verbal abuse. "As though Joe was acting as manager, everyone was torn to pieces," Howard says. "Usually these events ended with someone in tears."

Strummer's erratic behavior was obvious the third night, at Stadio Mirabello in Reggio Emilia. The show started off strong again, with the extended "London Calling," followed by fierce versions of "Radio Clash," "Safe European Home," and "Career Opportunities."

Strummer then paused to bring on a young female fan he had met earlier in the day to serve as translator. Calling her "honey" and "baby," the boozy singer launched into his appeal, which the Italian gamely translated: "Has anyone noticed OUT THERE . . . They have all the bookshops, all the bloody restaurants, everything . . . How come I stand here in this SHITHOLE without even a toilet!?"

The crowd roared, and Strummer answered his own question— "Because they've taken all the money!"—and turned back to the woman, ordering her, "Now tell them, '*Let's get down!*'" As puzzled fans struggled to absorb this, Strummer coached his admirably patient translator through introductions of White, Howard, and Simonon. Finally, the singer introduced himself, with self-loathing nearly dripping from his tongue: "My name is the biggest fucker in the world! Get it?"

Strummer dismissed the woman with a curt, "*Grazie*, baby," and shouted, "Here is *Signore* Nick Sheppard!" Amazingly, the transition was seamless. When the guitarist ignited "Police on My Back"— which had now become his main vocal showcase—the set finally emerged from the theater of the absurd.

After urgent versions of "Are You Ready for War?," "White Man in Hammersmith Palais," and "Three Card Trick," Strummer paused again, this time to ask the crowd for requests. When an audience member called out for "Lover's Rock," the frontman responded with apparently genuine shock: "'Lover's Rock'!? Are you sure about that? You must be crazy, man, you must be crazy!"

It was a bit of inspired humor, taking dead aim at one of the least successful Clash songs ever—but then Strummer went on to yell, "We're all fucking crazy!"

Such a clichéd rock and roll outburst seemed desperately out of character.

While the band swiftly launched into a slam-bang rendition of "Complete Control," Strummer seemed anything but in control—a point underlined when the singer then introduced the feminist epic "Sex Mad War" by praising "the nice-looking women in Italy . . . *bella bella bella!*" Once again, the performance was dynamic. But even though the rest of the set was equally fervent and well played, no sober observer could fail to be concerned about Strummer's condition.

If anything, the tour's final show at Genoa's indoor Arena Palasport before more than ten thousand spectators on September 11 was even more electric and chaotic. White later described the show as "a riot," and he was not far off the mark. In many ways, the evening was a classic Clash performance, with just enough unpredictability and danger to keep any showbiz boredom fully at bay.

Introducing himself as "Harry the Fucker," Strummer once again put the knife in his own chest. Beyond that, he led the band through one of its most dynamic, wide-open shows. Sheppard recalls, "Joe was wild and excitable and wanted us to stretch out musically." One of the fruits of this came early in the set: a gorgeous "Spanish Bombs" that began almost a cappella with Strummer singing over somber drums and muted guitar before building to a ferocious climax.

If Strummer was a bit "off the rails"—in Sheppard's words—it could make for compelling theater. "Are You Ready for War?" started strong but partway through Strummer went off, abandoning the usual lyrics, ranting and raving. The band valiantly stuck with the singer, until he literally waved them off, barking an order for them to go into "White Man in Hammersmith Palais."

The band complied, but as Strummer hit the song's climax, he suddenly stopped. Yelling, "*Venga!* Franco says it's cool . . ."— apparently a reference to Italian promoter Franco Mamone—the frontman started inviting the crowd onstage.

It is not apparent why Strummer did this. Sheppard later speculated that the singer was bored and simply wanted to interrupt entertainment-as-usual. It is also possible that he may have felt too much distance from the crowd.

A few days before, Strummer had defended playing in this series of huge venues: "It's the only possible way. We cannot do five concerts in Genoa, five in Naples . . . Can you imagine what would happen if instead of being here we chose a small club? We do not want thousands of people forced to stay out of our concerts for the enjoyment of the privileged few."

This made sense. Yet this stance directly contradicted what Strummer had told another journalist seven months before. Vowing to play seven nights in one city if need be, Strummer had insisted, "We want to be bigger than anyone else but do it in a way that matters." Both Strummer and Simonon had often talked about the catalytic role of the crowd in fueling their performances. As such, they mourned the loss of intimate connection as their concerts' scale grew.

Whatever Strummer's reasoning, the barrier between artist and audience had been obliterated. Chaos reigned for several minutes as Strummer alternated between exhorting the crowd—"Italy, come on, come on!"—and wrangling with skeptical security. Once the stage was finally full, Strummer led the band back into a reprise of "White Man," the crowd and band singing and moving together.

Sheppard: "I thought it was great! We ended up on the drum riser as our stage. We had to leave the stage after one song. When we came back there were no monitors and one microphone!" Nevertheless, the next half hour of the show was a steamroller, going from punk to dub and back again.

An equipment breakdown stalled "I Fought the Law," but the band took the opportunity to uncoil an extended dub breakdown leading into "Bank Robber," followed by "Janie Jones." The band then kicked off "Tommy Gun"—only to take another left turn as White was unceremoniously pulled into the crowd.

White: "In 'Tommy Gun' I would take a sudden run to the edge of the stage, stop, lean over, and fire an imaginary salvo. It was great fun . . . until some bright spark in the audience grabbed the guitar's machine head and wouldn't let go . . . It was either me or the instrument so in I went!"

Sheppard: "All the crowds on that tour were really wild . . . I remember Vince getting pulled into the crowd and coming out with a shoe missing and his clothes fucked up."

When the song ended, a ragged White clubfooted it over to Strummer and asked for the band to go offstage so he could get a new pair of shoes. The singer was not having it. As White later wrote: "Joe glared menacingly at me. I don't think he saw me, not a bit. It was eerie. Eyes glazed, and like the messiah calling his followers to prayer he stooped low, and pulled the microphone to his lips . . ."

While the dazed guitarist looked on, Strummer slowly intoned, "ENGLISH . . . CIVIL . . . WAR!" White: "The crowd erupted. I started smashing out tuneless chords in wild abandon. A few people jumped up onstage and started leaping around. I quickly forgot how stupid I looked. Suddenly all the madness made sense."

With glorious chaos swirling around them, the band quickly knocked out two more numbers before exiting the stage: "Know Your Rights" and "Magnificent Seven." At the end of that shimmering punk-funk juggernaut, Strummer screamed, "I . . . WANT . . . MAGNIFICENCE!"

But what made for a gripping performance didn't necessarily align with mental health. While the show had been riotous, the after-show drama would be as well. While Sheppard, Howard, and Rhodes shared a meal at a fan's restaurant—"One of the only times I enjoyed Bernie's company!" laughs Sheppard—White, Vinyl, and Strummer descended into something close to hell.

It began as just another night of hard drinking and skirt chasing—but soon took a much darker turn. According to White, after the trio tired of the bar, a wretchedly drunk Strummer suggested that they go in pursuit of prostitutes. "Joe assured me it was great. A real experience. It had to be tried," White says bitterly.

When this pursuit was unsuccessful, a new drinking spot was found. Once there, White remembers, Strummer and Vinyl began to badger him about his guitar playing and supposed lack of commitment to The Clash. Startled, White tried to defend himself, only to face more barbed insults.

When Strummer upped the ante by insinuating that he had slept with White's girlfriend and then summarily dismissed White from the band, the guitarist lost control and began to slug the singer in the face—but he faced no resistance. Suddenly, Strummer and Vinyl were laughing, claiming it had just been a test.

White felt sickened—yet this was not the end. The next day, Pearl Harbour got a call from her husband, Paul Simonon. As Harbour later told Chris Salewicz, "Paul says, 'Last night we all got drunk, and Joe and Kosmo told me that I had to divorce you or quit the band.' I said, 'What did you say?' I was livid. He said, 'I don't know what to tell them.' I said, 'Fuck you. Divorce me if you want.'"

While the two eventually sorted out the matter, a furious Harbour took her revenge upon Strummer upon his return to Heathrow Airport, kicking and punching him in public while roasting his hypocrisy. Harbor: "'You, Joe Strummer, you think it's not rock and roll for Paul and me to be married, and you walk around London pushing a pram with an orange Mohican. You are a fucking idiot!'"

The double standard was real. As with White's attack, Strummer didn't resist—he just took the blows, as if hoping that the pain would somehow be redemptive.

While Harbour made enough of a ruckus to attract the attention of nearby police, the two patched it up by—ironically, given the role of alcohol in the initial fiasco—going out drinking the next night. Displaying the scabs on his shins to all who cared to look, Strummer found an unusual way to apologize. Harbour: "Joe took off my high-heeled shoes and poured champagne in them and drank it."

But if Strummer's relationship with Harbour was mended, other wounds were not so easily healed. Nor were the injuries caused to the unity of the band. What is one to make of this ugly series of events? Offering no excuses, but with clear regrets, Vinyl will only note that this period was "the unhappiest time of my adult life." If anything, Strummer seemed even more lost and forlorn.

Yet, against all odds, the tour had been a success. Sheppard told

Gray, "The shows were really good, and we played really well," later adding, "The gigs were full of freedom and experimentation musically, and we felt confident as a band. I loved the whole experience—the food, the people, the country."

While Sheppard admitted, "I didn't really pay too much attention as to why Joe was off the rails," this would become increasingly difficult. Strummer had once said his 1982 disappearance was a way of working himself out of a depression: "I had a personal reason for going . . . I just remembered how it was when I was a bum, how I'd once learned the truth from playing songs on the street corner. If I played good, I'd eat. That direct connection between having something to eat and somewhere to stay and the music I played—I just remembered that."

The singer was shrouded in shadows he seemed unable to shake. The dream of a reinvented Clash able to face whatever 1984 had to offer was fading away.

Soon enough, Joe Strummer would again disappear.

CHAPTER SIX
GOT TO GET A WITNESS

Joe Strummer in Granada, October 1984, wearing an *Out of Control* hat. (Photo by Juan Jesús Garcia.)

I've often lost myself,
in order to find the burn that keeps everything awake.
—Federico García Lorca

Women began organizing communal kitchens for the striking coal miners and
their families driven by desperation and a realization that clubbing together
makes food go further and sharing poverty makes it easier to bear. They devised
ways to raise money to fund the soup kitchens and soon many became more
politically active, joining the picket lines beside their male relations and friends.
—Alex Callincos and Mike Simons, *The Great Strike,* 1985

The man looked a bit rumpled, nursing a drink at a corner table in a bar in Granada, Spain. At first Jesús Arias didn't recognize him: "The guy was dressed like a lumberjack in a checkered coat and dockworker's hat. He was unshaven, unwashed . . . He looked like a hippie, really."

It was early October 1984, and Arias had come to investigate an unlikely tale. The Spanish punk recalls, "My brother Antonio called me and said, 'Hey, Jesús, yesterday we met Joe Strummer at Silbar. He is dirty and smelly but he will be there tonight again. Please come, we need someone who speaks English!'"

Startled, Arias pressed for more information. If anything, the details seemed even more incredible. "I came in and the bartender said, 'This foreigner wants to show you his lyrics,'" Antonio told him. Puzzled, the younger Arias had gone over: "It was dark in the bar, I didn't recognize him, he had a five-day-old beard and is showing me this small notebook with handwriting in English. I told him it was great but I'm really thinking, 'How can I get away?'" Eventually, Antonio realized it was Strummer.

The elder Arias wasn't convinced. Why would the lead singer of The Clash—a certified rock star—be skulking in a bar in Granada all by himself? Jesús explains, "There were rumors that Strummer had been around in the past, that he had a girlfriend from Granada, but no one I knew had ever seen him, and I was always skeptical." Nevertheless, he went to see for himself.

Silbar was a hub for the small Granada punk community. Any vaguely avant-garde art had long been repressed in Spain under the dictatorship of General Francisco Franco, former ally of Hitler and Mussolini. Rock and other progressive scenes had sprouted in the space that developed after Franco's death in 1975.

"All our friends, our bands—TNT, KGB, 091—went [to Silbar]," Jesús Arias says. "But Strummer? It didn't make sense." The Spaniard steeled himself, walked over to the table, and asked: "Are you Joe Strummer?" The man looked up from his glass and replied simply: "Yeah . . . What do you want to drink?"

When Arias answered, "Coca-Cola," Strummer called out to the bartender in his ragged Spanish, "Hey, let me buy a Coca-Cola for this guy!" He turned back to Arias and asked, "Do you speak English?" "I told him, 'Yes, I do, very badly,'" Arias laughs. "Joe said, 'Well, that's good enough for me!'"

Strummer proved to be an easy conversationalist and a good listener, but Arias could tell that not all was well: "At first, he was really happy and talkative. He liked Silbar and Granada, like it was a little London without all the critics. But soon you could tell he was really down, really sad. He was thinking all the time, crying all the time . . . He was drunk all the time."

Strummer had first visited Granada in the 1970s with his long-time girlfriend, Paloma Romero. Better known as Palmolive, drummer for two trailblazing female punk groups, the Slits and the Raincoats, Romero was from nearby Málaga. In addition to being the inspiration for "Spanish Bombs," she also introduced Strummer to another of his great loves: the art and life of Federico García Lorca.

Lorca was a leader of the "Generation of 1927," a loosely aligned group of artists who brought avant-garde ideas into Spanish literature. An outspoken socialist, Lorca was also gay at a time when this was anything but accepted. Even so, his literary voice earned him a fervent following.

One scholar described the writer's increasing depression, "a situation exacerbated by Lorca's anguish over his homosexuality." Other aspects of the poet's life seemed familiar to Strummer: "Lorca felt he was trapped between the persona of the successful author, which he was forced to maintain in public, and the tortured, authentic self, which he could only acknowledge in private."

After time in New York City, Lorca returned to Spain amid the growing tension that led to the Spanish Civil War. An attempted military coup against the elected leftist government soon led to civil war between Republicans—government supporters—and Nationalists under Franco's command.

Lorca had every reason to fear for his life as summary executions and mass killings became common after war erupted in early 1936. Yet he remained in his home region of Andalusia only to be abducted and murdered by fascist forces on August 19, 1936. Tossed into a mass grave beside other victims of the terror, Lorca's body was never found.

Lorca's mix of politics, art, and anguish resonated with Strummer. At the time, going to Granada was—in the words of Chris Salewicz—"a bit of a pilgrimage . . . [Joe needed] to get away from things, he [needed] a creative place to think. He wanted to visit the grave of Federico García Lorca."

Arias happened to be a student of Lorca's work, and he bonded with Strummer during late-night talks about the martyred poet. Arias knew the area near Viznar—not far from Granada—where Lorca was probably killed, and the two made plans to visit. Before they could do so, however, Strummer disappeared just as suddenly as he had appeared—"like a ghost," Arias says.

As this phantom flitted in and out of Granada, the miners' strike was past the seven-month mark and nearing a turning point. In mid-August, Ian MacGregor sent a letter to the safety inspectors at the country's coal mines. These "pit deputies" were not part of the NUM, but a smaller union with a long name: the National Association of Colliery Overmen, Deputies and Shotfirers (NACODS). They had not joined the strike, though some refused to cross NUM picket lines.

That was expected of any union worker. Yet MacGregor found this unacceptable. If some miners themselves were now crossing the lines, why shouldn't the pit deputies? He ordered all NACODS workers to cross picket lines or be fired.

This enraged the union. NACODS swiftly voted to go on strike, demanding that MacGregor's letter be withdrawn, and also insisting that the National Coal Board agree to binding arbitration over any proposed future pit closure.

This course of action would be devastating to the government's plans. By law, no mine could operate without safety inspectors; MacGregor's ultimatum would effectively shut down all of Britain's coal mines. Moreover, if arbitration became the last word on closures, the still-secret—and often denied—plan for relentless downsizing might well be stymied. Either way, this would hand victory to the battered but unbowed NUM. Feeling the heat, Mac-

Gregor scrambled to extricate himself from this self-created disaster by striving to delay the NACODS strike.

Thatcher once again had to prepare for desperate measures. Years later, the *Guardian* reported, "The secret list of 'worst case' options outlined to Thatcher by [her] most senior officials included power cuts and putting British industry on a 'three-day week'—a phrase that evoked memories of Edward Heath's humiliating 1974 defeat by the miners that brought down his government, and which must have sent a chill down Thatcher's spine when she read it."

The prime minister was adamant this must not happen. As a mid-October deadline for the NACODS strike approached, Thatcher applied immense pressure behind the scenes. Partisans in this conflict held their breath.

England in 1984 resembled a battleground. The United States, however, was victorious—at least if an advertisement that debuted in mid-September was to be believed.

"*It's morning again in America,*" a white male voice intoned over soothing orchestral music. Familiar morning scenes of a boy delivering newspapers, a man on the way to work, a farmer on a tractor, slipped from one to another. The warm voice continued: "*Today more people will go to work than ever before in our nation's history, with interest rates at about half the record highs of 1980. Nearly 2,000 families today will buy new homes, more than at any time in the past four years. This afternoon, 6,500 young men and women will be married. And with inflation at just one-half of what is was four years ago, they can look forward with confidence to the future.*" As wedding scenes melted into a vista of the US Capitol dome and American flags being raised, the narrator concluded: "*It's morning again in America—and under the leadership of President Reagan, our country is prouder, and stronger, and better. Why would we ever want to return to where we were only four short years ago?*" One final image—a montage of Ronald Reagan and the American flag—remained on screen as the music faded.

The portrait the ad painted was powerful—but was it true? A tightening of the money supply actually initiated late in the Carter era by his Federal Reserve appointee, Paul Volcker, had led to the brutal recession of 1982. While devastating for many, it had driven down inflation and interest rates.

Only some reaped the benefits. For unlucky tens of millions, it was anything but morning in America. The ad ignored the ongoing agony of inner cities and Native American reservations, the record bankruptcies of family farms, and the growing ranks of the homeless adrift on American streets amid a widening gap between the rich and the poor. While the morning sunlight shone upon corporations shaking off regulations and taxes, the sun was setting on Rust Belt ghost towns.

This was reality. But did America actually want truth? Mondale had promised to "tell it like it is"—including that tax increases were inevitable—but had run headlong into the Reagan machine's public-relations buzz saw.

The "Morning in America" ads—developed by a Madison Avenue dream team—were the first blow in a one-two punch that staggered Mondale. While Reagan himself stayed above the fray, his surrogates savaged the Democrat as a "tax-and-spend liberal." "Mr. Mondale calls this promise to raise taxes an act of courage," Vice President George Bush proclaimed. "But it wasn't courage, it was just habit, because he is a gold-medal winner when it comes to increasing the tax burden of the American people."

This rejoinder neatly evoked the recently concluded, hyperpatriotic Summer Olympics—boycotted by the Soviet Union and its allies amid Cold War tension—in delivering its hammer blow. It also twisted Mondale's vow to not lie into something like an insatiable hunger to raise taxes. Outrageous, yes—but as the Democrat's poll numbers dropped, it seemed America might want gauzy self-affirmation more than uncomfortable reality.

This was just as Reagan's henchmen hoped. The retired actor was a master showman, and this was his "role of a lifetime," as biographer Lou Cannon put it. Leslie Janka, Reagan's deputy press secretary, admitted later, "This was a PR outfit that became president and took over the country. The Constitution forced them to do things like make a budget, run foreign policy, and all that, but their first, last, and overarching activity was public relations."

The *New York Times* acknowledged this in an article on October 14, 1984, "The President and the Press," which focused on how Reagan's handlers sought to stage-manage their agenda by keeping national media outlets on a short leash. Even when the rare presidential press conference did happen, reporters were given little chance to ask real questions. When they did, Reagan turned on his folksy charm to skillfully evade inconvenient queries, smiling all the while.

The Reagan administration stymied the press in more muscular ways, such as by barring reporters from covering the US invasion of Grenada, an event that provoked little public outcry. According to the *Times*, "Many people outside the Government appeared to share the view expressed by Secretary of State George P. Shultz: 'It seems as though the reporters are always against us. And so they're always seeking to report something that's going to screw things up.'"

Whether due to carrot or stick, many agreed. "Reagan had been one of the least scrutinized presidents in our nation's history," the *Los Angeles Times* opined. Perhaps it didn't matter if the media had failed due to public indifference and administration manipulation, or had come "on bended knee," kowtowing before the imperial presidency as critic Mark Hertsgaard argued. According to the *New York Times*, the result was the same: "The press has seldom been relegated to a more secondary role in determining the national agenda."

Back in Camden, Sheppard, Howard, and White continued to bang away on their own. Simonon occasionally appeared, with Rhodes a more frequent but rarely friendly visitor. If the three hoped their strong performances under challenging conditions in Italy might lure their singer back to the fold, they were disappointed.

"Joe disappeared," White says. "It made no difference to us seeing as we never saw much of him anyway." Nonetheless, this time seemed different: "There was suddenly a lot of concern in the Clash camp about his whereabouts . . . He supposedly hadn't told anyone where he'd gone."

As worry rippled through the Clash ranks about a possible end to the band, White remembers, "Bernie told us that he'd broken up with Gaby and taken time away to sort himself out." Salter later told White this was not true. The disgusted guitarist "no longer gave a fuck. I was sure that His Royal Highness would resurface when required." Days turned to weeks and Strummer still didn't appear.

Rhodes eventually delivered a sign that the singer was out there somewhere—tapes of what were supposed to be possible new songs. Their arrival hardly inspired joy, for as Sheppard recalls, "They were just raw chords and shouting, no lyrics, no melody . . . Terrible rubbish." The three were somehow expected to polish these into something of worth.

The situation seemed absurd. White: "Bernie was very suspicious, very Stalinesque. It was all under wraps, just like top-secret information. I didn't think too much about it at the time, but—looking back on it—it just seems insane."

Sheppard agrees: "It started to get pretty nasty, pretty insecure. Attempts were made to explain what was going on, but they weren't convincing."

The trio put their backs into the task, but with dwindling hope. Sheppard explains, "The whole situation was very, very weird . . . It was if we had ceased to be a band of five people after our return from America." Each day without new songs left them no closer to a studio, no closer to making the landmark record promised.

Yet the rump of what had been—and might someday once again be—The Clash soldiered on, hoping to make something of the creative chaos handed to them, and for the "platoon" to somehow be remobilized.

Meanwhile, the much-sought-after Strummer rematerialized in Granada some three weeks after his first visit. He resumed his friendship with Jesús Arias and the members of his brother Antonio's band, 091, and made a new acquaintance, music journalist Juan Jesús García.

The two met in inimitable Strummer fashion. Arias: "Joe was so drunk he got lost in Granada. He ran into Juan Jesús García and told him, 'I don't know where my hotel is,' so Juan Jesús took him there." When a grateful Strummer offered García a gift in return for his kindness, the journalist asked for an interview.

"Joe said, 'Okay—let's meet at this place and time tomorrow,'" Arias recounts. "Juan Jesús thought Joe was so drunk he'd never remember but called me to translate in any case." When Strummer did appear, the trio embarked on a wide-ranging conversation that gave tantalizing glimpses into the singer's present thinking.

Wearing sunglasses and his *Out of Control* hat, Strummer spoke slowly and quietly, nursing a monstrous hangover. With Arias as go-between, García started off by asking why Strummer had come to Granada.

Juan Jesús Garcia, Jesús Arias, and Joe Strummer, Granada interview, October 1984. (Photo courtesy of Juan Jesús Garcia.)

Sipping his "hair of the dog"—*carajillo*, coffee with cognac— Strummer responded in a low, gravelly voice. "Obviously I am obsessed with Andalusia," the singer said, then adding a second motivation: "The atmosphere in London is . . . depressing, depressed." However, Strummer's most important reason was "to think . . . I wanted to see things clearly, to be objective. I think I am getting there."

Asked about the present situation of The Clash, the singer replied simply: "One of reconstruction." After a brief pause, he elaborated a bit: "To learn from all the mistakes of the past and to understand. To feel the pain of all the mistakes of the past and so to do it better in the future."

Pressed on the possibility of Jones returning to the band, Strummer held firm: "No, no. It will not be possible to be The Clash with Mick Jones. Because to be in The Clash, you must be able to self-criticize. And he doesn't like to be criticized."

García probed further, asking how The Clash kept credibility after the ejection of Jones and Headon. Strummer humbly responded, "I don't know. I guess it's because we have never tried to be anything but ourselves. We are what we are, nothing more. We don't try to imitate an archetype or anything like that." Turning to face the central critique of many current detractors head-on, Strummer asserted forcefully, "I don't want The Clash to be a parody of ourselves!"

Evidence of deep soul-searching lay beneath Strummer's words: "Above all, we have to be honest with ourselves, be able to self-criticize, to analyze ourselves. We have to play with the same passion before one spectator in an empty club as we do with thirty thousand in the audience. When people recognize this, they respect you. In this, we find The Clash's credibility."

Asked if The Clash's political stance was unaltered, Strummer's voice rose, immediate, emphatic: "Of course! I think the singer can be the madman outside of society, singing the truth. To be a singer you must live there always—*always*."

A skeptical García pushed back, "How can you be outside the record business in a capitalist world? You have to be inside!"

Strummer granted the point, yet persisted: "Yes, but the record company can never dominate you, if you have independence, a position of strength . . . [At the US Festival] they asked us to play for half a million dollars. We agreed, and with that half-million you can say to the record company, 'Don't fuck with us'—that is independence."

Shifting his angle, García then brought up attacks on The Clash by Crass and other newer punk bands. Strummer growled and launched a terse, enigmatic rejoinder: "These groups, they thought the game was . . . *easy*. They came for the game the way the animals come to the slaughterhouse."

When García praised the way *Sandinista!* and *Combat Rock* utilized a vast array of musical forms such as jazz, reggae, funk, and blues, Strummer dissented: "No, it's no good. There is no way that you can play better jazz than a jazz man. A jazz man plays jazz. The reggae man plays reggae. I am a rock man. I am not jazz or blues—I am a rock man, so now I will play rock."

The singer then connected past mistakes with lessons for now: "We lost the idea of unity on [those records] but we learned what we should do in the future: it is best to stick to one approach that you grab ahold of and realize deeply. This is the difference between *Combat Rock* and the new record: *Combat Rock* was the sound of confusion; the new LP will be the sound of clarity. *Mas duro*—HARDER. But more clear, because no jazz, no reggae."

Strummer suggested recording for the new record was imminent. While this would have been news to the rest of the band, García took it at face value and queried why he would come to Andalusia right before the sessions began. Strummer shot back, "I could not stand one more day in London!" adding wistfully, "I love Granada and I want to write songs for the new record here . . . Granada overwhelms me and gives me the peace necessary to write."

When García queried about his progress, Strummer was ebullient: "I don't want to boast, but I think it is the best writing of my life. The first days here I wasn't getting anywhere when suddenly—*flash flash flash*—there were millions of images in my head. It was fantastic. I got into a bar, I stood at the bar and kept writing."

Strummer's enthusiasm seemed real, as Antonio Arias's startling first meeting with him would suggest. But the weirdness of the encounter indicated something out of balance, as did the focus on words rather than music, given that the latter was the crux of Strummer's creative dilemma.

The singer's ever-changing mood also suggested it was all more complicated than he let on. At points, Strummer seemed almost schizophrenic. The happiness with his writing expressed to García contrasted with what he shared privately with Jesús Arias: "Joe would say, 'I'm shit, man . . . I've done nothing with my life!' I'd say, 'What do you mean? You are Joe Strummer!'" Magnified by alcohol, the self-doubt shaded close to self-hatred.

When García tossed a softball question—"Do you like some new musical groups?"—Strummer remained silent. When pressed, he finally gave an answer that was, in his own words, "all around town": "Before I had very fixed ideas. Now I am flexible, I know better than to be fixed. I want to be like the wind or water or trees or clouds; I want to understand everything. So, the answer is: I don't know."

When García pushed on this again, asking if Strummer was interested in popular new rock acts like the Pretenders or the Romantics, the singer responded obliquely: "I am interested in the eight directions." A puzzled García followed up: "What are these?" Strummer: "When I know, I will tell you."

"The eight directions" is a Hindu concept, used in this case apparently as his way of saying something like, *I am adrift, with no direction home.* So he was, for later in the interview, his "anti" stance of early 1984 reappeared. Ripping current music as "weak shit," Strummer called for a new musical revolution to be made by the people just learning to play now: "Let's go forward with the new generations!"

A sense of uncentered longing rose when Strummer discussed the nature of fame: "Once I was in strange countries with only a guitar and some shoes and nothing else. Once I have done this. I know there will be a time when I will live this life again. I am ready for this life. Success is good, but it doesn't kill me to be the bum again." If the return to this motif suggested an admirable humility, it fit uneasily with the reality of his wife and child waiting back in London.

The gap between Strummer's aims and his ability to live them yawned ever wider. First, the Clash frontman movingly recalled his former musical partner: "Mick Jones and I were best friends, wrote all the songs together, shared the same passion for Andalusia and

García Lorca. We had similar ideas about everything, I liked how he developed within the group, how he played guitar."

But, he continued, "Mick started to think that he was a rock star, and didn't like the self-criticism and self-examination that is part of The Clash. When the band started to get on the terrain of 'we are the greatest,' this was dangerous territory, where you can lose perspective on things. We lost the ability to communicate with each other, not just about musical differences. We didn't understand each other as people. That's why I told Mick to go."

Finally, Strummer confirmed that part of the schism was related to drugs: "Mick went crazy with marijuana—all day, spliff after spliff. It was unbearable. Drugs are a waste of time that destroys people."

This was essentially the antidrug stance Strummer had proclaimed across Europe and America for the first half of 1984. But Arias saw a darker side: "Joe was letting down his guard some by the time I met him. It could be funny, in a sad way. One night he was smoking joints, one after another. Then he tells me, 'I fired Mick Jones because he was smoking too much joints.'" To Arias, Strummer seemed unaware of—or at least unable to overcome—the contradiction.

Sensing Strummer's deep pain, Arias was sympathetic, but worried: "Behind the brave face, Joe was utterly lost." Strummer told García and Arias he had come to Granada to "detoxify from England." He had a curious way of doing this, marinating in alcohol, pot, and late nights, rarely shaving or bathing.

Rationalized by Strummer as an artistic catalyst or even a form of therapy, this "bum" lifestyle seemed more indicative of depression or addiction. Aware of this, the Clash frontman tried to not have too much alcohol during the interview, saying to a waitress offering a second *carajillo*, "No, one is enough. Lots of alcohol is for the nights, the day is for work . . . I have a lot of work to do right now." Still, Arias rarely saw Strummer less than mildly drunk during this period.

The anguish seemed unending. When not expressed in drug use, it came out in tears. Arias: "We had been in the countryside and were coming back to the city when Joe suddenly sighed: 'How wonderful it is to be to be alive!' When I asked why he said this, he said: 'I had a brother who committed suicide, I loved him. If he had come to Granada he would never have committed suicide!' and started to cry."

Arias: "I thought, 'This man is very sensitive'—and he was—but he kept breaking into tears at other times too. Then I realized he had a lot of pressure on him, he was coming apart." Strummer's guilt was deep and apparent as well; Arias saw him withdraw five thousand dollars from a bank and give it to a beggar on the street.

The scenario was deeply poignant. Most likely, the singer needed medical help for his depression, grief counseling, maybe even alcohol/drug rehabilitation. Instead, Strummer embraced his pain—as a soul salve and creative aid—and then apparently ran from it into his substance abuse.

García came away impressed with Strummer's humility and sincerity. Moreover, *Diario de Granada*—the local paper for which García wrote—had a genuine scoop. Much to his dismay, however, the article languished. Arias: "The editors didn't think much of it, they didn't know who Joe Strummer was, didn't care. Finally, on a slow news day two or three weeks later, they said, 'Okay, let's publish this.'"

This, of course, was part of why Strummer had chosen to come to Granada. "Here he was nobody," Arias says. "Joe told me, 'Being in Spain is like being in Kenya,' he could get drunk all the time and no one cared." By the time the *Diario de Granada* article appeared on November 18, however, Strummer had returned home to face his distinctly non-bum life.

As Strummer was wrestling with his demons and his creative process in Spain, extraordinary drama had been playing out in the United Kingdom. An Irish Republican Army bomb aimed at Margaret Thatcher and her cabinet at a Conservative Party conference in Brighton missed her but killed five others. Emerging defiant and unscathed from the attack, Thatcher's popularity rose.

Shortly thereafter, Thatcher pulled off another coup: by utilizing a spy in the labor union ranks and marshaling intense pressure, she was able to get the NACODS strike called off by the union leadership. Any hope of quick victory for the miners vanished with this decision, denounced as a "sellout" by Arthur Scargill.

As the *Guardian* later reported, "When [the NACODS strike] was called off, the relief in Downing Street was palpable: 'The news was announced this afternoon and represents a massive blow to Scargill,' read the 'secret and personal' daily coal report for Wednesday 24 October" that came to Thatcher's desk.

The impact of this sudden reversal was immense. After that day, few neutral observers could see any obvious road to victory for the miners. In addition, the advance work on the legislative front was paying off, as judges were siding with Thatcher's government against the union. As fines levied on Scargill and the NUM mounted, and control over union funds was taken over by the courts, the strikers were left even more bereft and impoverished.

Winter had once been seen as a possible savior of the strike, for increased heating demand might exhaust coal stocks and lead to power cuts, pressuring the government to give in. But coal supplies were still high, thanks to the careful stockpiling and the mines defying the strike in Nottinghamshire and beyond.

This left many miners among the only Britons lacking for warmth as frigid weather arrived. Some families began to scrounge for usable nuggets of coal from gigantic slag heaps. This was an exceedingly hazardous endeavor, and lives would be lost in the process.

As the police tightened their grip on the mining communities, violence flared. Union solidarity ran deep in these communities. More miners began to trickle back to work, and the struggle to enforce the strike became more intense. "A single scab brought a whole community onto the streets," according to Callincos and Simons. As a result, villages could be "cut off from the rest of Britain for days while the police occupied it like a conquering army."

Strummer was well acquainted with how vague laws against "sus"—"suspicious behavior"—were regularly used against non-white youth. He had often critiqued Britain's police force as "fascist." This bemused most white Britons, raised with the notion of the friendly neighborhood bobby. Now, however, the constabulary was becoming loathed in the mining towns as the brutal political pawns of Thatcher.

According to one village resident, "My kids now call the police 'pigs.' I didn't teach them, they've learned it for themselves. I used to see it on the telly, kids in Northern Ireland treating police like this, and thought the parents must be to blame. But now, you don't need to indoctrinate them. The police do it for them."

Betty Cook of Women Against Pit Closures agreed: "We would read in the press before, say about a young black boy claiming he was beaten up by the police, and we would think, 'He must have done something.' The strike taught us better; we began to understand [other] people's problems."

Police officials reported to Thatcher that miners "frustrated by the failure of mass picketing are taking to 'guerrilla warfare,' based on intimidation of individuals and companies." With the media largely under Tory control, this escalation—even if understandable—was likely to be self-defeating, as it reinforced Thatcher's narrative of "union violence" that eroded broader support for the strike.

The miners saw no choice; they had to win the strike or face death as an industry. Feeling let down by their brothers and sisters in other unions—many of whom feared confrontation with the Tories, lest their own jobs be lost—the strikers turned to each other, with astonishing resolve. As Callincos and Simons detail, "Women began organizing communal kitchens for the striking miners and their families driven by desperation and a realization that clubbing together makes food go further and sharing poverty makes it easier to bear."

While hardship mounted, these operations became essential for the strikers' families shadowed by hunger. Rallying supporters across the land, the women "devised ways to raise money to fund the soup kitchens and soon many became more politically active, joining the picket lines beside their male relations and friends."

For women like Cook, the strike also forced a reevaluation of roles previously unquestioned, as she bluntly told the *Guardian* in

2004: "During the strike, my eyes were opened and after it I divorced my husband. The strike taught me a lot, I had always been told I was stupid by my husband but I learned I wasn't." This newly awakened female power would be one of the strike's lasting legacies.

Woman feeding a child at a soup kitchen for Cortonwood strikers' families. (Photo © Martin Jenkinson.) Inset: *Coal Not Dole* button. (Courtesy of Mark Andersen.)

While the solidarity of the mining villages was being tested, so was that of The Clash. In photos taken by García in late October, Strummer's dog tags were obvious—a sign that he recognized that somewhere the rest of his unit was waiting. How would Strummer bridge the growing gap? "He didn't talk about the new band much," Arias says. "I never saw him confident about them."

Nonetheless, something seemed to shift for Strummer during his second visit to Granada. "*I've often lost myself / in order to find the burn that keeps everything awake,*" Lorca had written, describing something like the process that Strummer had used, first in Paris, then again in Granada, to try to find a way out of darkness.

If Strummer was unsure about his comrades, the new band was hardly feeling confident in him. Still mulling the mysterious tapes,

Sheppard, White, and Howard now received their next gift: sheets of music with nothing but chord patterns.

While these seemed almost equally useless, the blow was softened—because Joe Strummer delivered them in person during a short visit to the practice space, his first in months. But was anything really resolved? Or had Strummer simply buckled under the immense pressure of manager and record company to return?

This turn of events marked Strummer's reengagement with the band—though it would not be smooth. Strummer had intimated to García that the album would be out in February, suggesting recording was imminent. But The Clash's leader had returned with tidings that were not entirely glad.

Strummer's announcements were shared at a band meeting called at a Camden bar. The good news was that—after the latest three-month hiatus—The Clash would finally play live again: a pair of benefits for the miners' strike at the Brixton Academy in early December, with rehearsals to commence shortly.

The singer still seemed out of sorts, and this news came off in an ugly way. Sheppard: "Joe sat us down and said, 'Right, this is what we're gonna do. We're gonna play some benefits. It's a good publicity stunt.' I thought, 'Why the fuck would you say that? That sounds really cynical and stupid.'"

The guitarist remains adamant: "I didn't believe for a second we did those gigs to further our own career—keeping our heads down would have done that better. My response was, 'I don't care why you say we're doing them; we are and about fucking time!' If you're gonna have politics, go do something, you know?"

White found Strummer's latest pronouncement in sync with his own dark suspicions about the Clash mission: "My question mark over all of that, really, with Joe's integrity, with regard to those kind of things—did he believe them or not, or was he just kind of using them as a tool? Did Joe really care about the miners, what was happening in England? I don't know."

Strummer's confounding words suggested a continuing internal struggle with despair. White was feeling equally weary: "I didn't care about miners or Thatcher or Scargill or working-class struggle or fucking anything else for that matter." His lack of enthusiasm proved wise—for Strummer had another bombshell to drop, once he was sufficiently lubricated with alcohol.

White: "We're drinking cognac at lunchtime. Then on to beer and by three in the afternoon, Joe drunkenly informs me that Nick and I aren't good enough to play on the forthcoming Clash record." After all the touring and other work to build a powerful new Clash—labor that was clearly paying off, as the live shows proved—this sudden reversal seemed to make no sense at all.

Years later, White shrugged it off: "Nothing Joe or Bernie said seemed to have a basis in reality anymore. Things just changed from one day to the next, from one beer to the next . . . It was depressing." Sheppard agrees: "At the same time as the benefit news, it was presented to me and Vince that we wouldn't be on the record, and that we would be sent off to make some other record with somebody else . . . [It was] just more nonsense stuff."

Rhodes's destructive hand is apparent in this turn of events. The Baker doesn't hesitate to point the finger: "Joe's hesitation and lack of direction at the end can surely be attributed to Bernie's constant haranguing tirades and self-defeating windups."

What could be the aim of such tactics? Rhodes faced his own set of pressures, not least from their ostensible employer. As Vinyl points out, "Bernard had an ally in Paul Russell of CBS UK, the part of the company we had technically signed on with . . . He respected The Clash were unlike any other band."

Yet there was a financial reality involved as well as an artistic one. Vinyl: "The Clash was one of the few big sellers for CBS UK, it was a feather in their cap, so a lot was riding on a strong follow-up to *Combat Rock*."

This band of headstrong would-be revolutionaries was no record executive's dream outfit. "At the outset, The Clash was a hard sell," admits Vinyl. "But as soon as it isn't a hard sell, it becomes a hard sell again, do you know what I mean? Russell was like, 'We gave you the space, now where are the goods?'"

The weight was onerous even for the hard-boiled Rhodes. But it was not the only factor motivating his relentless push on Strummer. The record could indeed have been banged out long ago, per the singer's often repeated preferences.

Rhodes had another agenda that was not so open: the new album's musical direction. This was driven by an artistic intuition that The Clash must move forward, not back. Despite Strummer's repeated dismissals, Rhodes felt that any leap toward the future had to incorporate elements of the new electro-pop style.

Perhaps it's not a coincidence that this echoed the view of the banished Jones. While he had dropped both Headon—still lost in addiction—and the idea of launching another Clash, he had a new band: Big Audio Dynamite, a.k.a. BAD. By early October, the band—which emphasized the hip-hop and electronic elements that had sown such divisions in The Clash—was playing out to good reviews, including opening twice for the Alarm in the north of England.

Such moves by his nemesis would inevitably worry Rhodes and possibly Strummer as well. Rhodes likely viewed the new record as a way to respond to Jones by keeping the punk edge but adding "modern" touches.

How was this to be done, who would do it? Given that no one in the present Clash had been recruited with this in mind, and neither Strummer nor Simonon evidenced any interest or proclivity for this, it was unclear.

Rhodes's way with his platoon made this more difficult. In Granada, Strummer had touted the benefits of "self-criticism," urging "all musical groups in Spain and the world to self-criticize—this is the most important thing." That amounted to an endorsement of the approach that Rhodes had imposed on the band since its beginning, against which Jones had rebelled.

But if self-criticism in principle made sense, in practice it was often abused. Even as ardent a practitioner as Bernardine Dohrn of the Weather Underground admitted that the results were often "terrible." In the wrong hands—as often in Communist China and, it seems, in The Clash—this tool for democracy and growth could easily become cover for authoritarianism.

* * *

As The Clash prepared for its return to live action, America had gone to the polls. With economic conditions improving for many, and his campaign ads laying waste to Mondale, Reagan soundly thrashed his opponent, winning 59 percent of vote, and nearly all the electoral college tally. Mondale won only Minnesota—his home state—and the District of Columbia.

It indeed appeared to be morning for the Reagan forces, if not for the country. This triumphant second election seemed to signify a genuine mandate for the president to consolidate and complete his conservative counterrevolution.

The greatest victor, however, might be seen as apathy, for barely more than half of eligible voters exercised that right. Many of those opting out were low-income citizens who had the most to lose from a second Reagan term. They believed their votes didn't matter, pollsters reported, that the system was rigged. While not entirely untrue, their absence helped preserve that unhappy status quo.

Jesse Carpenter was one of those who saw the election as a circus. Carpenter had been awarded the Bronze Star as an Army private in 1944 for carrying wounded soldiers to an aid station in Brittany, France, under "unabated enemy fire," according to his medal award certificate.

Carpenter had returned home damaged. Slipping first into alcoholism and then homelessness, he now navigated DC's streets with his wheelchair-bound best friend, John Lamm. On the night of December 4, the pair came to sleep in Lafayette Park, across the street from the White House. Not long after dawn, US Park Police found Carpenter lying at the feet of his friend's wheelchair. He had frozen to death across the street from the presidential mansion.

The Community for Creative Nonviolence (CCNV)—a direct-action outfit that stood with DC's homeless—had befriended Carpenter and Lamm. After his death, they won Carpenter the right to a hero's burial at Arlington Cemetery. "He avoided death abroad to die on the streets here," said the Reverend Vin Harwell, presiding over the funeral. "His is a story of tragedy, a life disrupted by war, never to fully recover. It is also a story of national tragedy, because

Nick Sheppard. (Photo by Per-Åke Wärn.)

Center: "Outright outright dynamite / this is the one for the miners' strike." Joe Strummer in front of mining village backdrop, Dec. 6, 1984. (Photo by Per-Åke Wärn.)

SCARGILLS CHRISTMAS PARTY
WITH THE CLASH
AND OTHERS
THE ACADEMY-BRIXTON-LONDON S.W.9.

Joe Strummer.   (Photo by Per-Åke Wärn.)

Inset graphics clockwise from left: billboard for the miners' show; draft designs for buttons and posters; tickets to the miners' show; montage

Top left and right: The guitar interplay between White and Sheppard ignited the show.

You are invited to Stargill's Christmas Party with THE CLASH
BRIXTON ACADEMY THEATRE
THURS 6th DECEMBER 8.00p.m.
Tickets £5.00 inc. VAT
STALLS UNRESERVED SEATING
Nº 02028

Vince White. (Photo by Per-Åke Wärn.)

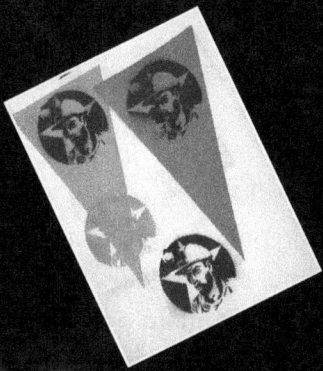

of mining villages for stage backdrop; bunting and stencil designs; button design. (All inset images designed by Eddie King.)

Paul Simonon. (Photo by Per-Åke Wärn.)

this is a nation where millions of Jesse Carpenters are homeless and without help."

Carpenter's unnecessary death was an indictment of a country grown cold and complacent. When Strummer visited DC in April 1984 on tour, he encountered homeless people sleeping on the street mere blocks from the White House. "What is Reagan doing for people like these?" he growled to a reporter, with the answer self-evident.

This might seem unfair. Only days before the election, Reagan had agreed to turn a dilapidated federal building near the US Capitol into a model shelter for more than a thousand men and women. This act of generosity, however, only came after one of CCNV's leaders, Mitch Snyder, embarked on a water-only fast that left him near death. It took fifty-one days and an election-eve appearance by a gaunt Snyder on top-ranking TV news show *60 Minutes* before Reagan relented.

Despite the actions of CCNV and its allies, the death of Jesse Carpenter made hardly a ripple across most of America. Yet only five days before, another tragic death—this one across the ocean, on a road near Rhymney in South Wales—would have a dramatic impact on the fate of a nation.

Support for the strike in South Wales had been so broad that the area had hardly seen any mass pickets. They weren't needed. As the strike neared the nine-month mark with desperation and deprivation growing, however, a few broke down and returned to work. Community anger over such "scabs" was intense, leading to daily confrontations as the returning miners sought to go to their pits.

On November 30, taxi driver David Wilkie was taking a strikebreaker to the Merthyr Vale mine under police escort, as he had done numerous times before. But this time, two strikers were lying in wait to drop a fifty-pound concrete block from an overpass onto the cab. The block crashed through the roof of the Ford Cortina, instantly killing Wilkie and injuring his rider.

The national revulsion over the killing was immediate and near unanimous, damaging support for the strike even among union partisans. Wilkie was not the first person to die—miners David Jones and Joe Green had been killed while picketing, and three children died scavenging coal—but his death came at a crucial moment, turning public opinion sharply against the strike.

Gloom spread across the mining communities. With Christmas coming, no money to pay for presents, and precious little good cheer to share, many die-hard union men had to make heartrending choices. Allen Gascoyne, NUM branch secretary in Derbyshire, remembers, "I had a guy come to me at Christmas in tears. He was losing his house. His wife was going to go, he'd got all these debts. I said: 'We've lost, kid, so get back to work.'"

Despite this advice, Gascoyne himself stayed out on strike, as did most miners, determined to hang on till the bitter end.

Such was the situation as The Clash prepared to mount the Brixton Academy stage to stand with the miners. Skeptics saw the band as a latecomer to the struggle. "Better late than never," Sheppard tersely countered. Commencing its first full rehearsals in nearly half a year, the new Clash threw itself into preparing for possibly their most consequential gig ever.

The Academy was putting itself on the line by hosting an event dubbed "Arthur Scargill's Christmas Party." As Simon Parkes recalls, "Established venues such as the Albert Hall and the Hammersmith Odeon wouldn't touch this gig with a ten-meter pick handle. The last thing they wanted was several thousand angry, hyped-up miners led by, horror of horrors, a punk band." Left unmentioned was the possibility of retaliation by a government that was always watching.

Nonetheless, both band and venue fully committed to the show. Long frustrated by The Clash's inaction, Eddie King was overjoyed to be stepping forward at last: "The police had cut off entire communities, beat up anyone trying to get to them, the government had effectively declared war on parts of its own country, its own populace . . . Everyone wanted to do something for the miners!"

King knew the score: "Thatcher had destroyed the entire industrial infrastructure, ripped out the heart of the country. Scargill and the miners were the only viable opposition. It was basically civil war—Thatcher stopped their benefits, seized the union funds, you got thousands and thousands of families without food or heating for their houses, kids dying scuffling for coal scraps.

"I was on retainer at that time, so only got paid a set amount," King continues, "but I went above and beyond because it was something we all really wanted to do." He designed T-shirts, buttons, banners, stencils—"even yards and yards of bunting!" he laughs—all featuring a miner juxtaposed with the Clash star.

The artist also created a special stage backdrop. King: "It was a massive collage of mining villages, I got photos and blew them up, put them together by hand, it took days and days of work. It was a labor of love." The result was stunning. "It was like a carnival at the Academy with pictures of miners everywhere!"

The upbeat vibe was needed. Asked by García in late October if he wanted to talk about politics or Margaret Thatcher, Strummer had let the question hang in the air for a few telling moments before offering a quiet "No." If this suggested despair about the momentum of events, it surely did not mean an absence of concern. Indeed, as the band practiced for the Brixton miners' shows, Strummer brought three nearly finished songs for the band to learn.

One spoke directly to the agony of the miners' strike. Sheppard: "'North and South' was brought to the rehearsals, and we worked that out quickly as a band, along with the two others. The idea was that I would sing it together with Joe."

"North and South" was an arresting tune, underpinned by terse, melodic guitar. Its lyrics mourned the gap between a northern England suffering the worst economic conditions since the Great Depression and a prosperous south reaping the benefits of Thatcher's financial initiatives. Focusing on "a woman and a man / trying to feed their child / without a coin in their hand," the song asked poignantly, "Have you no use / for eight million hands / and the power of youth?"

As unemployment rolls stretched toward four million, with youth joblessness at a scandalous level, this was no idle question. The song was perhaps Strummer's apology for six months of paralysis, and a vow that it was ending: "Now I know / that time can march / on its charging feet / And now I know / words are only cheap."

The song showed Strummer was well aware of the desperation growing in the mining communities. Admittedly, playing a benefit concert was of limited use. As such events had multiplied over the past few months, constituting a significant form of support for the strike, skeptical voices like Callincos and Simons asked how "a few rock concerts would cow a government which respects only power, and which had shown itself absolutely determined to crush the miners?"

In part, they were correct—music alone could not hope to stop Thatcher. But to agree that concerts alone are insufficient is not the same as conceding they have no value. At this moment, just when everything seemed to be turning against the miners, having the single most popular punk band in the country take their side was no small matter. Beyond the financial boost—"Having The Clash play for you could raise something like a small country's GDP!" argued King—there was the power of moral support, a precious bit of light amid the growing darkness.

Would it have made a difference if the band had engaged six months earlier, had toured the UK then, supporting the strike? Vinyl would later argue, "Tours take time to set up . . . Remember, this is a big band, everything will be under the microscope, you can't just play." Yet The Clash had rarely been stopped by such calculations—part of why the band meant so much to so many.

Even a fan as demanding as Billy Bragg would later concede, "It wouldn't have made the difference." But as The Clash took to the stage on December 6, 1984, it came bearing the frustration, anger, and pain built up over months of agonizing inaction amid the UK's ugliest, most consequential political face-off in decades.

Diverging from past set lists, White and Sheppard kicked it off with a rarely heard *Sandinista!* chestnut, "One More Time," standing on their own before five thousand roaring fans. White: "I opened the song with something original I invented and let it howl out with feedback. It was moody and heavy and different. I had my own style now and was going to let it show."

As White released his jagged guitar pattern, Sheppard met it with his own attack. Prowling the stage, the guitarists staked their claim to the song. Sheppard's guitar dropped away, leaving space for White's short interlude of reggae "chop" chords. This reverie ended suddenly, the duo generating a dissonant maelstrom.

When the guitars pulled back again, first Howard and then Simonon entered the fray, drums and bass punctuating the guitar squall. Finally, Strummer strode onstage, dressed all in white, with a black leather jacket and shades, and the crowd erupted. Hanging back as crisp reggae "chucks" bounced off crashing punk power chords, he let the tension build, as with the extended versions of "London Calling" in Italy.

Finally, Strummer stepped forward. Grabbing the mic, he chanted, "Outright outright dynamite / this is the one for the miners' strike," over and over. The song was a blistering denunciation of poverty and racism, channeling echoes from the American civil right movement and urban riots. As the tune settled into its familiar groove, the Clash frontman ripped out the song's opening lines, adjusted to fit the moment: "Must I get a witness / for all this brutality? / Yeah, there is a need, brother / you don't see it on TV!"

As in Italy, few would have guessed that both guitarists had largely crafted this radical rearrangement of the song, with Strummer working out his ad libs during the sound check. All the hours of work as a trio were paying off now. Sheppard: "We just took it and ran with it, basically. We'd been playing a lot together, and we had got very tight. We knew each other's vibe."

The reworked song demonstrated the power of the new Clash. While Strummer exhorted the crowd, "All together now / push!" the music dropped away, leaving only Simonon's bass. Then Strummer leaped back in, quoting Lee Dorsey's R&B hit "Working in the Coal Mine" over the spare pulse. After one final "down, down / working in the coal mine," both guitars reignited, followed by the rhythm section, launching the song toward its climax.

As the music slowed, everyone dropped away, leaving White's clipped chords on their own, walking the tune to its end—only to have Strummer slash through the lull, screaming, "London's burning!" Shifting effortlessly from dub to full-throated punk roar, the band was off into a Clash classic not played live in years.

Strummer ranted over tightly wound chaos as the band drove the song to its clamorous conclusion. With feedback still hanging in the air, Howard tapped out the intro to "Complete Control." Again the band was off, seamlessly going from one tune to the next. No recent Clash set had begun with such kinetic energy.

When the band finally paused, a delighted Strummer came to the stage's edge. Shading his eyes to survey the crowd, he called, "I forgot to say good evening!" The audience roared, and the singer went on: "We all know why we're here so I ain't going to go on about it. However, without meaning to disappoint, we asked Arthur to do 'Blue Suede Shoes' with us . . . However, he said he forgot the words and his wig doesn't go into a quiff anyway!"

His good-humored shout-out to the miners' leader completed, Strummer turned to the band and announced, "This is Radio Clash!" The song's spring-tight rebel funk was a breather from the breakneck pace, and the message underlined the band's mission tonight: to be an alternative source of information, helping to build a community of resistance to Tory rule.

A tip of the hat to Strummer's recent sojourns might be seen in the subsequent song, "Spanish Bombs." A sharp new guitar line opened the tune and then reappeared near the end, again showing that the band remained able to shape the older material to good effect. A spirited Strummer then paused to tout the American hip-hop group Run-DMC, as a parable of hope and despair in 1984.

"The other side of the coin is appearing," the singer asserted. "Look out the window and you have got Duran Duran and Wham! and Margaret Thatcher . . . the *Daily Mail* and the *Daily Telegraph* . . ." As his soliloquy faded, the singer grabbed his head and moaned: "Sometimes I can't see the light . . ."

Perhaps this was an indirect comment on the darkness of his past months. If so, the cloud was wiped away in an instant: "But when I hear Run-DMC can draw forty thousand people in Detroit, then I seem to think: 'Have no fear, *señor!*'" The singer's buoyant mood lifted "Rock the Casbah," "North and South," and "Are You

Ready for War?" A substandard new song, "Fingerpoppin'," then slowed the momentum. A clumsy comment on club mating rituals, the tune sounded flat and unfinished.

This would be the evening's last misstep. Strummer switched to bass to allow Simomon to lead the band in another rarely heard number, "What's My Name." While Simonon's limited voice had not suited "Police on My Back," it meshed well with this relentless tale of urban anonymity and gutter-punk grit. "The Dictator" followed, with lyrics rewritten to indict Thatcher and her "shock troops."

The song was played fast and hard, leading powerfully into yet another back-catalog barn burner, "Capitol Radio," decrying a media monopoly meant to "keep you in your place." Next the band downshifted to a moody "Broadway," whose introspection quickly gave way to the guitar explosions of "Tommy Gun," punctuated by Howard's double-time drum "machine gun" fire.

When the band paused, Strummer returned to a founding theme, introducing a revived "We Are The Clash" by pointedly noting, "When I say, 'We are The Clash,' I am talking about considerably more than five people." Tonight's version restored the "we can strike a match / if you spill the gasoline" couplet to the chorus.

As if to underline this idea, the band next crashed into a version of "Career Opportunities" that pitted the usual roar of its chorus with a spare dub take on the verses, opening space for a massive sing-along. As the crowd picked up this challenge, someone mounted the stage, grabbed a mic, and screamed, "Revolution, revolution!" before melting away into the masses.

"Revolution" was surely a lofty aim, especially at this moment in British history. Nonetheless, the cry communicated the mood at the Brixton Academy as the musicians exited, audience adulation ringing in their ears.

The band returned for two encores, the final one consisting of potent new number "Dirty Punk," "Jericho," and a slam-bang "This Is England," further developed and sped up from its Italian version and—inexplicably—missing its last verse. Strummer then introduced "an English folk ballad"—"White Riot"—that gained resonance from the fact that miners brutalized in the bloody Orgreave ambush now awaited trial on charges of "riot" that might mean life in prison.

Then the night was done. Despite the agonizing delays, the internal chaos, and Strummer's depression-verging-on-collapse, The Clash had risen up to give a performance for the ages. Moreover, nearly half of the set—nine songs in all—were unreleased, and included two sharp new ones. Even Chris Salewicz—no easy sell—had to admit the show was "fantastic."

The next evening was again packed. Simon Proudman, who had seen the new Clash in Bristol in February, later recalled the night's spirit: "There was huge excitement in the streets outside the Academy, this was the gig everyone wanted to see, and [we felt] The Clash were not going to disappoint us."

If some of the festive decorations had gone missing—"The punters stole them!" says an amused King—energy crackled in the air. UK reggae star Smiley Culture stepped to the mic to introduce the band: "For those of you who were here last night, it was wicked . . . Show them how much you love them . . . The Clash!" With that, White and Sheppard strode onstage.

This show was not as charmed as the previous evening. As White went to ignite "One More Time," his guitar malfunctioned. Frustrated, he stalked offstage, leaving a startled Sheppard to improvise. "I started playing a bit of the James Bond theme," the guitarist laughs. "Joe looked at me like I was crazy."

Despite the tricky start, Sheppard deftly brought the song around. White's instrument was fixed swiftly and he rejoined the storm of guitars, bass, and drums. Then Strummer lunged forward, even more emphatic than the night before: "I GOT TO GET A WITNESS / FOR ALL THIS BRUTALITY," he howled as the band accelerated. "YOU KNOW WE GOT A NEED TO, BROTHER / WE DON'T SEE IT ON THE TV!" Featuring a looser, spacier feel, this version of "One More Time" was almost as powerful as the previous night's rendition.

The downs and ups of the opening song foreshadowed the evening. While the band followed the earlier night's set list closely—

excising only "Fingerpoppin'," replaced by a chaotic take on "Brand New Cadillac"—technical glitches popped up here and there, and the band appeared a bit off at times. Regardless, the show was still powerful, and the crowd response fervent.

Standing still was rarely an option at Clash gigs, and this night was no exception. Proudman recalled the thrill of being "in the middle of a crush of a crowd moving backward and forward in excitement to the songs they loved. The band seemed to be enjoying it as much as the crowd. There was no Mick Jones, but no one in the audience cared as [we] shouted [our]selves hoarse."

Strummer paused during the show to acknowledge the question on many minds. After thanking opening acts Restless and Smiley Culture for "putting your money where your mouth is," Strummer had "another word as to the future: it's been two years since we made a record. Has anybody noticed that?"

When the crowd roared, the singer continued: "Yeah, me too. The fact is, we were waiting to see what was going to happen, we have to wait for things to go by. We've got a record, we're going to put it out in the new year, and we're going to be back." As the audience cheered again, Strummer raised his voice—and the stakes—even higher, yelling out, "We're going to make a comeback!" as the band launched into "Spanish Bombs."

While the words were passionate, they hardly reflected what had transpired over the past six months. Nor did they exactly speak the truth about the as-yet-unrecorded new album. As the band would soon discover, there can be a world of difference between having the songs for a new record and actually making it.

Yet picking up The Clash's fallen banner was clearly on Strummer's mind. After a surprise third encore sprang "Safe European Home" and "London Calling" on a startled audience already exiting the hall, Strummer called out one last time: "Great to see you here—we're coming back and better! Take a note, lads . . ."

While "London Calling" faded into the night, Strummer's words sent the crowd home with a promise and a mission. For two nights, this new Clash had gone back to war, a righteous burst of passion and artistry as 1984 drew to a close.

Now a powerful new album seemed within their grasp. Here was a chance to redeem the resurrected Clash; such art could touch hearts and minds, and maybe even help turn the world.

"I want you to show them how much you love them, because they are not going to be here tomorrow night, or the night after, here again," Smiley Culture had proclaimed on that second night at Brixton Academy, urging the crowd to "keep on calling them, man—The Clash, The Clash!"

This intro held more truth than Culture knew. In 1985, there would be a new record and live shows . . . but never again would The Clash play its hometown.

CHAPTER SEVEN
GONNA BE A KILLING

Kosmo Vinyl and Joe Strummer with Bernard Rhodes taking the lead. (Photo by Bob Gruen.)

Bernie wanted to reinvent The Clash. He had made up his mind that he was going to produce the record, hands down, and he wasn't going take, actually, much advice, or listen to anybody else.
—Michael Fayne

The trade union movement of Britain with a few notable exceptions has left this union isolated. We face not an employer but a government aided and abetted by the judiciary, the police, and the media. And, at this time, our people are suffering tremendous hardship.
—Arthur Scargill, March 3, 1985

ick Sheppard found it hard to believe either his eyes or his ears.

A session band stood before him, a makeshift version of "The Clash": Joe Strummer on guitar, Peter Howard on drums, and long-time Clash allies Mickey Gallagher and Norman Watt-Roy on keyboards and bass respectively.

While each musician was gifted in his own way, together they were anything but impressive. Sheppard recalls, "They were trying to arrange songs for the record, but it just sounded appalling . . . like bad pub rock."

With the triumphant miners' strike benefits over, the Clash camp had turned with laser focus to preparations for recording the long-awaited new album. Earlier plans of swiftly knocking out a raw punk record had been abandoned in favor of a far more amorphous process that veiled an immense—perhaps lunatic—ambition.

It seemed the height of insanity to bench Sheppard and White—as well as Simonon—for the duration of the sessions. Strummer had broken the bad news, but Sheppard had no doubt of its author: "I'm sure it was Bernie who decided that this group that he'd put together—me, Vince, Pete, Paul, and Joe—wasn't good enough to make a record live in the studio. So that was taken out off the table, and that void had to be filled. The record had to be made some other way."

The consequences of this development were staggering. After a solid year of work, of Sheppard, White, Simonon, and Howard playing together, honing the songs and their collective power as a platoon, a new outfit had to be suddenly fashioned from the pieces at hand. This "Clash" had to somehow revamp the songs and the sound for what needed to be a landmark musical advance.

Gallagher and Watt-Roy were obvious choices, given that they were skilled musicians who had worked together for years, including in past sessions with The Clash. Sheppard suspected that this gambit was Strummer's doing, a last-ditch attempt to salvage something of a live band sound and feel. The idea, however, stank of desperation—and sounded much the same.

Rhodes shared Sheppard's assessment, if for starkly different reasons. The manager had his own idea for the sessions, one that left little space for romantic notions of the "old-fashioned human and wood stuff" as Strummer had described his musical aspirations only months before. Not satisfied with control over the business, Rhodes seemed determined to insert himself into the creative process.

Strummer had tried to dodge the implications of benching his band by hastily assembling the new unit. But when Rhodes decided to—without asking—adjust the phasing on Gallagher's organ in pursuit of a less conventional, more "modern" sound, he short-circuited the whole idea. Once Gallagher realized what the unrepentant Rhodes had done, the keyboardist walked out, never to return.

Gallagher's exit served Rhodes's interests. With Strummer's ploy dispelled, the manager began to pursue his hyperambitious plan: nothing less than to painstakingly assemble a landmark record from components chosen by himself. Such an album would crown The Clash as one of rock's great bands with a breakthrough that strapped a punk engine onto a modern electronic chassis.

A skeptical Strummer had long been the main audience for Rhodes's brainstorming. His assent, however, could advance the project only so far. As such, the manager had struck upon Lucky Eight engineer Michael Fayne—with whom he had a warm, almost familial relationship—to be a key confederate.

Fayne would later wince at the recollection: "What Bernie was doing was flying to America, taping WBLS and all these radio shows playing hip-hop, and he was bringing it back. Bernie would make you listen to it for ten hours straight, man—seriously! He was trying to program me, 'cause that's what he would do, he would get in your head, and he'd get the message in. Then, he'd go: 'Right, now let's go buy a drum machine, let's try and bring that kind of flavor to The Clash.'"

This new obsession was simply the latest twist in a lifelong affection for R&B, soul, and other black musical forms, such as the vintage reggae records that Rhodes sold as a market trader in the seventies, alongside hand-printed silk-screened T-shirts he'd begun designing.

During his exile from The Clash, Rhodes had produced a handful of singles for Dexy's Midnight Runners, Subway Sect, and Johnny Britton. All appeared on Oddball Productions Limited, a company he had established in 1979. On returning to the fold in 1981, Rhodes had overseen remixes of "The Magnificent Seven" and "The Call-Up" that appeared, respectively, as "The Magnificent Dance" and "The Cool-Out." Both were credited to "Pepe Unidos," an alias for Rhodes, Strummer, and Simonon.

None of these ventures suggested an affinity for the stripped-down rebel rock the new Clash had vowed to tackle. Rhodes was someone who did not "want to be associated with mainstream rock and roll," former road manager Johnny Green says. "Bernard wasn't interested in that." He wanted to make something new.

Rhodes saw Fayne as key to this plan, the man to program the drum machine to his specifications. Fayne: "That's why Bernie was bringing in these hip-hop tunes, and trying to brainwash me with it—because he wanted more soldiers to push this down the band's throat, and move forward." Having dispensed with the guitarists and bass player, Rhodes was now preparing to sideline the drummer as well.

This prospect alarmed Fayne enough to register his concern: "I wouldn't even have used a drum machine, you know! It was so cold, and so removed to what the hell The Clash was about—it couldn't be any more alien. I, for the life of me, couldn't figure out why Bernie would go to that extreme. I remember trying to get into deeper conversation with Bernie about the whole situation and being told quite sharply, 'Listen, we are The Clash,' meaning him and Kosmo."

This shocking statement turned Strummer's populist anthem on its head, and defied any commonsense assessment of the band. But Rhodes was deadly serious. Fayne: "Bernie meant he and Kosmo were going to take the situation and make it work, regardless of what was going on. I thought that was quite arrogant, but it was kind of like, just letting me know who was boss."

This brusque rebuff was sufficient to get Fayne to fall into line, just in time to participate in the next step of Rhodes's plan. Fayne recalls, "Me and Bernie flew to Munich to find studios and to find personnel—I didn't understand it all at the time. It was my first trip out of the country, so I was just psyched to be out of the UK, you know? And we were in Munich, we went to loads of studios, and also went to see a few musicians. And it was only then that I realized that: 'Hold on a minute, there's something else going on here that I wasn't aware of.'"

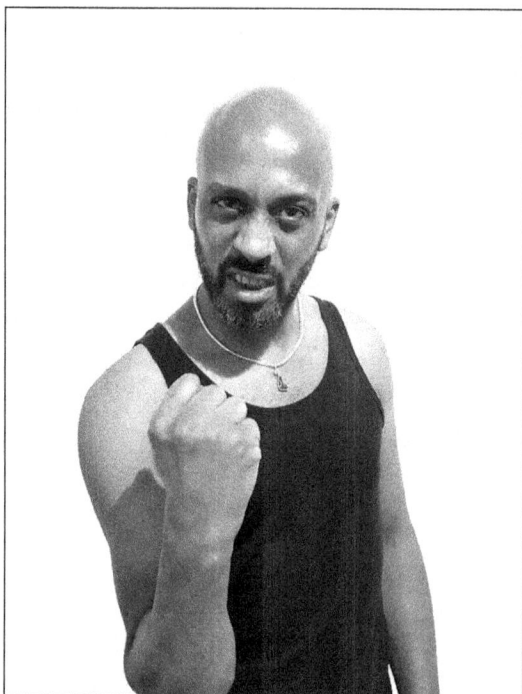

Michael Fayne still up for the fight, years after Weryton Studios baptism by fire.

The realization took Fayne's breath away: "Bernie wanted to reinvent The Clash. He had made up his mind that he was going to produce the record, hands down, and he wasn't going to take, actually, much advice, or listen to anybody else."

Sheppard would later attribute Rhodes's stance to panic: "What do we do with Mick Jones out of the picture?" However, it seems more born out of an ego-fueled contest with Malcolm McLaren, who had found success as an artist in his own right. Stretching in the same direction, Rhodes now saw himself as the one to build upon Strummer's songs, a mastermind producer like Menudo's Edgardo Díaz or Trevor Horn who had made UK hits like "Relax" and "Two Tribes" with Frankie Goes to Hollywood by replacing the band in the studio with session musicians, including, for a time, Gallagher and Watt-Roy.

Rhodes has never acknowledged any competition with McLaren, but it seems apparent. Quizzed about it in 2013 by filmmaker Danny Garcia, the indefatigable agitator responded that *he* was responsible for turning McLaren on to jazz, reggae, and hip-hop. Rhodes: "Fact is, I was producing records using different name tags well before (McLaren's '83 breakout hit) 'Buffalo Gals' was thought of."

While possibly true, such dismissals convinced few of those nearest to Rhodes. White: "[Bernie] wanted to be part of the band, really. He wasn't content with being just the manager. Malcolm had done this 'Duck Rock' thing, with hip-hop. I think he just wanted to get a bit of that, some artistic recognition."

Rhodes made a decision to remove the band from prying eyes and ears, away from its past haunts in London and New York. West Germany made sense on a number of levels. It was the homeland of electronic pioneers Kraftwerk and close enough physically to be practical, yet far enough psychically to provide the space—or, perhaps, the complete control—needed.

The vision was extraordinary. The Clash could at once retain its revolutionary message, advance musically, and continue its commercial ascent. Fayne: "In terms of The Clash aiming to be the biggest band in the world—I don't think Bernie Rhodes would start anything unless it was going to be that. Bernie always thought big. A lot of that driving force with The Clash being that was from Bernie."

To Rhodes, what was there not to like? The record label got a hit and the band got an artistically unassailable album, with radical politics front and center. He would be the director, orchestrating every piece into its proper spot in a vibrant panorama. Of course, human beings rarely like being treated like cogs in a machine, no matter how grand and wonderful. Never mind that there seemed little role for any of The Clash save Strummer—there was little room for *any* independent creative input in this vision at all. Even if successful, the human price tag of this approach was bound to be immense.

Such costs were already a harsh reality for the strikers and their families. Solidarity events like the Clash benefits and other outpourings of charity and cheer helped to warm what otherwise would have been a cold Christmas. In the new year, however, the weight of a day-to-day slog for survival with no end in sight set in.

A miner from Silverwood in South Yorkshire put it like this: "Before Christmas, people who were loyal to the union had something to look to. There were supporters bringing stuff down. We didn't feel so isolated. Now people are actually seeing the possibility of defeat."

With hope ebbing as spring loomed, the trickle of miners going back to work began to accelerate. Callinicos and Simons note, "The fact that there were no significant power cuts [as a result of the strike] was an important element in the demoralization." One disillusioned miner shared a take common among his brethren on strike: "We have been told all along: 'General Winter will do it for you.' Now General Winter is here, and it's not been done for us. We can see our backs are against the wall and we're saying: 'If we can't get out of this one way, why don't we get round the table for a compromise?'"

By now this was unlikely. Sensing blood in the water, Thatcher wanted unconditional surrender. Her hard-line stance horrified even some in her own party. Former Tory prime minister Harold MacMillan—while careful not to openly criticize Thatcher—took to the Parliament floor to commiserate with the suffering miners: "It breaks my heart to see what is happening in our country today. This terrible strike, by the best men in the world, who beat the Kaiser's and Hitler's armies and never gave in . . . the growing division of comparative prosperity in the south and an ailing north and Midlands. We used to have battles and rows [in this country], but they were quarrels. Now there is a new kind of wicked hatred."

To some, MacMillan spoke more urgently than the latest leader of the Labour Party, Neil Kinnock. Although a coal miner's son, Kinnock was also a rising politician who had no love for Arthur Scargill. He tried to walk a tightrope, cautiously supporting the miners while criticizing their leaders.

In part, this was driven by Kinnock's assessment of political reality, for he had been brought to his position by the landslide defeat of 1983. As Callincos and Simons point out, the election "reflected a massive exodus of working-class voters—only 39 percent of all trade unionists voted Labour in 1983." Since the electorate had moved to the right, so too must the Labour Party, Kinnock reckoned—and the new leader could ill afford to get caught up in a losing battle.

"From Kinnock's point of view, the miners' strike was a disaster," according to the SWP analysts. "It set up a roadblock across Labour's path rightward and allowed the Tories to attach to Kinnock precisely the sort of class-struggle politics which he was trying to drop. At the same time, a mere refusal to back the miners would bring down on Kinnock the wrath of the Labour left. So he sought to balance between the two sides in the dispute, calling for a ballot and supporting the strike; even-handedly denouncing both police and pickets; pressing the NUM into negotiations; and attacking Thatcher for her intransigence."

This sort of lukewarm support left the miners twisting in the wind. Feeling abandoned by the leadership of both the Labour Party and the broader trade union movement, the miners grew bitter and desperate. The majority of the NUM held out, still refusing to knuckle under to the Tories—but they were bleeding into the snow, with more of their brothers breaking down and drifting back. To cross a picket line was shameful and heartbreaking for a good union worker, but on one single day—"Black Monday," January 21—nearly six hundred returned to work.

At the same moment, a magnificent celebration unfolded across the Atlantic. Although frigid DC temperatures forced the cancellation of outdoor events, Republicans were marking Ronald Reagan's second inauguration in extravagant style. According to watchdog Senator William Proxmire—who awarded Reagan's inaugural committee one of his "Golden Fleece" awards marking the waste of public money—nearly sixteen million dollars of taxpayer money was spent for what appeared to be more the coronation of a king than a president.

If these glittering balls stood in sharp contrast to the suffering of the British miners, the juxtaposition of the homeless people outside the dazzling, bedecked halls was even more poignant. Refusing to join the revelry, the Reverend Jesse Jackson led seven hundred demonstrators in a counterinaugural protest march and prayer vigil near the White House in the snow and cold, delivering what UPI reporter Leon Daniel described as "a stem-winding demand for jobs and peace."

The protesters gathered in Farragut Square for a rally where the civil rights leader described President Reagan as a "Robin Hood in reverse, who takes from the poor to give to the rich." Then, with Jackson wearing a sign saying *Jobs Not Bombs*, they marched to within a block of the White House, where they kneeled in prayer before heading on for a final rally near the Washington Monument.

An especially powerful moment came when Jackson halted the march near the Monument grounds to chat with a homeless and jobless veteran named Benjamin Franklin Jones. Sitting on a steam grate and huddled under a blanket for warmth, Jones described his plight to Jackson—a telling illustration of the distance between the idealism manifest in the nearby monuments and a more ugly reality experienced by millions of Americans.

The encounter seemed to fire Jackson's oratory to new heights of outrage and eloquence. "There's a hole in Reagan's safety net," the minister proclaimed as protesters stood in the snow at the foot of Washington Monument. "There are more millionaires at the top and more poor people at the bottom." After attacking the inaugural festivities as "vulgar ostentation" filled with 'private airplanes, long limousines, and $25,000 dresses," Jackson returned to the hope-filled themes of his mentor, Martin Luther King Jr. "There will be peace in the valley!" Jackson shouted to the cheers of the crowd. "There will be food for the hungry!"

Jackson's words were just the sort that had often stirred Strummer into creative action, energized by a passionate belief he sought to emulate and embody. Hope was in short supply for the beleaguered Clash frontman, however, as it was for so many in his country. Just when Strummer was needed to defend his vision of a platoon banging out a blistering return to the original fire and fury of The Clash, the singer was oddly passive, even resigned in the face of Rhodes's coup d'état.

Fayne knew that the new musical direction "was definitely not coming from Joe." Strummer might have been open to it, as he saw punk as a wide-open spirit of defiant truth telling, rather than a narrow style. On the 1984 US tour, he had dismissed musical labels as meaningless with vigorous good humor: "I refuse to be boxed into anything . . . Punk, funk, junk, skunk—what the hell difference does it make? Does it speak the truth or is it a waste of time? That's my criteria. I couldn't care if it was a chorus of choir girls with tinker bells jangling. If it spoke the truth, then that would be it, and there would be no saying it wasn't."

This stance notwithstanding, Strummer had ejected Jones partly due to deep musical differences, including the use of electronic drums and synthesizers. Rhodes's vision should therefore have seemed a leap in the wrong direction. The singer, however, was in no shape to fight back. Fayne: "By then, Joe was punch drunk, you could see in his eyes that he just didn't have anything else to give. He would have gone along with anything Bernie said. 'Cause he was hemmed into that situation. He had all of these responsibilities; everyone's looking at him to do this, that, and the other. You've got Bernie going, 'You've gotta do this, you've gotta do that.' And to go through all that turmoil in his personal life too . . . It was an impossible situation."

Strummer made the fateful decision to engage fully in Rhodes's quest, even though it opposed his own vision, repeatedly aired across the US and Europe. As The Clash's face, its songwriter, and the voice that brought the tunes to life, Strummer was essential to Rhodes as no other band member was. Strummer was also the only one who could thwart the manager's new dream—but he did not.

The Baker argues that the singer viewed Rhodes as a surrogate paternal figure, a role that loomed even larger with the sudden loss of Strummer's actual father. Their relationship was charged and powerful, if not entirely healthy.

In George Du Maurier's 1895 novel *Trilby*, a stereotypical Jewish character named Svengali seeks to hypnotize, mold, and manipulate a young girl, all to turn her into a great singer. Rhodes clearly saw himself in this role vis-à-vis Strummer, once asserting, "He was nothing without me."

Asked by one of the authors of this book to clarify exactly what role he played artistically in The Clash, Rhodes drew a parallel to Andy Warhol's involvement with the Velvet Underground in the mid-1960s, saying, "Without me, you wouldn't *have* a group to be writing about." The combative manager sometimes even claimed to have single-handedly invented punk rock.

Such pretensions of grandeur could seem laughable, but were not entirely delusionary. Rhodes had been present at punk's creation, and played an indispensable role in assembling not only The Clash but, to some degree, the lead singer's persona. Strummer knew all of this, recognizing that, for all his myriad faults, Rhodes carried an undeniable spark of genius.

Perhaps Strummer's reluctance to split with his longtime mentor was, in part, because the singer was finally on the rebound creatively. By late December, Strummer had four more new songs beyond the trio debuted at the strike benefit shows. Strummer threw himself into polishing the songs, ones that expressed the hope and liberation he longed to feel, to make real for himself and others.

In particular, Nick Sheppard was impressed by "Movers and Shakers" and "Cool Under Heat," which he deemed "soul songs," anthems in the spirit of Curtis Mayfield. Taken together with the other new songs, "Life Is Wild" and "Play to Win," the quartet suggested that Strummer wanted to impart a sense of optimism amid one of the darkest moments for both himself and his country.

Fayne recognized the atmosphere created by the strike in the new tunes: "The strike had an impact on the whole country. If you're a political writer, you have to echo [what is] around you.

Otherwise, you don't make sense. So it's depressing, right? The strike really showed the disparity between rich and the poor, the powerful and the weak. If you're a writer, you go, 'Let's try to bridge that gap!'"

Fayne knew this wasn't easy—and that Strummer keenly felt Jones's absence. Strikingly, Strummer seems to be exhorting himself as much as the Clash audience in these songs. They became a way to cheat the darkness, to shake off the shroud, to somehow break through to the other side.

Although any role in the upcoming recording remained unclear— Rhodes was seeking session guitarists to supplement Strummer's limited skills—Sheppard and the others helped demo the songs in advance of the journey to Munich.

Sheppard laughs at the recollection. "It was typical Bernie! On Christmas Eve, I was ordered into Lucky Eight to overdub guitar onto 'Life Is Wild' and some of the other newer tracks." While Rhodes had issued the directives, he was scarcely seen. To the musicians and engineer, this was all for the best. Fayne: "When we did the demos, Bernie was hardly around . . . It was a case of the band coming in and laying them down." In the absence of the oft-dictatorial manager, Sheppard recalls, "It all went very well, and Joe was very pleased with the results."

Such moments gave a glimmer of what might have been, had Strummer held his ground, and the original "new Clash" been allowed to exercise its collective power. "Play to Win," with a chorus that evoked Strummer's love for an iconic American pioneer spirit, seemed a bit incomplete. But the others were potent additions to what was now a bulging portfolio of new songs. All exuded a sense of defiance.

Fayne, however, harbored no illusions: "Bernie knew when it got to the actual recording session he was going to step in and really take over . . . He had heard the songs, and had kind of picked the ones we were going to do in Munich."

Some of the neo-Clash's best songs—the monumental "In the Pouring Rain," as well as "Jericho" and "Sex Mad War"—inexplicably would not be chosen, perhaps because Rhodes did not see them as easily adaptable to his new approach. Whatever the reason, their exclusion hinted at a possible disaster lurking.

Meanwhile, a catastrophe of far greater magnitude still loomed. With Reagan's reelection, few saw any obvious exit from the nuclear standoff between the two superpowers. The American president could hardly be expected to back down, having earned four more years to pursue his aims.

For its part, the Soviet leadership seemed a bit stuck, with war hawks ascendant, partly thanks to Reagan's aggressive rhetoric. As power transitioned from one ancient, ailing leader to another—Brezhnev to Andropov to Chernenko—the course toward a devastating East-West collision remained unchanged.

Behind the scenes, however, Reagan was feeling chastened. While he did not yet know about the near miss averted by Stansilav Petrov's diligence, briefings he had received after the Able Archer 83 maneuvers made him realize, perhaps for the first time, that the Soviet Union genuinely feared a US first strike.

This assessment was buttressed by information that Thatcher's government received on Able Archer from a highly placed Russian spy, Oleg Gordiesvsky. Thatcher aide Rodric Braithwaite explained, "What Gordievsky made clear was that the rhetoric that she and Reagan were using was terrifying." The informant's report, Braithwaite noted, "gave an insight into the way officials and senior people in the Soviet system felt about the Western threat to them. Reagan and Thatcher had only ever thought the other way, about the Soviet threat to them."

The significance of this shift was huge. As analyst Peter Burt wrote in 2013, "Previously secret documents obtained under the Freedom of Information Act reveal that, rather than climaxing in a nuclear Armageddon, the [Able Archer 83] moment became a turning point for Thatcher's cabinet, pushing [them] to rethink their relationship with the Soviet Union." It also did so for Reagan himself.

US words and actions had almost sparked global holocaust. According to Burt, "Thatcher herself apparently delivered the chilling message to President Reagan, hoping to convince him to moderate his rhetoric and actions. Gordievsky's analysis was an epiphany for Reagan—who met the spy personally—convincing him that the time had come for a new relationship with the Soviets."

Wide-ranging arms-control talks had been arranged for January 1985 in Geneva. The jockeying for position beforehand, however, suggested any breakthrough was unlikely. Reagan made it clear that his "Star Wars" initiative was not up for discussion. The Soviets, in turn, said that without progress on this front, no advance could be expected elsewhere. The momentum toward global conflagration seemed likely to remain unchecked.

It was unclear how either side could back down. This was the danger inherent in the incendiary rhetoric that both Thatcher and—especially—Reagan had used. Then, at this critical juncture, a new player was introduced into the mix.

On December 16, 1984, Margaret Thatcher welcomed a rising Russian leader to her country home, Chequers. Little known outside of his country, Mikhail Gorbachev was from a younger generation than the old-line Soviet leadership. With an engaging personality that distinguished him from typical Eastern Bloc apparatchiks, Gorbachev had won growing praise from Soviet watchers who suspected that present leader Konstantin Chernenko was terminally ill.

Gorbachev had signaled his top priority the day before in remarks upon his arrival at Heathrow Airport. "Opportunities for the prevention of nuclear war exist," the Soviet insisted. "These opportunities must be used to the full."

At Chequers, Gorbachev pressed this agenda. Years later, he described how "I unfolded in front of Margaret a diagram divided into one thousand squares. I said that if all nuclear weapons stockpiled primarily by the US and the Soviet Union were divided into one thousand parts, then even one of them would be enough to cause irreparable damage to all life on earth. Why continue the race, what is the point of this insane competition?"

Thatcher responded that the arms race had been forced upon the West by the Soviet Union's buildup, and its failure to renounce world revolution as its aim. Gorbachev countered, "It was the US that had started it all—it invented the nuclear bomb and used it in Japan, when there was no military need for it, just the political calculus." The US drove this deadly race, Gorbachev concluded. Thatcher demurred, arguing the West simply sought to deter aggression.

While a dogged defender of the Soviet system, Gorbachev exhibited a sense of humor that left Thatcher astonished. The Russian leader later recounted, "At some point, our conversation became so tense that some of those present thought that it would have no continuation. And then I said to Margaret that I had no instructions from the Politburo to persuade her to join the Communist Party of the Soviet Union." Grasping the joke, Thatcher broke into laughter, her smile suggesting that a connection of lasting importance was being forged.

For five hours, Gorbachev and Thatcher contended. At the end of the session, Thatcher was left heartened. In a back-channel note to Reagan, the Tory prime minister relayed, "I certainly found [Gorbachev] a man one could do business with," adding, "I actually rather liked him."

Communist and capitalist find common ground: Gorbachev and Thatcher, December 16, 1984. (Photographer unknown.)

✳ ✳ ✳

Even as die-hard capitalist and committed Communist were finding common ground, relationships within The Clash were deterio-
rating dangerously. By January 1985, the action had relocated from
London to Munich's Weryton Studios. Fayne recalls, "Bernie really
liked the studio manager and the vibe of the place. It was a little
sterile for a punk record, I thought—it was ultra-clean, they were
ultra-modern, but I was just glad to be along for the ride."

Working with Norman Watt-Roy and various German session
musicians, Fayne and Rhodes quickly began constructing rhythm
tracks for the songs slated for inclusion. Meanwhile, Strummer had
returned to Spain, this time with Gaby Salter and their daughter
Jazz. Jesús Arias was struck by the difference in Joe's mood: "He
was really happy and upbeat, excited for the album to be recorded."

This positive attitude would soon be tested. Once in Munich,
Strummer realized the reality of the tortuous process he had accepted. Many of his songs needed to be torn apart and reconstructed
in radically new ways, piece by piece, with session musicians. Progress was agonizing.

Rhodes was proving no more amiable in his new role, and the
atmosphere was tense. Simultaneously laughing and cringing,
Fayne recalls, "We found these German musicians—drummers,
string arrangers, all sorts of people—it was crazy. One day we had
a shitload of these people into the session . . . I actually don't know
what happened to this day, because it was so chaotic!"

Given the scope of Rhodes's vision, some turmoil was unavoidable, but Fayne felt the manager-cum-producer's naïveté made it
worse: "Bernie would have an idea, and he'd think, just because
you have an idea, it's going to work! Okay, you do have to have an
idea, right? But then, you have to construct a framework around
it, in order for it to become something of substance. And he didn't
bother with any of that. He'd just sort of shout, 'Right, you do this
and you do that,' and, 'You do that, and you do this,' you know?
And it was just chaos."

Rhodes's drive was undeniable—but the path he had chosen
was treacherous. Fayne: "He had this utopian vision of The Clash
becoming an even bigger band. If he could just modernize it, and

spruce it up a bit, he could create something new. But if you have something that works, if you want to 'future-ize' it, you tweak it. You don't fucking come in a room and paint everything, and then decide the curtains are wrong. You don't, because then you lose the people that love you for who you are." This sensible take was lost on Rhodes.

The Clash had not made its name by following common sense, though—and Rhodes was no mere manager. He had always been part of the band. Years later, an older and wiser Strummer acknowledged, "Whatever The Clash was, it had a lot to do with Bernie." Not all was wasted effort. Rhodes was slowly gathering his team, including enlisting Weryton engineer Hermann Weindorf—whom he dubbed "Young Wagner"—to play keyboards and synthesizer.

When none of the German guitarists proved adequate, Sheppard was suddenly and unceremoniously summoned. Although the guitarist was glad to be included after all, any relief he felt dissipated under a deluge of bad news. Sheppard: "I'd come up with these guitar lines in the demo sessions with Joe, but once we got to Munich, they were dismissed out of hand by Bernie . . . because I'd come up with them: 'You came up with that, it can't be any good.'"

The brutal dismembering of the group to which Sheppard had given so much of himself over the past fourteen months had also left him demoralized: "By the time I got to Munich, I didn't feel like I was in The Clash at all. I didn't feel like I was part of any commando gang that was going to take over the world with rebel rock. I just kind of went with a guitar and no idea of what I was going to be faced with."

Meanwhile, three of the five nominal Clash members remained in London, unsure if their services would ever be required.

For Simonon, this was neither unusual nor necessarily unwanted. His bass skills were solid but he was hardly a virtuoso, and he had often absented himself from past sessions, especially as Jones's musical ambitions had grown. In this case, he had intentionally stepped back, explaining, "Mick was in charge during *Combat Rock*, so I thought Joe should have his chance." This made some sense—except that Strummer was not actually running the show.

For the others, the exclusion was insult added to injury. Sheppard knew the cost of Rhodes's constant manipulations: "Things got incredibly surreal, and dysfunctional. Me and Vince, Pete, probably Paul as well, and I think Joe—we all started feeling very divorced from any semblance of a group."

This may have been precisely Rhodes's intention, for any group solidarity could have foiled his plans. It's true that The Clash had never put much stock in recording in a conventional way. While both their first record and *London Calling* had been banged out as a unit, this was the exception rather than the rule. Little of *Sandinista!* had involved all four members playing at the same time. Indeed, key bits were done by hired hands, such as the iconic bass riff of "Magnificent Seven," which was written and played by Norman Watt-Roy.

The current situation was unprecedented, however. Rhodes was neither a trained musician nor a very experienced producer. A cornerstone punk ethic was that "anyone can do it, you learn by doing." But rarely had anyone with such a thin musical background taken such a central role in a band as popular as The Clash. Fayne: "At the time, I wasn't a producer myself, I was barely an engineer, but even I thought it was *crazy*. I thought it was suicide." If Rhodes's stance was "punk," it was reckless as well as destructive to the cohesion of the actual band.

Probably no one felt the sense of betrayal more keenly than White. Ground down by Rhodes's never-ending mind games, the musician was almost relieved to skip the sessions. Even so, White had worked hard to sharpen his guitar skills, as was obvious by the growing power of his live fireworks with Sheppard. To be excluded was not simply a blow to his ego, but just another brick in the wall separating him from Strummer, who he had seen as the band's rightful leader.

White was already incensed by the singer's collaboration in Rhodes's "divide and conquer" strategy. His disgust had been made worse when, by chance, he saw Strummer lighting up a spliff in secret after one of the miners' shows. "So what was that NO DRUGS POLICY he was always banging on about to the thousands of fans at shows and radio interviews and rags?" White later wrote. "He's the star and nobody really cares about being TRUE to any PRINCIPLE whatever."

Howard was feeling similarly. At the same Brixton show, Rhodes had corralled the band for a meeting and suddenly asked them what they each would do with a million pounds. "I suppose it was intended to get us to think about what our priorities were," Howard related years later. "But it came off in an ugly way, as generally was the case with Bernie."

Like the others, Howard recognized this as the setup for a brutal "self-criticism" session. No longer willing to toe the Clash line, White gave an intentionally cynical response involving girls, booze, and a sea cruise—and got the lashing he fully expected. Likewise, Sheppard chose to tweak the lion's tail by joking that he would use it to get his somewhat protruding ears done. "I was giving Bernie the needle, as he had gotten a nose job," Sheppard laughed later.

Perhaps the cheekiness of Sheppard's remark gave the manager pause, for Rhodes didn't rise to the bait. According to White, Sheppard went on to talk about creating a nonprofit recording studio to help new bands. As the rest of the band gave suitable answers, the meeting wound up without further eruptions. White recalls groaning inside at Strummer's idea to split the money between a revolutionary group—seemingly Nicaragua's Sandinistas, still facing a US-backed "secret" war—and the workers of Corby, a devastated UK steel town.

When White bemoaned Rhodes's query and Strummer's response to Sheppard and Howard, the drummer exploded. "Don't you get it, Vince, don't you fucking get it?" White remembers Howard as shouting. "Don't you realize Joe already has a million quid? Whatever he wanted to do with a million pounds, he's done it!" Recalling Strummer's comfortable home off Portobello Road—bought outright, with cash, Strummer had told White—the guitarist realized Howard was right.

The longtime squatter agonized over such contradictions. Still, this was little comfort for those still on meager weekly wages, treated like expendable cogs in the Clash machine. Strummer was also hurting, under immense pressure—but that didn't make anything better for those he failed to protect. Howard and White came to a bitter conclusion: the singer simply couldn't be trusted. "Joe was sparking off in all directions," White recalls. "The separation between him and the band was complete. Separation was everywhere. There was no healing it."

Such divisions were everywhere in the not-so-United Kingdom. Perhaps the most painful were erupting in the mining villages themselves, as family members turned against one another over whether to stay the course of the strike.

As the strike entered its eleventh month, agony and deprivation was growing daily, as was the number of miners breaking rank and going back to work. Any realistic hope of victory was ebbing with each defecting miner. The NUM knew the strike was becoming unsustainable. Yet to surrender meant the loss of tens of thousands of jobs, most likely the death of their industry and their communities.

As the noose tightened in early 1985, the *Financial Times* announced, "The mineworkers' strike, as a living entity with some sap left in it, is over." The "end game" was now in motion, the paper said: "Mr. MacGregor and the prime minister have an aim . . . to ensure that the end of the dispute makes it wholly clear that 'Scargillism,' which they define as a mixture of industrial coercion allied to revolutionary ambitions, must be seen to fail, and fail utterly."

Yet, as Callincos and Simons argue, "The Tories weren't invulnerable. Early 1985 saw turmoil on the world's financial markets, as the dollar soared and the pound sterling sunk lower and lower." The *Financial Times* admitted, "Anxiety about the oil price and the rising dollar may have triggered the sterling crisis, but it seems fairly clear that the effects of the miners' strike played an important part." To the SWP duo, "The costs of the strike had been enormous . . . £4 billion seemed like a minimum—far more than Thatcher had spent to reconquer the Falkland Islands."

The war comparison was apt, and the mining communities had borne the brunt of the conflict. The battle-weary country was growing unsettled by the suffering, and the government was nervous about its sliding popularity. According to Callincos and Simons, "A MORI opinion poll published in the *Sunday Times* on February 10 showed Labour and Tories running neck and neck. Only 34 percent of those polled thought Thatcher 'a capable leader,' her lowest rating since June 1981, and 60 percent thought the government were handling the miners' strike 'badly.'"

This is why those authors argue, "Had the NUM held firm, the government's nerve might have cracked, and the miners at least won terms which secured the reinstatement of [fired] strikers. As it was, the nerves of a section of the miners' leaders cracked first." This may be too harsh, for the NUM itself was on the verge of splintering, with a Thatcher-sponsored breakaway union rising in Nottinghamshire, and the rank and file increasingly despondent and divided.

Scargill used his little remaining leverage to try to avert the worst outcome: the union accepting the government's right to close mines for loosely defined "economic reasons," i.e., not making enough profit. As Callincos and Simons point out, "If the NUM was faced with defeat, there was more than one sort of defeat. One was devastation—unconditional surrender by the leadership, and the disintegration of the union as a fighting organization. The other was a defeat in which the miners held together, preserving their organization and fighting spirit."

The emotional mettle of The Clash was under similarly extreme stress. The disaffection of White and Howard lessened slightly when Rhodes beckoned them to join the rest in Munich in February. The manager did not want to spring for airfare, however, so the duo had to ride in an equipment van with no working heater through an unusually frigid German winter.

"Maybe that was one of Bernie's punishments," White laughs. "We didn't know what we did [that was so] bad. And suddenly, me and Pete were driving across Europe. I'll never forget it—it was in January, with subzero temperatures, the fucking van froze up. The radiator froze, everything froze, the van was totally freezing! And we arrived there, in six feet of snow."

Barely escaping frostbite, Howard and White arrived only to

find themselves twiddling their thumbs, waiting in the hotel room for a call that might never come. When, at last, White—but not Howard—was asked to the studio, he soon came to regret making the trip. Initially impressed by the progress on recording, White swiftly found himself in a Kafkaesque mind fuck, where nothing was ever good enough and endless retakes were required, punctuated by Rhodes's tirades.

White was not alone in his assessment of the seventh hell unleashed at Weryton. Fayne felt the heat too, seeking to satisfy Rhodes's idiosyncratic directives: "The sessions were very labored, you couldn't really find the vibe. It wouldn't have been so painful if it wasn't so contrived. It was awful—I felt like I was a soldier involved in a massacre, who was saying, 'I'm only obeying orders.'"

If freedom helps fan a creative spark into flames, such liberty was hard to find. Fayne: "I wasn't doing the work on my own. I had Bernie sitting there. He'd go, 'Right, we need some of that.' So I would program that in: *dah-dah-dah*. Then Bernie would say, 'How about if we do this and that?' I didn't have carte blanche."

Sheppard has a similar take: "Bernie was out of control, nothing was good enough. And when he didn't like something, he's going to tell you in the nastiest way he can." Unlike Fayne, however, Sheppard didn't dismiss the concept out of hand: "Bernie was making a brave attempt to do something. I don't think he thought he was Mick. He was trying to make a record with everything in it. He wanted to make a punk record and a rap record and a modern record."

Yet such a vision required expertise as well as passion. Sheppard: "He didn't have the tools necessary to do it. As Joe said, he was trying to create something: 'Can this thing be packaged? Can this thing be invented? Can you do this?' Bernie's idea was good—but it was being done by someone without a musical bone in his body, and no interest in listening to anyone else."

Nonetheless, granted Sheppard, "A good idea executed poorly can be better than a bad idea with all the technical skill in world."

However powerful Rhodes's concept might have been, his ultracontrolling follow-through was further shredding the band's fabric. "I was trying very hard to arrange things, I did rough mixes, got very involved," Sheppard says. But as the sessions dragged on and on, past March and into April, the guitarist got ground down: "It was like a war of attrition, you just kind of gave up. I had no critical faculties left. I just did as I was told, stopped asking if it was good or bad. It wouldn't have made an ounce of difference anyway, because no one would have listened."

Fayne felt the same—and saw a similar exhaustion growing in Strummer: "He was definitely putting on a brave face, 'cause I know Joe—when he's happy, you know, he's got this laugh, which is so contagious. He's like a little boy, you know, his face would light up, and he's got this naughty smile. And that was gone. And when you're done, you're done—and Joe was done." Even the ostensible bandleader was not exempt from Rhodes's mania, as White explains: "Joe was under his tutorship—he sent Joe for singing lessons!"

Nonetheless, Strummer refused to break with Rhodes. Disgusted with the endless not-so-merry-go-round, Sheppard unloaded all of his angst to Strummer over drinks. "I was going on about I was done with it, that I couldn't take it anymore," says the guitarist. "And Joe stopped me and said, 'No, I don't want to hear it, I have got to believe in this. I've got to believe this is the right thing.'"

Utter, unassailable belief is one of the most powerful forces on earth—though it can still be vanquished. And so it was when, on March 3, Arthur Scargill emerged from Congress House, the London headquarters of the Trades Union Council. Cheers from gathered unionists erupted as he walked to the podium. But when Scargill announced that the NUM executive board had voted 98-91 to return to work without an agreement, shock waves sailed through the crowd.

No matter how unlikely victory seemed, the idea of surrender smelled like betrayal. Even at this late date, pockets of resistance remained, notably in South Wales, where just 6 percent of miners had gone back, and the act of crossing a picket line was enough to make an outcast of anyone who dared to risk it.

From a strategic perspective, however, there no longer seemed any point in denying reality. More than half of the NUM membership had returned to work in February, amid gleeful threats from MacGregor: "People are now discovering the price of insubordination and insurrection. And boy, are we going to make it stick."

While Scargill had argued in the board meeting to stay the course, he had lost the debate. Now this hero of the working class was booed and jeered by his own. The BBC reported that cries of "no no no!" rang out, and "grown men were in tears, [while] others chanted, 'We will not go back to work!'"

The labor leader's voice was ragged with emotion: "We have decided to go back for a whole range of reasons. One of the reasons is that the trade union movement of Britain with a few notable exceptions has left this union isolated. Another reason is that we face not an employer but a government aided and abetted by the judiciary, the police, and the media. And, at this time, our people are suffering tremendous hardship."

The NUM had held fast on principle, refusing to accept the closure plans. But the union could not prevent them and would not cause more pain to their loyalists for no gain. With this decision, something precious had died—and it was nothing less that Britain's post–World War II socialist dream.

All that remained were the eulogies. Years later, Tony Benn, often thought of as Labour's left-wing conscience, spoke in praise of the miners' struggle: "They were skilled and courageous men who had built the prosperity of Britain. They were treated like criminals by Mrs. Thatcher . . . It's a story that will never be forgotten." Labour MP Dennis Skinner added, "It was an honorable dispute. It was the only strike I can recall that wasn't about pay but was about saving jobs for other people."

Neil Kinnock also felt the pain. Later he said, "I was deeply saddened by everything in those long months, especially around Christmastime 1984, when things were really bad and it was obvious the miners were going down to a completely undeserved defeat and were still sticking it out. You could not fail to be impressed by the sheer guts of that. It was desperately depressing."

Nonetheless, the Labour leader placed the blame at Scargill's door: "Once he refused to [hold a national ballot], the strike was doomed, because sympathy action by other groups of workers was always going to be limited, and there was always going to be division in the miners' ranks. And a divided force made Thatcher's job of hammering the miners much easier."

Kinnock's relatively neutral stance also facilitated Thatcher's assault, however. While Scargill made mistakes, time would prove his central claim: Thatcher aimed to close not simply twenty mines, but seventy-five in total, a plan that would herald the beginning of the end for the UK coal industry. If not for this lie—never confronted, much less countered by Kinnock, who busied himself criticizing Scargill—there is little doubt that the miners would have voted for the strike, a strike they would likely have won.

Thatcher was able to use brute force and deception, marshaling the might of the police, the courts, and most of the media to accomplish perhaps the most crucial aim of her second term: breaking the power of the National Union of Mineworkers. This was a massive win, but one gained without integrity.

If something akin to murder had happened, the NUM was determined to stand proud. On March 5, the vast majority of striking miners returned to work, often marching in step with brass bands, carrying their union banners. A few die-hards continued to hold out for several weeks, before grudgingly giving in. More than seven hundred miners had been sacked over the course of the year, and scores of others faced "riot" charges that might mean life imprisonment.

While it was bitter for the miners not to be able to protect such members from retaliation, as Callincos and Simons write, "Whenever they returned, the miners did so defiantly and with pride. They were beaten, but they had held out for a year against the worst that the state could inflict on them . . . The miners had, in A.J. Cook's words, fought the 'legions of hell.' They, and the women who had endured with them the longest major strike in British history, were all heroes, every one of them . . . They deserved better than what was in store for them."

The prognosis was not hopeful. The *Guardian*—one of the few major UK papers to be supportive of the miners—mourned the consequences that would follow: "The defeat of the miners will be seen as a landmark in the decline of the industrial working class and advocates of political strike action. It is unlikely that the unions will again mount such a general and coordinated challenge to the authority of the state . . . Union strength and membership was in decline well before the miners' strike, and that process is likely to accelerate."

Scargill remained at the head of the NUM, but the union's back was broken. Having brought the NUM to heel, Thatcher was now free to pursue her "free market" agenda largely unfettered. Still, bitter rage simmered across broad swaths of Great Britain. Those who felt treated like trash vowed never to forget this humiliation, to find a way to take their revenge somehow, someday.

The same week that Scargill's star was falling, another was rising. As suspected, Chernenko had been deathly ill, and passed away on March 11. Mikhail Gorbachev was elected general secretary of the Soviet Communist Party only three hours later. At age fifty-four, he was the party's first leader to have been born after the Russian Revolution of 1917. Unbeknown to Gorbachev's colleagues and the world, another Russian revolution was beginning.

As this new era dawned, the 1985 Clash revolution was grinding forward. While a couple of the dozen songs slated for the album had escaped relatively unscathed, most were radically rearranged, even rewritten, featuring electronic drums, synthesizers, and an eclectic array of sampled sounds, as well as guitar and bass.

The result could seem like a jumble. Sheppard: "Bernie didn't know when to stop. His idea of producing was to cram every conceivable space with something—and he had forty-eight tracks to work with!" Given the painstaking layering of the songs, assembled bit by bit, with each instrument overdubbed separately, it was hard to get a clear sense of the success of the sessions.

One outcome was obvious, however: The Clash had never been so divided, demoralized, or exhausted. "Making the record," Sheppard recalls, "was quite a long—and pretty horrendous—process. It seemed like an age and I was there for most of it. Joe was there for all of it, and I was the second-longest-serving member, if you like, followed by Vince, followed by Pete and Paul."

Late in the game, an unexpected bone was tossed to this ragged pack: a minisession with Howard and Simonon. As all five musicians stood together for the first time in months, the unit swiftly knocked out two tracks for use as B sides.

"Sex Mad War" and "Out of Control" were now "Sex Mad Roar" and "Do It Now." Both were outstanding songs, with revamped lyrics that showed Strummer's perfectionism as a wordsmith. The former also featured a new coda with eerie interplay between Sheppard and White, hinting at the unit's untapped potential.

But the session was rushed and unsatisfying, with no chance to overdub or further hone the tunes. The dense, claustrophobic mix made it hard to pick out many of Strummer's words. Above all, it begged an uncomfortable question: why were these and other blockbuster songs relegated to the back drawer—or left undocumented—instead of forming the heart of the planned album?

This was the closest the band would ever get to Strummer's original vision for the album: the punk platoon unleashed, guns blazing, for posterity. That idea had been the light on the horizon, the beacon toward which the new Clash had been straining, shoulders to the wheel. It had been their chance to refute the critics and redeem all the frustration of the past sixteen months. The sessions had turned darkly bitter, an experience as likely to kill dreams as to realize them.

The tension in the band was building toward an explosion. In late April, just as the sessions were winding up, it finally came. Sheppard: "On the last day of recording, I was doing some backing vocals. Bernie was on my case again, and I really fucking lost it with him, told him he was a piece of shit, and all that. I really had a go, something I'd never done before . . . It was quite emotional."

Sheppard's rage cut through the thick wall of diktat, silencing the irascible manager. "Kosmo was there at the time, at this meeting or conversation where I'd lost it with Bernie," Sheppard says. "And he suggested that we go off as a group and do something, because we hadn't been a group for so long."

The idea struck a chord. Sheppard: "So me and Joe went out for a walk around Munich, which we really hadn't done that whole time. We bought some oranges, ate them, and talked. Out of the blue, one of us said, 'Well, the only thing we can do is go busking. What else are we going to do, go and pick fruit or paint pictures? We're a group, let's just fuck off and go busking.' So that's what we decided, that's the thing that we would do as a group. We'd go off busking."

The idea seemed off-the-wall for a massive band like The Clash, an exceedingly chancy prospect. No matter, a soul-weary Sheppard thought—as likely as not, it would turn out to be more loose talk. "We went back to England—I had another fucking run-in with Bernie at the airport—and I just went home to my flat in Wapping and said, 'Thank Christ that's over.' And then Joe said, 'Right, let's go.' To his credit, he was like, 'Yeah, we're gonna go do it.'"

The Clash was about to embark on its final tour, a last stand the likes of which the rock world had never seen: a ragged, passionate offensive, waged with simple weapons amid the ruins of the band's—and the country's—shattered unity.

CHAPTER EIGHT

MOVERS AND SHAKERS COME ON

The Clash and friends take to the streets on their way to Ripon and St. John's College, York, England, May 8, 1985. (Photo courtesy of the *York Press Gazette & Herald*.)

We feel we were getting involved in release a record, go on a tour, do this, do that. We began to ask ourselves, What is this all about? And we decided that if we can't get it with three acoustic guitars and a pair of drumsticks, on a walking tour of England, then . . . We are looking for an answer. We want to know if rock and roll still means anything. This is our attempt to find out if it does.
—Joe Strummer, May 9, 1985

During fiscal year 1985, no funds available to the Central Intelligence Agency, the Department of Defense, or any other agency or entity of the United States . . . may be obligated or expended for the purpose of which would have the effect of supporting, directly or indirectly, military or paramilitary operations in Nicaragua by any nation, group, organization, movement, or individual.
—The Boland Amendment

ive figures stood under a bridge next to a canal. As the musicians faced one another, strumming guitars, moving in and out of shadows, an occasional ray of morning sun glinted off their black leather jackets.

This barely secluded spot in the open air seemed an unlikely rehearsal space for one of the world's most popular rock bands. Nonetheless, The Clash had found itself there, in Nottingham, where the north of England begins.

Armed with acoustic guitars and drumsticks—tapped vigorously on the bridge's bricks by Peter Howard—the unit ran through several of its own songs, plus rock standards like "Come on Everybody" and "Stepping Stone." A few moments later, having honed their skills sufficiently for the adventure ahead, the musicians left the shadows, heading for a nearby shopping district.

This was not the only odd locale to recently host The Clash. The previous afternoon the quintet had stood on the shoulder of the M1, one of the UK's main motorways, thumbs out, seeking to hitch a ride. They made unusual-looking hitchhikers. As Howard laughed later, "We all turned up wearing leather jackets, leather jeans—we must have looked like the fucking Village People!"

If the men were arguably hilarious in appearance, the distance between their Woody Guthrie-esque mission and the rock-star attire mirrored the creative tension in the unit's founding ambition: to be simultaneously the biggest band in the world and sociopolitical revolutionaries.

The mission's intent was serious. Recording the new album in such a dictatorial way had strained the band's fragile unity. Even Rhodes seemed to recognize that it was critical to restore some modicum of internal cohesion. While hardly converted to a more sensitive style of management, the Clash kingpin knew that the record he was shepherding would need a band behind it.

Rhodes's assent was duly acknowledged at a band meeting shortly after the return from Munich. As if reflecting the unsettled nature of the group itself, Rehearsal Rehearsals was now history. This longtime Clash stronghold had been lost, under pressure from upscale development planned for the Camden Market area. So the gathering itself took place in yet another peculiar context: a posh Kensington Hilton hotel meeting room.

During the confab, Rhodes was so amenable to a shared band "holiday" that White later credited the concept as "one of Bernie's better ideas." The controlling manager actually had not initiated this trek, however, and was no doubt nervous about the band being on its own, out of his grasp.

Strummer later told UK rock writer Jon Savage that Rhodes "sensed that The Clash had become too prey to his ideas, he realized he had it under his thumb too much, and there wasn't a lot of life in there. What he expected us to do was to go up north, somewhere like Bradford, and live in a house while we did, I don't know what." But what Rhodes "expected" was not foremost in the band's mind. Strummer: "We just went up and kept moving."

A picture of Jesus had been prominently featured at the back of The Clash's US tour bus, not far from a huge black, red, and gold banner reading, *REBEL PUNK*. This latest trek was in the spirit of that itinerant peasant rabble-rouser. "Won't take nothing for my journey now," goes the civil rights anthem "Keep Your Eyes on the Prize," echoing Christ's admonition to his disciples: "Take nothing for the journey except a walking stick—no bread, no bag, no money in your belts."

So it was with The Clash, more or less, which was making a leap of faith of its own. "We went to a pub on the North Cascade Road in London," Howard recalls. "We had consumed an inordinate amount of alcohol—and Joe said, 'We're going right now.' And I said, 'We can't do this, I don't have a bank card, I don't have a credit card.'" But, as Howard knew well enough, turning back wasn't an option.

White recalls, "We were allowed to take ten pounds as starting money. No more. No bank cards. The rest was up to you. You had to survive on what you earned, playing in the streets. If you couldn't make it like that, you didn't deserve to call yourselves a band." Though it later turned out that apparently both Strummer and Simonon brought credit cards as a last resort, the spartan nature of the endeavor was real enough. Most importantly, all would share in any hardships.

Feet would not be sufficient locomotion for this journey, however, and the band was proving to be a hard sell to passing drivers. Tired of languishing on the roadside, the group made a tactical decision to split up in order to seem less imposing. White explains, "Joe told us to meet at the pub nearest the train station in Nottingham." The musicians duly fanned out down the road.

Now on his own, White was aware of the absurdity of the situation: "The world-famous Clash, stadium rockers, standing with guitars, our thumbs out, one by one trying to flag rides holding out bits of cardboard!" He was the first to be plucked from the roadside.

While White's journey proved uneventful, Howard had a more entertaining time: "We are all decked out in these leathers, right? The guy who picked me up looked me up and down, then basically spent the whole trip to Nottingham kind of hitting on me: 'Well, you must have had a homosexual experience in your life . . . Maybe when you were at school . . . ?' And I was going, 'No, really, honestly, actually, I haven't.' And he said, 'Yeah, but have you ever thought about it?' And I was kind of going, 'No, no, I'm just in this band, actually . . . sorry.'"

Slowly the troops reconvened in the preordained pub. Only the lead singer remained unaccounted for. At last, with his bandmates' anxiety growing, Strummer arrived just before closing time with two female fans he had serendipitously met at the train station. The duo agreed to put the band up for the night. Howard: "Yes, we met in the pub, got a place to sleep from people we didn't know. The next morning we did our rehearsal under the bridge. It's all terribly cinematic . . . A fucking great idea for a movie, in fact."

Setting up near the shopping precinct, the band nervously launched its busk, setting out a guitar case for coins. The Saturday-morning shoppers proved to be a tough crowd, however, unimpressed with the musical wares on offer. Having accumulated only £2.38—according to White—after an hour's labor, the band decamped to a nearby sidewalk outside a sprawling Marks & Spencer next to a record store.

Confident in their new venue, the band worked up versions of the reggae classic "Rivers of Babylon" and the Buddy Holly/Rolling Stones/Bo Diddley–beat chestnut "Not Fade Away." Curiosity seekers began to circle about. Soon, someone recognized the band, and coins began to fill the guitar case: £20 in less than an hour, enough to buy food and drink at a nearby pub.

From there, the band went to busk at a central gathering point, Old Market Square, and then on to numerous other spots, including "a tiny pub set in a cliff" according to White. The interactions were unpremeditated, unforced, marked by the sheer surprise of discovery, the pleasing shock of the seemingly impossible.

One Clash fan, Stuart Nock, was making his way to the Garage Club with a friend after a gig. "We could hear the strains of someone busking 'Career Opportunities' floating down the street," Nock later wrote. "I remember commenting that 'someone thinks they're The Clash.' We rounded the corner of the small street the Garage was on—and there were The Clash playing out on the street!"

The sight was jarring but energizing, dissolving the barriers between performer and audience. Nock says, "There were only three or four people watching. As we got up to them they had just finished the number. Joe asked what we wanted to hear. Someone said 'White Riot' and they just launched into it. [Later] they came into the club and held court in the bar and were very friendly." This turned out to be the last show for the evening, for, as White remembers, "our voices were shot already . . . and Joe reckoned we better rest up or we'd never make it."

This first day set a pattern of impromptu hit-and-run performances—"eight or ten a day," Strummer later told Jon Savage—lasting any where from ten minutes to an hour. While this modus operandi would be refined over the days ahead, the essence remained: playing for free for anyone who wanted to hear, for as long as their voices could hold out, then crashing on the floors and couches of fans.

The impact was immediate, as even the cynical White admits: "As the sun went down [on the first day] already a sort of camaraderie had developed. With no ten-ton trucks and television sets and scaffolding and stage barriers and separate hotel rooms and sound check and tour itinerary and no Bernie, we were stripped naked. We were in this together. Equal. Nothing to lose or gain." For a band hammered into pieces over the past months, this was a welcome balm.

Meanwhile, Ronald Reagan was finding no such reprieve from his most prominent annoyance: the Sandinista regime. The FSLN had convincingly won an election organized for two days before the US presidential contest. Reagan had denounced the electoral exercise as a "Soviet-style sham" and arranged for the most prominent opposition parties to boycott. Though hardly perfect, the election was seen by international observers as more free, fair, and inclusive than those organized by the US amid the terror in neighboring El Salvador.

Nearly as irksome to Reagan as the Sandinistas was the US Congress—in particular, one representative named Edward Boland. A Democrat from Massachusetts, Boland had made it his mission to thwart the US "secret" war on the Nicaraguan government, which—having been belatedly debated on Capitol Hill—was not "secret" anymore, and of dubious legality.

After initial reports of a clandestine anti-Sandinista campaign to arm, organize, and direct "contra" counterrevolutionary forces were confirmed in 1982, Boland had sponsored an amendment to the 1983 Defense Appropriations Act to prevent the use of US funds to overthrow the FSLN. Reagan had chafed under these restrictions, and ordered his underlings to find a way to quietly circumvent the ban, exploiting inadvertent loopholes in its language.

This quest blew up in Reagan's face. When it emerged that the CIA had mined Nicaraguan ports in violation not only of the intent of the Boland Amendment, but of international law, congressional leaders were outraged. Their spines were further stiffened by pressure from a rising grassroots movement that pledged to resist US war in Central America.

On March 5, 1985, the *Los Angeles Times* reported: "The consequences of congressional ire snowballed quickly. By the beginning of this year, Reagan's policy on Nicaragua was dead in the water.

The contras were militarily stalemated and politically divided; the CIA was under public fire for mismanaging the program; and Honduras, the key US ally in the [campaign to overthrow the Sandinistas], was increasingly nervous about the relationship."

A vibrant peace movement opposed Reagan's Central American policy. (Button and bumper sticker courtesy of Mark Andersen.)

Boland was determined to strengthen his ban. As the nonpartisan Congressional Research Services (CRS) noted, "The continuing appropriations resolution for fiscal year 1985 provided that: 'no funds available to the Central Intelligence Agency, the Department of Defense, or any other agency or entity of the United States involved in intelligence activities may be obligated or expended for the purpose of which would have the effect of supporting, directly or indirectly, military or paramilitary operations in Nicaragua by any nation, group, organization, movement, or individual.'"

This legislation, the CRS added, "also provided that after February 28, 1985, if the president made a report to Congress specifying certain criteria, including the need to provide further assistance for 'military or paramilitary operations' prohibited by this statute, he could expend $14 million in funds if Congress passed a joint resolution approving such action."

Given how badly Reagan had botched public relations for his "contra" campaign, congressional support for a renewed effort was unlikely. So the administration took a new tack, seizing the tools at their command to effectively declare economic war. Using a visit by newly elected Nicaraguan president Daniel Ortega to Moscow as proof the regime were "Soviet puppets," Reagan announced a ban on US travel and trade with Nicaragua on May 1, 1985.

Coming as The Clash prepared for its busking adventure, this escalation was opposed by most of America's allies, who saw it as simply feeding and justifying authoritarian tendencies growing within the FSLN. Moreover, it seemed patently insufficient to dislodge the Sandinistas. As a result, the administration continued to seek a way to push the shooting war forward, by hook or by crook.

Meanwhile, The Clash had traveled to Leeds. When hitchhiking had proven futile, Strummer reconvened the group to plot the next move. The decision was made to pool their remaining busking funds to pay for bus tickets.

This slight concession to reality could not mask the radical nature of what The Clash was doing. If the US tour was a bit out of bounds simply for not being tied to the release of a new album, this jaunt was truly off all the maps.

Sheppard marvels, "The tour had no commercial themes, nothing to sell. I actually didn't think about it that much, other than, 'What a great idea! Fuck, let's go and do that, that'd be great!' We went, literally, 'Well, what's the first place we can go? What's the first town up the M1? Nottingham. All right, we'll go there first. Where should we go next? How much money have we got? Well, we've got enough to get to Leeds—well, we'll get the bus to Leeds.'"

Even the bus could become a performance venue. One fan named John saw The Clash "on a late-night National Express bus from Nottingham to Leeds. It was very exclusive—just me, them jamming at the back, and the coach driver."

The absence of basic practical considerations could leave the band in sticky situations. Sheppard: "We arrived in Leeds at ten o'clock at night or something. We're like, 'Fuckin' hell—we're sitting in the bus station tonight!' But we just found this club, and we started busking outside it. These two guys literally walked out of the club, and went, 'Fuck me, it's The Clash!' And they were the guys that put us up that night, looked after us, took us home, cooked us breakfast, all that stuff."

Howard echoes Sheppard's recollections: "The theory was that we would live off what we got. I mean, that's what we did. And it was fucking amazing. There wasn't any intention to make it a commercial idea, it wasn't, 'What can we do with this?' Nowadays, every bit of it would be filmed for TV or something. But it wasn't like that, you know—and that made it quite compelling."

The lack of commercial calculation is still astonishing. Tony White—who saw the band play to passersby in Leeds' Royal Court Park—later wrote, "There were no ads in the music press or the broadsheets, no announcements, no press releases or friendly music journalists tagging along with their photographers. There were no publicity campaigns or photo-ops and no daytime TV coverage. Neither were there tour T-shirts, posters, or merchandise of any kind."

The whole affair was so far outside of normal rock business practices that Tony White hesitated to call it a "tour." While this reticence was understandable, it nonetheless reflects commercial, rather than artistic, criteria. If a "tour" refers to a band going from town to town playing for audiences, what else could this be?

The rejection of commerce in favor of pure enjoyment and artistic striving revealed the power of communal creation and release, past consumer pigeonholes. This was definitively off the capitalist-rock-biz path, especially for a band of The Clash's popularity. Underground critics who dismissed the group as opportunistic poseurs might well have been silenced by this action. What more powerful refutation of the corporate money machine could there be?

Not everyone saw it this way. In Leeds, The Clash found itself on the turf of Chumbawamba, a rising anarcho-punk band who shared a squat in Armley, a historically working-class industrial district. Initially one of many bands inspired by Crass, the group was now finding its own voice, driven in part by its experiences during the miners' strike. Guitarist/vocalist Boff Whalley recalls how the band "began a process of unlearning some of the insular and antisocial ideas we'd picked up from an insular and antisocial political movement."

Whalley was referring to the anarcho-punk scene that had produced what were now being called "peace punks." This subset of punk emphasized vegetarianism, nonviolence, animal rights, and a fierce commitment to anticorporate action and independent labels.

Chumbawamba set a high standard even within this DIY crowd by initially releasing its music on only easily duplicable cassette tapes.

By 1985, however, the band was beginning to show an artistic creativity and ideological flexibility that set them apart from "peace punk" peers. Journalist Aaron Lake Smith would later write, "The British miners' strike was a decisive event in Chumbawamba's political evolution . . . Diet and lifestyle became less important than solidarity with organized labor." The band recorded a benefit single for the miners, distributed pamphlets and food to workers' families in the nearby Frickley, and even started a theater troupe to perform for miners' children.

According to Smith, the strike "was the first crack in what would soon become a fissure between Chumbawamba and the [anarcho] punk scene . . . Chumbawamba worked to incorporate themselves into their community in Leeds rather than to be punks standing apart from it. They chose to venture into uncomfortable situations with people who were different from them. As Chumbawamba became closer and closer with the miners, they distanced themselves from 'the punks,' whom they increasingly viewed as petty, hardline, ineffective, and humorless."

Still, the conversion was not yet complete. When band members heard the startling news that The Clash was busking on the streets of Leeds, Whalley and vocalist Danbert Nobacon began planning a direct action protest . . . of The Clash.

This was not very surprising. Anarcho-punk originators Crass had drawn initial inspiration from both Sex Pistols and The Clash. However, they swiftly turned on their catalysts, lambasting both as sold out to the corporate rock world and, in the case of The Clash, in thrall to warmed-over socialist politics.

Chumbawamba echoed this in a key early song, "Rock 'n' Roles," that savaged the scene as simply "one more method of keeping us in line / one more fashion called punk this time." The lyrics argued, "This planet is being destroyed, bit by bit by bit / and rock and roll is helping to kill it," before concluding, "We're shouting loud but we're facing a wall / of sexist, drugged-up rock and roll."

For them, no band embodied this sell-out more than The Clash,

especially since they had left the underground with the diverse musical flavors and commercial success of *London Calling*. The Clash's
revival of Vince Taylor and the Playboys' hit "Brand New Cadillac"
was seen as especially egregious, with its references to an unnamed
treacherous woman as "my baby" who forsakes love for an expensive car and, implicitly, a man who can afford such luxuries.

Both Strummer and Simonon admitted to having been a bit
seduced by drugs, money, ego, and other of rock's self-indulgent
charms. The duo hardly celebrated this, though, and the ejection
of Jones and Headon was part of a determined effort to regain The
Clash's moral and artistic footing. The busking tour was the most
fervent expression of this drive toward purification and revival.

That motivation was lost on Chumbawamba at the time. Bassist/
vocalist Dunstan Bruce later denounced his "former idols," saving
special venom for "a pallid version of The Clash, sans Mick Jones"
that now "roamed the streets in search of lost credibility." Bruce:
"They'd done the America, champagne, and [cocaine] thing, and
they came back over here trying to prove that they could still relate
to the kids . . . To me, it just smacked of insincerity."

Bruce's passion on this issue, and that of his bandmates, was
undeniable. Their grip on the actual reality of the now not-so-new
Clash was less certain, however. But if Chumbawamba had the
quintet in their gunsights, The Clash had its own gripe with another
punk-related group.

In Nottingham, when Howard had noticed the Alarm was
there in town too, with plans to play Leeds next, an impish notion
formed in his head. In 1984, Strummer had denounced the band as
"an imitation of a shadow of The Clash." Although this may have
been unfair to a band with an obvious debt to The Clash but its
own sound and style, it was nonetheless heartfelt.

Fate, reasoned Howard, had given them the chance to take
some minor revenge: "I had the idea of playing outside the Alarm
gig. I was saying, 'The Alarm are so, kind of, hairstyle Clash wan-
nabes, that we should go and fuck 'em up, go over there and busk
outside. Everyone who's going into the gig will be late going in.'"
While White remembers Strummer emphasizing a desire to play

for Clash fans rather than to simply be a wrench in the works, there was a confrontational aspect to the affair. Sheppard: "We thought it would be a really good windup, very punk rock, for The Clash to play outside an Alarm gig."

The stage was now set for a face-off between three equally earnest, socially conscious bands, all of which had supported the same side in the miners' strike.

As The Clash gathered on the front steps of the venue—the Leeds University student union building—a ripple of disbelief ran through the hundreds of Alarm fans waiting for the doors to open. Memories of what happened over the next half hour vary wildly. White recalls the band kicking off its set with two new songs, "Movers and Shakers" and "Cool Under Heat," while Clash fan Tony White remembers a "blinding version of [reggae classic] 'Pressure Drop'" that segued into "Garageland." All agree that the band played at full tilt, generating a powerful sound that carried far in the early evening air.

As The Clash bashed out their songs on acoustic guitars, with Howard banging on a borrowed snare drum on a simple stand, the long, snaking line of concertgoers broke. A huge mass quickly formed, enveloping the band, making them almost indistinguishable from the crowd. Close to a thousand people gawked, sang along, or shouted with disbelief outside the hall.

Word traveled inside to where the Alarm was in the midst of its sound check. According to lead singer Mike Peters, "I distinctly remember [Alarm roadie] Redeye bursting onto the stage during the sound check and announcing that Joe Strummer and The Clash were busking to the fans outside the venue. I didn't believe him at first and thought it was a windup but soon realized it was true. So I dropped everything and ran outside to see what was going on."

By the time Peters arrived, Strummer was locked in a dispute with the Alarm road crew. Sheppard laughs, "Joe spent pretty much the whole gig talking to the roadies, who'd come out very upset that we'd done this thing—he was trying to reason with them, or protest, or whatever, I don't know. He didn't sing any songs really. He just talked to these guys while we sang all the songs—hilarious!"

Left: The Clash amid the crowd outside the Alarm show. (Photo by Tim Beasley.)
Right: Leeds' *Other Paper* article, ghostwritten by members of Chumbawamba.

As Peters watched, members of Chumbawamba moved through the throng. "We came prepared . . ." explained a blurb published in the *Leeds Other Paper* credited to "Dennis the Menace" and "Minnie the Minx." "We had a banner, our voices and a handheld hydraulic paint dispenser. The banner read: *As well as marketing safe rebellion, CBS makes parts for the Cruise murder missiles.*"

This claim, which indicted The Clash for effectively funding possible nuclear holocaust, was incendiary. Nobacon, the banner's main author, "originally read of this connection in a fanzine in the early eighties and took it on trust." To his dismay, he later discovered it was apparently false information.

For now, however, the war was on. With Strummer still mid-argument, the rest of The Clash was in full fury, having barely the space to play, nearly swallowed up amid the crowd. Now just yards away, Nobacon took aim and Whalley prepared to unfurl the banner. According to the *Other Paper* communiqué, "They sang 'my baby drove up in a brand new Cadillac . . .' We gave it to them in their ugly faces."

Suddenly, Strummer, the band, and bystanders were drenched in a spray of bloodred paint. Chaos erupted, according to Nobacon: "We shouted things, we got called 'wankers.' We got bottles thrown at us . . . We split." Chased through the crowd, the duo laughed while making their escape. While exhilarated at the time, both Nobacon and Whalley would later look back on the action with ambivalence.

The Clash seemed to take little notice of the act of sabotage, racing through songs variously remembered by those present as "White Riot," "Clash City Rockers," "Police on My Back," and/or another reggae standard, "Johnny Too Bad." Sheppard: "I don't really remember the paint, none of us really noticed, until we all left and realized we were covered in it—it didn't actually affect us at all. We didn't know it had happened, because there was so much else going on."

The performance ended as quickly as it began, again leaving contending memories. White: "Some security from the venue came out and roughly told us we better leave. We were quickly out of there."

Peters remembers, "The door to our own gig opened and the fans rushed in to get down to the front."

Howard: "The Alarm was waiting for the audience to come in, so they could go onstage.'" Sheppard similarly recalls completing their guerrilla mission and leaving as planned. With a crowd following on their heels, the paint-spattered group walked around the corner and set up outside the Faversham Pub, playing for all comers.

One Alarm partisan, Steve Fulton, called the prank "bizarre and ugly," accusing Joe Strummer of "playing the bully" and "looking the worse for it." By contrast, Peters called Strummer "my hero," saying, "I felt sorry for Joe and the band, they were obviously trying to prove some sort of point . . . I could relate to what they were trying to do, as it was the way the Alarm had demonstrated itself in the early days, busking on the subways and performing outside [unfriendly venues]."

While Peters undermined his gracious words with a silly claim—"Here Joe was imitating the Alarm with acoustic guitars"— he was correct that Strummer and company were out to make a point, if mostly to themselves. Their mission, roughly, was to redis-cover the joy of playing music, to be among the people, away from the rat race—above all, to feel themselves as a living, breathing musical unit, not pieces in Rhodes's grand dream.

Even the paint failed to dampen the band's spirits. Not know-ing why the attack happened, or what issues were involved, they tended to blame the upset Alarm roadies. In addition, Sheppard re-counts, "At the time, we thought it was really cool. We had blood-red paint all over our leather jackets, it was mad, it was art . . . this Jackson Pollock effect, and it was blood-red, like a badge of honor."

While Strummer "got hit with most of the paint," according to Sheppard, he apparently also took it in stride. After all, The Clash had been dealing with disillusioned followers since 1977. Far from aping the Alarm, the singer was revisiting his own busking roots, savoring the simple satisfaction of creating with his back to the wall, scrambling and scraping to make his way by wit and will in the streets. By that measure, the day had been a resounding success.

When the broader motivation for the spray-paint protest emerged, Sheppard took exception: "I found it quite offensive when [Chumbawamba's Bruce] said, 'Multimillionaires going back to busking, trying to get street cred.' There was no ulterior motive from me, Joe, or anybody else. It was literally, 'How about this? Let's go and do this. That'd be cool. Yeah, all right. Let's go and do it.'"

Simonon echoes Sheppard's sentiments: "[The busking tour] was like starting out fresh again, it was great. 'We'll meet you in Glasgow in a week's time,' and the idea was to leave everything behind other than the guitars. You couldn't take any money with you. We survived by our wits."

Recalling the embattled December 1976 tour with Sex Pistols, the Damned, and the Heartbreakers, Simonon continues: "It was as exciting as the Anarchy tour, you never knew where you were going next. I remember we were in Leeds, it was two a.m., outside this black club, and people were coming out and really digging us."

Conveniently, such situations could help with finding a place to sleep. Simonon: "There were two guys and they were shocked it was us. They said, 'Where you staying?' And we said, 'We're not staying anywhere,' so they invited us to stay at their mum's! The money we made from busking meant we could go further, we didn't have a plan of where to go next. There was no rules. You didn't have to be on the so-and-so plane at twelve o'clock."

The next day, May 8, The Clash headed to nearby York. Starting out in St. Sampson's Square, the band busked for passing shoppers then made its way up Petergate to York Minster, one of Britain's grandest churches. "By the time we got to York Minster, there was a line of three to five hundred people behind us," Howard remembers. "I was playing my drumsticks on a dustbin lid." The Clash held forth to their gathered fans and a puzzled crowd there simply to celebrate V-E Day.

By now, the band was regularly playing outside in public, without any permits, to growing crowds. The combination was bound eventually to draw the attention of the authorities, and it did that day. The band was impossible to miss in such a high-profile spot. After a couple songs, the law intervened.

Howard: "The police were all around us, saying, 'You've got to stop now, it's getting out of hand, there could be damage—if you don't stop, we will arrest you.' The drummer laughs: "In England, the beat cops have the pointed hats, and the ones in charge have the flat hats—so one of the flat hats comes over to us and says, 'You've got one more number, and then you've got to stop. Could you make it 'London Calling'?"

The band complied with the order's first part, but defied the second, instead breaking into "I Fought the Law"—with Howard drumming on the doors of the church itself—before decamping to a nearby pub, Hole in the Wall, to drink and chat with their followers. It was not the last time police would appear on this tour.

The next day at noon, the band materialized at King's Square, a popular outdoor shopping district where Howard used a bench as his instrument. Stuart Heron—who had seen them the day before at York Minster—recalls, "The square was packed and again the band sounded great." As this was a popular spot for street entertainers, Heron notes, "This time the police did not try to move them on."

The musicians then paraded through York's streets, strumming guitars Spanish-style. With about a hundred fans joining in, they made their way to Ripon and St. John's College for another impromptu show. Howard played a drum loaned by a fan.

Word was starting to get out. The York shows inspired an outpouring of local write-ups, ranging from incredulous ("Clash in York? Now Pigs Fly!"), to jesting ("Punks March on Minster!"), to straightforward and supportive ("Carefree and Trouble-Free as Fans of Superstars Jam the Centre of City"). After an interview Strummer gave to a local radio station was sold to BBC Radio One without permission, the whole nation knew. While Strummer was angry about this chicanery, the chat was a window into the tour's ardent sense of mission.

Asked why a band with millions of record sales would leave the financially secure pop world to play on the streets, Strummer responded, "We feel we were getting involved in 'release a record, go on a tour, do this, do that.' We began to ask ourselves, 'What is this all about?' And we decided that if we can't get it with three acoustic guitars and a pair of drumsticks, on a walking tour of England, then . . ." Strummer's voice trailed off, then resumed, even more urgent than before: "We are looking for an answer. We want to know if rock and roll still means anything. This is our attempt to find out if it does."

While Strummer disavowed any intent to be "really preachy," he expressed the disaffection of post–miners' strike Britain, where shadows of rage and despair were lengthening: "We're going to have to have an English revolution in about ten years. I think it is possible, and I would like to be involved."

The desolation of the increasingly postindustrial north was evident everywhere, especially as the band moved to Sunderland, where Sheppard's brother lived, and then nearby Newcastle. This had been hard-core mining country, as indicated by the expression "carrying coals to Newcastle." Now, the present was grim and the future seemed even bleaker, with fury and hopelessness festering.

Even White took note: "The farther north we go, the more angry it gets." Later he recalled how Strummer engaged in Sunderland with local Socialist Workers' Party militants, who tried to get him to sign on like the powerful soul-punk band the Redskins had done. Strummer deftly resisted: "I totally respect where you are coming from, but I can't be seen to affiliate with any particular party." He later defended the SWP activists to an unimpressed White: "Don't be too hard on them, Vince, they are trying. The system is unfair, it has to change."

While White was often bored by the politics, the devastation shocked him. After visiting one depressed area, he wrote, "The houses were mostly boarded up with metal and wood. Rows and rows of derelict [small homes]. It was a depressing sight I would see over and over again in the north. Shipbuilding, cotton mills, mining towns—the whole lot had gone to pot. The great British industrial wave had receded, leaving vast communities high and dry . . . just carrying on, going nowhere. Whole communities had been destroyed by the present government."

This was the bleak vista Strummer had sketched in "Three Card Trick," "In the Pouring Rain," "This Is England," and most recently "North and South." Sadly, it was not simply the north of England, but the Rust Belt of Reagan's America, the South Bronx, Native American reservations—so many places across the world. The desperation resonated with Strummer's personal pain, and helped to fuel powerful newer songs like "Cool Under Heat"—which spoke of "sorrow upon sorrow / ganging up in your head"—and, above all, "Movers and Shakers."

This song was first heard in public on the busking tour, and its message might be seen as the trek's credo. Preserved on an audience tape from Newcastle's Station Club on May 11, the unfamiliar song was greeted respectfully, with little of the raucous singing along that was coming to characterize these shows. Clapping his hands and howling at the front of The Clash's acoustic assault, Strummer sought to make its hopeful, determined energy palpable nonetheless.

Strummer had once argued that the best songs came from a

place of "concrete and hunger." If so, "Movers and Shakers" was surely one of those. Opening with a stark vignette from the devastated South Bronx—"The boy stood in the burning slum"—the song immediately stakes its claim: "Better times had to come."

While some critics would dismiss these lines as hyperbole, few who spent time in the South Bronx during the late seventies or early eighties would react that way. At the time, arson was rampant. Often slumlords were literally burning down their own buildings for the insurance payoff, leaving vast patches of vacant lots, with parts of the neighborhood looking like bombed-out nightmare-scapes.

Yet tens of thousands of people lived there nonetheless, seeking to make a living, to raise families, to build better lives amid economic collapse. Here African American and Puerto Rican teenagers, working with the most basic materials, found their voices and created hip-hop. Strummer evokes that tale: "Fate lay in the hands that clap / muscles to move / the power to rap." Out of adversity, something beautiful had risen: "He went up on money street / Waving an' popping to the beat / off his wits and on his feet / he worked a coin from the cold concrete."

Homeless people now crowded American sidewalks, on what Christian-anarchist advocate Mitch Snyder called "a forced march to nowhere." For Snyder, this evoked not simply Okies and vagabonds during the Great Depression, but the genocide of Native Americans on the "Trail of Tears." In the second verse, Strummer finds another protagonist stepping out of this despair "with a red bandanna and rapid wipes . . . where the highway meets the lights."

Once again, the singer would face criticism, this time for celebrating "squeegee men" and thus seeming to accept a brutal system that drove humans to such undignified toil. This appears to miss the point, for people need to survive before any revolution can be made, and that effort is common sense: "This man earns 'cause it's understood / times are bad and he's making good / down on him, but he's got it beat / he's working coin from the cold concrete."

If such lines hardly carry the sledgehammer impact of "Clampdown's" "kick over the wall / cause governments to fall," they complement more than contradict those sentiments. In such dire straits, the mere preservation of the creative, fighting human spirit in however small a way can be revolutionary.

As the song pauses before racing to its denouement, it becomes clear that Strummer is, in part, seeking to lift his own flagging spirits. Riddled by pain and self-doubt, the singer offers gentle encouragement: "When I see you down / and I say / That ain't no way through / Hey! That ain't no way through."

The cry "Movers and shakers come on!" could be understood as Strummer's call to his better self, insisting, "You've got what it takes to make it." All the brooding about the new Clash, all the self-loathing over how he had failed them and himself, comes out: "Movers and shakers come on / even if you have to fake it."

The final verse brings it home, to Strummer's own story of being a busker living in a dead-end squat "when a friend was anybody with food to eat." "It was a lousy life / with a leaking roof," the singer admits, but "we got up to find the truth."

Having started the song with the birth of hip-hop, the singer now brought it around to punk's genesis. "One day I was a crud, the next I was a king," Strummer said in 1977, speaking of seeing Sex Pistols for the first time. The power of that moment kicked him into action, and resonated across the years: "Make a drum from a garbage can / allow your tongue to be a man / when that beat propels you off of your seat / you got it made in the cold concrete."

All the pain, doubt, and depression is cast away as Strummer cries, "Movers and shakers come on!" urging any and all forward. As he does, one last desperate shout of "COME ON!" echoes, met by raucous applause. If the song cataloged troubled situations far from the stricken towns of northern Britain, the defiantly upbeat message could hardly be more relevant to them.

While The Clash played many songs on this journey—new ones alongside their classics, as well as rock and reggae standards—their biggest hit, "Rock the Casbah" was unaired. Yet its antifundamentalist theme, born in reaction to the excesses of 1979's Islamic Revolution in Iran, was gaining increasingly relevance.

Just as the new Clash had begun to coalesce at Rehearsal Rehearsals eighteen months before, a new phenomenon burst into

Western consciousness. Around dawn on October 23, 1983, a militant connected to a new Iran-sponsored Islamic guerrilla group, Hezbollah, drove a truck heavily laden with explosives into the US Marine barracks in Beirut. Two hundred forty-one people died in the resulting carnage, introducing Americans to "suicide bombing."

A new frightening energy was surging against the arrogant ways of capitalist and Communist alike, while also largely rejecting Western concepts of human rights and freedom. In Afghanistan, the United States supported mujahideen fighting the Soviet invaders and its puppet government, but also found itself denounced as "The Great Satan" by Iran's Islamic Republic for its own misadventures.

The revolutionary regime went to war in 1980 with neighboring Iraq, ruled by a quasi-socialist dictator, Saddam Hussein. The US had broken off relations with Iran after the hostage crisis, and animosity lingered. Reagan moved to support Hussein and his regime, reckoning that the enemy of an enemy is a friend.

The blowback was immense. Westerners—especially Americans—in Lebanon became targets for shadowy Islamic groups over 1984 and the first months of 1985. While some were government operatives like CIA officer William Buckley, most were not. Iran-linked groups abducted the likes of Peter Kilburn, a librarian at Beirut's American University; Catholic priest Lawrence Jenco; Presbyterian missionary Benjamin Weir; and Associated Press reporter Terry Anderson.

Reagan had benefited from the political damage inflicted on Jimmy Carter by the Iranian hostage crisis, and hawkish Republicans since Nixon had excoriated their opponents for making the US look like "a pitiful, helpless giant." Now it was Reagan who was helpless. The Marine barracks bombing and spate of kidnappings were deeply embarrassing and infuriating to him.

While The Clash was on the busk in northern Britain, Reagan reached out to Israeli prime minister Shimon Peres, asking for his help in winning the release of the hostages in Lebanon. According to the *New York Times*, at about the same time, Manucher Ghorbanifar, an Iranian exile who was "under pressure from Iran to find arms in the West, made contact with a Saudi businessman, Adnan M. Khashoggi, who introduced him to Israeli operatives."

The *New York Times* later noted that Ghorbanifar "had raised the issue of ransoming hostages in a meeting in Hamburg, West Germany, with Iranian officials and Theodore C. Shackley, a former CIA agent." In due time, the *Times* continued, a secret CIA memo "suggested the possibility of selling arms to Iran as a way of blunting Soviet moves in the region" and freeing the hostages.

In public, Reagan continued to blast the idea of "making concessions to terrorists." Behind the scenes, an operation involving this unlikely cast of characters—plus a few more—was taking shape.

Far from this cloak-and-dagger scenario, The Clash was confronting another ugly reality. If the US tour had provided what Sheppard described as "a cocoon" at the outset of the miners' strike, this jaunt destroyed it. The band could offer little but salve for wounded souls, though that was appreciated. "We are lads that don't have a lot of cash, we're in college or we're on the dole," one fan told York Radio, speaking for many peers. "So, today, after ten years of success, to come around places like York and Leeds and play gigs that are free, that really means a lot to us lot."

Whether by instinct, design, or coincidence, their travels took them through the heart of poststrike Britain. Sheppard would later revisit heartbreaking conversations he had with members of mining families, ruminating, "The busking tour wasn't really about music, it was about us getting back in the real world."

Years later, the *Nottingham Post* reported that The Clash played a miners' benefit at a much-loved independent record store, Select-aDisc. They also performed at The Bunker in Sunderland, where Billy Bragg had done one of his own strike fund-raisers. One fan, Tony Keen, remembers the band dedicating "North and South" to the miners at another show. Even White was photographed wearing a miners' strike benefit T-shirt during this time.

It is hard not to wonder what this sort of tour could have done during the strike itself—to help keep spirits up, to raise awareness and funds, to rally the troops. While such a tour had been deemed impossible before, the mere fact of what The Clash was now doing made that claim seem no longer credible.

The music—when it was audible to the growing crowds—was also stronger than ever. The acoustic guitars and voices mixed well. Howard was a marvel, inventively using whatever percussion "instrument" he had at hand; Tony White saw them twice, lauding the drummer's "fantastic drumstick work."

Bootlegs from York and Newcastle reveal the band gelling in its new acoustic format, but there was also a more intangible factor at work. What the songs lost in volume—lacking any amplification—they gained in emotional ballast.

For a London band to play "North and South" in this context was very significant, but other songs resonated as well. "Garageland" had seemed a bit defensive opening the warm-up shows before the US Festival, but a bootleg version from the Newcastle Subway sounds utterly convincing. "Career Opportunities" had sounded sound hollow on a Shea Stadium stage, yet rang true on the streets of northern England. The pathos of "Straight to Hell" was even more poignant, performed in the very places where "railhead towns feel the steel mills rust."

This was as close as The Clash would ever get to Woody Guthrie playing around campfires for hobos and migrant workers. When Strummer later described this as "the best tour we ever did," he was no doubt thinking of such communion: singing "hard-hitting songs for hard-hit people," in Guthrie's words.

This point, while real, could be overstated. The Clash were playing bars, colleges, and shopping districts, not union halls, picket lines, and immigrant camps. Still, their accessibility to the audience and the powerful interchange with them was astounding, heartening, and unprecedented for a band of its stature.

Playing at Grey's Monument in Newcastle, the band ran afoul of the police again. The landmark honored Charles Grey, a peace advocate and champion of civil and religious liberty. Not surprisingly, the plaza was a popular venue for street musicians, religious speakers, and protesters. It was not a spot the busking Clash was about to miss.

"Joe just kind of appeared and said, 'We are The Clash,' and they started playing," one fan recounted years later. "A large crowd quickly gathered and the police turned up and duly got 'on their back.'" Sheppard laughs: "These Newcastle coppers told us to move on. That was the only time I felt threatened in the whole tour. They breed them rough up there [in mining country] . . . We just looked at these fucking tough guys and went, 'We're not arguing with them!'"

The Clash "went about thirty yards off in the direction of the central station and started playing again by an underpass," the fan recalled, "by which time I couldn't see them any more in the melee that quickly developed." From there, they went on to busk at the Exhibition Park Subway, before decamping to The Station, then bouncing back to Sunderland for sets at Gollum's Bar and the Drum Club.

Many of the shows seemed magical. "Joe was fearless, absolutely fearless on that tour," Sheppard says.

Howard echoes those sentiments: "Joe was unstoppable. Everybody's saying, 'Let's go and busk outside a university, or in a student-y area . . . because, you know, they'll go fucking crazy, they'll have us all for dinner, and they'll give us this, that, and the other. And Joe was going: 'No, let's find the roughest fucking club, let's go and busk outside there.'"

A larger lesson was present, as Howard notes, one rarely learned in the typical rock star "bubble": "There you have a classic example of the things that you start to learn about people, because you really wouldn't know too much about that, in the environment of being driven to a gig, and having security, and nobody allowed backstage . . . and all that kind of stuff." The drummer pauses, and then continues: "But all of a sudden, you've got, like, really hard-bitten people coming out of a club, and then we'd play like 'Pressure Drop' or some other reggae classics. And as soon as we started playing, these Rastas sort of visibly wilted, then one maybe would kind of know who we were. And you'd be in this situation with people who, if you saw them [back home], you would shit yourself. Then, all of a sudden, you're in their house. You're drinking their rum. You're sitting there, you're eating their food. And actually, it became one of those, if you like, real experiences. That's why it was really good."

Sheppard: "We were looked after [on that tour]. It was amazing, the hospitality and respect we were shown by people." The connection was visceral and direct; Strummer later said, "I never felt closer to our audience than on that tour."

Howard: "A lot of people who saw us busking didn't say, 'It's a shame they had a dustbin instead of a drum kit,' they said, 'I've seen The Clash now.'"

Sheppard: "Necessity is the mother of all invention, right? It was a mixture of luck, and working it, and that was what was cool about it. It was a really organic thing: 'How do we make this work? Let's latch onto these guys, they actually live here. What songs are we gonna play? How do we get to the next town? What are we gonna eat? Fuck, I'm cold—let's go and buy some fabric, and cut it into red strips, and make scarves' . . . that kind of thing, you know. And we pulled together, man—it was great. That's what was good about it. We all pulled together."

The power of the platoon had reappeared. This happy development, however, highlighted how far this tour was from the dehumanizing process of recording the new album, marching to the rigid cadence of Rhodes's electronic drums. The destructive aspects of the Clash manager were high on the agenda for at least Sheppard, Howard, and White, who tried to get the message through to Strummer. Sheppard: "One of the great things about that busking tour is that we spent all of our time together. And we had some pretty serious sit-down discussions: 'You know what, Joe, that Bernie guy's fuckin' . . .' We said what we thought, you know? And he listened. He listened."

Howard agrees: "I would sit there and go, 'I don't really know what the hell Bernie and Kosmo are up to. I don't know *what* they're talking about anymore. Every time they come in, there's a different harebrained scheme, something else, you know—something else that's even more fucking wack than the last time . . . I suppose we were gently trying to convert Joe to getting away from Bernie. I didn't think he was the right man for the job at the time. I thought Bernie was doing the wrong thing by everyone involved. I *did* feel that getting away from him for a certain amount of time would give us all a bit of perspective."

Strummer took it all in, sometimes commiserating with his bandmates, but giving little indication of his own position.

There was little time for sustained reflection. When the musicians arrived in Edinburgh, Scotland, on May 13, they were back to the streets. Every new town could be hard at the beginning, and Edinburgh was no exception, with indifferent shoppers hurrying past them.

White wrote later, "We were there for nearly an hour, and not even a penny." Yet the guitarist was not really worried, having seen how the band's fervent support protected them: "The Clash reputation was there, everywhere, providing a soft buffer against any real hardship." As if to prove this point, the band asked a young guy in a biker jacket where they should go and he pointed them to La Sorbonne, a run-down haunt largely frequented by students.

One such student—and longtime Clash fan—Martin McCallion, had been shopping for a new wallet in a department store on Princess Street when he walked out to an astonishing sight: The Clash in full fury on the sidewalk. Although the musicians were finishing up, they announced the upcoming La Sorbonne show.

McCallion hurried to rally his friends at the nearby university: "There were no cell phones or Internet at the time, of course. We didn't even have phones in our rooms, just one for the whole floor out in the hall. But I called up everyone I could think of to tell them about The Clash playing La Sorbonne."

By now, the band had settled into the semblance of a routine: busking in the streets during the day to promote a slightly more conventional show at a club or pub at night, which helped raise the money to get to the next town. A bootleg of the Newcastle Exhibition Park Subway set captures Strummer inviting the crowd to the Gateshead Station that night. There, in turn, Strummer announced to the crowd, "We're on the bum," before passing the hat for "some drinking money."

The La Sorbonne show was everything McCallion and his friend Tony Keen had hoped for: "La Sorbonne was a small kind of ratty space, with a tiny stage. It was comfortably full, and you could hear and see the band just a few feet away. They didn't have amps or microphones, but they were incredible!"

In another fortunate twist, The Clash had been introduced to Jimmy Boyle, whom Sheppard describes as "a real hard-nut criminal who had kind of turned his life around." Once called "the most violent man in Britain" after being jailed for murder, Boyle had experienced an awakening via art therapy programs while in prison, ultimately becoming a renowned sculptor.

Sheppard: "Boyle started the Gateway Exchange, a halfway refuge, an attempt to get people off heroin, which was big in Glasgow and Edinburgh at the time. He brought us over to check it out." Sebastian Horsley, one of Boyle's coworkers, described the initiative as "a sort of last-chance saloon for people coming out of prison, coming off drugs, and those with mental health issues."

After Gateway, Boyle also introduced The Clash to Wester Hailes, a sprawling "council estate"—equivalent to a US public housing complex—that was home to both heartbreaking social problems and innovative programs of social uplift. The band was deeply moved, donning Gateway Exchange shirts for several gigs.

Strummer remarked at the time, "We have the highest regard for the Gateway and for communities like Wester Hailes. We met the people there and heard about what is happening, everyone feeling a part of something, realizing that, by getting together, they can improve their situation."

Boyle also used his contacts to get a show at Coasters, a well-known club, the following night, May 14. The Edinburgh word-of-mouth assured that "the small acoustic shows" were no longer so small. "A time had been set and word had been spread," White remarks. "Things were getting out of control." As the crowds grew, police moved in, shutting down a couple of gigs before they began due to what White remembers as "fire regulations."

Coasters was larger than most of the other venues and reasonably well established. The Clash built anticipation with a busk in the nearby shopping district. One fan later reminisced, "The band played . . . on Princess Street at the corner of The Mound where there is a speakers' corner, where basically you can spout off as long as you're not offensive. They played quite a few numbers before heading off to Coasters with a large following running after them."

The space was mobbed. McCallion and his friends barely got inside, ending up crunched in a back corner, with more than 1,300 other attendees. After the small La Sorbonne show, this was "overwhelming and not really much fun," McCallion said. "So many people were singing along, and we were so far back, you couldn't really hear the band. I don't think we stayed the whole way though."

If the night was unsatisfying for those in the back, many others closer to the action were once again transported. Tellingly, the band opened the set with "North and South" before racing through nine Clash classics, with "Pressure Drop" and "Johnny Too Bad" thrown in for good measure.

Sheppard was astonished: "There were about a thousand people in this room. And you could have heard a pin drop when we played, because we didn't have any microphones, we didn't have any amplification. So if you wanted to hear us, you had to shut up. So we'd do a song—and it would be absolutely silent. And then we'd finish, and there'd be this massive roar—it was quite surreal and amazing."

White had a more jaundiced view: "No one could hear anything . . . Later I realized people were just showing up for the band name, the event."

If partly true, White perhaps misses a central point. As the busking shows grew larger, the band receded and the populist idea that "we are The Clash" became very real. On a live tape from Coasters, one can hear the beat set by the band but not the guitars. No voices are distinguishable except the crowd howling en masse. It was extraordinary: without amps, microphones, or light shows, something grew that was considerably more than five people, sounding immense and undefeatable.

Sounds' Mandy Rhodes attended the Coasters show, and wrote an article entitled "There's (Still) a Riot Going On" lauding the band: "Today The Clash could easily pack any venue they chose. They could follow the dubious example of the Stones if they cared to and charge outrageous prices for a ticket to the spectacle. Instead, they are turning up all over the place from tiny bars where they are greeted with disbelief and open arms to the front door queues of gigs by such as the Alarm . . . to busking on one of Edinburgh's busiest streets."

When Mandy Rhodes asked Strummer the purpose of this "bum tour," the singer responded in an urgent, show-ravaged rasp: "We're doing the tour for ourselves, we enjoy it more this way. We wanted to get out on the streets again, back to our roots, and find out what direction we should take."

The interviewer was well aware of the political subtext. In the late seventies, Strummer had argued, "As a group with flash appeal, we can use our privilege to get the message over, tell the people to rise up." How then, Rhodes wondered, "would the band would go down in an even more downtrodden 1985?"

Strummer sounded defiant: "You saw the spirit of the crowd tonight. They made the night. They have the potential and the energy to change the system. We want Reagan and Thatcher out, we want a change in the system. We're not saying that we have the answer, though, not at all. That's why we are doing this tour, to talk to people, maybe to find a way to create change."

If such talk might seem over-the-top idealistic, what Mandy Rhodes had just witnessed made it seem anything but: "The energy of the audience at the shows was unquestionable. Largely consisting of the young and unemployed, the common allegiance was against 'the system' that deprives them of work, accommodation, and any measure of self-respect . . . More now than ever the message of The Clash has to be sung loud to pick up on the feeling in the land."

The writer was impressed by the vehemence of both band and crowd: "They were inspired and united for once, if only to hear the call for change . . . Regardless that The Clash played without amps or microphones, the message was as loud and clear as ever . . .

Using only acoustic guitars and an oil can for a drum, they belted out a battle cry and the feeling was one of solid unity."

She found no artifice involved: "When such vast amounts of money can be made out of pop, The Clash seem to see their role as a vehicle for others to use. It is the people who must advocate and demand the changes, but the band will help by getting people together in one place to listen to the sounds of defiance."

Such a politically charged rave in the pages of *Sounds*—whose stock in trade often seemed to be cynical takedowns—was unusual. Mandy Rhodes's words are an indication of the special power of this unique moment. The writer granted it might be "a dream world" of "self-delusion" but the hope generated was palpable.

If the tour showed that rock still "meant something," where could it go from here? The limits of the journey were apparent, as the band pressed against the bounds of what was possible without amplification, arrest, or outright mayhem.

For now, The Clash moved on to nearby Glasgow. Once again, the band arrived late but had good luck. Art school student Gillian Farmer was at a café/bar called Nico's with two friends when the band came in on May 15. Startled, she built up her courage and walked over to ask Strummer for an autograph. "Sorry, we don't do that," Farmer recalls him responding, coolly but graciously.

Undeterred, Farmer struck up a conversation with White, asking about where the band was staying. When he responded that they didn't have a place, Farmer blurted out an offer to stay at her flat, "never expecting for a second they'd say, 'Well, that would be really cool.'" She was shocked when White swiftly agreed, turning to Strummer to say, "Hey, Joe, it looks like we have a crash for the night!"

Thus began a whirlwind of shows in what would be the last stretch of the busking tour, starting at the nearby Fixx Pub on Miller Street, not far from Barrowlands where the new Clash had first played in the UK only fourteen months before. Farmer helped them make connections at other spaces, including the Rock Garden pub, the Cul-de-Sac bar at the nearby university, and Vic's Café at Glasgow's art college.

"Phones were ringing off the hook," Farmer says, as the word spread about the next day's shows, beginning at three p.m. at the Rock Garden. One lucky fan, Paul Henderson, "met The Clash by chance, sitting on the stairs of the art school." After going for a beer, Henderson went to the impromptu gig at the Rock Garden, and was riveted: "The crowd was singing along so loudly!"

Another fan, Tony McCormack, was headed to the pub for an afternoon pint: "When I turned into Queen Street, I saw a large crowd congregated around the door and they had door staff on too, which was very unusual for Thursday lunchtime." When the doorman told McCormack that The Clash was playing downstairs, he first thought it was a joke, "as he knew I was a Clash fanatic."

When it became clear this was not a put-on, McCormack begged without success to be let in. He waited nonetheless and then cornered the band when it emerged. Told that the group was headed to the Cul-de-Sac, McCormack rushed there. The show, however, had been canceled due to congestion.

McCormack was not deterred. "The Cul-de-Sac doorman said they were going to Dukes next, so off we went!" McCormack was beginning to doubt his judgment "when the door opened and in walked The Clash . . . no hangers-on, just the five of them." McCormack offered to buy them a beer, only to have Strummer reply, "No, we'll get you one, as we're playing for beer and food."

The place was soon packed. The band kicked off with "Pressure Drop," "Guns of Brixton," "Bank Robber," and "Brand New Cadillac." With a hundred folks milling around outside, the authorities came to investigate. "Strathclyde's finest turned up to be met with 'Police on My Back,'" McCormack remembers. "[The Clash] were told to get outside as there were too many people inside and a mob outside."

This directive was actually welcome. Farmer recalls, "Joe saw all the people outside and said, 'Let's give the people what they want!'" Once outside, according to McCormack: "The Clash duly broke into 'I Fought the Law.' Loads of wee Glasgow women were hanging out their windows [to see what was happening] as a couple of hundred Clash fans sang and danced about like maddies."

When the band went into "Straight to Hell," McCormack recounts, "it was eerily quiet." The ever-resourceful Howard played the drum part on a windowsill. McCormack: "The police panicked as more and more people turned up and sent The Clash back inside and only let the number back in that met with fire rules."

Stuck outside in the resulting chaos, McCormack and his friends waited till the band left, then followed them in a cab to the Mayfair Reggae Disco. McCormack explains, "They did a storming set of all the famous Clash reggae stuff, finishing with 'White Man in Hammersmith Palais.'" From there, The Clash headed off to a final set at the Windjammer Pub, but McCormack went home, savoring a day of Clash-chasing that had been "perfect."

The Clash-mates roused themselves the next morning, going with Farmer to perform what would be their final show of the busking tour—and, as it turned out, the final time they would ever play in the UK. The gig was at Farmer's school, the Glasgow School of Art, in a space above Vic's Café, at noon on Friday, May 17.

The show's atmosphere was "unbelievable," Farmer says. "It was packed, people at the door, just clambering to get in." The band began with "Cool Under Heat," then swiftly ran through "Straight to Hell," "Guns of Brixton," "White Man in Hammersmith Palais," "Pressure Drop," "Bankrobber," "Police on My Back," and "Brand New Cadillac." "Everyone [was] cheering and singing along," Farmer recalls. "They were so massive, everyone knew all the words to all the songs."

Photos from the concert capture Sheppard, White, and Simonon playing at gale force. According to Farmer, Howard was in back "hammering the hell" out of a plastic chair, the treble of the metal arms punctuating the bass sounds created by the seat and back. Resplendent in a fiery-red quiff and dark green *Kent State* T-shirt, Strummer was raging out front, riding the thunderous acoustic hurricane as the band brought the show to an end with a rampaging "White Riot."

Then it was over. Later, Farmer would remember Strummer as distant and quiet that last day in Glasgow. "The only time I caught Joe in a good mood was dancing to [a record of] 'Route 66,'" Farmer later wrote. "He really didn't seem to be in a happy space—until he got on the stage, then it was incredible."

This moodiness could have been ordinary brooding, or just an exhausted singer protecting his tour-ravaged voice. Nonetheless, Farmer felt that "looking back, it did seem to have the sense of something that was coming to an end."

The band decamped for the train station from Vic's Café. Farmer went with them, stopping to have a curry and then seeing them off on a train to Manchester, ostensibly to continue the tour there. But this, like rumored plans to play Liverpool, Carlisle, and Birmingham, was not to be.

Sheppard: "We set up to start busking in the city center of Manchester and Joe had completely lost his voice. And we realized, 'We can't go on, because you're in a bad way, man, you've gotta go home now.'"

Years later, Strummer ruefully said much the same, admitting to Jon Savage: "We didn't get to play in Manchester, 'cause my voice had gone by then."

It was a sudden, intuitive end to what had been an extraordinary seventeen days. Sheppard "We just went, 'That's enough. We can't do any more than this.' So we got the train home. It was a bit sad, really, when we finished, but there you go."

The tour seemed like a new beginning for The Clash. Sheppard says, "It would have been a great thing to do originally," instead of the somewhat forced California jaunt. Certainly these two and half weeks had been a marvelous balm for the band, going a long way to restore urgently needed solidarity.

But had The Clash found the answers they had been looking for? At least one de facto member of the team remained outside this newfound unity: Bernard Rhodes. As it happened, he held the ace of spades in his hand.

CHAPTER NINE
KNIFE OF SHEFFIELD STEEL

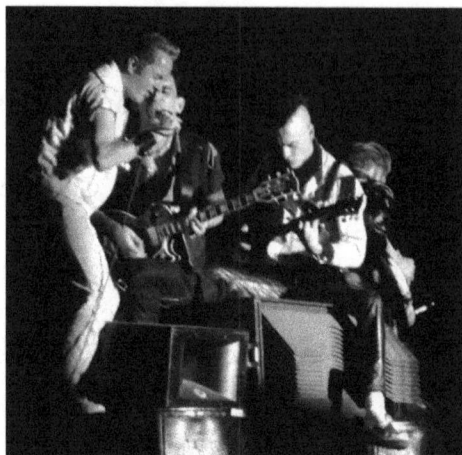

Strummer, Sheppard, White, and Simonon scale the speaker stack, Roskilde Festival, June 29, 1985. (Photos by Per-Åke Wärn.)

Bernie needed something earth-moving, ground-shaking, monumentally amazing. And so, what the world has been given is Bernie's idea of a monumentally earth-shaking, amazingly modern genius record.
—Nick Sheppard

The massacre now is over / and the order new enshrined . . .
—Old English folk ballad, c. 1986

The five members of The Clash stood closely together, singing
Toots and the Maytals' "Pressure Drop." With guitar, bass, and
drums silenced, the voices surged and swelled on their own,
brassy and determined. Onlookers joined in, howling out the lyrics.

The spare words contained a compelling message. Brought to
a global audience by the film *The Harder They Come*, the song told of
karmic justice. As author "Toots" Hibbert explained, "It's a song
about revenge, but in the form of karma: if you do bad things to
innocent people, then bad things will happen to you. The title was
a phrase I used to say. If someone done me wrong, rather than fight
them like a warrior, I'd say: 'The pressure's going to drop on you.'"

The Clash had often sung the roots-reggae classic like this on
the busking tour. The five voices intertwined with each other and
the audience's, the melody ringing out clear and strong. The sound
was stirring, and suggested unbreakable solidarity.

The scene evoked their audacious sojourn across northern Britain, immersed in their audience, living off what they earned each
day. But now the band was not scuffling on concrete, playing for
spare change. The Clash was onstage at the Roskilde Festival in
Denmark, before more than fifty thousand fans, most of them essentially invisible to the musicians standing on a distant stage.

It was June 29, 1985, nearly six weeks since the band had
last played, without amps and microphones above Vic's Café in
Glasgow. The shift of venue can only have been jarring. Yet The
Clash did not show it onstage. Most likely they were just glad to be
playing again for a live audience, however far removed.

Beyond the several-dozen busking gigs bashed out over barely
more than two weeks, this was only the seventh show The Clash
had done in almost thirteen months. This was an astonishingly lan-
guid pace for rebel rockers who had promised to outwork metal
bands and banish lightweight pop as 1984 dawned.

The group had returned from its triumphant, energized trek
through the north only to find itself falling into the rabbit hole of
the new album once again. The lyrics of "Pressure Drop" took on
another relevance—for the weight had descended squarely on the
weary, heartsick Joe Strummer.

Certain pretenses were falling away. Vince White was working late one night on final bits for some of the songs at Strummer's house when the singer began rolling and smoking one joint after another. White was already aware that Strummer had fallen off the wagon, and didn't make a big deal of it, even joining in, though pot was not his preferred vice.

According to White, an abashed Strummer still sought to explain this deviation from his public pronouncements, saying, "I'm under so much pressure." When the guitarist reassured him, "Don't worry about it, it's only rock and roll," Strummer went on: "I know what you think about spliff, but I was under so much stress, like Bernie and that . . . A friend was round, it was there . . . and I just smoked it, you know? I felt so much release, and it all—the pressure, Bernie, the band, everything—just DISAPPEARED!"

If this seemed facile self-justification, the weight was real—and working on the album only made it heavier. The laborious process, with each move dictated by Rhodes, killed virtually every bit of joy the singer found in the creative process.

Even the good bits carried a double edge. Whereas busking had reawakened his love for the simple, organic interplay of humans and instruments, the new record being born was anything but. Yet Strummer saw Rhodes as somehow essential to The Clash, and to himself as a person. How could the singer shatter this bond to preserve the one with the band, to remain true to himself as an artist?

While Simonon remained vaguely neutral and curiously disengaged, the position of White, Howard, and Sheppard was clear—the band's biggest single obstacle was one of its main creators. If Strummer knew they were right, he couldn't seem to find the strength to face down the manager. How could he, when Rhodes was a Clash cofounder as well as a father figure?

There was no easy answer, and a spiritually depleted Strummer found it hard to muster the determination. His mother was clearly terminally ill, and the singer had recently learned he was to be a father for the second time. The conflicting pulls were immense, and Strummer had chosen the path of least resistance, drifting closer and closer to disaster.

After the busking tour, Strummer had finally attempted to confront Rhodes. But the resourceful manager turned it against his detractors. Sheppard: "As soon as we got back to London, the whole fucking power trip was back. We had this meeting in Holland Park—a fucking conference room in a hotel, for God's sake!—it was weird, you know? We started off: 'Joe has talked to Bernie about how we feel.'"

A breakthrough seemed imminent, but it was not to be. Sheppard: "Bernie just turned it around: 'This man's Joe Strummer, he's a hero, he's a god, he's a voice of the people, how dare you . . . You're all just scum. You're this, and you're that, you're a coward, you're middle class'—that type of stuff—and just built Joe up."

Rhodes skillfully reframed the argument to portray the band as selfishly burdening an already overwhelmed singer. He got his hoped-for result: Strummer—and, apparently, Simonon—did not definitively stand with the others and Rhodes emerged firmly in control. Sheppard sighs at the recollection: "If you're told 'You're brilliant' enough, you believe it. And Joe *was* brilliant, he was the voice of a generation, and all that stuff Bernie said. But this move just got us straight back into his power play, basically. And Joe let him do it."

Sheppard allows, "It was maybe the last time Bernie was able to do a number on Joe," but the turning of the tables was deeply dispiriting to the band. A crucial opportunity to set a new course had been lost.

Strummer later offered a self-acquitting version of the events to Jon Savage: "When we came back to London after that busking tour, we felt we had something good going inside the group, but as soon as we came back and met Bernie and Kosmo in Holland Park . . . Bernie didn't like that it was slipping out of his control, so somehow he put a stop to the good feeling that we had." This is an odd way to describe the verbal abuse Rhodes unleashed on the dissenters on their return, a situation where Strummer had much power but chose not to use it.

Michael Fayne had been amazed by the busking tour, but harbored few illusions: "You're out there hitchhiking, you're depending on each other, on people you don't know . . . You have faith that you're gonna have a place to sleep, you're gonna get enough money to be able to get to the next town somewhere, and so forth . . . and it was great, right? But then they finished, and you've gotta come back and face reality, the reality you've created in the first place."

For Fayne, the issue was clear: "Joe never got rid of Bernard, so what did they think was gonna happen when they got back, you know? Bernie's not gonna just disappear! They came back, and all of the incredible vibe of that tour dissipated—because Bernie's back in control, essentially."

Rhodes's trump card was his grip on Strummer. Fayne: "Without making Joe sound weak, what happened is almost like Stockholm syndrome," referring to the way hostages can develop sympathy for their jailers. "Joe had been captive for so long by this person, man, he actually believed he couldn't take up shit with him. Bernie can get in your head. I've seen Bernie make grown men cry—this guy is fierce, man! I mean, I've never met anybody like him, you know?"

Rhodes's ace in the hole was not simply personal—it was contractual. Having already been ejected once from the band, he had sought to be protected this time around. Strummer was now bound to Rhodes by law. There could be no easy exit from this not-so-congenial embrace.

For their part, the miners had fought the law but had not won. As a result, they were now at the mercy of Thatcher's National Coal Board. As Jonathan and Ruth Winterton reported, "Within one month of the end of the strike, the NCB had announced twelve pit closures . . . Two months after the strike ended, the first closures were announced in Yorkshire"—the starting point and heart of the strike. "Over a few months, fourteen [more] units were to be closed, with manpower reduced at other sites."

The NUM could do little to stop this savage downsizing. Its smaller sister union of safety inspectors, NACODS, fought a few rearguard actions to ensure that the closures went through the proper review procedure. As Thatcher had intended, however, they could only slow the bleeding, not stop it. One of the pits slated for closure was Cortonwood, where the strike had begun.

While the miners were at work again—at least till their pits closed and they were let go—the divisions remained. Even as they worked side by side, strikers shunned those they still derided as "scabs," refusing to even speak to them.

These fractures split the mining towns themselves. Even families were torn apart by choices made and promises broken. The vitality of these hamlets depended on the pits, for even those not employed there counted on the money miners would spend in the community. The closure of a mine could effectively doom the village itself. The residents knew this, so any betrayal during the life-or-death strike was hard to forgive. Years would pass but many wounds remained unhealed.

The divisions in The Clash were nearly as bitter. Rhodes's brutal reassertion of authority, added to Strummer's abdication, was a hammerblow to Sheppard, White, and Howard. They were now totally at the manager-cum-producer's mercy.

While recording had relocated to London studios, the mind games continued. White recalls working for days with Strummer to get guitar fills that both loved—only to have Rhodes summarily dismiss the lot. A disgusted White laments, "Joe made a half-arsed attempt to stand some ground. But it wasn't nearly enough."

White went back to the fretboard, working for "three days and nights" on tight, rehearsed guitar parts. Once again, Rhodes berated him, and at one point brusquely ordered him to play three impromptu notes very slowly. When it wasn't quite right, White was made to do it again and again. After four hours and dozens of takes, a still-unhappy Rhodes summarily dismissed the demoralized guitarist.

White was not the mercurial manager's only victim. Fayne remembers, "There was one particular day where Bernie came into the studio. I was blazing it, just listening to the guys. The door swung open, and he ran into the room, picked up a mic stand, and started to smash the drum kit up, while Pete was sitting there . . .

Oh, it was wild, man! Pete just jumped up and tore off, and Bernard walked out."

As usual, there was a point. Fayne: "Bernie didn't want any connection with the past, you know? He wanted to take this forward, to control it, to mastermind the whole thing, and what they were doing was a bit too reminiscent of what it was."

This had its value, but to Fayne, the madness overwhelmed the method. "If he'd had a pair of ears, in two seconds Bernie would have gone, 'Oh, man, that's wicked, man! Carry on.' But he didn't. He was tone deaf, he didn't know a tune if it slapped him in the face." The cumulative damage was serious; Howard, for one, had come to loathe Rhodes and regret being in The Clash at all.

Then worrisome mixes of the new record began to circulate. White recalls being horrified to hear "The Dictator" with "weird synthesizer sprayed all over it . . . out of tune." When he pleaded with Strummer, calling it a "bloody ridiculous mess," the singer responded, "It's brilliant, it's wild!" White: "Joe brushed me off . . . [He] was locked into his own world."

One late addition to the record at least provided some fun. Several dozen of the Clash family and friends were invited into a studio to do backing vocals for the songs. The massed voices conveyed the sense of something immense and communal. Sheppard: "I think they were added to make that connection of when that massive crowd sings 'We are The Clash,' the idea is that The Clash belongs to the audience, you know—the audience are as much the band as the band is."

The backing vocals evoked the titanic sing-alongs of the busking tour. Sheppard: "It was done after the tour, but I don't know if Joe had come up with the idea as a result of the busking. I have a feeling it was more to do with Bernie, to be honest, and as I've said before, you know, Bernie did have some great ideas." In any case, the guitarist remembers that night fondly, unlike most of the recording.

White had found a new rehearsal space and, with Sheppard, Howard, and sometimes Simonon, poured frustrations into relentless practicing. Sheppard: "Basically, me, Vince, and Pete found a fuckin' horrible rehearsal room in Finsbury Park and did nine- or ten-hour days for two, three months. We went there every day, and we played the set, and we turned into a different band, as a result of the busking tour, and as a result of all that training."

Asked how they could push on so intently given the circumstances, Sheppard demurs: "We had nothing else to do, really." Yet their dedication to The Clash, however battered, was also real. Ironically, with recording finally done and Rhodes distracted by mixing the album, some creative space developed. Sheppard: "We had no supervision from Bernie at all. Paradoxically, that gave me a lot of self-confidence. The three of us certainly got very, very tight."

The grind proved productive as the trio gelled more and more as a unit—and finally got a chance to show it when three European festival shows were announced, starting in late June with Roskilde in Denmark. Sheppard was glad for the respite from the endless rehearsals but had few illusions about the motivation for these performances: "These were moneymaking gigs, big festival shows." Even so, the band came to them with something to prove.

The six agonizing weeks since the return from busking also seemed to be belatedly solidifying something for Strummer. Sheppard: "We were on the bus on the way to Roskilde, Bernie was ranting as usual. But this time I saw Joe give him a look of pure hate and disgust . . . Later I realized that Joe had stopped believing in him." Soon it became clear that the showdown meeting had slowed the disintegration of Strummer's relationship with Rhodes, but not reversed it.

This was hardly the best time for internal combustion, however. Roskilde was the band's biggest show since the US Festival. While The Clash were one of the headliners, the context was now quite different than 1983. While other bands had scaled the top of the charts, The Clash had gone more than three years without a new record, much less a new hit—an eternity in the fickle world of pop music.

The band's star was in danger of fading. Nonetheless, the musicians remained ambivalent about playing the game on anyone's terms but their own. The pressure from CBS was growing, adding to the internal tensions, friction that burst into the open at a shambolic preshow Roskilde press conference.

Although often viewed as Rhodes's cat's paw, in a way Kosmo Vinyl was as much his captive as Strummer was, and nearly as weary. While The Clash was immensely important to him, he was worn down by the constant struggle. In principle, the exhausted consigliere was on the way out, but he just couldn't seem to find the will to finally make the break. Years later, Vinyl was loathe to discuss what happened that day at Roskilde. Even so, it is clear that he had been wound up tight by Rhodes beforehand and dispatched on a mission of confrontation.

The acrimonious press conference came off like a page torn out of a farcical US Festival playbook. Vinyl regularly interrupted the proceedings, sparring with the assembled journalists as well as Strummer, seeming to supersede him as the band's voice. Even the normally reserved Simonon joined the conflict. Asked if punk was dead, the bassist snapped, "It stands right in front of your eyes!"

The local newspaper, *Göteborgs-Posten*, blasted the band over the contentious exchanges, opining, "The Clash is obviously a band in big trouble." Sheppard recalls, "We didn't take part in any question-and-answer scenario. We were there for a bit, and it was chaotic." He and the others soon left.

Adding to the bad vibes, Strummer griped about the festival for being allegedly money hungry. It seemed an odd critique, given that the band was being well compensated for playing. It was also arguably misinformed, for the festival retained some of its original hippie idealism, donating much money each year to various charities. Strummer was likely unsure about the wisdom of playing at all, given his skepticism about the stadium-rock world—but of that he said nothing.

The rancor foreshadowed what would be a consequential, if hardly smooth performance. Both an audiotape and a video recorded by fans document the show. The latter conveys palpable excitement in the crowd, bopping restlessly to reggae before the band's set, with homemade Clash banners waving, all eyes focused on the empty stage.

Ironically, The Clash found itself amid another strike, although of a far less essential commodity than coal: Carlsberg & Tuborg, the leading Danish beer brewer, was facing a lengthy and determined work stoppage. This made for a significantly more "dry" festival than usual, a situation Vinyl wryly noted. Rebounding from his odd performance at the press conference, the punk raconteur provided a spirited, good-humored introduction for the band.

As Vinyl bounded off the stage, Howard set down a terse, relentless rhythm. Recognizing the introduction of "Complete Control," the audience began to spontaneously sing the *"whoaoooah whoaoooah"* backing vocals. As they did, White and Sheppard hit the song's clarion chords, simultaneously becoming illuminated by spotlights. Mostly hidden in shadows, Strummer began to sing as the tune gathered momentum, the focus still on the guitar duo.

When the song exploded into full force, the singer leaped onto a walkway that extended into the crowd, his white denim fatigues shining in the intense lights. While Strummer sported his usual *Mohawk Revenge* T-shirt, he had not worn that hairstyle for some months. Vinyl, however, had recently trimmed White's coif into the war cut, maintaining the band's Mohican quotient.

Strummer urged the crowd on, shouting out off mic, dancing at the edge of the walkway, his leg pumping. Simonon, Sheppard, and White bounded around the stage behind him, with the rock-steady Howard anchoring it all.

When "Complete Control" crashed to its end, the frontman greeted the crowd, announcing, "London calling to the faraway towns!" as the band launched into the next song. Strummer's desperate ranting of the US Festival was nowhere to be seen, replaced by a palpable desire to engage the distant audience as an ally.

Although White and Sheppard had now been part of The Clash for nearly two years—and Howard even longer—Strummer still introduced them as "the new boys." Years later, Sheppard laughed good-naturedly about this, but was quick to emphasize, "By then we completely owned the material, be it old or new."

Such confidence showed in the performance. The band segued smoothly from "London Calling" into energetic versions of "Janie

Jones" and "Safe European Home"—the latter's catchy two-note guitar opening reappearing for the first time since 1978—then into a newly dusted-off "Hate & War" with Sheppard on vocals.

The impact of the busking tour was noticeable, with the interplay of the four members out front authentic and unforced. Strummer leaned easily on Sheppard's shoulder as the guitarist kicked out the opening chords to "Garageland" and all four regularly clustered near the mic on the walkway, rubbing elbows as if out on the streets playing for spare change.

When a spooky "Armagideon Time" slowed the tempo, the band appeared relaxed, in command of the gigantic stage. Simonon even set down his bass for a turn at break dancing at the beginning of "Magnificent Seven." Strummer, in turn, led Simonon, Sheppard, and White out onto a massive speaker stack for the song's climax, the three guitarists sitting and playing, with Strummer on his feet singing.

After the musicians climbed down from their perch, they launched into "Rock the Casbah," an animated Strummer prowling the stage with the mic stand on his shoulder. As the guitars crashed into one another, the singer climbed onto the opposite speaker stack, jumping down to shout out the climatic "Allah!" at the end of the song, his arms opened to the heavens.

Strummer's banter between songs was lighthearted. He checked to see how many folks understood English, and joked about the famously ugly English weather to kick off a revamped "Three Card Trick." This was the first public evidence of the radical musical surgery involved in the new album; the song was now hitched to a jaunty ska chassis. While the changes were not necessarily improvements, the tune fit nicely into the groove the band had crafted.

As Clash shows went, this one seemed strikingly free and easy—possibly too much so for some tastes. In the shadows, Bernard Rhodes was seething, incensed that the show organizers were apparently ignoring a preshow directive not to film the band for rebroadcast. Determined to assert himself, he turned to Vinyl, dispatching his loyal lieutenant to the mic at the end of "Three Card Trick."

The evening's good vibes came to an abrupt end as Vinyl came running onstage, waving the band back and commandeering the microphone. As the confused musicians retreated, Vinyl gruffly announced, "Hallo, hallo! If you don't stop filming the show up here, there will be no more show . . . There will be no more show while they continue filming—everybody stop!"

This was a jarring intrusion. Even if the promoters were breaching an agreement, this unnecessarily disruptive protest would inevitably stall the band's momentum. But Rhodes was rarely one to use a scalpel when an ax was available.

As the unit regrouped, Strummer reached for a gentle way to restart the set, beginning an a cappella version of "Pressure Drop." The singer motioned to his band to keep their instruments silent, while encouraging them and the audience to join in the chorus. After a few rounds, the band kicked in, launching the voices to the far reaches of the festival grounds.

Strummer poured it all out, jumping up and down, leg pumping, rousing the crowd. Then, as the song neared its end, Strummer again silenced the instruments and beckoned all—including Howard from behind the drum kit—to sing together at the front of the stage, creating a huge chorus with the crowd.

It was a powerful moment and an implicit rebuke to the acerbic manager. Sheppard: "That was our nod to the busking thing, when we did 'Pressure Drop' at Roskilde, and Pete jumped off the drums, and we all sang it, kind of, a cappella. It felt good, like we were together again."

With connection between audience and band reestablished, Strummer stepped back for a blazing Sheppard-led version of "Police on My Back," followed by Simonon taking the lead on "What's My Name." Bouncing back to the mic, Strummer asked for "some help to sing 'Spanish Bombs'!" The band kicked off the song, seeming to have hit its stride again.

Suddenly, the stage went dark. The music grew quieter and slowly dwindled to silence midsong. Silhouettes of Strummer and Vinyl could be seen in urgent conversation. The crowd erupted in confused whistles, cheers, and chanting as shadows contended vigorously with one another onstage.

After a few minutes of dimly glimpsed chaos, the lights and PA came back on to reveal Vinyl midrant: "If they do not stop filming entirely, there will be no more Clash tonight. They say they have stopped but they haven't. So if they do not stop, there will be no more Clash AT ALL!"

Amid boos, whistles, and cheers, Vinyl incited the crowd: "We come here to play for the people here at the festival, not a bunch of arseholes sitting at home on television. And all these people are trying to do is rip you off!" The raspy Cockney-toned agitator paused, then shouted, "Now, do you want the filming stopped?" As the crowd roared its assent, he asked, "Do you want The Clash?" When the affirmative tumult grew even louder, Vinyl beckoned the band back onstage, roaring, "Well, let's hear it then: The Clash, THE CLASH—come on!"

Unlike Strummer's US Festival exhortations, this seemed less like an attempt to impart a crucial message and more like a tantrum from a prima-donna band. The unit itself, of course, was the main victim of the interruption. Strummer was visibly peeved, as once again they had to fight desperately to regain lost momentum.

As the band hurried back on, Strummer barked, "Let's go, let's go!" Even while scrambling to their positions, White and Sheppard ignited a sledgehammer "Clash City Rockers." The upbeat performance faced considerable inertia; one might have thought it made more sense to just pack it in for the night.

Instead, Strummer anchored himself at center stage, rallying the band to the attack. Often The Clash played its best in the most challenging of circumstances, and this night was no exception. With short, sharp commands, the singer urged the band through "London's Burning," "Clampdown," "Bankrobber," and into a moody "Broadway." This sprint seemed about far more than simply pleasing the crowd; it held the sense of a band fighting for communion with its audience.

It was odd, then, when Strummer began "Broadway" singing to himself, turned away from the crowd, hand to his head. The singer channeled the song's downtrodden protagonist as if tens of thousands were not there, just a "bum" giving testimony to a passerby on the street. "I'm telling you this mister / don't be put off by looks / I been in the ring / and I took those right hooks," Strummer sang, his head jerking back, miming the jarring blow. "And I've worked for breakfast / and I ain't had no lunch / I been on delivery / and received every punch . . ."

As the music rose and the song's hobo came out of his shell, so did Strummer. Turning to face the crowd, the frontman roared out the words. While White and Simonon joined him up front and Sheppard stomped in the back, Strummer turned one of *Sandinista!*'s lesser numbers into an urgent soul exorcism.

Even as the song's last jazzy sigh dissipated and Strummer allowed himself a satisfied "Yeah . . ." White peeled off the brittle, relentless opening notes of "Brand New Cadillac" and the band was off again, rampaging through the rest of the set: "I'm So Bored with the USA," "Tommy Gun," and "I Fought the Law."

Feedback screamed, and Strummer pointed to Howard, calling out the final salvo, a blistering "White Riot." Sheppard, White, and Simonon careened around Strummer, driving the song to a thunderous climax. The band bounded offstage briefly, and then charged back for a rough-hewn reprise of "Garageland."

This repeat was unprecedented, suggesting Strummer had a point or two to underline. The song was a vow of continued commitment to the band's roots, surely relevant given the size of the venue. However, as Sheppard notes, it also could be seen as "a coded reference to the backstage issues" with Rhodes, who held Strummer in thrall with one of the "contracts" that the song references.

One of the few details that Vinyl remembers from that night is "how angry Joe was at me and Bernard" for interrupting the show. The disruptions of the band's performance echoed the way Rhodes had thrust himself into the album, to the dismay of the actual musicians and, often, to the detriment of the music.

For Sheppard, the band's solidarity in the face of obstacles was heartening: "Looking back, I felt a sense of release. The worse the backstage machinations got, the better the gigs, both musically and emotionally, so I was really happy at Roskilde." White also recalls feeling good about the show—at least until one fan told him back-stage how much better Mick Jones was than him.

It had been a gripping, determined performance. While *Rolling Stone* would later headline a short clip of the show as "The Clash End on a Low Note," it might have been the last great Clash show, against all odds—including the impediments thrown in the band's path by its own management.

Yet there were some other notable critiques. The *Göteborgs-Posten*'s July 1 review commented on the set's lack of new material: "This year's Clash are just a pathetic echo of the past." Per-Åke Wärn, a Swedish photographer who had been impressed by earlier neo-Clash shows seconded this: "I felt like I was watching a Clash cover band."

This take held some truth. Festival shows tended to be what White derisively described as "playing the greatest hits." The absence of new songs was striking, especially since the long-awaited record was supposed to emerge soon.

Sheppard had his suspicions: "There's probably some kind of conversation somewhere between Joe and Bernie as to how we're gonna represent these songs eventually. How do you recreate this [new] record with real people? There isn't a drummer on it, so how do you go out and play those songs?"

Strummer was in charge of the set list, so the paucity of newer material might have also suggested growing discomfort with the direction taken in the studio, combined with disenchantment toward Rhodes. It also hinted at doubts about the worth of the new songs—and, by extension, the power of the neo-Clash.

White—hardly in the best shape himself, facing excruciating stomach pain from stress and excessive alcohol intake—would later write about a conversation with Strummer not long before the Roskilde show where the singer admitted to his deep depression. White responded to him with typical flippancy: "Have a fucking beer, man. That will cheer you up."

White remembers Strummer reacting with stark self-awareness: "A beer? You think it is that easy? That simple? There's no way I can't do that. One beer leads to two. Then three and another and

WE ARE THE CLASH * 315

another. I will end up drinking ten. Or twenty. Or fifty. It won't stop." Although White says that Rhodes was present and was able to help Strummer lift his spirits, the broader challenge of what was likely a combination of clinical depression and alcoholism was simply pushed aside.

While Strummer wrestled with intensely difficult issues, including how—or whether—to press forward with the new Clash, the Reagan administration revealed no qualms about its course in Central America. Effectively barred from arming the contra rebels—who Reagan called "freedom fighters" in the mold of George Washington, despite their bloody deeds and scant popular support—the government was making the rounds to allies to drum up financing, with very mixed results.

As The Clash had prepared for its return to action at Roskilde, the CIA had helped draw the feuding contra factions into a single entity, now known as the United Nicaraguan Opposition. On paper, this made for a more effective and supportable entity; in reality, little had changed. The contras remained better at sowing terror and killing civilians than defeating Reagan's Sandinista nemesis.

With Congress blocking its way, and facing battlefield reverses, the Reagan administration decided to make a play straight out of a spy novel: it would sell arms to Iran through the shadowy brokers Khashoggi and Ghorbanifar, in order to free the hostages held by Iranian ally Hezbollah. Most incredibly, White House aide Colonel Oliver North was to direct the middlemen to channel the Iranian payments to the contras, neatly dodging the congressional ban.

The timing was exquisite. According to the *New York Times*, on July 1 President Reagan publicly denounced bartering with terrorists; yet only two days later, National Security Adviser Robert McFarlane met with David Kimche, who was in the US on behalf of the Israelis who had met with Khashoggi and Ghorbanifar. In this meeting, the arms-for-hostages deal was first outlined.

On July 16, McFarlane met with Reagan and came away empowered to go forward with the Iranians and Israelis. Selling arms to an enemy in order to ransom hostages held by terrorists, then using the profits to evade US laws forbidding military aid to the contras, was audacious. It was also most likely illegal and surely politically explosive. Richard Nixon had faced impeachment for less.

Three days before Reagan chose to wager his regime on this desperate ploy, The Clash played the Rockscene festival in Gue-henno, in a remote region of France. For Sheppard and the others, Rockscene came off as an impersonal event: "We literally flew in, did the gig, and flew out." It was a bit odd for them to be there, for, as *Rolling Stone* reported, on that day—July 13, 1985—"seemingly every major rock act on earth played the Live Aid concert for African famine relief, hosted primarily in Philadelphia's JFK Stadium and London's Wembley Stadium and broadcast to over a billion people worldwide."

Even if slightly diminished by the lack of a recent hit, The Clash was a glaring omission from the Live Aid bill. When a disappointed White inquired why the band wasn't playing, Vinyl explained that bad blood existed between Strummer and show organizer, Bob Geldof, formerly of the Irish punk-pop act Boomtown Rats.

Neither this explanation nor the reappearance of the *Sex Style Subversion* banner as the backdrop at the show pleased White, much less Howard or Sheppard. Yet the band played well, with Strummer once again refraining from confrontation, despite his aversion for the stadium setting.

The only barb came from Vinyl, who marred an otherwise rousing introduction with a slap at the festival's name—"I'm sure the promoter would like me to address you as 'Rockscene,' but I can't think of a name that is more fucking patronizing in the world!"—before calling out once again to "hip-hoppers, punk rockers, young ladies, pill poppers, black toppers, and showstoppers!"

White was upset not to be playing Live Aid, and was left cold by the audience and vibe that day. Sheppard remembers the show more favorably, feeling that the band presented itself powerfully, albeit with a "greatest hits" set that once again contained only a single new song, "Three Card Trick."

But if all seemed copasetic onstage, behind the scenes division was deepening. Strummer took White aside before the show to say he was splitting with Rhodes who—ironically enough—had stayed back home to watch Live Aid. By now, White never knew what to believe when Strummer spoke. Nonetheless, he came away sensing that the end of The Clash—or another new beginning—might be near.

Bedeviled by Rhodes's never-ending windups, and Strummer's erratic behavior, White turned to Simonon with his worries about the band's fate. According to White, the bassist was the picture of equanimity: "Ever since this band began it's been on the cards. There hasn't been a single day when it might not end at any moment . . . even in the beginning. I don't worry about it. I just take each day as it comes."

When White asked if Simonon was annoyed to not be included on the new album, he shrugged and replied, "Bernie knows what's best. He is . . . difficult, but it's for the best." Eventually, Simonon would question the wisdom of his faith in the manager. For now, White knew he, Sheppard, and Howard were on their own.

Two weeks later, the band was at yet another festival, this one set up by the then-Socialist government of Greece in a partnership with the French Ministry of Culture. No tapes of the show survived, and once again The Clash, alone among all the bands on the bill, refused to allow filming.

Both Sheppard and White remember it as a barnburner. White: "It was a blinding show. At the final count I realized I played my best. And we as the band had reached our best." Nursing his tender stomach, White also played the show entirely sober for the first time and found it surprisingly satisfying.

Sheppard felt the same, viewing the night as one of the best realized of the more than 120 concerts the new Clash had played: "Athens and the few other shows we did after the busking tour made the group musically. There was another corner that we turned there, in terms of a dynamic." It didn't hurt that there were 40,000-plus fans on hand, as frenzied and fanatical as the Italians had been the previous fall.

To Sheppard and White, horizons still seemed to beckon for the band.

If the guitarists were cautiously bullish about the future, the singer was harder to read. In public, Strummer gave no indication of doing anything but staying the neo-Clash course. An interview for Greek television in advance of the Athens show underlined this stance. The film crew interviewed an animated Strummer in a *Straight to Hell* T-shirt with fifties-style rolled-up sleeves, hair slicked back, and dog tags glinting in the sun on a busy London street.

In the clip, Strummer shared hopes for the future: "We have a new record that is going to be released sometime in September . . . and we just wanted it to be up—'up,' as in not 'downer' music. We are sick and tired of people complaining and not coming up with any answers." This echoed his past ambivalence about "protest" music, much of which seemed uninspired "complaining" to him. Strummer: "I don't think complaining music goes a long way to anything."

Pumping clenched fists, then snapping his fingers, the singer went on: "We wanted to deal with reality, but we want it to be 'up' so when people hear the record they felt like they can get outside and deal with their lives, rather than . . ." Strummer fell silent, pointing to the ground with both hands—indicating people being depressed all the time, presumably—before sweeping his arms across the camera frame and declaring, "There's too much heroin in London!"

Oddly, he did not reveal anything about the record's radical musical shifts, simply responding to a question about differences from the old Clash by saying, "We're a bit more rocking now," before appearing to lampoon modern synth pop with an air pantomime of keyboard playing contrasted with guitar.

After dismissing love songs and describing his preferred lyrical subject matter as "reasons for living," Strummer celebrated the fact that the current Greek government was Socialist and denounced Thatcher's regime, calling it "the opposite of a Socialist government," and proclaiming, "It doesn't work."

More specifically, the Tory approach didn't work *for everyone*, as was suggested by the growing national divide. While granting that London's economy was buzzing, Strummer urged the journalists to "travel up north and see what they've got there—they're really crying for some kind of a life, that's all they want, a life!"

The eye-opening experiences on the busking tour seemed palpable as Strummer pressed his point: "We tried a conservative government and it doesn't work. I'll tell you one thing for sure: next election here in this land, they are going out!"

This Strummer seemed as passionate as in early 1984, covering much the same ground. Dismissing definitions of punk that saw it as "a special hairstyle or a brand new leather jacket or a certain kind of studs," Strummer argued, "Punk was an attitude that just said: 'We don't believe you.' We were being told we didn't have a right to exist because we were too unemployable, there was no future for us—and punk had the guts to step up and say, 'I don't believe you! I have the right, I have been born the same as you and I have the right to exist!'"

The singer was smiling but emphatic, first clenching his fist, then pointing straight into the camera to declare, "That is punk and that is why we will go forward!"

It was a gripping performance, albeit with a few worrisome elements. Strummer seemed slightly manic. He also seemed a bit off center, ending the chat by sweeping up the female interviewer for an impromptu jig, laughing as the camera rolled. Even so, the overall impression was of a singer still up for the fight.

With such a Strummer back at the helm, the promise of the new Clash seemed redeemable. Despite all the internal chaos, at least Sheppard and White hoped the band still might be coming together, not falling apart.

Much depended on the new record. Fan anticipation was high, the album was soon to be out, and European dates had been set for October, with tour plans for the Far East and beyond in the new year. Although Howard remained dubious, Sheppard and White dared hope that Strummer would finally split with Rhodes and definitively side with them, and all would be well.

This scenario was possible, perhaps even plausible. Sheppard, White, and Howard continued to put their backs into rehearsals as if it were reality. And yet Strummer didn't always share his true

feelings with them. A radically different course of action was beckoning the beleaguered singer.

At the Rockscene festival, Strummer had attacked Reagan from
stage for allegedly continuing to push the world toward Armageddon. However, after months of go-nowhere arms control talks,
something was starting to shift.

On July 3, the Soviet Union announced that Mikhail Gorbachev
and Ronald Reagan were going to meet—the first summit in eight
years, since before superpower relations froze over with the invasion of Afghanistan and Reagan's election. Given how close the
world had come to nuclear holocaust in late 1983, "to jaw-jaw is always better than to war-war," as Winston Churchill had once said.

Gorbachev's arrival, combined with Reagan's post-1983 conversion, would open a hopeful new era. Initially, Gorbachev viewed
the elderly president as "not simply a conservative but a political
dinosaur." Reagan was similarly skeptical, despite Thatcher's
advice—refusing to give up his "Star Wars" missile defense plan,
for example—but the personal relationship that developed helped
to thaw the ice.

Reagan deserves praise for facing down right-wing attacks for
supposedly becoming "soft" on the USSR. Still, as American foreign
policy analyst Strobe Talbott argues, it was Gorbachev who "changed
the dynamic" and took the real risks: "Gorbachev was determined
to take the Soviet Union in a radically different direction—away
from the Big Lie (through *glasnost*), away from a command economy
(through *perestroika*), and away from zero-sum competition with the
West. Reagan came to recognize that Gorbachev's goals, far from
being traditional, were downright revolutionary."

Had Strummer been aware of these shifts, it might have been a
ray of hope penetrating the thick clouds shrouding his mood. This
darkness gave birth to a new realization that came—definitively,
dramatically—after hearing the near-final mixes of the new record,
the fruit of Rhodes's own revolutionary vision.

Whatever the quality of Rhodes's contributions to the new album, no one should doubt the depth of his commitment. In the
months after the return from Munich it became an all-consuming

passion. "Bernard would have never let us take the time in the studio that he took mixing the album!" Vinyl laughs.

Even someone as traumatized by the tortuous process as Sheppard would later admit, "Bernie's basic vision, mixing punk and electronic music to update the Clash sound, in itself, had something to it." By now, the results of this experiment were becoming clearer. "This Is England" had been chosen as the first single, to be issued before the album itself. Rhodes mixed and remixed it endlessly, knowing the song would set the stage for the broader press and fan reception.

This was one of the songs the trio felt best about. "The drum machine was based off something Pete had worked out, together with a hip-hop track," Sheppard recalls. "I took a bit from an old soul song, 'Clean Up Woman' by Betty Wright, and kind of turned it backward for the riff." The result was comparable to what had been done earlier with "In the Pouring Rain."

The breakthrough was presaged by adjustments already made over months of live performance. The studio version took the advances, realized them more fully, added new dynamite, and blasted the song into the stratosphere. While Sheppard was irked that his spaghetti western bits were scrubbed by Rhodes in favor of what he called "ever more snub-nosed punk guitar," in this case at least, the nonmusician's instincts seem on target. The sound was multilayered, but still somehow lean, relentless, hungry, and mean—much like the triumphant Thatcher regime, circa 1985.

The words, of course, bitterly recounted how it felt on the other side, the losing end. Strummer's partly revamped lyrics vividly evoked cutthroat economic policies, racist violence, police brutality, the Falklands, tabloid sleaze, and social desperation, all leading up to a heart-crushing climax: "Who dares to protest / enough to react like a flame? / Out came the batons / and the British warn themselves / This is England . . ." The song sketched a claustrophobic world that afforded no room for dignity, levity, or redemption—it was the sound of brutal defeat, like "a boot stamping on a human face, forever," in the words of Orwell's *1984*.

Although the edited 45 rpm version omitted the climatic verse, even this truncated take was an astonishing achievement, going a long way to justify Rhodes's brusque artistic interventions. Utilizing mournful synthesizer swells, sampled voices, and grim yet engaging drum machine beats, all strapped to a pile-driver riff, the song was a wrenching requiem for the post–World War II English dream Thatcher had now so thoroughly vanquished.

Some of the other songs also turned out well. "Dirty Punk" captured the power glimpsed in its live version, driven by a raw guitar assault, convincingly presenting Strummer's neo-punk credo in word and sound. CBS even considered releasing it as a single; Sheppard later argued it could have been a hit, and he had a point.

"Are You Ready for War?"—inexplicably renamed "Are You Red..y?"—was sped up, with keyboards, drum machine, and guitar bursts replacing the original's tight punk-funk grooves. Sheppard hated this revision which, among other things, lost his "DJ scratch" guitar bits and the "sea shanty" swagger. Yet the revamp remained compelling in its own way.

"Dictator" was also profoundly revised; Rhodes's everything-and-the-kitchen-sink production approach was in full effect. Still, it was mildly improved, given that the original had been one of the less successful of the new tunes. White's distaste for the wild synthesizer flourishes was understandable, and the Central American radio announcer jabbering in the background could also be off-putting. But while some later deemed it "unlistenable," the resulting aural assault could also be riveting.

"Three Card Trick" and "North and South" were slightly diminished, but were still outstanding tracks. Like several other cuts, "Movers and Shakers" was hobbled by clunky electronic drums, but a catchy mariachi hook—perhaps echoing the lost Strummer/Vinyl demos—played well off the singer's passionate words.

Other tracks were nearly crippled. "We Are The Clash" was more impressive as a demo two years before. The collective rallying cry so forcefully driven home in countless concerts was nowhere to be found. This polished version added new lyrics that lost the sweep and urgency of the original, muffled guitars that hummed along far too pleasantly, a disjointed multitracked solo, and rinky-dink electro-drums.

Even worse, the song now sounded derivative, its new opening evoking a tepid "Anarchy in the UK." Elsewhere the massed backing vocals worked, but here they recalled second-string British punk band Sham 69. This was hardly the breakthrough Rhodes had sought, and surely not the paean to communal power Strummer had first envisioned.

Such missed chances abounded. "Life Is Wild" begged to be a raw punk rave-up, but was yoked to boppy synth-drums and keyboards. "Cool Under Heat" struggled to breathe, burdened by an oddly unbalanced mix and splotches of gratuitous synth dribblings. While the choruses were rousing, the verses dragged, trading its live soul swing for a clumsy shuffle.

Some songs were simply misbegotten. While "Fingerpoppin'" sounded decent, the lyrically slight song ranked as average new-wave disco. "Play to Win" had actually regressed from its unfinished demo; while the chorus remained, the verses were gone, replaced by cheesy sound effects and uninspired repartee between Strummer and Michael Fayne.

The engineer later fondly remembered the "live in the studio" interplay as perhaps the only spontaneous moment in the entire process. Nonetheless, like "Fingerpoppin'," "Play to Win" should have been relegated to a B side, replaced by a neo-Clash gem like "In the Pouring Rain," "Jericho," or "Sex Mad Roar."

The record was indeed unique, if also sometimes a bit of a car wreck. Rhodes's ambition was energizing; success at realizing it more problematic. "Bernie needed something earth-moving, ground-shaking, monumentally amazing," Sheppard sighs. "And so, what the world has been given is Bernie's idea of a monumentally earth-shaking, amazingly modern, genius record."

The guitarist quickly admits, "A lot of the ideas on the album are good ideas. They're just not arranged musically." Calling Rhodes's approach "chucking shit against the wall, seeing if it sticks," Sheppard contrasts this with the work of Mick Jones: "You could call Jones a genius, someone who can arrange brilliantly. And so, his arrangements of various samples are incredibly musical."

This critique is poignant. Moreover, at the time, Sheppard, White, and Howard knew the record did not represent what was possible with the new material and musical prowess that the neo-Clash had amassed, had the band been allowed to engage the challenge itself with appropriate production support.

"The record is not at all representative of the people that were in the band," Sheppard argues, while also granting this was not unprecedented: "You could probably level the same comment at most of *Sandinista!* and *Combat Rock* too, if you think of the other people that played there. For instance, the bass player that was on [the new record] is on 'Magnificent Seven' and most of *Sandinista!*"

Sheppard feels a critical difference lies in who was in charge: "It's also about the creative control. On both of those records, Mick is pretty much in control of the creative process, at least until you get to the Glyn Johns mix of *Combat Rock*."

Yet Jones, despite his artistry, had increasingly lost the plot. And Rhodes's bold effort was not the "unmitigated disaster" some would later claim. Even Sheppard and Howard later agreed there was value in having a nonmusician involved. "That's why punk worked, isn't it?" grants the drummer.

Rhodes's vision, however imperfectly executed, could be exciting. Strummer's critique of past records as going in too many directions at once had also been taken to heart. In this sense, the record was arguably an advance on *Combat Rock*, more conceptually unified and politically direct, and nowhere near as self-indulgent as *Sandinista!*. Other than a couple of inexplicable choices, the songs were strong, something the production sometimes obscured, but could not destroy.

The new record was not the raw punk return-to-form that Strummer had promised and fans expected. And this was not all bad. Did The Clash exist simply to fulfill such expectations? Moreover, Strummer had agreed to this new direction, since trying to recapture a hallowed past might not be the noble course.

Regardless, Strummer was now horrified by the results. In a stunning reversal, he threatened to take action to stop the record from being released. An acrimonious divorce ensued, for Rhodes refused to waver and Strummer would not be mollified, choosing to let the house fall down rather than relent. Even though contracts existed compelling Strummer to promote the album, he simply walked away. Rhodes would have his album, but he would not have his lead singer.

Strummer later told Jon Savage, "I fell out with Bernie after we returned from Munich where we recorded the tracks—somewhere between that and when he began to mix it." Savage: "So the LP's release was something you had no control over?" Strummer: "Absolutely none."

This account is a bit off, as various band members recall Strummer as hearing early mixes and—in White's case—even defending them. The essence, however, seems true enough.

"Maybe the busking tour put Joe in a different reality," Sheppard muses. "It put us all in a very, very different reality for a while there. 'Cause let's face it, that's what Joe is. He's Woody Guthrie, Bob Dylan, a minstrel, a troubadour. Imagine going back—after doing the tour—and listening to that record. Joe Strummer is not a guy that you associate with drum machines and synthesizers."

One might ask why the singer hadn't seen this before. The erratic swings suggest he was worn down by years of struggle in The Clash, by personal grief, by the pressures of family, art, and addiction. So he put his trust in Rhodes, who was more than a manager, or even a mentor, almost a surrogate father. If that trust proved to be misplaced, Strummer's blindness was a very human one.

This turn of events had enormous consequences for Strummer and the band. Sheppard: "Joe pretty much disappeared off the scene very quickly after the end of that relationship [with Rhodes]. I was at sessions where the record started to get finished in England, sessions that Joe had nothing to do with. He had disappeared, we didn't know where he was—turns out, he was in Spain."

In Granada, Jesús Arias found Strummer drinking heavily, shrouded in darkness: "He had nothing good to say about The Clash, about the new record . . . He didn't want to talk about any of it." The two went to find Federico García Lorca's final resting place in the middle of one drunken night. "Let's dig him up," Arias recalls Strummer insisting. But the area was a spacious plain where perhaps hundreds of victims of Franco's fascist forces were buried in a mass grave. Recognizing the futility of this quest, Strummer dissolved into tears.

Arias used their time together to revisit a past topic of conversation: Mick Jones. Arias: "Joe was very down about his personal situation—his father dead, his mother dying, Mick Jones gone . . . I told him. 'Paul McCartney and John Lennon on their own, good—but together they were the Beatles! Mick Jagger and Keith Richards alone, okay, but together they are the Stones! You and Mick are the same . . .' I said this over and over."

Outwardly, the singer still resisted this notion, but inside something was shifting. Jones and Rhodes had cofounded The Clash more than anyone else; a soul-weary Strummer couldn't imagine the band without at least one at his side. If Rhodes was out . . . then Jones was back in. How this could work legally, personally, or artistically was unclear, but he began to try to make it so.

In Strummer's absence, band matters began to unravel swiftly, first resulting in blown tour dates. The Swedish daily *Expressen* reported in September, "The Clash has been forced to cancel their whole tour of Europe including three shows in Sweden. Only half of the band's original members are part of today's band—two years ago they sacked guitar player Mick Jones who has now teamed up with former drummer Topper Headon to claim equal right to the name Clash."

According to Thomas Johansson of EMA Telstar, the promoter for the Swedish shows, "They've worked all weekend in England trying to solve the conflict, [but] if Strummer and his band go on tour under the name 'Clash' there's risk of Jones and Headon being able to stop them from collecting the money from the gigs."

This seemed odd, as the new Clash had already played Scandinavia numerous times, including at Roskilde less than three months before. However, Johansson said, "It's not until now that the former members have put their threat of suing into action and contacted a lawyer." *Expressen* reported that even the "This Is England" 45 and forthcoming album might be abandoned: "Currently the band's label CBS don't know if they will be able to release the records or not."

The story was convincingly told, but it was not true. Sheppard later called it "a smoke screen" meant to cover for the fact that "there was no band to play the shows" because The Clash's singer was nowhere to be found.

Strummer now believed he had made a catastrophic error, and was trying to make it right—but it was too late. The steel wheels were rolling, and the train couldn't be turned around. On September 22, a single of "This Is England" appeared with "Do It Now" as the B side of the 45, and "Sex Mad Roar" added to the 12-inch.

Eddie King had parted ways with the band after a dispute with Strummer a few months before. Nonetheless, his striking images graced the single's cover, put into final form by Julian Balme, who had been recruited by Vinyl to step into the breach.

Two Mohawked punks—one female, one male—were pictured in front of a revised Piccadilly Circus, bursting with Clash commentary: *Mohawk Revenge, Cool Under Heat, Club Left, Discussion Disco, Sex Style Subversion*. Mixed in were an advertisement promising "eternal sunshine," as well as one for a strip club and a casino—with a skull and crossbones next to it—and a sign saying, PARTY PLANNED. Looming over all of this, as if in judgment, was a video-screen version of the Lady Justice statue from the London courthouse. Balme: "Eddie was really forward-looking, and his work has been terribly overlooked . . . The Clash was always visually aware, and, to my mind, Eddie's graphics were brilliant, always breaking boundaries," all while tipping his hat to punk's past.

The visuals packed a punch, and the song hit even harder, with the hastily recorded but potent B sides worthy additions. As the first shot in a vinyl neo-Clash offensive, it startled those not expecting to hear synthesizer and drum machine contending with punk guitar. Nonetheless, it was well worth the lengthy wait, seeming to promise a similarly accomplished album soon to come.

CBS hoped that this brash electro-punk Molotov cocktail would find favor with the record-buying public. A promotional onesheet prepared at the time proclaimed, "In light of the band's three-year absence from recording and performing, it is certainly no under-statement to say that radio, retail, and most important of all—the legions of dedicated CLASH fans and fanatics who buy the records and concert tickets—are all literally dying for this record."

"This Is England" sleeve, designed by Eddie King and Julian Balme.

This ignored the nearly six months of touring the band had done in 1984, as well as numerous shows in 1985. Still, it suggested CBS was ready to pull out all the stops. There would be yellow and orange versions of the cover art, an extensive advertising campaign, and selected dance remixes. A UK video of "This Is England" was to become available in time for the American release, with plans for additional videos. The onesheet concluded: "All these elements are coming together to herald the return of one of the premiere punk bands of the 1980s, and the release of one of our most important records for 1985."

But as "This Is England" rose to #24 on the UK charts, warning signs were flashing. When Sheppard, Howard, and White went out with Vinyl to film footage for a video, neither Strummer nor

Simonon appeared. No videos or live shows would ultimately materialize to support the single. It sank off the charts just before the new album, *Cut the Crap*, appeared a bit over a month later.

The name was apparently drawn from a snatch of dialogue in the dystopian film *Road Warrior*. While it was intended to bluntly communicate the new Clash's initial mission—to vanquish both the weak-kneed pop music and the ugly right-wing politics of the moment—to the demoralized White, Howard, and Sheppard, it seemed as clumsy as some of the synth-and-drum-machine-saddled songs. They had no say in the choice, just as they had no control over the music.

Cut the Crap cover, designed by Eddie King and Julian Balme, with photo help from Mike Laye.

They were still needed, however, to flog the record with live performances, a mission made considerably more difficult by the fact that their singer was missing. White later recalled Rhodes as convening a band meeting to announce that Strummer had gone "mad . . . He's lost touch with reality." Yet the never-say-die agitator would not be deterred: "The Clash has always been an idea . . . Now, how to take that idea to the next level!"

"[Bernie] was saying, 'We'll find another singer and carry on—*seriously!*" White says with a shudder. "He certainly had that intention." This seemed insane. The skeptical trio were still drawing their wages, however, so had little to lose from lingering around to watch the ensuing chaos. White, for one, still hoped their erstwhile leader would return, somehow, some way.

Any hope they had of Strummer riding to the rescue like the cavalry in his beloved western movies was soon dashed. The singer did eventually convene them to officially announce he had split from Rhodes, but informed them at the same time that he intended to try to reform the original band with Jones, even though this utterly betrayed the entire rationale for the past two years.

Their services were no longer needed, with a small severance payment offered as a consolation prize. The trio who had suddenly been made redundant might have been excused if they felt treated a little bit like trash. Sheppard recalls Howard as floating the possibility of rerecording the album without Rhodes, but Strummer's reaction made it clear he had closed that chapter and moved on.

Strummer then asked that they not join in any effort by Rhodes to continue on, and all three agreed. It was short but hardly sweet, as Sheppard explains: "We had the meeting at his house, he said, 'I'm not going to go on, and I'd ask you not to'—and that was it. 'That's the end, here's a grand, sorry—see you later.'"

Shortly thereafter, Strummer was in hot pursuit of Jones to try to get him to rejoin The Clash. As Jones had gone to the Caribbean on vacation, a hilarious quest involving Strummer pedaling around an island on a borrowed bicycle ensued.

While Strummer succeeded in tracking down his former best friend and creative partner, Jones was unwilling to abandon Big Audio Dynamite. Not surprisingly, he enjoyed having complete artistic control, and the unit had its own album coming out soon. The spurned Strummer took a listen to the results of Jones's efforts and swiftly dubbed it "the worst shit I ever heard."

This reaction was to be expected, given the duo's vast musical differences. What Strummer heard was a more artful, but far less political or guitar-driven version of the hybrid Rhodes was attempting. The encounter scarcely repaired the relationship between Strummer and Jones, and it suggested how misbegotten the whole reunion idea had been in the first place.

While this last-ditch idea was dying, another idea was in similar straits. First, Rhodes tried to convince Simonon to take over the vocal spot. When that predictably failed, he got Vinyl to arrange open auditions for a new singer. The whole business unfolded at the Electric Ballroom, where Sheppard, White, and countless other aspirants had strutted their stuff two years earlier, when the possibilities of a retooled Clash seemed limitless.

Sheppard joined in, not really intending to continue on but simply getting leads on possible personnel for a new band: "It was truly surreal—Bernie and Kosmo had somehow convinced themselves it could be done." It could not, but Rhodes's desperation was understandable. The album was about to launch, and it would be nearly impossible to promote it, as the band that made it could not perform. Like Strummer, Rhodes likely recognized the bitter taste in his mouth: defeat.

There were, of course, matters far weightier than the fate of a record or a band. While The Clash was in its death throes, so too was the Cortonwood colliery, the cradle of the miners' strike. After the stoppage officially ended, the local union had kept the fight alive in its pit by refusing to collaborate in the mine's closure.

The truth was unavoidable, however: if the union kept fighting the closure, it would lose sooner or later. If later, its members—already stretched beyond reasonable bounds by the suffering of the strike—would forfeit even the token severance payments that might mildly cushion their looming joblessness.

A Sheffield daily, the *Star*, later reported, "Early in October 1985 the Cortonwood men took a heartbreaking decision to abandon their fight to save their colliery. Faced with the prospect of depriving [those who retired voluntarily] of up to £30,000 each if they prolonged the closure battle, the Cortonwood NUM branch withdrew its objections."

As a result, "miners' leaders at the NUM's Sheffield headquarters, the Yorkshire NUM's Barnsley headquarters, and at Corton-wood were silent about the votes to give up the fight, which won with a three-to-one majority at the doomed pit." Three hundred and twenty miners lost their jobs right away; another three hundred and seventy transferred to other mines, with unemployment delayed for some months, or at most a few years.

For these workers and tens of thousands of others like them in what was once the industrial heartland of Britain, a particularly resonant metaphor from "This Is England" might have come to mind: "this knife of Sheffield steel."

Sheffield made the best steel in the world, so it had been said, when the future seemed bright. But that moment had passed, taking lives, dreams, communities with it. Once the toast of the industrial world, towns in Britain's beleaguered north, like those in America's Rust Belt, faced the bleakest of prospects. "The wrong side of a scissor blade" they surely were, and the knife was in Thatcher's—and, across the sea, Reagan's—hands.

Was this pruning "superfluous branches . . . that bearing boughs may live"—or something more akin to murder? To those tossed on the scrap heap, Sheffield steel now cut the flesh of those who created it, a working class that had defeated fascism, awed the world with its industrial accomplishments, and built the might of Great Britain, an island-nation that once ruled a vast global empire.

Workers created this wealth, but did not own it. After the crushing of the miners' strike, fewer and fewer remained who felt it was worth asking why.

On October 25, 1985, the Cortonwood colliery closed for good. "The last cage-load of miners on a production shift came up at lunchtime, to be met by a posse of journalists," the *Star* detailed. "Many miners, still bitter about defeat in the strike, refused to speak, but those who did made it clear they believed the fight had been worthwhile."

Cut the Crap arrived in this heartless Britain that was striding boldly into the new, treading thoughtlessly on the old. Lacking all but the most basic promotion, it would rise to #16 in the UK charts, and

#88 in the US, before falling away into an abyss, already cast off and disowned by most of its makers.

The album's vast political ambition could nonetheless be glimpsed dimly via a "CLASH COMMUNIQUE OCTOBER '85" on the inner sleeve. Dashed off by Rhodes, it was nestled next to the lyrics for three of the album's twelve songs—the only ones Strummer had apparently left behind before his abrupt exit.

The grammatically eccentric blurb read: "Wise MEN and street kids together make a GREAT TEAM . . . but can the old system be BEAT?? no . . . not without YOUR participation . . . RADICAL social change begins on the STREET!! so if your looking for some ACTION . . . CUT THE CRAP and Get OUT There."

Even more than the risky, erratically realized music, this earnest screed came off a bit awkward, even cartoonish. White predictably found it horrifying—"more soap-powder rebellion"—but even a sympathetic observer could see it lacked the nuance, depth, and humor Strummer had so often brought to The Clash's radical politics. Much like the album itself, the broadside presented an inviting target.

Reviews in the UK music press were predictably merciless. Mat Snow wrote a withering NME critique, "No Way, Jose," a sarcastic smack at "José Unidos," the pseudonym chosen by Rhodes to suggest that Strummer had coproduced the record. *Melody Maker*'s Adam Sweeting likened *Cut the Crap* to a shipbuilder trying his best to recapture old glories, only to see them "banged back together by a man holding the blueprint upside down." Only Jack Barron in *Sounds* refused to join the hazing, bestowing 4.5 out of five stars on the album.

More measured responses could be found in the USA, with the self-appointed dean of American critics, Robert Christgau, awarding it a B+. Although that seems a fair assessment, a steady stream of invective and dismissal would rise, tarring the record—and the whole neo-Clash experiment—as a failure.

If this take was unfair and ahistorical, such were the times into which the record had been born: an "England grown cold" in the words of Jon Savage. This context mattered. It gave birth to the neo-Clash experiment and provided the effort with lasting relevance, no matter its ultimate defeat. Indeed, those last songs, even when never fully realized, had much to offer to the challenges of that moment, and of many moments yet to come.

In his definitive 1991 punk tome *England's Dreaming*, Savage called *Cut the Crap* "an ambitious and moving state-of-the-nation address with innovative use of rap rhythms and atmosphere." This hardly reflected the critical consensus about the deeply flawed yet important record, but was not far off the mark.

By then, praise mattered little, for the band once called The Clash had long ceased to exist, except in the hearts and minds of its fans.

CHAPTER TEN
AIN'T DIGGIN' NO GRAVE

Immigrants being evicted from "The Jungle," October 2016. (Photo by Philippe Huguen/AFP.)

Constant revolutionizing of production, uninterrupted disturbance of all social conditions, everlasting uncertainty and agitation distinguish the bourgeois epoch from all earlier ones. All fixed, fast-frozen relations, with their train of ancient and venerable prejudices and opinions, are swept away, all new-formed ones become antiquated before they can ossify. All that is solid melts into air, all that is holy is profaned, and man is at last compelled to face with sober senses his real conditions of life, and his relations with his kind.
—Karl Marx and Friedrich Engels, *The Communist Manifesto*

As for the future, your task is not to foresee it, but to enable it.
—Antoine de Saint Exupéry

R iot police encircled a restless, angry mass gathered on a cool fall day. Shoving ensued where the lines briefly intersected, as frustration and fear threatened to burst into violence. A new life lay beyond the police line, but raw hope was hardly a match for batons and body armor wielded with military discipline.

It could have been the British miners facing off with police, struggling to save jobs and communities, but it was now thirty years later and two hundred miles to the east of the coalfields where that titanic conflict had decided the course of a nation. This was the new world born of that losing struggle—and others like it—playing out its contradictions at a sprawling shantytown called "the Jungle."

This makeshift colony of immigrants nestled at the edge of Calais in northwestern France, just across the English Channel where the two countries were now connected by a heavily trafficked tunnel. These people had mostly fled desperate areas of the Middle East and Africa, riven by grinding poverty or devastated by wars that ignited after the disastrous US invasion of Iraq in 2003. Having lived through untold horrors, they now hoped to make their way to a better home.

On this day in October 2016, a sign at the Jungle's entrance claimed over eight thousand ragged, weary souls lived there—perhaps 1,500 of them children—but no one really knew for sure. What was clear, however, was the determination of French officials to dismantle the camp, to disperse the mass, and, in the process, most likely dash dreams of making it to the United Kingdom, their promised land.

The Jungle had become a flash point for conflicting visions of Europe and the world. Some saw the camp as a festering sore to be lanced, its residents scarcely more than animals, with walls needed across once-open borders. Others saw the Jungle in more human terms, not without danger, but filled also with suffering and aspiration, a prick to the consciences of rich Westerners.

On a concrete overpass just outside the camp, an anonymous yet acclaimed graffiti artist called Banksy offered his take: a life-size stencil of billionaire Steve Jobs, cofounder of Apple, portrayed carrying a small bag of clothing like a refugee in one hand and an original Mac computer in the other.

A statement made the connection: "We're often led to believe migration is a drain on the country's resources, but Steve Jobs was the son of a Syrian migrant. Apple is the world's most profitable company, it pays over $7 billion in taxes—and it only exists because [the US] allowed in a young man from Homs." Banksy's words were backed up by money and supplies donated to the camp.

Some well-intentioned souls tried to preserve the artwork behind glass, but such was a pipe dream, as the reclusive street artist knew. Soon enough, even more anonymous hands had made his art their own. The figure of Jobs now formed the I in a huge black and red message: LONDON CALLING.

The scene suggested that if The Clash had ended with a whimper more than a bang thirty years before, its reverberations continued to ripple into the world.

"I know human misery / down in dusty shanties," Joe Strummer sang in "The Dictator," mocking inequality and indifference: "But my palace ain't for you scum." The song had sought to make the suffering of the "third world" real for "first world" audiences. Now the worlds were merging into one in the Jungle, equidistant from the wealthy European capitals of Paris and London.

Although this rising reality of "one world, not three" was something The Clash had struggled for, this new vista was hardly the stuff of its dreams. Sometimes the Money God seemed ascendant everywhere, with profit forever worth much more than people, who were largely pawns on the chessboard of global finance. "We ain't gonna be treated like trash," vowed "We Are The Clash," but all across the human frontier, millions upon millions of lives were being thrown away.

This was not how it was supposed to be. If The Clash, the miners, the "New Deal" Democratic Party, and so much else had gone to the ground in the hard-fought mid-1980s, the promise of a new world dawning seemed immense. With opponents defeated, Reagan and Thatcher had turned to realize their vision of vast horizons with liberty, economic growth, and prosperity for all.

"The Big Bang" became the name for the explosion of financial deregulation unleashed by Thatcher in 1986. Part of a broader "bonfire of regulations," it ushered in a new era where the market was allowed free rein, offering myriad profit-making possibilities to the corporate sector and, thus, it was said, to the economy as a whole. While the US savings-and-loan crisis that erupted around the same time—abetted by Reagan's similar deregulation—suggested danger as well as opportunity, few in power took notice.

By 1986, dark clouds of Rhodes's legal reprisals against Strummer loomed. The band was all over except for lawyers and accountants clocking billable hours. Freed from touring, recording, and rehearsals, the members mostly retreated to their own corners to contemplate what life held next.

The wreckage was significant, but not without bits of mordant comedy. Sheppard describes an increasingly forlorn Rhodes: "So I started getting woken up every morning by Bernie. The phone in the flat was a pay phone in the hall, and it would ring every morning, I'd be in my fucking pajamas, on the phone with Bernie, half asleep, and him going on about, 'You shouldn't be listening to fucking Roland Kirk—you should be fucking out there, and doing this, you know, you're not happening,' and all this. At one point I finally said, 'Bernie, why are you ringing me? *Why are you ringing me?*' And he said, 'Beause there's no one else.'"

Among the missing was Kosmo Vinyl, who had no stomach for legal contention. The consigliere finally made good on his desire to leave the music business behind. Devastated by the band's collapse and disgusted with a country he saw falling fully into Thatcher's grip, Vinyl made a new home in New York City.

Rhodes did manage to gain full ownership of *Cut the Crap*, among other concessions. But while he was undeterred in his fight for the Clash carcass, others were more reflective. Michael Fayne, for one, defends him: "Bernie paid my bills, and bought me clothes—treated me like a son! So I've got a lot of respect for Bernie, in that way, because of the way he treated me."

Still, Fayne admits, "But I know how he treated some other people," adding, "Bernie should have just started a whole new band, without Joe, without all those guys—I don't know why he didn't do that. I suppose, if you've got a cash cow, you want to milk it for as long as you can. I think that's basically what was going on."

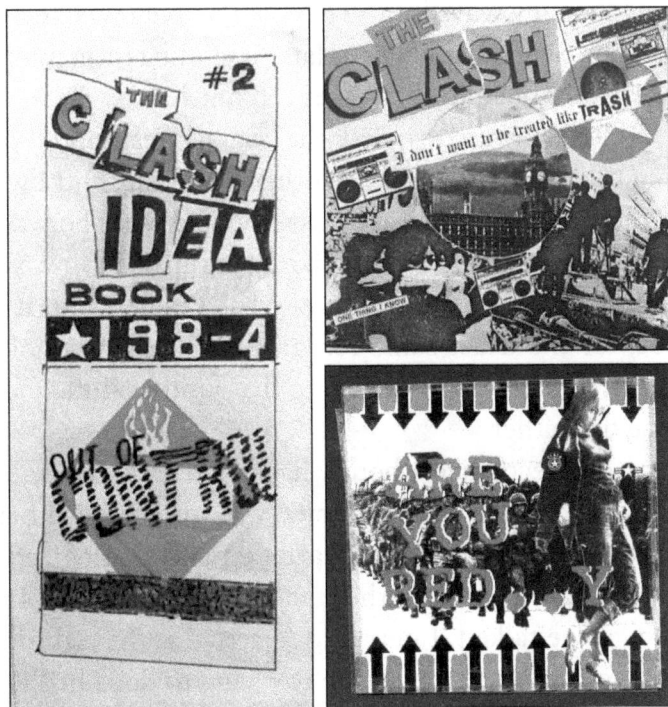

Left: "We can strike the match / if you spill the gasoline"—draft of a never-produced *Idea* matchbook cover. (Designed by Eddie King.) Top right: draft of "We Are The Clash" sleeve for a never-released single. (Designed by Eddie King.) Bottom right: draft of sleeve for never-released "Are You Red..y" single. (Designed by Julian Balme.)

This is not entirely fair to Rhodes, for his idealism was real, albeit largely untethered to any consideration for others. He was a man who dreamed big, and dreamed of revolution. The Clash was perhaps his greatest dream. Letting go of this band was not easy for the irascible but dedicated manager.

Similarly, White found it difficult to move on, indulging in gratuitous sex and excessive drink after also breaking up with his longtime girlfriend. When he confronted Strummer about his abdications as bandleader, the singer admitted, "It's all my fault." But seeing Strummer seeming whipped and broken proved a slender satisfaction. "There was no arguing with Joe, he just agreed with everything you said, even if it was wrong," White later wrote.

White's time in The Clash would leave lasting damage, almost as if he had fought in a war, or joined a pernicious cult. This comparison might seem over the top, but the experience was deeply dehumanizing in many ways for the newer members who felt chewed up and spit out. Strummer knew it, later confiding to an interviewer, "I hope we didn't fuck up their lives too much."

Like White, Howard carried the scars: "Year upon year, we were being told this, that, and the other by Bernie, and I would go on about the fact that I couldn't possibly take what he was saying as read. And Joe was saying, 'It's like being in the army, you have to . . . Unless we all agree to follow what's being told, it doesn't work.' But, for the exact same reason I wouldn't have joined the fucking army, I didn't respond well to that kind of stuff, and I don't think Vince did either."

Howard did recognize Rhodes had good intentions, however hard to discern. When the drummer was about to quit midway through the 1984 US tour, the manager actually apologized for the ugly outburst that had caused the standoff, saying: "Look, I'm sorry about the way we talked. I'm trying to arrive at the right idea, but we weren't getting there. What we're trying to do is brilliant—it's big, it's amazing—and I have to be harsh on you in order to get the best out of you."

Rhodes's uncommonly contrite words mollified the drummer who, to his lasting regret, returned to the fold only to face another year and a half of dictatorial chaos. Howard: "We were constantly being battered from side to side on many, many levels: musically, emotionally, sartorially. Every single thing that we did was up for ritual and public annihilation. Not that many people do respond that well to that. Making things difficult for us did not succeed in bringing out the best; it just succeeded in making things difficult for us."

Yet the trio had persisted. Sighing, Howard explains: "Other than the glamour of the situation, of being in a band everyone knew, the reason why everybody threw themselves face-first into it was because there was a kernel of truth somewhere, buried underneath the negativity, where everybody kind of went, 'Yeah, yeah, yeah—you're right, that could be it!' If we just—as Joe had done—exorcised our middle-class demons, and stopped being 'musos,' we could actually do something pure, something revolutionary. You did kind of feel like, 'Okay, if I look hard enough, if I try hard enough, it *might* be there.'"

This aspiration reflected the band's staggering ambition, and perhaps it could have been realized. But it could also be a highway to hell. Sheppard seemed to come through better than the others. "Whatever you can say about Bernie, he never let us be pampered rock stars, never let us get comfortable," Sheppard says. "Of course, he took it too far, but it had some value."

Howard echoes this: "I think Nick can ride things quite well. And Nick had a far purer punk ethic than any of us did, 'cause he was in the Cortinas and he saw the start of it. Whereas I was listening to fucking prog rock, you know? Now I can see the chaos of any of those things is actually the value of it. That's the whole fucking point. I can see that now. But at the time, it wasn't clear."

Ongoing failures to follow through made it worse. After the break-up, Strummer told White, "I'll see you're all right, make sure you're sorted, get some money . . . you all will," meaning the three who gave so much only to be jettisoned.

Perhaps Strummer's low spirits paralyzed him, or maybe the legal chaos created by his untimely departure was too great to make such payments possible. In any case, no money appeared. Soon even the meager wages stopped, and there was one more broken promise to add to the pile.

Ironically, none of the three had signed formal agreements when joining The Clash. So they were not entangled in the legal mess, but also could not pursue compensation for their creative work, and had no rights to anything. By contrast, Rhodes had audaciously claimed songwriting credit equal to Strummer for *Cut the Crap*.

Howard: "I never had a contract of any description at all. It's funny, actually. In all of this, the thing that I think I'm most angry and most bitter about is the fact that I didn't get any money. They got a *lot* of money, and I didn't get any."

While Fayne expresses relief that he personally was never bound to Rhodes by contract, he adds, "I feel a little bit sorry for Pete, Nick, and Vince, in the sense that I think that Joe afterward definitely felt that he should have stood up. He should have fought, you know, that's what he should have done."

Howard understood Strummer's dilemma to a degree: "After getting rid of Mick, Joe relied on Bernie a great deal more . . . which meant he was probably a little bit lost. He made a decision—and one thing Joe did do in life is, if he made a decision, he would go the whole fucking way with it, you know. Whether you're making the right decision, or the wrong one, it's just doing it, and living the consequences. And I think that's what Joe actually did."

The singer had walked a rough road, but he hadn't truly seen the neo-Clash experiment through. As White bitterly notes, "At the end, Joe realized he'd made a mistake—but rather than just deal with Bernie, he just got rid of the whole thing. He decided to fold the whole thing, drop everything like a stone, like a hot potato, and denounce it all, rather than take responsibility for what he had pretty much engineered. That was typical of Joe, at that time, in his fashion, to completely run out on everything—and that included me and Nick and Pete and Bernie."

Strummer found some distraction after the break-up producing an album by the Spanish band 091, but this was hardly smooth sailing either. The singer would soon largely disappear from public view, parenting a second daughter, Lola, while dabbling in acting and film soundtracks. Julian Balme recalls, "In the late eighties I worked in Notting Hill, around the corner from Joe's house, and I'd often bump into him in the neighborhood. I do remember him being totally, totally lost . . . He'd given it his all but now was running on empty."

Not all was darkness. Strummer relished his fatherly role in many ways. Freed from road warrior demands, he was able to be more present for his kids. He was also able to visit his beloved Sandinista Nicaragua while making films, and headlined a short, chaotic "Rock Against the Rich" tour sponsored by anarcho-agitators Class War in 1988. But Strummer's guilt never seemed to lessen.

When one of this book's authors interviewed Strummer in 1989, the ghosts of the mideighties were still palpable. Asked what advice he'd give musicians just starting out, Strummer's response hinted at *Cut the Crap*'s lasting trauma: "Always play the music the way you want to play it rather than the way that somebody you don't fully know or trust can get in and change it. The better the musician is in control in the music, the better it is going to sound. I'm not saying that nonmusicians can't contribute—because they can—but [you] can't trust their judgment all down the line. I'd like the musician to be in control of the music."

Asked directly about the final version of The Clash, Strummer demurred: "An idea only exists in a framework of time. Like we can say Marcel Duchamp putting out the urinal in an art gallery and saying, 'This my piece,' is much better when we consider it was 1917. Completely shocking—we can't imagine how shocking that was, of its time! Punk rock was of its time. We didn't really realize in 1984 that an idea drowns like a fish out of water, out of its time. We thought, 'Let's do an experiment to find that out . . .' We didn't know we would find that out, but I think I found that out, that punk was of its time, and it couldn't go again."

Strummer even seemed to welcome this passing, in part for the weight taken from his shoulders: "Now we have rap and other things that are heavy, heavy like 'Fuck tha Police' and all that. As far as I'm concerned, I've just got to drift off somewhere and try not to annoy people. That's how I see my role: try to write something good, try to record it good, maybe play it around on stages sometimes, maybe not. Maybe do film sound . . . I just try to keep useful. I don't see myself as having any influence left, or any message left, really."

Asked if he hoped his music could still inspire change, Strummer was guarded: "Well, that would be nice, but . . . Life is a funny ride. You go up and you go down. I think both experiences are interesting."

Strummer dodged when pressed on how The Clash connected to his work now: "I can't think of an answer to your question. All I know is: I write a song—why, I don't know. And when I get up on the stage and sing it—why, I don't know. There is no answer. Why does the sun rise? Why do we get up in the morning? Why do we drive the automobile down the right-hand side of the road? Why don't we just do a U-turn and drive it up the other side of the road? I don't know why . . ."

A sense of profound melancholy was impossible to miss. In "Clash City Rockers" Strummer had sung "You got to have a purpose / Or this place is gonna knock you out sooner or later." In these post-Clash years, one friend described Strummer as "a soldier without an army." While the absence of The Clash as a source of purpose for him was significant, the challenge likely ran deeper.

Over recent decades, depression has become more recognized as a medical condition, not a personal failing, with treatment options growing. Bruce Springsteen, an artist who was profoundly touched by The Clash, later shared details of his own bouts with darkness. As the New York Times reported, Springsteen "credits medication and the resolve of his wife and bandmate, Patti Scialfa, with being able to survive the onslaught." Springsteen: "During these periods I can be cruel: I run, I dissemble, I dodge, I weave, I disappear, I return, I rarely apologize, and all the while Patti holds down the fort as I'm trying to burn it down."

Much of this seems to echo Strummer's own struggles, which were no doubt worsened by often high-functioning but very real addiction. By the early nineties, the acting out had capsized his marriage with Gaby Salter. Sadly, attitudes and knowledge were more limited at the time, and Strummer was loath to seek help. Nor had the Clash camp been set up to provide such enlightened palliatives.

For some, the sense of an immense opportunity missed is haunting. Fayne: "Joe was tired, really needed help . . . He needed The Clash! Because if he'd had The Clash at the point when all this shit went down, he could have got it all out, in an honest way, and it would have worked. It would probably have been the best Clash album ever, with all those emotions, 'cause you can't fault Joe for his writing. The problem is if you don't have the vehicle, you don't have the vehicle."

By this, Fayne meant Strummer needed the Jones/Headon Clash. Apparently Strummer felt the same at the end, even telling Antonio Arias of 091 that a "This Is England" couplet—"I got my motorcycle jacket / but I'm walking all the time"—was an oblique comment on the failings of the new band. This needn't be a slam on those involved, only an admission of a lack of chemistry. Yet a strong case could be made that Strummer did have what he needed, if only he had trusted it.

As these pages show, Strummer's comrades never threw in the towel—he did. White: "Joe didn't have enough belief in his own vision. He gave too much credit to Bernie for the success of the band, for creating him as 'Joe Strummer.'" The singer's true failing might be that he trusted Rhodes, then lunged for Jones, but didn't stand by the unit who for two years honorably upheld the Clash banner.

All three have mourned the lack of opportunity to prove their mettle—and, by extension, that of the entire neo-Clash experiment—in the studio. Even Howard, who has tended to be the most dismissive of the unit's musical accomplishments, admits, "When the five of us were together, there was a certain calm—which was always invaded by Bernie and Kosmo—but if it had been allowed to continue, had been trusted a little more, it could have produced something of lasting worth."

Sheppard: "Who am I to say what the record would have sounded like? Still, things were definitely getting better [musically]. For example, the interplay between me and Vince continued to develop, to get strong. So if we were left to our own devices, as a group of five people, I think we would have made a record that would have done justice to the songs—and there were some great songs. I think we would have made a good record, yeah. Fuck me, it's not that difficult!"

Sheppard is quick to admit, "That's neither here nor there—because that didn't happen." Yet if history has any use, it is to provide lessons—and there are lessons aplenty in this ambitious yet failed misadventure.

But as The Clash's former members sifted the ashes, Reagan and Thatcher pressed their advantage, remaking the world in their image. This was not all bad. In 1986, Reagan defied pressure from the nativist wing of the Republican Party to pass immigration reform, legalizing millions of undocumented migrants, including many driven to the US by his bloody Central American wars.

Growing respect between Gorbachev and the American leader helped end the Cold War, pulling the world back from the abyss. Indeed, the two came close to abolishing their nuclear arsenals at the Reykjavik summit of October 1986. Even though the meeting ended without an agreement—due to Reagan's insistence on keeping his pet "Star Wars" program—it set the stage for dramatic reductions not only in superpower tensions, but in actual nuclear stockpiles.

Not all went well for the ascendant conservatives. Reagan's "Iran-contra" gamble crashed on October 5, 1986, when a plane running arms to the contras was shot down. CIA employee Eugene Hasenfus survived but was captured by the Sandinistas. Princeton University history professor Julian Zelizer recounts, "The scandal was enormous, resulting in Reagan suffering the worst fall in approval ratings since those numbers were tracked, leaving the White House paralyzed, struggling to survive."

Unknown artist weighs in on Iran-
Contra scandal and Reagan legacy, 1987.

By rights, this should have brought down the administration. But while high-level officials were convicted in court for their actions, the "Teflon president" walked away unscathed. As Zelizer notes, "Not only did Reagan stay in office—he ended his two-term presidency with a historic breakthrough [by signing] a major arms agreement with the Soviet Union."

And yet, while Reagan was victorious in many regards, he failed to extinguish either the Sandinistas or El Salvador's FMLN. The latter fought the US-backed military to a standstill, and ultimately emerged as a powerful electoral force after a peace agreement was signed. El Salvador remained violent and impoverished, however, with a network of savage gangs sprouting from the postwar ruins.

As for the Sandinistas, they lost a 1990 election, but bounced back under the leadership of Daniel Ortega to regain power in the twenty-first century, despite splits in their movement. While their idealism peeled away over time, replaced by growing authoritarianism and corruption, they proved to be far more than a Soviet pawn. If the FSLN did not live up to their initial promises, the same might be said for the Reagan policy that lit the fires of war in the region, but did little to heal the devastation.

Across the ocean, Thatcher would win a third election in 1987, albeit with a reduced percentage of votes and a smaller parliamentary majority. She would fall in 1990, toppled by public outrage over the so-called "poll tax" and a rebellion inside the Tory party. While the grassroots uprising against the poll tax was sweet revenge for many active in the miners' strike, the Conservatives remained in power, with Thatcherite rule fully entrenched by then.

As for the miners, Arthur Scargill's prophecy turned out to be true: the industry was square in the Tory bull's-eye. Relentless rounds of pit closures were followed by privatization. The decline was abetted by competition from cheap imported coal and other power sources. By the end of the 1990s, only 13,000 remained of a work force that had been over 200,000 before the strike. While some heralded this as a victory for efficiency, the pain it caused for workers was horrific.

While Thatcher remained unrepentant, some of her henchmen later admitted to regrets. In 2009, Norman Tebbit, secretary of trade and industry during the strike, acknowledged, "Many of these communities were completely devastated, with people out of work turning to drugs . . . because all the jobs had gone. This led to a breakdown in these communities with families breaking up and youths going out of control. The scale of the closures went too far."

Time revealed the righteousness of the strike in other ways as well. A steady drip of revelations unmasked the Tory lies: proof of a closure hit list, of Thatcher's direction of the dissident miners' antistrike effort, of brutality, espionage, and deceit from the state forces, seen especially in falsified police statements whose discovery led to the dismissal of all charges for those arrested at Orgreave. Such news stoked old furies, but could not change the course already set.

That path was solidly to the right. Both Labour and the Democrats would return to power in the 1990s, in the form of Tony Blair and Bill Clinton, but much had been surrendered to facilitate this revival. When asked in her waning years what she considered her greatest achievement, Thatcher replied, "Tony Blair and New Labour. We forced our opponents to change their minds." By this, she was noting the obvious: Blair—who Joe Strummer came to revile as "Tony Baloney"—won his office by remaking socialist Labour into a kinder, gentler Thatcherism.

Similarly, Reagan's crowning victory might be seen in the rise of Clinton and other Democrats who advanced the conservative agenda in ways the happy warrior never could have. Reagan had demonized "welfare queens" supposedly living high off the public dole, a racist trope that was effective at splitting working-class whites from the Democratic coalition. But it was Clinton who "ended welfare as we know it" through "welfare reform."

So too with the self-destructive "War on Drugs." According to the Drug Policy Alliance, "The presidency of Ronald Reagan marked the start of a long period of skyrocketing rates of incarceration, largely thanks to his unprecedented expansion of the drug war." The *New York Times* reported, "During the Reagan years, drug use was also increasingly stigmatized, making the subsidizing of treatment more difficult politically, and the prison population soared as harsher penalties were imposed for use, possession, and sale of illegal drugs."

For those who viewed drug abuse as a crisis that required public health intervention, not criminalization, these results were disheartening. Clinton once again sought to beat the Republicans by co-opting their "law and order" agenda. By the time Clinton left office, the US prison population was continuing on its way to over two million, nearly five times what it had been at the dawn of the Reagan era.

Perhaps the biggest surrender was the way Clinton Democrats cozied up to Wall Street and big business through "free trade" deals and financial deregulation, including the destruction of the Depression-era Glass-Steagall Act separating the investment and consumer banking industries. These changes were intended to unleash economic energies, and they surely did. But only some benefited.

As this "neoliberal" vision surged, its ideological rival—the "centrally planned" economies of the Eastern Bloc—dissolved, beginning with the fall of the Berlin Wall in 1989. Although the demise of the Soviet Union was surely a step forward for freedom and genuine socialism—which would be political democracy made real by economic democracy, not a corrupt "dictatorship of the party"— it also supported an emerging narrative of capitalism's inevitable triumph.

"There is no alternative," Margaret Thatcher had often said, and more and more people seemed to agree. One optimistic analyst, Francis Fukuyama, dared to suggest in 1989 that "what we may be witnessing is not just the end of the Cold War, or the passing of a particular period of postwar history, but the end of history as such: that is, the end point of mankind's ideological evolution and the universalization of Western liberal democracy as the final form of human government."

Fukuyama was hardly the first to entertain an "end of history"— he cited Karl Marx as the idea's "best-known propagator"—but his was a capitalist version of the vision. "Modern conservatism is entirely about the effort to turn selfishness into the great human virtue," economist John Kenneth Galbraith had once argued. Reagan and Thatcher had done a pretty good job selling the notion.

"Greed is good," proclaimed wheeler-dealer Gordon Gecko in the 1987 film *Wall Street*, capturing the zeitgeist. Reagan's "trickle-down" economics went global; the unfettered pursuit of profits for a few would ultimately benefit all via the market's magic, its greater efficiency and innovation. This was not entirely untrue. Mountains of money resulted, but the bounty was not shared equitably. As Vinyl wryly noted, "'Trickle-down' turned out to mean them pissing on us!"

One of the most conspicuous symbols of this was the explosion of the housing market, manifest especially in the gentrification of once-blighted inner-city urban areas. Even hardscrabble neighborhoods like Brixton and the South Bronx were not immune as untold wealth moved into real-estate speculation.

The division between those who benefited and those displaced was stark. As a select few grew astronomically wealthy, the many remained stuck. While elected leaders could have tried to level the field a bit, this seldom happened. The political system was increasingly captured by the power of concentrated money.

Like many others who came of age in the punk era, Peter Howard laments what three decades of an unfettered "free market" approach has done to a London that's still burning—not with boredom, but with the stench of gentrification and an ever-rising cost of living that effectively rules out a lot of creative risk-taking.

As Howard notes, without squatting—a practice that temporarily lifted the pressures of paying rent—he would never have shed his home city of Bath to pursue his dream. Such leaps of faith are more daunting with astronomical rents and so many people working longer and harder, for less and less money.

The resulting cultural void morphs into an emptier vision, one driven solely by the brute logic of survival. "If you can't afford to live in London, you don't come here. I mean, if you were in Notting Hill in 1977, everyone you saw was *fucking amazing*," Howard asserts. "They had a dress code, or a musical thing they were pursuing, they were in bands. People can't afford do that anymore. There is no 'other' thing that they think is worth pursuing [beyond money]."

If the "free market" was ascendant, and socialism discredited—for reasons both sound and utterly bogus—capitalism with a human face was hard to find. Barriers between countries fell and institutions like the World Trade Organization (WTO), International

Monetary Fund (IMF), and World Bank gained more and more control, making neoliberal policies essentially mandatory. National self-determination seemed quaint. If one country adopted policies that stymied the rich, the money would simply flow to more hospitable environs.

"How does a nation—the largest democratic unit the West can claim—exercise its will in a world where capital can roam free and traders can undermine the will of the people by simply shifting resources to countries where labor is cheaper and unions are weaker?" asked *Nation* writer Gary Younge. The question was inescapable, but no answer was obvious. This reality fueled a global race to the bottom on wages, working conditions, and environmental practices.

Far from upholding tradition, the "free market" was generating change at a shockingly unprecedented pace. Was Margaret Thatcher a punk rocker as conservative analyst Niall Ferguson had waggishly asserted? If punks had sometimes celebrated chaos and their forebears, the Situationists, had wanted a "revolution of everyday life," the free market brought it in spades.

The untrammeled pursuit of profit enabled by computer-age technology was corrosive in so many different ways. Marx and Engels had foreseen this in *The Communist Manifesto*, arguing, "Constant revolutionizing of production, uninterrupted disturbance of all social conditions, everlasting uncertainty and agitation distinguish the bourgeois epoch from all earlier ones. All fixed, fast-frozen relations, with their train of ancient and venerable prejudices and opinions, are swept away, all new-formed ones become antiquated before they can ossify."

This constant swirl of change brought vast moneymaking opportunities, but it could also unsettle human society to a frightening degree. The poetry of lines like "all that is solid melts into air, all that is holy is profaned" should not distract from the agony that was implied, the loss of meaning and direction for lives now adrift in an ever-shifting commodity stream.

For Marx and Engels, this dislocation would strip away illusions, enlightening in the most concrete, hopeful sense—the development of class consciousness that would shred the false promises of capitalism: "Man is at last compelled to face with sober senses his real conditions of life, and his relations with his kind." While the full accuracy of this optimistic interpretation remained to be seen, some element of truth was present. This never-ending disruption, mixed with the growing inequities, was bound to generate a potent backlash.

In part, this was seen in the ascent of Islamic fundamentalism. Terrorist groups such as al Qaeda and, later, the Islamic State fed off the pain generated by the West's economic, cultural, and military imperialism. Although most Muslims opposed such entities—and indeed were their main victims—the brutality fed a new narrative. After the 9/11 attacks in New York City, Washington, DC, and Pennsylvania, Islam was seen by many as the enemy in a "clash of civilizations," replacing vanished Soviet communism.

A more hopeful face of dissent came with the Zapatista uprising in Mexico as the North American Free Trade Agreement (NAFTA) went into effect on New Year's Day 1994. On November 30, 1999, a motley band of protesters shocked the powers-that-be by shutting down the World Trade Organization meeting in Seattle. This was the first of a series of street confrontations with elite institutions of global capitalism, stretching from Washington, DC, to Quebec City, to Genoa, to Davos, and beyond.

As protest swung back into the headlines with Seattle, Strummer had found his artistic and spiritual footing again with a new band, the Mescaleros. With these compatriots as collaborators, Strummer revived his past fire in songs both new and old. In interviews, he began to resemble the punk rabble-rouser of yore again, if with greater humility and ever-present self-deprecation.

"I'm proud that we have ridiculous aims, because at least then we ain't gonna underachieve," Strummer had said amid the neo-Clash fervor of early 1984. The reinvigorated singer may have remained unwilling to reprise such ambition, but he paid homage to those with similarly lofty aims, in particular the DC punk band Fugazi.

Formed in 1986, Fugazi had its roots in "straight edge" progenitor Minor Threat and "Revolution Summer" luminary Rites of Spring. The unit was part of a wave of subterranean bands that rose to stratospheric heights of popularity for the underground. Beginning with Nirvana's 1991 hit "Smells Like Teen Spirit," some of these vindicated Strummer's 1984 aim of bringing "rebel rock" to the top of the charts, thanks in no small part to MTV and major label backing. Fugazi stood out in its resolutely independent stance, refusing to sign a record deal, make videos, or otherwise accommodate the corporate-rock world.

Strummer had once dismissed such outliers as a "tempest in a teacup." Having finally escaped his CBS-contract straitjacket, however, the singer had something of a new perspective. He now seemed to recognize that the musically ferocious, clean-living, and politically radical Fugazi—dubbed "America's Clash" by none other than Sounds—had accomplished much of what he, Simonon, Rhodes, and Vinyl had stretched toward in their failed attempt to reinvent/purify The Clash.

Ironically, The Clash had scored a posthumous #1 UK hit themselves, thanks to the use of "Should I Stay or Should I Go" in a Levi's advertisement. Strummer was ambivalent about this, but as he had not written the song, he had little say in the matter.

When the subject came up in a 1999 interview, discussion ensued about the ugly intraband legal battle sparked when Dead Kennedys' lead singer Jello Biafra turned down a similar request for use of their song "Holiday in Cambodia" for a commercial. When an interviewer suggested that Biafra didn't accept the offer simply because the price wasn't high enough, Strummer wryly noted, "They always said that, didn't they? Everybody's got their price . . . But what about Fugazi?"

This was no idle query. Acclaimed punk/hip-hop photographer Glen Friedman recounts a head-turning Fugazi anecdote: "I witnessed the legendary music mogul Ahmet Ertegun coming backstage to try to get this 'unsignable' band to sign with him. He offered them 'anything you want' and said, 'The last time I did this was when I offered the Rolling Stones their own record label and $10 million.' Fugazi politely declined and [band cofounder] Ian MacKaye then changed the subject and continued to talk about their shared love of [the music of] Washington, DC."

Such tales led Strummer to remark, "Ian's the only one who ever did the punk thing right from day one and followed through on it all the way." When the singer returned to DC in 1999 for his first show there in a decade, he paid tribute to Fugazi during a fiery new song, "Diggin' the New." In a SPIN interview in 2000, he singled out Fugazi as embodying "the true spirit of punk"—a compliment MacKaye later returned, referencing the audacious busking tour of 1985.

Twinges of Strummer's regret over the fall of the neo-Clash experiment can be detected here. Still, nobility can be found in defeat as well as in triumph. If the last version of The Clash, like the band as a whole, failed to accomplish their lofty aims, the effort was hardly in vain.

Sadly, Strummer never seemed to stop apologizing for that time, even once going so far as to say, "We never played a good gig after Topper left."

This was silly and insulting. White called Strummer "an asshole" for the remark, then made his broader case: "Joe kind of artfully manipulated The Clash II period in his subsequent interviews as to say it was all just a big mistake—but clearly it wasn't, 'cause it was two years of touring, you know?" Yet while Strummer admitted to liking "This Is England" and the busking tour, the overall sense he left was one of embarrassment, especially over the firing of Jones.

Rhodes offers no apologies, while resisting revisiting the time in any depth. In 2013, he told this book's authors, "A few years ago I was approached by publishers to do a book giving my side of the story, but I had no time . . . Though the past is quite important to me, the future is where my thoughts are most active." (Ironically, a Rhodes memoir is now slated for release in the fall of 2018.)

Nonetheless, Rhodes's anger and pain is evident: "To sum up: I had an idea for a great, creative, and politically radical rock group. Found the people, got the thing moving, success arrived, parasites moved in and drugged the musicians with bullshit, etc., in the process gradually erasing our close friendship. My role with the group—particularly Joe—became 'I take the blame, they get the credit.'"

Although Rhodes may have a point here, he is not above his own historical revisionism, claiming, for example, "It was [Joe's] idea to have a drum machine on *Cut the Crap* and of course I had to deal with it."

The manager is on firmer ground in arguing, "Fact is, the album works good, the artwork is cool, and 'This Is England' still inspires." Rhodes's website contains a couple of dozen fan reviews of *Cut the Crap* that share this more upbeat view, defending the record as "unjustly neglected," "a solid punk masterpiece," and "an all-out return to the punk ethic the band had been straying from." The headline of another section of the website reads, "Popular Thieves and Unknown Originators." It is clear in which category Rhodes sees himself, and not without some justification.

Intriguingly, Rhodes's old ally Simonon defended *Cut the Crap*'s exclusion from the *Sound System* box set, saying, "It's not really a Clash album," due to the absence of Jones and Headon. Yet overall, the bassist has been far less apologetic about the era than Strummer, in one interview reaffirming directly to Jones, "We were right to fire you." While Simonon has belatedly criticized Rhodes's role, he nonetheless insists that the final Clash "had some really good songs."

This seems more accurate than Strummer's dismissals. Michael Fayne recalls that time as "a baptism by fire," but says, "Something good came out of that. Without that experience, where would I be?" For him, the band's mix was too combustible, the aims too impossibly high, but all the more glorious: "The Clash were always gonna fail, if you look at the initial ingredients and characters. They were always gonna fail, that was inevitable. But, man, what a way to go out!"

Describing the distance between The Clash's rhetoric and its reality as "Grand Canyon wide," White remains skeptical about its impact in any form: "Thanks to the music, you could feel better about yourself . . . But if you took on that revolution, in any meaningful sense, [music] is more like a kind of steam valve, you know, where people let off steam. It's arguable whether it's actually getting people to accept the system itself, by being able to listen to loud punk rock music, rather than get out and destroy some of the shit."

Even White can't mask his pride in the band's power, however: "A lot of people saw The Clash Mark II and got a lot from it, were influenced by it, in a positive way . . . You can't deny it." While disgusted by the hypocrisy, when pressed, the guitarist grants that The Clash might have been "a lie that told the truth."

Howard has a similar take: "Beyond all the breakdowns, Joe had a pure intent, and I think he believed Bernie had those pure intentions as well. The politic of the band was important, just saying, 'What the fuck are you doing? What are you doing here? Why are you enjoying this, in this way? It isn't about *that*. Think about *this*.' To be able to plant a seed of 'just think' is fucking amazing, incredibly potent."

This was by no means easy. Howard: "Joe wanted to say, 'Just think,' to a bigger audience, which is a bit of a conundrum, because you're doing something that relies on communicating with a small audience. Joe was genuinely agonizing about this, going, 'Look, it must be possible to do something good to a big audience. Why isn't it possible? It doesn't have to be shit. Come on, let's do it.'"

While the drummer's bitterness is apparent, so is a respect that can supersede the pain: "I have pondered it for many, many years, and I think that fundamentally pure intent was the reason why we all committed ourselves so much to it, were so affected by it, almost incapable of just walking away from it."

Though Howard asserts, "It went on far longer than it should have," nonetheless "there was something of importance, a real potential. It failed—but having said that, I can't think of a single thing, at the moment in music, that's even attempting this, that would even have part of that conscience. I can't think of anything."

Of the three "new boys," Sheppard views it all the most philosophically, with flashes of easy self-deprecation: "What's interesting about that whole thing is that The Clash is important culturally—

far more important than bands that sold a lot more records. If you actually analyze what The Clash did, it's very little, in concrete terms. I mean, they didn't introduce a bill for gun control, or try and get a 'health care for all' program through. We're talking about a pop group, you know, who took drugs, and played songs, and drunk a lot, a bunch of guys, troubadours, wandering the world singing their songs. It's a phenomenon, you know? Maybe, for our generation, The Clash *was* the band that mattered."

Sheppard sometimes speaks of The Clash in the third person—as if he hadn't been in it for two years—but pride shines through: "It's ancient history now, in human terms, but it moved people, made a lot of them look at themselves, at their lives, enabled them to do something that they maybe wouldn't have done if they hadn't heard it, which is very interesting, quite surprising. The lyrics obviously touched people, and enabled people, but I think so did the music. [The Clash's] gift was purely about somehow releasing something in other people."

Howard, White, and Sheppard all regard the busking tour as the most powerful validation of the neo-Clash experiment, but for the last of the three, there was a special significance: "When we were in York, we met a couple of wonderful, hilarious guys who were miners—or had been miners—one of whom was called Spartacus, because his dad had seen the film the night before he was born!"

The memory brings a smile to Sheppard's face as he continues: "And he was a fucking riot, hilarious—he was like the Johnny Cash song 'A Boy Named Sue.' Imagine growing up in a mining village being called Spartacus! These guys are tough, man. These guys don't take any prisoners. They're fucking . . . they're miners, for fuck's sake. And he's called *Spartacus*, you know? And we're in York, sitting around in the kitchen of somebody's house, after a bunch of busking gigs, and we've had a few beers. These two guys were like a duo of comedians, just had this fantastic, surreal play off each other—they had us in stitches."

Not all was for fun, however: "In the middle of it, Spartacus turned around and said, 'In that whole period, you know, when we were on strike, and it was really bleak, it was winter, it was fucked . . . We had no money, we had nothing, the one thing we had to keep us warm were those two nights in Brixton, when we came down and watched The Clash.' They were big fans, obviously—that's why they were there—and they said, 'That gave us real warmth, and comfort, and hope.'"

His voice thickening with feeling, Sheppard brings the story around: "And I thought, 'Well, fuck, you know—that's vindicated the whole time I've spent in this band, and that one thing, that's enough. I don't care what the NME thinks of my time in the band. I don't care what anybody thinks of my time in the band—because if I've done that, that's enough, you know? To me, that'll do."

Many argue that Sheppard's Clash was not the genuine article, that no unit without Jones or Headon could be. Yet this is hard to sustain. Was the Chimes version not real, the first album not The Clash? Was it not The Clash playing on the Anarchy Tour, or at the US Festival? If the final Clash played with fire and creativity, touched its audiences, inspired them, does this not matter?

Ultimately, Sheppard makes a convincing case. A similarly passionate Vinyl seconds the emotion: "Okay, Thatcher won—but at least we put up a fight, right? At least we said, 'No, we ain't going along with this, no fucking way.' Like the miners, we tried to do *something*, even if it weren't enough in the end."

A fuller sense of the importance of these lost battles of 1984–85 became clear on a single shocking day more than twenty years later. On September 29, 2008, the world economy nearly melted down, with feverish profit-seeking collapsing into a near-catastrophic downward spiral across global markets.

While the chain of events that caused the stock market nosedive and subsequent world recession—the worst since the 1930s' Great Depression—are complex, the crisis represented the fruit of the Reagan/Thatcher era as clearly as a devastating flood follows a massive rain. British journalist Seamus Milne later wrote, "A generation on, it is clear that the miners' strike was more than a defense of jobs and communities. It was a challenge to the destructive market- and corporate-driven reconstruction of the economy that gave us the crash of 2008."

Capitalism had not resolved its potentially fatal internal contradictions nor answered the questions of equitable distribution, democracy, or sustainability. Milne's words ring with truth: "The vindication of the miners' stand is well understood thirty years later . . . [Their defeat] brought us to where we are today: the deregulated, outsourced zero-hours modern world."

The crushing of the strike cleared the way for this resurgent capitalism at just the wrong time for the world's environment, as best-selling author Naomi Klein has pointed out. Global warming emerged into broad consciousness shortly after the events described in this book. In fact, as the *New York Times* has reported, "The recognition that human activity is influencing the climate developed slowly, but a scientific consensus can be traced to a conference in southern Austria in October 1985"—even as the poststrike lament, "This Is England," was falling off the charts.

For Klein, this climate crisis is less about carbon, as such, and more about capitalism. The British miners' strike might be seen, ironically enough, as a failed bulwark for the environment against what Klein derisively calls the "market fundamentalism" preached by the Reagan/Thatcher regimes.

This is so, even though many on the left now regard coal mining itself as a brutal relic of the past. Such attitudes are understandable. But while the danger of the work—and coal's contribution to eco-catastrophe—is undeniable, nothing that exists today would have been possible without the toil of untold miners over the past two centuries. This sacrifice can never rightly be forgotten, in moral terms, nor can the political import of the NUM's desperate last stand.

Is our society's top priority the protection of people, of all life on earth—or is it profit for the few? For Klein, the trajectory since 1985 is clear: "The past thirty years have been a steady process of getting less and less in the public sphere. This is all defended in the name of austerity, balanced budgets, increased efficiency, fostering economic growth. Market fundamentalism has, from the very first moments, systematically sabotaged our collective response to climate change, a threat that came knocking just as this ideology was reaching its zenith."

Like climate change, the 2008 economic crisis made one thing, at least, obvious: *history has not ended.* Although swift action by elite policymakers helped avert the worst possible consequences of the meltdown, the curtain had fallen on one era, and a new drama began to unfold, offering profoundly uncertain outcomes.

In America, hope was fueled by the election of the nation's first black president, Barack Obama, at the head of a vibrant multicultural coalition, followed by the Occupy Wall Street movement of 2011 and the insurgent 2016 presidential campaign of democratic socialist Bernie Sanders. Economic inequality was back on center stage, and socialism no longer seemed a dirty word. Between the cracks in capitalism's seemingly immaculate veneer and the withering of authoritarian pseudosocialism, broader political horizons again seemed possible.

Darker forces, however, were also unleashed. The rise of Rupert Murdoch's Fox News as the source of a right-wing "alternative reality" seemed the logical culmination of the reactionary power of the tabloid assault on the miners. This media powerhouse helped foster the Tea Party movement in America, which took Reagan's antigovernment rhetoric to new depths of fanaticism.

In the ensuing chaos, an egomaniacal billionaire con man was able to ride the surge of desperation and disillusion into the White House. Donald Trump revived Reagan's "Make America Great Again" slogan and the "law and order" mantra of Nixon. Benefitting from a covert Russian hacking campaign, he coarsely summoned the ugliest bits of America—racism, misogyny, anti-immigrant/anti-Muslim bigotry, greed, and more—to build a movement that narrowly won the electoral college, though not the popular vote.

Trump is surely disgusting as a person—"morally bankrupt and pathologically dishonest," in the words of the *Washington Post* editorial board—yet he has a certain malevolent genius. While Trump is hardly "a champion of the forgotten millions" as one commentator claimed, he did speak to a very real pain.

Top: Bitter fruit whose roots stretch back to 1984–85.

Left: Kosmo Vinyl resurrected the spirit of The Clash with a fiery "Cisco Kid" art series opposing Donald Trump.

When factories and mines closed, dreams died with them, and lives turned to self-destruction. For the first time in modern history, life expectancy actually began to fall for America's white working class. In 1984, Joe Strummer blamed Reagan's rise on the drug culture; in 2016, blue-collar areas suffering an epidemic of opiate addiction voted disproportionately for Trump.

As the New York Times wrote, 2016 "brought to the surface the despair and rage of poor and middle-class Americans who say their government has done little to ease the burdens that recession, technological change, foreign competition, and war have heaped on their families."

Earlier that same year, British politics were rocked by the triumph of "Brexit," when UK voters narrowly chose to leave the European Union. Although this move promised to severely injure the country's economy, it was sold as a reassertion of national sovereignty eroded by economic change and immigration.

The pain that helped birth both President Trump and Brexit can be traced right back to Reagan and Thatcher, together with erstwhile opponents who shifted rightward for political expediency. Trump scratched out his win with the help of the Rust Belt, where working-class voters deserted the Democratic ticket. The margin was slender—some forty thousand votes switched in three states would have reversed the verdict—but sad and scary nonetheless.

Similarly, Brexit triumphed thanks to defecting Labour voters in England's north, including depressed coal-mining areas like Newcastle, Sunderland, and Stoke-on-Trent. If Brexit, like Trump, was powered by anti-immigrant animus, it also reflected class desperation. As the *Nation*'s London correspondent D.D. Guttenplan noted, "The losers in globalization's race to the bottom [used] the only weapon they had to strike at a system that offered them nothing."

"The god that failed" here was the "free market" deified by Reagan and Thatcher. Yet a left now seen as drifting away from class struggle did not benefit. *New York Times* columnist Eduardo Porter has noted how the market-fundamentalist gospel was "brought down by right-wing populists riding the anger of a working class that has been cast aside in the globalized economy that the two leaders trumpeted forty years ago." The rise of this aggressive far right inevitably evoked the specter of Europe's fascist past.

For Vinyl, the moment seemed frighteningly familiar. The aging agitator returned to the fray, fashioning his art into a weapon. Working relentlessly, Vinyl spat out a series of neo-Situationist "Cisco Kid vs. Donald Trump" broadsides in the months before the US election, all to no avail. Vinyl: "The morning after Trump won, I had the same feeling of utter defeat as after the miners were beaten and The Clash had broken up—just sick to my soul."

Vinyl was not alone in his darkness. As Trump and his administration touted "alternative facts," George Orwell's *1984* shot to the top of the *New York Times* best-seller list. Global tensions that had receded after the end of the Cold War reignited, stoked by what the *New York Times* described as Trump's "chilling language that evoked the horror of a nuclear exchange" in threatening North Korea with "fire and fury like the world has never seen." As a result of the president's bellicose rhetoric—along with the looming threat posed by climate change—the hands of the Doomsday Clock were moved to two minutes before midnight in January 2018, even closer than in the fear-drenched days of 1984. Meanwhile, Muslims faced attacks and immigrants endured a renewed wave of deportations, with all bracing for far worse perhaps yet to come.

This moment was pregnant with danger. But possibility also glimmered. The massive protests that greeted President Trump, the raucous town hall meetings fighting to preserve health care, the surprising Labour surge led by Jeremy Corbyn, the outcry after the terrible Grenfell Tower fire, born of the Thatcherite "bonfire of regulations"—all suggested what Vinyl already knew from his Clash years: the future remains up for grabs, the final tale is not yet written.

At The Clash's second-to-last show ever in July 1985, the mouthy firebrand had roared, "This here rhythm ain't never gonna stop— it's gonna rock you to the front till the very last drop!" Later, he worried that the words might seem pretentious. In fact, they not only evoke the irrepressible spirit that made The Clash a band that touched lives deeply and indelibly, but also carry meanings that still resonate.

Vinyl was talking about the power of art and audience, how this communion could generate an energy that was particularly powerful at the stage front, the nexus between band and crowd. The word "front," however, also echoes The Clash's martial metaphors. The extraordinary force that pulled one into the vortex of performance could also push outward, propelling the listener onto a battlefield, to the front line where human need cries out for defenders.

Joe Strummer's old namesake Woody Guthrie evoked a similar concept:

Wherever little children are hungry and cry,
Wherever people ain't free.
Wherever men are fightin' for their rights,
That's where I'm a-gonna be . . .

No human being has the strength to take that stand every day, with untiring consistency. Strummer's foibles described herein recall Phil Ochs's famous disclaimer, "I could never be as moral as my songs." Still, while knowing that words—including his own—could often be all too cheap, Strummer refused to surrender, continuing to believe that time can march with charging feet.

In mid-1982, as the centrifugal forces that would rend and reassemble The Clash gathered, Strummer told Mikal Gilmore, "I'll tell you what real rebellion is: It's something more personal. *It's not giving up.* Rebellion is deciding to push ahead with it all for one more day. That's the toughest test of revolt—keeping yourself alive—as well as the cause . . . It's the only rebellion that counts: not giving up."

This was a simple yet critical insight. Vinyl recalls how Strummer kept a NUM button on his leather jacket for years after the band's end: "When I asked about it, Joe told me, 'A miner gave it to me—how heavy is that? It doesn't get any heavier!'" If this was a tip of the hat to the "never say die" miners, Strummer also knew that wearing badges was not enough, that action spoke loudest.

His best tribute to that lost struggle came when Strummer mounted the stage in support of striking firefighters only a few weeks before his untimely death in December 2002. Mick Jones was in the audience. During the encore, Jones spontaneously joined his old partner for three songs, including "White Riot," the anthem they had come to blows over during the long run-up to their final fracture.

Fate brought the pair together onstage one more time, not on a lucrative reunion tour, or for suits holding big-money tickets at a Hall of Fame soiree, but for striking workers, fighting the harsh winds of post-Thatcher austerity. That night, the best spirit of The Clash lived again, if only for a few moments—just as it can any time, anywhere that human creativity, determination, and compassion rise.

If the band "The Clash" is gone forever, such an idea of "The Clash" can be with us always. "Ideas matter," the biblical scholar

Marcus Borg has written, "much more than we commonly think they do, especially our worldviews and values, our ideas about what is real and how we are to live. We receive such ideas from our culture as we grow up, and unless we examine them, we will not be free, but simply live out the agenda of our socialization."

Borg's point that our sense of what is possible is often constrained by our society could have come from Joe Strummer himself. In 1984, the Clash frontman insisted, "Money doesn't get us anywhere. I'm talking about preventing the world from going backward, finding a decent economic order where the poor are taken care of and everyone gets an even break. I'm talking about getting the world round to that kind of sanity, which is chiefly what we're trying to do in The Clash."

Realism met determination in the singer's words, and the call to action was clear: "We ain't just some shitty rock band trying to fake our way through. We are really trying to make a difference. People ask me, 'Can The Clash change anything?' Of course we can't. But we can be a chink in the blinds."

This last point is crucial. Strummer strained to write songs of deep worth, to perform them with fervent passion. But he knew that it took an audience to make them truly live, not just in ecstatic moments, but in changed lives, in new consciousness, in action. Strummer was trying, in the best punk fashion, to point the listeners away from the "stars" onstage and back toward to their own power, their responsibility to be participants, not just spectators.

A quiet reminder of this challenge can be found lurking in the pages of *Sound System*'s "Service Manual": the words "It's up to you" written in ten languages, signaling a global intent. This simple phrase recalls Strummer's insistence from a Brixton stage, standing with the striking miners, that "The Clash" meant not simply the five members of the band, but everyone in their audience.

This audacious idea, of course, is only as true as anyone makes it, with blood, sweat, toil, and tears. But to act, one first has to believe, past jarring reverses, even seeming defeat, that, somehow, some way, a better world is possible.

"As for the future, your task is not to foresee it, but to enable it." In sacri-

ficing his life in a world war against fascism, Antoine de Saint Ex-upéry honored this vow, inspiring others to act on life rather than accept it as is. This "enabling" of the future is the gift Sheppard spoke of, the "chink in the blinds" Strummer conjured night after night onstage, giving the best of himself in the process.

This is *the rhythm that ain't never gonna stop,* the radical claim Strummer staked in "North and South." As a bleak Christmas approached for tens of thousands of strikers, as the lifeblood of their embattled families and communities oozed into the earth, The Clash spat out words of hope and defiance: "We ain't diggin' no grave / We're diggin' a foundation / for a future to be made."

Tens of thousands of lives were touched by such Clash nights in 1984–85, even if subsequent dismissals or revisionism have sought to erase this inconvenient truth. Small, persistent pushbacks have grown, however. Visitors to Duke's Bar in Glasgow, for example, now walk past a small round plaque commemorating The Clash's busking show there—a lifetime ago, on May 16, 1985, before the forces of "market fundamentalism" overtook the lives of those who witnessed it.

This all might seem to be dead, dusty history, of little use beyond nostalgia. Yet while the energy of such an experience, in all its ragged, one-off glory, can be tamped down for a period, it can never be completely controlled. Nor, perhaps, can the participants feel compelled to simply settle for less, ever again.

If the last stand of The Clash has elements of tragedy and farce, it is more nearly defined by such sparks of persistence and passion, squeezed out over two years of striving. That time was dedicated imperfectly but powerfully to an idea of how the band might be purified and reinvented to the point where boundaries between fan and performer dissolved, and vast windows of possibility opened.

We are the clash—we are the rub between what is and what can be, between reality and possibility, the arena where truth can bring transformation. And, as Joe Strummer knew, truth often means descending into the house of suffering.

In many ways, this book has been a journey to that place of pain. It has no tale of unvarnished triumph to share. It can hope, however, to carry the ring of truth, of hard-fought battles, stinging defeats, and saving lessons learned. Above all, it seeks to faithfully transmit the restless, contradictory, fully human spirit of the band it celebrates, critiques, and tries to resurrect, in however limited a fashion.

Those now reading this book might be seen as part of the only Clash alive in flesh and blood. If so, take these words as a call to battle. Win or lose, we must spend ourselves again and again on those barricades, in a thousand ways large and small. Anything less is not worthy of The Clash, this band that truly mattered.

"When I say. 'We are The Clash,' I mean WE . . ." Joe Strummer in *Hip Hop Punk Rock* T-shirt with Clash fans at Chicago's Sears Tower, May 1984. (Photo by Eddie King.)

ACKNOWLEDGMENTS & SOURCES

We Are The Clash book Kickstarter event. (Photo by Mark Andersen.)

Any book as ambitious as this one will necessarily rely on a vast array of sources to have any hope of success and/or credibility. Four key works were fundamentally important to us, even though our interpretations sometimes differ significantly from theirs, and any errors are, of course, our own. They are: Vince White's *Out of Control: The Last Days of The Clash*; Danny Garcia's film and companion book, *The Rise And Fall of The Clash*; Nick Hall's film *I Need a Dodge!: Joe Strummer on the Run*; and Chris Salewicz's *Redemption Song: The Ballad of Joe Strummer*. Vince, Danny, Nick, and Chris were all exceedingly generous with their time and sources. Their works not only form an essential complement for *We Are The Clash*, but their kindness exemplifies what is best about the ongoing Clash community, as did the support, patience, and inspiration of Kosmo Vinyl, Nick Sheppard, The Baker, Johnny Green, Jesús Arias, Jon Savage, Gaby Holford (née Salter), Alex Michon, and Caroline Coon. Mark Jenkins was crucial in helping us edit and condense this book—an immense amount of work that he did out of love, for no compensation at all. Alex Dent made lots of great suggestions, particularly to add a new opening to the introduction. Kate Crane/*Smashpipe* and Joseph L. Flatley/TheVerge.com also helped spread the word. Robin Bell rescued us at a key moment with his film production skills, and Luca Lanini and Federico Vacalebre stretched to fill us in on the Italian tour of September 1984. Similarly, Charlotte Manning, Niall McGuirk, Chris Magee, Nichola, and Chris Tipton/Upset the Rhythm provided amazing hospitality during Mark's research trip to the UK and Ireland, as did Colin Coulter and everyone with the "Clash in Belfast" conference. Craig O'Hara of PM Press and Tim Merrick of *The Clash Blog* also provided key support and encouragement, while much respect is due to Justin Sullivan of New Model Army for the use of his penetrating, heartbreaking lyrics from "The Charge" for the epigraph that begins this book and helps open Chapter Nine. Antonia Tricarico, Saverio Giovacchini, Athena Viscusi, and Alexandra Getz Escudero assisted us with translations, while Maura Pond helped set up our wearetheclash.com website. Words can't sufficiently express our gratitude for these extraordinary contributions—thanks so much, brothers and sisters!

At the same time, both Ralph and Mark have been working on this book in some sense since we each first heard in early 1986 that the new Clash had broken up, archiving clippings and puzzling over unanswered questions. The mystery behind this sudden dramatic crash, the lofty ambitions precipitously abandoned, the enigmatic album *Cut the Crap*—all of it intrigued and haunted us, marked indelibly as we were by this final chapter of the Clash saga. By the mid-1990s, Ralph had become the first journalist to seek out Vince White, Peter Howard, and Nick Sheppard to try to piece together the tale for *DISCoveries* and *Goldmine* magazines. In addition, Ralph recorded conversations around that same time with Johnny Green, Raymond Jordan, Viv Albertine, and numerous other key Clash players. For his part, Mark interviewed Joe Strummer in 1989, seeking illumination about what had happened. Strummer's responses are published here for the very first time, with maximum thanks to Ian MacKaye for locating the original tape and digitizing it.

These early interviews were supplemented by in-depth follow-ups conducted between 2012 and 2017 with Nick, Peter, and Vince, as well as with Kosmo Vinyl, Jesús Arias, and a broad array of other participants or observers such as Bernard Rhodes, Eddie King, Michael Fayne, Julian Balme, Billy Bragg, Chris Salewicz, Danbert Nobacon and Boff Whalley of Chumbawamba, Per-Åke Wärn, Gee Vaucher and Penny Rimbaud of Crass, Mark Jenkins, Kris Needs, Robin Banks, Jeff Slate, Bill Daly, Tony Keen, and Martin McCallion. Although we didn't interview Paul Simonon, Mick Jones, Nicky Headon, or Terry Chimes, we thank them for their priceless contributions to a band that has meant everything to us. The *Joe Strummer Slept Here* interactive documentary by Stephen Hay and Graham Roberts, based in part on the recollections of Gillian Farmer, was invaluable. We also benefited from insights and memories of literally dozens of other Clash observers and analysts—whom we've tried to acknowledge in the text—helping us to reconstruct this era with accuracy and sensitivity.

Our political sources were crucial and broad-based as well. While both of us have our own vivid recollections as activists during the Reagan/Thatcher era, the main basis for our parallel narratives was intensive research. Rather than clutter the book with footnotes, we've tried to note our sources in the text itself. Particularly central works included *The Great Strike* by Alex Callinicos and Mike Simons, *The Age of Reagan: A History, 1974–2008* by Sean Wilentz, *Margaret Thatcher: At Her Zenith: In London, Washington and Moscow* by Charles Moore, Thatcher's own memoir *The Downing Street Years;* as well as *The Miners' Strike Day by Day: The Illustrated Diary of Yorkshire Miner Arthur Wakefield* and *Yorkshire's Flying Pickets in the 1984–85 Miners' Strike, Based on the Diary of Silverwood Miner Bruce Wilson* (both edited by Brian Elliott); and *The 1984–85 Miners' Strike in Nottinghamshire: If Spirit Alone Won Battles: The Diary of John Lowe,* edited by Jonathan Symcox. David Cortright's *Peace: A History of Movements and Ideas* and Lawrence S. Wittner's *Confronting the Bomb: A Short History of World Nuclear Disarmament Movement* and *Toward Nuclear Abolition: A History of the World Nuclear Disarmament Movement, 1971-Present* were key resources as well. Mark's interview with Jason Toynbee at Open University also informed our discussion of neoliberalism and The Clash.

We are also blessed by all the photos and memorabilia Clash friends shared over the years of working on this book, most of which could not be included here. Thanks must go to Bob Gruen (with much help from Sarah Field!), Mike Laye, Eddie King, Kosmo Vinyl, Juan Jesús Garcia, Per-Åke Wärn, John Harris and John Sturrock of reportdigital.co.uk, Tim Beasley, Martin Jenkinson, Jan Bengsston/*Schlager* magazine, *Creem* magazine, the *York Press Gazette & Herald*, and Philippe Huguen/L'Agence France-Presse for their beautiful photographs and art. We found a number of anonymous shots on the Internet, some of which were truly compelling. *We offer our most sincere apologies to any photographer who didn't get credited properly for any image used in this book. Please let us know right away so we can correct this omission in future editions, okay?* Thanks so much!

We don't really consider this project over and done with, and we wish to keep learning more about this era, filling in blank spots, honing our understanding and insights. As such, we are eager for any additional recollections or feedback, the most valuable of which will be shared on wearetheclash.com, our ongoing resource for education and activism. (In order to pass along your thoughts, Mark can be reached at wearefamilydc@gmail.com and Ralph at chairmanralph@yahoo.com.)

Andrew Matey proved himself a superhero by helping us access the full collection of Clash live recordings—he is another testament to the generous spirit of the Clash community. Justin Cudney went above and beyond, designing and printing our Kickstarter *We Are The Clash* posters and postcards, as did Jason Lobe, Brian Duss, Stephen Jeter, and Robert Winship in filming, crafting, and editing our Kickstarter pitch video. Matt Connolly deserves kudos for helping get the rewards out when Mark and Ralph were overwhelmed by other demands, as do Juan Risso and Angie Hunter for computer help.

Special thanks also must go to Bobby Polsky, who gave Mark his first Clash II bootleg in fall 1984, as well as to Danny Ingram—Mark's comrade Clash fanatic and original DC punk friend—and to Greg Carr, an original Montana punk friend. Along the same lines, Ralph thanks his late musical brother-in-arms Anthony Salazar, for teaching him those first Clash songs—an experience that ignited the desire to express himself musically, and to write about "the only band that matters" in the first place—not to mention his unflagging enthusiasm. (Rest assured, my friend, I've put those countless phone calls, conversations, and shared press clippings to good use.) Ralph gained further reinforcement for his original dream from his first editors, Jeff Tamarkin (*Goldmine*) and John Koenig (*DISCoveries*), whose support proved equally invaluable—as did the encouragement of Clash stalwarts like Johnny Green and Raymond Jordan, plus Vince, Nick, and Pete (of course), and a few Clash City confidantes whose names must remain behind the scenes, for now. Thank you, one and all.

We also must thank our stalwart—and very patient—Kickstarter supporters: A. Margaret Andersen, A. Binovi, A.J. Kandy, Aaron Dukes, Abby Moser, Allison Chang, Annie N, Armando Gonzalez, Azazel, Barry Shank, Bartosz Glowacki, Benita Raymond, Berrin Ozbilgin, Bert Queiroz, Bill Daly/Crooked Beat Records, Blain Myhre, Bobbie, Bonnie Schlegel, Brad Sigal, Brendan Hoar, Brendan Sweeney, Brian Lombardozzi, Brice Lipman, Brien Stewart, Bruce Carter, Burke Stansbury, Calista Redmond, Candace, Carl LeVan, Carlos Salinas, Carol Inagal, Caroline Klibanoff, Carolyn Sasich Leitko, Carrie Crawford, Casey Neill, Cassandra J. Perry, Cate Cohen and all the others at Mark's Clash Kickstarter event at St. Stephen's, Charlotte Manning, Chris, Chris Schneidmiller, Christina Ross, Christoph Paul, Christopher Corrigan, Christopher LaMarca and Katrina Taylor, Claire Packer, Clarissa Peterson, Clark Lobenstine, Colin Bill, Corbin Dallas, Craig Keenan, Craig Wedren, Dan Treado, Danielle Kurzweil, Daoud Tyler-Ameen, Darius Kanga, Dave Berman, David Comay, David Levine, David Maydoney, David McConnell, Deidre Swesnik, Dolores G. Perillan, Don Irwin, Donald Hargraves, Donna Wilson, Doug Abeel, drivenbyboredom, Edward Hoyt, Elana Brochin, Ellen Chenoweth, Emily, Eric Damon Walters, Erica, Ferruccio Martinotti, Frank Gasque Dunn, Fred Solowey, Gavin Malette, George Washington Burton, Gertrude Sunsted, Greg Hymel, Gregory Jay Bloom, Gretchen Brodtman, Hard Art

DC 1979, Heather Booth, Heather Jameyson, Heidi Phelps, Helen French, Holly Wilson, Hovey Kemp, Iain Ross, Iselin Gambert, James Caparas, Jane Morrow, Jason Kooken, Jason Yawn, Jennifer Fox-Thomas, Jeremy Grant, Jess Owens, JG Sylvester, Joe Iosbaker, John Hilla, Jon Bolduc, Jon Hancuff, Jon K. G. Allanson, Joseph Hunter, Jud Branam, Juliana Paciulli, Julie Meyer, Justin Cudney, Kate Crane, Kathleen Kent Abate, Kathleen Ryan, Katie, Katy Otto, Kerry White, Kevin Dunn, Kevin Erickson, Kevin Johnson Jr., Kevin Tucker, Kevin Young, Kimberly Righter, Kristin Valentine, Kristina Hunken, Kurt Sayenga, Lale Kuyumcu, Lawrence P. Keitz, Leah Gold, Leann Trowbridge, Lenny Flatley, Linc Kinnicutt, Linda Hsu, Linette Robinson, Luther Gaylord, Mara Cherkasky, Marc Poe, Marian Currinder, Mark Anderson, Mark Haggerty, Mark Jenkins, Mark Kennedy, Mark Lance, Mark Lansing, mark p, Markus Kampschnieder, Marty Key, Matthew Saliba, Matt Siblo, Maura Pond, Megan Kuhn, Meghan Adkins, Mia, Michael Cotterman, Michael Horstman, Michael Markarian, Michael T. Fournier, Mike Paarlberg, Minna Morse, Mo Sussman (RIP), Molly, Molly Neuman, Morgan Daniels, Nalinee D, Nance Morris Adler, Nathan Larson, Neil Soiseth, Nicole Thomas, Nomnaut, Noreen, Omar Ronquillo, Patricia Mullahy Fugere, Pete Chramiec, Pete Perry, Peter, Peter Hogan, Ran Zilca, Richard Johnson, Richard Siegmeister, Rob Thornton, Robert Egger, Robert T. Bryan, Robin Bell, Roger Gastman, Roland Schrebler, Rudy Rucker, Ruth Hildenberger, Ryan Bell, Ryan Shepard, Sadie Dingfelder, Samantha Linscott, Sara Beauchamp, Sean Knight, Scott Favorite, Scott Sommers, Shawna Kenney, Small Axe Films, some fella, Soren Huseyin Ozdeger-Andersen, Stephen Jeter, Steve D. Lambert, Steven Wisnieski, Suki Valentine, Tarock Music, Tim Fitzgerald, Tony Ross, Tracy Lingo, Travis Morrison, Tyler Sonnichsen, Valerie Pletcher, Vic Bondi, Vige Millington, Wendy Lyon, William, William J. Fleming, and William Reintzell.

Last but not least, we must thank Johnny Temple, Johanna Ingalls, Ibrahim Ahmad, Alice Wertheimer, Aaron Petrovich, and all at Akashic Books, for their belief in this book—we couldn't wish for a better ally in this fervent effort to help the last years of The Clash come alive again.

ABOUT THE AUTHORS

RALPH HEIBUTZKI saw The Clash Mark II on May 10, 1984, at Michigan State University. Since he had not witnessed the classic lineup, the backstage drama of Mick Jones's departure hardly kept him away. If anything, the pro- and anti-Jones debates playing out in the music press spurred him to buy a ticket for the gig at one of the many midsize college venues that were the band's theater of battle on their "Out of Control" tour—or "campaign," in Clash-speak—that spring.

Energized by the razor-sharp, heartfelt performance and potent original songs, Ralph touted the new Clash to all who would listen, eagerly awaiting an album that had the potential to match the raw, jagged brilliance of their first record. When *Creem* ran an article questioning the new lineup's promise, Ralph did what came naturally to any die-hard Clash fan: he called the magazine's Detroit headquarters and spent forty minutes debating with the author, Bill Holdship.

The wait for the promised new record turned out to be agonizingly long. Weeks turned to months turned to a year, and no album appeared. When *Cut the Crap* finally did materialize—nearly a year and half after Strummer had vowed to "go into the studio and bang it out"—the results initially left Ralph confused and disappointed, so distant were they from his expectations. Nonetheless, the excitement, passion, and meaning of the 1984 live shows stayed with him.

In addition, the yawning distance between Strummer's words and the record's reality piqued his curiosity. Several years later, Ralph would become the first writer to seriously excavate that era with a series of articles based on interviews with most of the key players. Bit by bit, an alternative Clash Mark II history emerged from Ralph's first foray into punk rock archeology.

As Ralph dug deeper, he found much to admire—from the combustive intensity of the new material, to the band's reborn political engagement and brash underdog gestures like its busking tour of northern England and Scotland. Only The Clash—armed with little more than some acoustic guitars and Pete Howard's drumsticks—would play for free in any available public space without sitting down for a formal press interview, let alone any new record to promote.

One idea runs through all of this like a red thread: the notion, as Joe Strummer constantly declared throughout the whole impromptu exercise, that the performer onstage is essentially no different and surely no more important than the people in the audience. This credo lies at the core of punk rock, an ethic that Ralph took to heart when he soon began taking up the guitar and performing himself.

Those initial forays to London to ferret out the lost history of The Clash formed an essential backdrop to Ralph's ventures into folk-punk music, spoken-word performance, and political activism through his involvement in groups like the Hillsdale County Coalition for Peace and Justice.

Those ideals also motivated Ralph's first book, *Unfinished Business: The Life and Times of Danny Gatton*, and is a driving force in all the projects that he has pursued since then, based on the immortal dictum reportedly handed down by Rhodes at the outset of The Clash's existence: "Look about your situation, and sing about what really matters."

If anything, the neo-Clash era had an even more powerful impact on **MARK ANDERSEN**, if in a somewhat different way. Having grown up feeling trapped by rural working-class life in Sheridan County, Montana, Mark first encountered photos and lyrics of The Clash in *Rock Scene* magazine as a teenager in 1977. It quickly became his favorite band, and helped inspire him to leave farm/ranch work behind to attend Montana State University and become a radical activist there.

Having excelled as a student, Mark was accepted into the Johns Hopkins School of Advanced International Studies in Washington, DC, in 1983. It was a heady moment for a kid from nowhere. Massive loans were assembled to pay for a degree that was a ticket into the lower echelons of the American ruling class.

However gratifying in some ways, the career path that loomed—and the cost at which it came—unsettled Mark. When he read interviews in 1984 with Joe Strummer that questioned The Clash's past direction, despite their Top 10 success, and called for a return to punk roots, it resonated deeply with him.

While Mark never saw this version of The Clash live, the interviews, photos, and bootleg recordings he tirelessly sought out helped to catalyze a second personal revolution. Heartened by the band's example, Mark abandoned his elite-oriented career path, spending time in war-torn Central America, including as a *"brigadista"* helping harvest coffee in Sandinista Nicaragua in defiance of US policy. At the same time, he dove into the DC punk underground, cofounding the activist collective Positive Force DC in the "Revolution Summer" of 1985.

Mark's immersion in this fertile, influential, and legendarily anticommercial DIY scene—which gave birth to phenomena like straight edge, Riot Grrrl, and emo while nurturing bands such as Bad Brains, Minor Threat, Fugazi, Bikini Kill, and Nation of Ulysses—would lead to cowriting *Dance of Days: Two Decades of Punk in the Nation's Capital* and authoring *All the Power: Revolution Without Illusion.* Driven by that initial spark, Mark has done inner-city outreach, organizing, and advocacy for over thirty years, most recently with We Are Family DC. (For more information, visit wearefamilydc.org or email info@wearefamilydc.org.)

Ralph Heibutzki photo by Lisa Quinlan Heibutzki.
Mark Andersen photo by James Lathos.

"I started out a hippie, and I ended up a punk. I'd say the difference was, hippies were trying to believe in the illusion of an alternative world, and punks knew that to create that alternative world something had to be done."

Is punk rock something you grow out of?

"Never! You see, punk rock is like the Mafia. Once you're made, you're made. Punk rock is not the clothes or the music. Punk rock is an attitude, the don't-give-me-any-bullshit-'cause-I-can-see-right-through-to-the-heart-of-the-situation attitude. Because I'm wise to the tricks of the world. We're sick of all the bullshit. Give us some truth. That's the energy of punk rock."

—Joe Strummer

The Clash.
The Future Is Unwritten.

Flyer design by Mark Andersen, photo by Bob Gruen.